Dialogue with Photography

Dialogue with Photography

PAUL HILL & THOMAS COOPER

Farrar / Straus / Giroux   *New York*

Library of Congress Cataloging in Publication Data
Dialogue with photography.
Includes bibliographies and index.
1. Photographers—Biography.   I. Hill, Paul,
1941-   II. Cooper, Thomas Joshua, 1946-
III. Camera (Lucerne)
TR139.D52   /   770'.92'2 [B]   /   78-25851

The interviews in this book originally appeared in
Camera magazine, Lucerne, Switzerland, and were developed
with the editorial counsel of Allan Porter

Acknowledgments

This book is a dialogue with individuals who have helped shape the art of photography in the twentieth century. The men and women we interviewed over the past four years are all recognized masters in photography, and their contributions to art movements such as the Bauhaus, Photo-Secession, Group f/64, Dadaism, Surrealism, and Social Realism were seminal and remain significant: every interview was a history lesson in itself.

We wish to express our gratitude and appreciation to the persons interviewed and to their families for their generous help and consideration in making Dialogue with Photography *possible. We have gained immeasurably from their goodwill and understanding.*

And to the following friends our heartfelt thanks for their labors on our behalf: Angela Hill, Isabella Jedrzejczyk, Alain Jullien, Cynthia Wootton, Gerry Meaudre, Helena Srakoćić (Photographers' Gallery, London), Carlos Guardia, Bernard Plossu, Jean-Claude Lemangy (Conservateur au Cabinet des Estampes, Bibliothèque Nationale, Paris), Sue Davies (Director, Photographers' Gallery, London), Jonathan Bayer, Deborah Baker, Sue Garfinkle, Angela Thompson, Valerie Bayliss, Lewis Ambler, Gerry Badger, Georges Herscher (Publisher, Editions du Chêne, Paris), Christopher Seiberling, Eileen Hose, Raymond Moore, Jim Hughes (Editor, Popular Photography, *New York), Raymond and Barbara Grosset (Agence Rapho, Paris), Arthur and Debra Cardoza, Peter McArthur, Kay Ketchum, Dr. Rod and Maxine McArthur, Chuck Putnam, Susan Kismaric (Department of Photography, Museum of Modern Art, New York), the staff of the Lee Witkin Gallery Bookshop (New York), the staff of the Robert Self Gallery (London), Minette Burgess and James Enyeart (Center for Creative Photography, Tucson), Sherry Suris, Steve and Gloria Zorich, D. W. and Nelsie Cooper, and the directors, staff, and students of Trent Polytechnic (Nottingham).*

To our colleagues at Camera *magazine (Lucerne) special thanks, most especially to Allan Porter, Editor-in-Chief, who so kindly suggested the title for this book, and to his assistants Renata Wagner and Maja Hoffmann.*

And finally, to our editor at Farrar, Straus and Giroux, Nancy Meiselas, who had the faith in us to compile our efforts into this book.

P. H. & T. C.

Contents

PAUL STRAND / 1

MAN RAY / 9

CECIL BEATON / 21

JACQUES-HENRI LARTIGUE / 33

BRASSAÏ / 37

ANDRÉ KERTÉSZ / 44

GEORGE RODGER / 50

HENRI CARTIER-BRESSON / 74

ROBERT DOISNEAU / 80

HERBERT BAYER / 111

HENRY HOLMES SMITH / 132

HELMUT GERNSHEIM / 160

BRETT WESTON / 211

MANUEL ALVAREZ BRAVO / 224

ELIOT PORTER / 237

W. EUGENE SMITH / 253

LAURA GILPIN / 282

IMOGEN CUNNINGHAM / 293

WYNN BULLOCK / 313

MINOR WHITE / 338

BEAUMONT NEWHALL / 377

INDEX / 413

Dialogue with Photography

Paul Strand

(1 8 9 0 – 1 9 7 6 / A M E R I C A N)

Paul Hill

When did you first become interested in photography?
I would say it was when I went to the Ethical Culture School,
which was a school with a much higher grade of intellectual
standing than the average public school at that time. By
accident—one of the accidents of life, seemingly—a man
named Lewis Hine was assistant professor of biology there.
He was passionately interested in photography, and later became a very good photographer. But at that time he was

feeling his way. He was doing all the photographic work for the school; he photographed the graduation exercises and the school play and the athletic events—probably when I did a back somersault off the horizontal bar, he got it with the flash light, or at least I hope so. One day, there was a notice put up on the board saying that Lewis Hine would have an extra-curricular class in photography and I was keen to join it. I put my name down. They built a little darkroom upstairs, and we began. I think there were four or five others in the class, none of whom became photographers. This must have been around 1906.

It should be clear that at that time Lewis Hine himself had not yet become a photographer in the sense that we know him. I don't remember seeing any of his work at that time, except the things he did for the school in which he used an open flash pan that went off with an enormous explosion that sounded as if the whole place was being blown up! He was very adept at it. But the one thing that was significant for me was on the day that he took us all down to a place called the Photo-Secession Gallery at 291 Fifth Avenue, where there was an exhibition of photographs. I walked out of that place that day feeling, This is what I want to do, this is what I would like to do in my life. From then on, it was a struggle to try and fulfill that dream. That was a decisive day. I had seen what was happening in photography throughout the world.

On that day there began for me a relationship with photography—grandiose as that might seem—but it was a very slow process. I read the other day that Minor White said it takes twenty years to become a photographer. I think that is a little bit of an exaggeration. I would say, judging from myself, that it takes at least eight or nine years. But it does not take any longer than it takes to learn to play the piano or the violin. If it takes twenty years, you might as well forget about it!

Did you ever work with Hine on any of his projects?
No, never. I used to meet him occasionally, by chance. We were always good friends. But I did not really appreciate what he was doing at that time. I was concentrating on the things I was doing myself. He must have come around to "291" when

I had an exhibition there (1916), and he must have been very proud.

He was a modest man and he did not take himself seriously. He did not think of himself as an artist. He was not the "artist type," but he was "*the* artist." He had an amazing eye.

What happened when you took your first portfolio to Stieglitz?
I used to go and see Stieglitz about once every two years. I did not go there to bother him unless I had something to show. He was a great critic for me. I showed my work also to Clarence White and Gertrude Käsebier. They were very sweet to me as a young fellow, but not very helpful. They said what I had was not bad and so on, but it was not very constructive criticism. But from Stieglitz I got very great criticism, which I took extremely seriously. I learned an enormous amount from what he had to say.

In the meantime, I was trying to make a living. I was in business as an office boy and did all sorts of other odd jobs—salesman, telephone operator. But I took the summer off in 1915. I was in a fortunate position, though, because I could always have a room with my family without rent and two meals a day. So in 1915 I put together a group of work that included "Wall Street," "City Hall Park," abstract photographs, and some other things of New York. I took the work to show to Stieglitz for criticism. I felt I had done something better and that I had gained an enormous amount from his criticism. We were alone in the gallery. He was very enthusiastic and said: "You've done something new for photography and I want to show these. I'll give you an exhibition and I want to put them in *Camera Work.*" Well, I was absolutely dumbfounded and happy at the same time—a very good combination! That afternoon he said: " '291' is your place too, you belong here. Come in whenever you want. There is a room in the back where you will meet other people who also come here because they feel that there is a relationship between their lives and what is going on in this place. You will meet some of the painters like Marin, Hartley, and Dove." Then he called: "Steichen! Come here a minute—I want to show you something." So this man came in—a young, tall, very well-built, strapping fellow. We were introduced and Stieglitz said: "Here is a man who has done something in photography that I have not seen done anywhere. I think we should show these things." And Steichen was very nice and very friendly, and he agreed. After that I went on working—I was on the verge of doing the portraits which I did in 1916. I did "The Blind Woman" and all those things with the idea of photographing people without them being aware they were being photographed.

What was it like to be a member of the Stieglitz circle?
I react very badly to that phrase, but I suppose you cannot do anything about it since it has been coined.

"291" was a place where a particular kind of work was being done, and it was through Steichen, really, that modern art at that time—Cézanne, Braque, Picasso, Brancusi—came into the Photo-Secession Gallery. Stieglitz was very glad to have these things because he found that this art was being trampled on in the same way that photography was. Photography as an art was denied, ridiculed, attacked—especially by the academic painters, who thought that the camera might take their livelihood away. The acknowledgment of the validity of photography as a new material, as a new way of seeing life through a machine, was questioned and fundamentally denied. Well, here were these pictures by the Cubists, which were also looked upon as the work of idiots. I used to hear people at "291" say that some of these painters should be in a lunatic asylum, they should be punished, they shouldn't be allowed to do these things!

There was a fight going on for the integrity of a new medium and its right to exist, the right of the photographer to be an artist, as well as the right of Picasso and other artists to do the kind of work they were doing, which was a form of research and experimentation into the very fundamentals of what is, and what is not, a picture. It was said around 1910, when Steichen sent over the Cézanne watercolors and the Rodin drawings, that this was a kind of photography. I'm not sure I agree any more. It was all right in those days, but I think it is very important for young photographers to find out about the whole development of the graphic arts, not simply come along and show photographs that could not stand up to a Cézanne for a second. You cannot claim that photography is an art until your work can hang on the same wall.

An interesting thing in relation to that movement happened when I was making a portrait of Picasso in 1956, when he was seventy-five. We were out in his garden, and he asked me if I knew Steichen and Stieglitz. I said that I knew them very well. He said: "You know, they were the first ones to bring my work to America." I noted he said Steichen *first*, not Stieglitz. Steichen was very important. He was a photographer who made contributions in other ways besides photography. The whole cultural life, as far as painting was concerned, was changed by his bringing modern art to America. And I, as a photographer, was in the middle of it—fascinated. I was learning from these people what photography was, and what painting was, and so on. And all the abstract things I did were consciously directed at finding out what these fellows were talking about, and seeing what relationship it had to photography. The "Bowls" were simply things that were in the kitchen, and "Shadows of the Porch Railing" was done at Twin Lakes, Connecticut, on the porch of a house where we were living. I must have learned quite a lot, I think, because I went out the following year and made "The White Fence," and I have never made a purely abstract photograph since! I have always tried to apply all that I learn to all that I do. All good art is abstract in its structure.

In the ferment of World War I, there was also a great deal of unrest in America. It was a time of new thinking and new feeling about various forms of culture, sharpened later by the catastrophic Crash of 1929. Many, many millions of people were on a boat on a rough sea. People who have made their mark in American cultural life were enabled to do so by their talent and with the help, though not much, of federal government grants. In photography the outstanding contribution was Roy Stryker's Farm Security Administration file of photographs taken by Ben Shahn, Dorothea Lange, Walker Evans, Jack Delano, and many others who went out to photograph what was happening to people during that period when there was so much suffering. Every one of those photographers had an assignment. They were not given a camera and told: "Here, go out and make some pictures of anything you like." Not at all. They were sent out to take photographs of the dust storms and of the displacement of thousands of people who, because of the storms, became migrant workers. The result was that American photography got an enormous shot in the arm. It continued the dual traditions of fine art and social documentary photography.

At the same time, there were developments in American documentary filmmaking which were similar. While Stryker was doing his thing in Washington, we in New York made six movies for Frontier Films. This was an educational cooperative of young film artists, which I had the honor of being president of for five years. Frontier Films finally had to disband because of World War II. Wars are very shattering affairs for cultural work. During the war, I worked on several films, but I wasn't very valuable, I wasn't a young man any more. So in 1944 I went back to still photography.

How would you define documentary photography or filmmaking?

In my understanding, it means an interest in the life and times in which you live—what's happening to the people and the society around you. Very often, what you might call the fine arts ignore this aspect. On the whole, I am attracted to those artists who are interested in a large panorama, and not to those who are strictly concerned with their personal likes and dislikes. I am attracted to those who are more interested in everything that exists outside of themselves. That is the final source of all the best art, and it's a source which has hardly been tapped.

We are beginning to live in a period of great changes, and these changes bring much befuddlement and confusion to all sorts of good people who now find themselves lost. They don't know what is happening around them.

I was very interested to read about a painter-friend of mine whose work showed no awareness or interest in the world—in the tensions, the conflicts, the whys and the wherefores. The painter was interested in the work of Goya, particularly the paintings Goya made of war. He said: "Ordinarily, I don't think I could bear to look at those events, but now I can." I was very happy to read that. For those who are meandering and don't know where to go, Goya's a very good place to begin!

Why did you come to live in France?
After I had completed *Time in New England* with Nancy Newhall, which was published in 1950, things in America made it difficult to find my way from one clear goal to the next. McCarthyism was becoming rife and poisoning the minds of an awful lot of people. Then there arose the question of where do I go from here. That decision finally took shape in a very old idea, that I would like to make a book about a village, a small place. I liked the idea of being confined to a small place and then having to dig into that smallness. But I did not want to choose a village in America during McCarthy's time, when his ideas were doing very bad things to my fellow countrymen. It isn't that I am disloyal to my country—I had just finished a book on New England, so I couldn't be accused of being a renegade or an ex-patriot or anything like that!— but *there is* the rest of the world, so I came to France with my wife.

We started to look for a village in France, and finally we found Yvelines, where there was a young poet who was interested in doing the text for my book. He and I started traveling around France; there were many villages, but we didn't know how to go about it. The French have a way of closing up their shutters about seven o'clock at night, and we never saw a soul outside on the street. It was very depressing. We felt excluded from what was going on, but we kept traveling extensively, all over the country, and I started to photograph the things I found in France that I'd never seen anywhere else. The upshot was that we made a book from photographs taken all over the country, from Brittany to the South of France, up to the mountains, and so on.

We settled in Orgeval; it's a good center for all the work that I have done since.

Do you believe that, with your retrospective, the final barrier to seeing photography as an art has finally been broken?
I don't want to give the impression that I brought this about single-handedly. All I would say is that this exhibition was such a force, and the response was so strong, that the opposition has become less and less.

Is there a philosophy of life that you have tried to show in your photographs?
I find in most cases that what the artist says about what he is going to do, or what he has done, is an inadequate and not very meaningful statement. The thing is the work itself, and in a sense the artist should not be asked for the philosophy of life upon which he bases his work. The work *is* the basis. The work is *the thing itself.*

April 1974

BOOKS OF STRAND PHOTOGRAPHS

Ghana: An African Portrait. Text by Basil Davidson. Millerton, New York: Aperture, 1975.
Living Egypt. Text by James Aldridge. An Aperture Book. New York: Horizon Press, 1969.
The Mexican Portfolio. Preface by David Alfaro Siqueiros. New York: Da Capo Press, 1967.
Paul Strand: Photographs 1915–1945. Text by Nancy Newhall. New York: Museum of Modern Art, 1945.
Paul Strand: A Retrospective Monograph. Millerton, New York: Aperture, 1971.
Paul Strand: Sixty Years of Photographs. Profile by Calvin Tomkins. Millerton, New York: Aperture, 1976.
"Paul Strand Portfolio." *Camera Work,* edited by Alfred Stieglitz. New York, No. 48 (October 1916) ; No. 49–50 (June 1917).
Time in New England. Text edited and selected by Nancy Newhall. New York: Oxford University Press, 1950.
Tir A'mhurain. Text by Basil Davidson. An Aperture Book. New York: Grossman, 1968.

Man Ray

(1 8 9 0 – 1 9 7 6 / A M E R I C A N)

Why did you take up photography?

I was a painter for many years before I became a photographer. I bought a camera one day because I didn't like the reproductions of my work done by professional photographers. At just about that time, the first panchromatic plates came out, and you could photograph in black and white, preserving the values of the colors. I studied very thoroughly, and after a few months, I became quite expert. What interested me the most were people, particularly their faces. Instead of painting people, I began to photograph them, and I didn't want to paint portraits any more. Or, if I painted a portrait, I was no longer interested in creating a likeness. I finally decided that there was no comparison between the two, photography and painting. I paint what cannot be photographed, something from the imagination, or a dream, or a subconscious impulse. I photograph the things that I don't want to paint, things that are already in existence.

I had grown tired of painting. In fact, as I've often said, to master a medium you must despise it a bit, too. That means that you must be so expert and sure of yourself in that medium that it is no longer amusing or interesting to you—it becomes a chore. So I began to paint without using brushes, or canvas, or palette. I started painting with air brushes, an air gun, and compressed air. It was a wonderful relief to paint a picture without touching the canvas. I painted practically three dimensions because, with the air gun, if I wanted a thin line, I'd draw close to the surface, and then if I wanted to model a shade, I went moving in a third dimension. That was a marvelous thing at the time; it relieved my depression about painting, especially since I was being attacked so much for my abstract work. So it became another medium, and when I had satisfied my curiosity, I would stop and perhaps go back to painting for a while.

But I continued to make photographs, reproducing my work and doing portraits of people who came into the studio. I hoped one day that I would be able to make a living out of it. All pupils ask the classical question: "How do you become successful and famous?" I've talked to thousands of pupils and there's only one in ten thousand who might make it. It requires time and persistence, and a certain passion, a certain mania.

What has been your passion? What has been your mania? Somehow, it seems that play is a very important part.
Well, it's all play. The motive? What am I after? The pursuit of liberty, first. When they said I was ahead of my time, I said, "No, I'm not, I'm of my time, *you* are behind the times." But I continued. I jumped from one thing to the other, or did two things at the same time. I had my hands full, and that was enough to keep me going. Then, when I came to France, I immediately met all the young revolutionary crowd, the Dadaists and so forth. I had brought a few works with me, and they thought my work was absolutely in line with what they were advocating. So I collaborated with them and we published magazines and gave exhibitions. I tell youngsters now, "You are all going back forty or fifty years. Why don't you create a new movement of your own? Find a new name for it, that's what you should do, not go back to the past." I'm not a historian, I was always the worst in history class, a disgrace to my instructor.

Did you feel isolated in America because of the sort of work you were doing?
For the most part. I began to paint and exhibit a bit around 1912. My first big show was in 1915, in a gallery on Fifth Avenue that was devoted to young American painters, but they just didn't know what I was driving at.

What was the name of that gallery?
Danielle's. Danielle was a prosperous man who had a big saloon and a lot of money, and a friend of mine—a poet—persuaded him to open an art gallery. The whole New York

School became involved with it. They were all very nice people, but I was on an entirely different track. When I got out of school and started thinking about what I wanted to do, I decided that I must do the things that one is not supposed to do. And that has been my slogan.

I was invited to the Armory show in 1913, but at that time I didn't have anything I thought was important enough to exhibit. And when I saw the show, I was glad that I hadn't participated. There were all the Cubist paintings of Picasso and enormous Picabia paintings, Duchamp's work, the riots over the "Nude Descending the Staircase." I said to Duchamp one day, "You know, if you hadn't put the title 'Nude Descending a Staircase' on the canvas, that picture would have passed unnoticed the way the Picabias did." Ever since then, I've always attached titles to my objects. They do not explain the work but add what you might call a literary element to it that sets the mind going. It doesn't do it to everybody, but the few people that I expect will respond to it do.

At that time, did you show your work to Alfred Stieglitz?
Oh, yes, I used to go to Stieglitz's gallery. It was a few blocks away from the technical publishing house where I made my living as a draftsman. Whenever he had a new exhibition, I'd rush up to his gallery during my lunch break. It was interesting because here was a marvelous photographer who had opened an art gallery; he didn't show photographs, instead he showed modern art. Around 1912, there was an exhibition of Picasso's collages—you know, a few charcoal lines with pieces of newspaper painted on; another time, there was an exhibition of Cézanne's watercolors—a whole unpainted sheet, with just a few touches of color. The white seemed to be part of the painting, it had been done in such an artful way. I came around quite often, and Stieglitz and I got to know each other. We talked a little bit, but I was very young then, and very timid too, and hadn't gotten anywhere yet with my work. He invited me to have a show at his gallery. I said all right, when I have enough things, but I never did. I was just then getting interested in photography, too, and I began to use it to reproduce my paintings. I wondered why Stieglitz was so interested in modern art, showing abstract things—Brancusi sculptures,

Rodin's quick watercolors. I thought: Well, because he's a photographer and photography could not compete with modern painting. We never discussed it, but I felt that he wanted to give photography the value it deserved. He was a secessionist compared to other photographers, and the idea of seceding or revolting had always appealed to me. I was a revolutionary. And so I went on, more and more determined to do all the things that I was *not* supposed to do. When I came to Paris, I was told I should stick to painting. Stieglitz told me to ask for support from a rich coal baron who had bought one or two of my paintings at an exhibition. This man was very nice and immediately gave me a check, saying that he would be in Paris the following year and would see what I had done. I offered him some paintings, but he said, "No, I want to see your new work, and I'll take it out of that." When he came the next year and saw that I was totally involved in photography and making thousands of dollars, he said, "Oh, no, you're an American. You must go back to America. You mustn't stay in Paris and you mustn't give up your painting." I told him that I didn't plan to give it up, I had lots of time for painting. I only worked two hours a day at photography, and that was enough. But sometimes I would work ten hours a day in the darkroom, because, when I started, I was fascinated by optics and chemistry and would do everything myself. People ask: "What camera do you use?" I say: "You don't ask an artist what paints and brushes he uses. You don't ask a writer what typewriter he uses." Anyway, I regard the camera as an aid, in a way. Many painters, especially nowadays, started using a camera—like Warhol, or even Ingres, who painted all his nudes secretly (he would make daguerreotypes from which he drew his nudes). All the nineteenth-century painters were against photography, because they were afraid it would take their bread and butter away from them. Once, Ingres was asked what he thought about photography, and he answered: "I think it's wonderful, but you mustn't say so!"

You have said that you were a revolutionary even within your family. Did your family have an interest in art at all?
None. The fact was, I wanted to paint, it was a passion, I was mad about painting. I don't know where I inherited it, or how

I got the contagion. It seemed like a disease; the smell of turpentine and oil would intoxicate me as alcohol intoxicated others. And then, of course, as in all bourgeois families, the idea of being a painter was not acceptable to them. So, finally, I had to get away from home. I got a little shack out in New Jersey, went to my work at a drafting office, and would then go back out there and paint. I arranged that I would only have to go into town three times a week, the other half of the week I could paint. I didn't care about money or anything, I just wanted to paint.

Did you pay much attention, at this time, to what was happening in photography at the Photo-Secession Gallery?
I didn't see all their exhibits. I knew Steichen, of course, who was a painter to begin with—well, a decorative painter. He wanted to be a society painter, as I did, too. I thought I'd paint beautiful ladies the way Singer Sargent had done. I wasn't really interested in photography, I never was, as an artist. In the thirties, I even published a little booklet called *Photography Is Not Art* through my literary friends. Of course, everybody, including Stieglitz, was trying to prove that photography was art. Since then, my old photographs have been collected, exhibited all over the world, and even honored with medals in Europe. So people would ask me: "Well, do you still think that photography is not art?" "Oh," I'd say, "I don't know what art is, myself. I think the Old Masters weren't artists, they were just good photographers before the camera was invented." Now I would say: "Art is not photography"— which is still more confusing.

Do you find yourself making art *now, but using your photographic past?*
Everything is art. I don't discuss those things any more. All this anti-art business is nonsense. If we must have a word for it, let's call it art. And, if it's different from anything else, that is the real revolution. The mere fact of calling it a negative thing is not sufficient to destroy it, if that's what they want to do. The Futurists of 1911 advocated burning down all the museums, and I agreed with them, too, although I loved the Old Masters. To me, they were more than painters, they

were blacksmiths, they were a force, a Goya or a Uccello, or even a Manet, later on. Why, those men used a brush the way a blacksmith would handle a hammer.

Is there anything at all that's related to photography in the work you are doing now?
Everything is related to photography, because it all has to be photographed in the end. There are half a dozen books and catalogues of mine with color reproductions, and everything is there—rayographs, photographs, black-and-white rayographs, color reproductions.

What work are you doing now?
Well, it's a secret, because I don't like to show the things I do immediately, sometimes I wait years. There have been large exhibitions of all my graphic work, lithographs and etchings, but this is a sort of panorama from my early work. Here, in Paris, they accept everything I do, there is no hesitation at all. But some of the American publishers want to change things; they want to take this out or put something else in. I say: "This is my work. If you want to do something different, sign it with your name, create something, but don't try and change my work."

I never touch a camera myself, any more than a movie director does. People say: "Do you take the photographs yourself?" Always. Even if somebody else pushes the button, I take the photograph. You don't ask an architect whether he built the building himself, you don't ask a composer whether he plays the whole piece himself. I have enjoyed the last year, since I haven't wanted to produce any more original work, at least not for publication. The things I exhibit, the things I reproduce, are works that have been going on for the last sixty years, they have no date. Some of the French critics are very intelligent. One critic commented that all the things I've been exhibiting, all the reproductions I've published (some of which were done forty or fifty years ago) could have been done today!

There are no dates in my career. I have several mediums at

my fingertips. Photography was just as incidental as painting was, or writing, or making sculptures, or just talking. In 1963 I wrote a book called *Self-Portrait*, at the instigation of an editor in New York who wanted a book about the twenties and thirties. I said: "Well, I started long before that and I finished long after that. I'm still around, you see, so you can't really fix a time. I'd have to start from the very beginning and go to the very end." So, the book starts with my actual birth, and ends with my return to Paris in 1951, after having spent ten years in California during the war.

Where in California?
I lived right on Vine Street in Hollywood. I had a beautiful studio there, in a courtyard with palm trees and humming-birds and flowers. I forgot that I was in America at the time, just as I forget now that I am in France. I live within my own four walls, it's my life. I don't attach any importance to the outside world. I think that a few people is all one needs for companionship or acceptance. I can only deal with one or two people at a time.

You asked me what I am doing now. Well, it is the same thing that I have been doing all my life. When I have a show, people ask: "Is this your recent work?" One day I shouted: "I have never in my life painted a recent picture." By living my way, I have been able to emphasize my own personality. I consider individuality the most important thing. In a preface to a catalogue for an exhibition in a museum, I wrote: "This exhibition is not for the public, it is only for one person—for you who are here." Well, at first they thought that was a little too tough. But finally they got it, they understood what I meant. I never think of pleasing the public or arousing their interest. I despise them just as much as they have despised me through the years for the things I've done.

I have been accused of being a joker. But the most success-ful act to me involves humor. In America, for instance, much of the Dadaist activity is like comic strips in the newspaper. Theirs is provincial humor, appreciated only by the people immediately around them. It hasn't got the universal quality that the European movements once had.

Why did you return to Paris in 1951?
Well, after all, I had spent twenty years in Paris before the war. It had become impossible to stay with the Germans all around me, and it was fortunate that I did go back to America; otherwise, I'd have ended up in a prison camp. The Germans let me go, after looking at my passport very carefully to see that I wasn't involved with any of the political activities in France. I practically had to escape.

I had a wonderful time in California. I did a lot of photography and a lot of painting, and I was no longer working for anybody but myself. That had been my ideal. I was able to do all the paintings that I had been planning for ten or twenty years before—paintings I had never been able to realize. Some of them were from photographs of abstract mathematical subjects, which I used because they were man-made, they were *not* from nature.

That in itself is a rather revolutionary idea, isn't it?
Absolutely. But all those paintings are gone now. I came to Paris in 1951 and found this studio by chance. I settled down and started all over again, a sort of second life. I painted like mad from 1950 to 1960.

Did you become disenchanted with America?
Oh, no, it had nothing to do with that. I thought Hollywood was a wonderful place. And when I stopped in New York on my way back to America in 1940, they had set up a big studio for me at *Vogue* or *Harper's Bazaar*. I was doing all their fashion work, and celebrities, theatrical and movie people. I said: Well, I've been through this terrible war, and need a little vacation now. I was really on my way to Hawaii and Tahiti, I was going to disappear. I had left the studio in Paris with everything in it, not knowing whether I'd ever see the things again. A lot of my paintings were hidden away in a cellar, but I found some of them seven years later when I came back to collect them. It's just that I feel freer here, that's all. There's a proverb about a prophet in his own country. I didn't want to be famous or anything, I just wanted to be comfortable and have enough to live on and do my work.

I lectured a lot in America, and was well paid for that. I had pupils in California, the wives of movie producers who had nothing to do and wanted to learn photography or painting. I even had a waitress who would come in her spare time for lessons in painting. She became a good painter and later a professor of art in a university. I was very successful as a teacher, but I wouldn't teach formally. The Art Center in California gave me an exhibition and tried to get me to teach. I told them I was against education. I could teach only a few people, one at a time. I've always had one or two students in my studio in Paris learning photography.

Bill Brandt came to you, didn't he?
He was my pupil. He came to my studio and asked if he could study with me. I told him I couldn't teach him anything, but he could watch and help. He fiddled around a bit and finally became a photographer, as Berenice Abbott did. I had three or four others, and they all are famous photographers now.

Did any other photographers come to see you, people like Cartier-Bresson or Brassaï?
There is a snapshot by Cartier-Bresson of me and Duchamp, taken just before Duchamp died. We were sitting here over a game of chess, and Cartier-Bresson took a snapshot. He sent it to me when I had my last exhibition, saying: "If you need a photograph for publicity, you can use mine."

Can you explain your relationship with Atget?
I discovered him! But I don't consider that to my credit. Atget lived a few doors from my studio in Paris in the twenties. He had albums which he printed on a little frame, putting it outside his window to dry in the back yard in the sun, and as soon as he had the prints, he put them in a book. You could go to him and buy a print for five francs, and then he'd replace it. They were all the French size (18 x 24 cm.). I begged him once: "Lend me some of your plates and I'll make some prints on modern paper." "Oh, no," he said, "that's not permanent." His prints all faded if you exposed them to the light,

because they were washed in salt water to fix them. They were the kind of prints that photographers made as proofs for their sitters so that they wouldn't be kept as permanent things. Anyway, I would drop in once in a while and pick up a few prints. He had thousands of them: he'd photographed so much in his lifetime. But he said he was making documents for painters. He was a painter himself, he painted landscapes. I finally acquired about thirty or forty prints and gave them to Beaumont Newhall. They're the ones that have been most reproduced, because they have a Dada or Surrealist quality about them.

Atget was a very simple man, almost naïve, like a Sunday painter, you might say, but he worked every day. When I had a couple of his things reproduced in a Surrealist magazine in the twenties—a crowd standing on a bridge looking at the sky, at an eclipse—he said: "Don't put my name on it. These are simply documents I make." You see, he didn't want any publicity.

Did Atget explain why he didn't want any publicity? He was living in very poor circumstances.
Very poor. He had no money. He had been an actor once, in a traveling show, I think. I was away from my studio for a few weeks on a trip down south when he died. At that time, Berenice Abbott was my assistant. I had known her in New York as a young girl of eighteen; she was a sculptress. She had come to Paris a month or two before me. She was starving, and I asked her to come and help me, because I was loaded with work. All the painters—Picasso, Braque, Matisse—were asking me to photograph their work. When Atget died, she went to his studio with her brother and got his collection of negatives, which she was later able to publish in France. She was very enthusiastic about it. She became a very good photographer after a couple of years with me and then went off on her own.

I don't want to make any mystery out of Atget at all. He was a simple man, and he used the material that was available to him when he started in 1900—an old rickety camera with a brass lens on it and a cap. I've taken photographs that way, too, when my other cameras broke down. I've even taken photographs without a lens on my camera. Once, I had to photograph a painter and I arrived with my studio camera and tripod and everything. I started to set up, but I'd forgotten the lens. I knew the size of my lens because I prescribed my own glasses, I knew optics so well. I knew that my lens had a 12-inch focal length, but of course I realized it would be a very fuzzy picture. I had a roll of tape and taped my own eyeglass lens onto the opening in my camera and just let the black cloth down, with a little hole in it, to diaphragm it. I opened the cloth and let it down, and I got the portrait of Matisse—a beautiful, soft-focus photograph with all the details visible.

Do you feel it is a burden to be a historical figure in the art world?

It's a nuisance, an absolute nuisance. They drag me on television and on radio, and there are newspaper and magazine interviews. I discourage them as much as I can, of course. But an artist has to rely on publicity, otherwise he can't have exhibitions. I gave up photography professionally twenty years ago, although when I feel like doing a portrait, I do one. I make some prints, but not by myself. I have two or three laboratories here in Paris, and they do wonderful work for me. There's been so much progress in printing and the mechanics of photography, but there's no progress on the creative side of it.

There are two or three collectors who have a couple of hundred of my prints, and the Museum of Modern Art has about 150. The Metropolitan had a traveling exhibition. I wasn't there for it, but they sent me photographs—one from Pasadena, one from San Francisco, one from Washington. I get all the catalogues from the exhibitions of my work, and sometimes the collector is a bit of a photographer himself, so he slips in some of his own photographs, to see if he can get noticed along with me. But that's a mistake: you should never show your work with that of a master, it only makes you look worse. I never show my works with painters who are considered greater than I am. I want only one-man exhibitions, just as I want a one-man audience!

April 1974

Man Ray (catalogue). New York: Alexander Iolas Gallery, 1974.

Man Ray (catalogue). Los Angeles: Los Angeles County Museum of Art, Lytton Gallery, 1966.

Man Ray, by Sarane Alexandrain (translated by Eleanor Levieux). Chicago: J. Philip O'Hara, 1973.

Man Ray, by Sir Roland Penrose. Boston: New York Graphic Society, 1975.

Man Ray: Photographs—1920–1934. Introduction by A. D. Coleman. New York: East River Press, 1975.

Man Ray: Portraits. Introduction by Fritz Gruber. Guttersich: Sigbert Mohn, 1963.

Photo-graphics (Man Ray). From collection of Arnold H. Crane (catalog). Milwaukee Art Center: Milwaukee, Wisconsin, 1973.

Photographs by Man Ray: 1920 Paris 1934. Hartford, Connecticut: James Thrall Soby, 1934.

Self-Portrait. Boston: Little, Brown, 1963.

New York Dada: Duchamp, Man Ray, Picabia, by Arturo Schwarz. New York: Hacker Art Books, 1973.

Cecil Beaton

(B O R N   1 9 0 4 / B R I T I S H)

Pavel Tchelitchew

When did you become involved with photography?
At a very young age, about eight or nine. My sisters' nurse
taught me how to do things properly. My attempts were simple
to begin with. I used a Kodak 3a, also a smaller Kodak. I
photographed scenes with my sisters in them, and I tried to
make them look like pictures that were being done by the
photographers of the day. I was particularly interested in
photographs of the Edwardian Age, so I would pose my sisters

as if they were in paintings, like actresses. I did pictures of them which were sensational as photographs.

Sensational?
In the sense that they were avant-garde.

What photographs inspired you at that time?
I liked the photographs I saw in *The Tatler* and *The Sketch*, and also those in the photographers' shops in Bond Street —big, high-falutin', high potential, terrific backgrounds. When I started, lots of people liked that kind of photograph, and I gradually became more interested. I left my sisters' nurse behind me! I went off on my own. I sent my films to Selfridge's because I couldn't afford the time to process them myself. When I got the negatives back, I would go to work retouching them, making them look like *proper* photographs. Nanny used to help me with the processing in the bathroom when I was very young.

Was there any art background in your family?
No, none at all. My father took some photographs, but they were always intended to be straightforward. Mine were never straightforward!

How did your family react to this?
They didn't look much. My mother was interested, she posed a lot, but my sisters and father didn't pay much attention to it. They thought it was all rather a bore.

At what age did you decide that photography was something you would devote a great deal of your time to?
I don't think I ever thought of it in terms of the time spent. I never really anticipated that I would grow up and take photographs for a living. I was just keen to try and get a lot from photography, and be as independent as I could. It was only when I was eighteen that I decided I'd like to take it up seriously, and when I was twenty I decided I would love to have a studio, which was a feeling I'd never had before. But

I never did have one. My best pictures were always done in the drawing room at home, or in other people's houses.

What about at Harrow, a very traditional public school, what did your contemporaries think of your taking photographs?
They didn't see them, they weren't interested.

What about when you moved on to Cambridge University?
They were more interested in them there.

Did you photograph student life at the time?
No, I was taking studio pictures, mostly of the people working in the theater at Cambridge and the productions I was involved with.

What were you studying?
I studied many things, but I never followed through. I failed dismally. I think I went to one or two lectures.

What did you spend your time doing?
Mostly taking pictures, and in the theater.

How did your interest in the theater begin?
I joined the Amateur Dramatic Club around 1924 or 1925, and they gave me my first part.

As an actor?
No, as an actress!

Apart from your involvement in the theater, were there any other artistic influences when you were at the university?
Yes. There was a person named Le Bas. He and I were very intimate with one another. He had a little car, and I used to go to London with him. We went to see the exhibitions at the Lefevre and Leicester Galleries. We used to see all that was going on.

What art interested you?
I cannot remember. I wasn't interested in the conventional painters, though.

Did you think that photographs could hang in a gallery along-side paintings?
No. Photographs just weren't exhibited as photographs. Very few people would ever bother to give their permission to have an exhibition of photographs. It was only in America, during the twenties and thirties, that they were accepted.

How did you get your first show in 1930 at the Cooling Gallery, London?
I just met Mr. Cooling. I thought that I would have an exhibition of paintings and drawings in one gallery, and photographs in another. I had a lot of pictures in that exhibition.

Was it at Cambridge that you also began to paint?
I began to paint at the same time, in a very miserable way.

When did you find that you were more and more drawn toward set designing?
At Cambridge. I was very interested in it. Lebas also was interested, and he and I sort of fought with one another as to who would get certain jobs.

How were you making your living at that time?
First of all, I had to study with my father at his business; I failed utterly at that. I was very bad at business, a complete flop! I had to go to another office and accept a much lower income; in fact, I think I was paid a pound a week.

Doing what?
Office work, writing out invoices. Suddenly I made up my mind to have an exhibition. I put together enough to have a show at the Cooling Gallery, and they were so delighted and surprised that they used my things as an advertisement. I also designed book jackets to make some money, but not many, perhaps one book a season—certainly not enough for my financial needs.

Whom were you taking photographs for at that time?
Mostly for people who liked my photographs. I took photo-

graphs of well-known people and gave them to *The Tatler* in particular.

How did you get to know these people? Through the theater?
They were not really well known by the general public, but by people interested in the theater and in the arts. I did put a certain number of pictures in *The Tatler* and *The Sketch* which were influenced by the *Book of Beauty* magazine. I eventually produced a *Book of Beauty* of my own.

Did you photograph people in a particular style right from the beginning?
Yes, right from the beginning. I had in mind that I wanted to do something completely different, completely new, something that would be completely absorbing. I did not want to make the people look like themselves, I wanted to disguise them.

Were you affected by any surrealistic work that you saw at that time, or was your very individual style something that you came to through the theatricality of the settings that you were designing?
It was very surrealistic in approach, but it didn't strike the Surrealists until about five years later, when it became much more salubrious to act in a professional way, unprofessionally!

Were you influenced by any of the Surrealists?
I think I was influenced by people like Dali.

One senses in your photographs a sense of humor about the whole process, and also a sense of theatricality. Could you explain further?
I think that the sense of humor was very much based on keeping it quiet, not letting the public know about it, not letting the person know. It was that kind of humor I was using. I thought that the sense of theatricality was very important, but again, it must be played low, especially with some people.

*Did you have the sense that you were creating a sort of pic-
torial drama, a little piece of theater?*
Yes, I think I did have that. I had a very strong sense of
theater. It was natural that my feeling for the theater should
be expressed in the work that I did.

*There is a Caligari-like feeling in many photographs of yours.
Was there a style of theater or literature that you were particularly interested in?*
The Caligari aspect was obviously there. I painted on walls
things that looked like enlargements of pictures. I think my
sets were made up of things that were dramatic in their feel.
    I worked in the revue before moving on to the larger
theatrical arena. I had two careers—photography and set
designing. They overflowed constantly.

*When you were talking about your sense of humor, and the
fact that you had to keep fairly quiet about it, was this because you didn't want the sitters to know that in fact there was
an implied social comment on the sham and superficiality that
you saw in some of the personalities you photographed?*
I think that's putting it awfully bluntly, but I suppose you're
correct.

*Your work seems to eulogize all the superficial and flamboyant
things of the period, but at the same time one has the feeling
that you were teasing the people you were photographing.*
That is very true.

Was it a financial decision to join Vogue *as a photographer?*
No, I think not. I wanted to join *Vogue*. They were very
interested in the sort of things that I did.

Did they understand them?
Yes, I think they did, but they didn't assist me at all. They
would suddenly say, That's far beyond a joke, that isn't feasible,
that isn't factual; but they did give me a platform, and they
liked what I did.

Did they censor you in any way?
Yes, they did.

Could you describe a case where you went too far?
I could show you photographs that were not accepted. There was a photograph of a woman's legs with a wonderful arrangement of leaves below the waist; then beautiful legs, sandals; and then beautiful leaves around the bottom. A wonderful picture.

Did you find yourself working in a vein that was similar to anything being done at the time?
I wasn't really. I think my work was quite outside everything else. I didn't feel contemporary at all. *Vogue* would have cashed in; they would have had someone taking pictures like me if they could have, but they didn't.

Vogue *had a rather rich tradition of photographers preceding you, people like Steichen and De Meyer. Did they influence you?*
Yes, enormously. Steichen influenced me in a particular way: he forced me to use a different camera, an enormous camera, not my little Kodak. De Meyer was an all-around influence on me; I think that he could do wonderful tricks with illusion. He is very much to be respected.

Did De Meyer's rather unusual life style, during the time he was working for Vogue, *interest you?*
No, I was ignorant of that.

So the influence was purely through his images?
Absolutely. His work interested me enormously. The silvery quality, the romance, the lighting, all those were very important.

Did he also hide people, disguise them?
He did. Yes.

When you found that you no longer had to rely on Steichen, what did you want to do?
I felt freer to work in the same areas he did. I think that he

did extraordinary things with portraiture, but I also felt I could upset the apple cart and just make them *my* way.

Did you see yourself as an illusionist, a magician?
I didn't see myself at all in that light. I would just take a picture and be amused to feel that I had captured something that happened to coincide with the idea that I had in mind.

You said that Vogue *gave you a platform—freedom. Why, then, did you photograph only society figures and business personalities of the time? Were you told to do this, or was it done out of choice?*
Choice.

Did you make the sets that you put the sitter in as well? It seems that you virtually created an entire environment.
I did it on purpose. I bought the materials; every little ornament was placed by me.

Did you feel yourself creating images that would last?
No, I didn't think of that at all.

How did you feel during the Depression, photographing what a lot of people at that time thought was trivial? Were you involved in any political movement?
No, not at all. I enjoyed only the things of the moment.

When you saw the work of people like Bill Brandt, who photographed the depressed North of England, did you feel that you should have been involved?
Yes, but I only felt that much later.

Before World War II?
During World War II I felt that.

How did you get a job as an official war photographer?
I didn't get a job as any sort of photographer. A friend of mine said: "I think you would do well at the Ministry of Information." They opened my eyes to reality. My life was

suddenly enlarged enormously. I photographed the shipbuilding yards in Newcastle, also the Air Force and the Navy in England. I took the photographs, and then sent them to the Ministry of Information, and they used them. They sent me to China, India, and Africa—all over the world.

How did you feel about the soldiers you photographed?
They seemed to be very real. They weren't dressed up as anything, they were just themselves.

Is this when you became aware of what you felt you should have been aware of in the thirties?
It was a different thing. I can't say anything belonged to the thirties, because I *did* belong to the thirties, and I just took photographs. Then in the forties I was different, and I took different sorts of photographs.

Did you see your work, even the fashion, as a kind of documentation?
The fashion work was more a fantasy. But the documentation of the war was the real thing.

In the thirties, how did you come to be commissioned to photograph the British Royal Family?
That was entirely due to good fortune. Princess Olga asked me to take some pictures of her at Buckingham Palace, where she was staying as a guest. Three days later, Queen Elizabeth, the present queen's mother, asked me if I would go and take some pictures of her. It was terribly overdue! I was longing for it. I had had nothing but rebuffs from Queen Mary, the wife of King George IV, but I was received with open arms by the Queen Mother, as she now is. Since then I have photographed all of them.

What was it that you most enjoyed about photographing the Royal Family?
Well, photographing the Queen Mother was very exciting, because everything was open to one. There were the gardens, the cottages, the house, the rooms; everything was just there

ready for my asking. And it was the same with other members of the family.

You've been well known publicly as a photographer of the Royal Family and for being associated over a long period of time with one of the enigmatic characters of the twentieth century, Greta Garbo. Was it through photography that you two first met?
No. Absolutely not. She was the one person I wanted to photograph. I knew her pretty well before I dared to ask her to be photographed. She only said: "Will you take some pictures of me for my passport."

Do you still keep in touch?
Yes.

Are there any major figures in photography whose work you admire?
Most of the early Victorian photographers, and more recently, people like Avedon, Penn, Norman Parkinson, and David Bailey.

Many of these photographers have been great portraitists. What do you consider to be a primary ingredient of a good portrait?
I think just the head! The face must tell you something.

Have you any thoughts on photographic education?
I think it's interesting, particularly if the enthusiasm comes from the student. You can't teach people photography, they've got to learn how to do it the best way possible for them. They can learn from looking at pictures taken by well-known people, but they don't really get intimate with the medium until they've made a few bad shots!

There is a gap of thirty-eight years between your show in 1930 and the one at the National Portrait Gallery, London, in 1968. Why?
I wasn't interested in showing pictures. I had nothing to offer.

Presumably, people asked you?
I suppose so.

Is there a central philosophical concern in your photography?
It's just a question of whether I can do something that pleases
me. If it does, it will very likely please the subject and an
audience. That's the test of the matter. But it has to please
me first.

Would you like photography to go in any particular direction?
No, I have no ideas about that.

Are you involved at the moment in any photographic work?
Obviously I am tied down [Sir Cecil suffered a stroke in 1974],
but I am very much involved in thinking about the medium
in much wider terms than I ever have before.

Because you've had a chance to see more?
Yes.

What are the conclusions you are coming to about the medium?
I think creativity is a question of taste. If it comes through,
if it isn't too extraordinary, it'll be there—innate taste, style.

*Where would you place photography among your many in-
terests?*
Oh, I think I would put it fifth.

What would you put first?
I don't know!

September 1976

SELECTED BIBLIOGRAPHY

Beaton Portraits. Foreword by Roy Strong. London: H.M. Stationary Office
    for the National Portrait Gallery, 1968.
The Best of Beaton. Notes on the photographs by Cecil Beaton; introduction
    by Truman Capote. New York: Macmillan, 1968.

The Book of Beauty. London: Duckworth, 1930.

British Photographs. New York: Hastings, 1944.

Cecil Beaton's New York. London: Batsford, 1938.

Chinese Album. London: Batsford, 1945.

The Class of Fashion. New York: Doubleday, 1954.

Far East. London: Batsford, 1945.

The Happy Years—Cecil Beaton: Memoirs of the Forties. London: Weidenfeld and Nicolson, 1972.

Images. Preface by Dame Edith Sitwell; introduction by Christopher Isherwood. New York: House and Maxwell, 1963.

Indian Album. London: Batsford, 1945.

Japanese. London: Weidenfeld and Nicolson, 1959.

The Magic Image: The Genius of Photography from 1839 to the Present Day, by Cecil Beaton and Gail Buckland. Boston: Little, Brown, 1975.

Near East. London: Batsford, 1943.

Photobiography. London: Odhams, 1951.

Portrait of New York. London: Batsford, 1948.

The Parting Years: Cecil Beaton's Diaries 1963–1974. London: Weidenfeld and Nicolson, 1978.

The Strenuous Years: Diaries 1948–1955. London: Weidenfeld and Nicolson, 1973.

The Wandering Years: Diaries 1922–1939. Boston: Little, Brown, 1961.

The Years Between: Diaries 1939–1944. New York: Holt, Rinehart and Winston, 1965.

Jacques-Henri Lartigue

(B O R N   1 8 9 4 / F R E N C H)

Paul Hill

How did you first start taking photographs?
My father was a businessman; during the holidays he used to
take photographs for fun with a huge camera, and I used to
amuse myself by looking through the ground-glass screen. As a
child I did a lot of painting and writing, and one day my
father gave me the camera and I started to take pictures. I
was then six years old, and the camera was a 13 cm. by 18 cm.
on a tripod. It had a dark cloth, and after you had focused,

you pulled off the lens cap and counted one—two—three and
then put it back.

Were there any artists in your family?
No, but they were all very gifted and intelligent people, many
of them inventors and scientists. My grandfather invented the
monorail.

Is it true that you had a strong sense of play as a child?
Yes, exactly.

What was your greatest passion when you were younger?
Sports.

*Did you become aware of what other photographers were
doing as you became a little older?*
No, not at all. I didn't know anything about that until I was
fifty years old. I did like looking at the photographs in *Vogue*
and *Harper's Bazaar*, though.

As a painter, how do you regard photography?
I have two pairs of eyes—one to paint, and one to take photographs. There is little relationship between the two.

Do you think of photographs as documents or art objects?
I take photographs with love, so I try to make them art objects.
But I make them for myself first and foremost—that is important. If they are art objects at the same time, that's fine
with me. In fact, it is what I write in my diary that excites me
most; I write with love, and try to express things the best way
I can.

Which contemporary photographers do you like best?
I like a great many—all for different reasons, because they all
make different images: landscapes, portraits, carefully composed pictures like those of Hiro, and so on.

*Do you resent the fact that you are better known as a photog-
rapher than as a painter?*

For forty years I was known as a painter. Since the war I have been known as a photographer—each one in its turn.

Is photography still important to you?
Yes, more and more.

Do you see the world with the same tender eyes as you did as a child?
Fortunately, I am still a child. It seems to me that human beings tend to get more and more "down" as they get older. One must try always to remain childlike, gay, happy.

Is there anything that you feel should be happening in photography today?
I think just about everything has been tackled, but it may be that things will be done again, only better and differently.

Can one learn to be a photographer? How would you teach photography?
First, one must learn how to look, how to love. It's the same with painting and writing.

Is a special environment necessary?
I don't really think so. I don't think that you learn to have nervous enthusiasm, either. It comes from the guts. I couldn't teach anyone. It's the same with writing. All you can teach a writer is how to fill his fountain pen and take hold of a sheet of paper!

Do you think that there is a European style of photography?
No. Each photographer has his own style and his own character.

Your work is always presented in a gay, lighthearted way. Is there a darker side to your life?
I have thousands of unpublished photographs. The ones which have been published were well selected. I am a bit of an egoist, and I make pictures for my own pleasure and not necessarily to show them. I never work to order.

Are you happy to fill the role of a lighthearted man?
I am lighthearted, therefore I am happy . . . not the other way
around!

April 1974

BOOKS OF LARTIGUE PHOTOGRAPHS

*Boyhood Photos of Jacques-Henri Lartigue: The Family Album of a Guilded
Age.* Introduction by Jean Fonolin. New York: Guichard-Time-Life
Books, 1966.
Diary of a Century. New York: Viking Press, 1970.
Jacques-Henri Lartigue. Aperture History of Photography Series, Number 5.
Millerton, New York, 1976.
The Photographs of Jacques-Henri Lartigue. Introduction by John Szarkow-
ski. New York: Museum of Modern Art, 1963.
Women. New York: Dutton, 1974.

Brassaï

(B O R N   1 8 9 9 / F R E N C H ,
B O R N   I N   H U N G A R Y)

Paul Hill

Is it true that for a long time you took no interest in photography?

Yes, that is true. Until the age of thirty I had never even held a camera; photography was unrelated to any of my other interests. But, for five or six years, from 1924 on, I led a nocturnal life in Paris, sleeping by day and walking by night. During these walks through the city, I saw many marvelous images in the fog and in the rain. I began to look for a way of expressing what I saw, and it was at that point that I thought of photography. Around 1930 a woman lent me a camera, and for months I devoted myself to night photography. André Kertész gave me some advice, but he never lent me a camera, as is often said, and I never worked in his studio. In my first years in Paris, I was working as a journalist and I asked several photographers to illustrate my articles. I asked Kertész to supply photographs for three or four of these articles. In 1933, I published my first photographic album, *Paris de nuit*. A few months later, it was published in London by Batsford with the title *Paris after Dark*.

Why did you choose photography as your medium of expression?

The choice was not easy for me. I was equally gifted in drawing, sculpture, and painting. Do you know what Picasso said when he looked at my drawings in 1939? "You're crazy, Brassaï. You have a gold mine and you spend your time exploiting a salt mine!" The salt mine was—naturally—photography! But I have always believed that a medium of self-expression should not be chosen without regard for the given period. One should use the media of the times: photography, television, the cinema. Curiously, just as I was disdainful of photography for a long time, the century has also been very slow to recognize its importance. Only in the last ten years or so has photography been considered worthy and been accepted in art galleries and museums as an artistic expression of our era. I do not disavow my drawings or my sculpture or my tapestries, but as far as I'm concerned, contrary to what Picasso thought, photography has proved to be my "gold mine," and my best and most original medium of expression.

So you became a professional photographer. Were you upset by the fact that you had to do what you were told and were often asked to fulfill assignments that did not interest you and were spiritually antithetical?

Your question is very important, especially for those photographers who do not have an independent income and must work for a living. There is always the danger of prostituting one's gifts simply in order to live and to survive. The most difficult thing in life is to make money doing what you like to do. After a brief period of slavery—I too have worked for a hairdressing magazine!—I achieved complete freedom. When I first started working for *Harper's Bazaar*, circa 1937, I was asked to take fashion photographs. I categorically refused. I was able to arrange to photograph only what I wanted to photograph for the magazine. That was how I chose to make portraits and to photograph the studios of several artists, including Picasso, Braque, Matisse, Bonnard, etc., etc., and to travel. Carmel Snow was a wonderful woman, with a remarkable intelligence and flair. She preferred that I suggest subjects that I would like to photograph, rather than rely on her to tell me what to do. Twice a year, when she came to Paris to see the collections, we would have lunch together at the Plaza-Athenée. It was at these meetings that we would decide together the photographic themes for *Harper's* upcoming issues. Alexey Brodovitch, the magazine's art director, never gave me any directives, but he liked my photographs very much and his layouts reflected the feeling of the photographs.

You and Cartier-Bresson are often called the pioneers of documentary photography. How do you react to this description?
I would never consider myself a "photojournalist" or a "photoreporter" because I have never taken photographs of topical interest for a newspaper. Usually, in reporting, the photographs are presented in series with an accompanying legend or text. Without this explanation, often they do not stand on their own. But, for me, I have always maintained formal perfection: the structure or composition of a photograph is just as important as its subject. This is not an aesthetic demand, as one might assume, but a practical one. Only images powerfully grasped—streamlined—have the capacity to penetrate the memory, to remain there, and to become, in a word, unforgettable. It is the sole criterion for a photograph. But that doesn't mean that, for me, photography is nothing but art for art's sake. If I look back over my photographs, I must admit that I have always been reporting, but reporting *in depth*, on the city and the times in which I lived. Prewar Paris had much

more personality than the city today—the effect of so-called progress has been to strip away the specific character of the people, the streets, the *quartiers*, and to bring them all down to the same level. My *Paris secret des années 30* has been described, especially in the United States, as a vast social inquiry into the underworld of Paris. At that time, no one thought of photographing the cesspool cleaners, the inverts, the opium dens, the *bals musettes*, the bordellos, and the other seedy spots with their fauna. It is not sociologists who provide insights but photographers of our sort who are observers at the very center of their times. I have always felt strongly that this was the photographer's true vocation. My future publications will verify, I believe, that my inquiry was not limited to underground Paris or to the Paris night but included many other aspects of the city and other social classes as well.

You said once that a successful drawing is always superior to a photograph.
No, I never said that. Napoleon once declared that he preferred a drawing to a long report. Today, I am certain he would say that he would prefer a photograph. In reality, it was Picasso who preferred a drawing to a photograph, because it was a more direct, a more spontaneous expression of a personality. And, in that sense, he had a point.

And did he also tell you that photography could never provide the same satisfaction as drawing?
It's true that drawing does give you a greater satisfaction, but it is a narcissistic one. In photography you can never express yourself directly, only through optics, the physical and chemical processes. It is this sort of submission to the object and abnegation of yourself that is exactly what pleases me about photography. What is extraordinary is that, despite this submission and this abnegation, the personality of the photographer shines through all the obstacles. In the end, images convey personality just as strongly as in a drawing. But if you seek personal expression in photography, you will soon become aware of limitations. Photography reflects the infinite variety of subject matter offered by the natural universe. But

the range of vision of the "great photographers" is extremely narrow. They must confine themselves to their own peculiar obsessions and types of images which can express character and feelings: Weston's is the sand dunes of New Mexico; Ansel Adams's is vast cosmic landscapes; Arbus's is monsters; Atget's the streets of Paris.

How did your attitude to the cinema evolve?
The purpose of film is to express movement. I made the film *Tant qu'il y aura des bêtes* because I wanted my ideas on this subject clarified. It was a twenty-three-minute short based solely on movement, without a word spoken. It won a prize in the 1956 Cannes Festival, where it was shown as the official French entry. It is the one and only film that I have ever made. As a result of this success, I have had many offers from producers urging me to make other films like that one—just as I received many offers after *Paris de nuit* to do a *London by Night* or a *New York by Night*. But the idea of exploiting a success has always offended me. No doubt it is the secret to making money, and many artists—even very great ones— keep working the same vein during their whole life. Picasso was perhaps the only twentieth-century painter who had the courage never to exploit a successful mode or style. In the course of his life, he had twenty or thirty periods, any one rich enough to support an artist for life—the blue period, rose period, classicism, etching, lithography, sculpture, etc., etc. But he abandoned each and started again from zero.

Why have you stopped taking photographs?
According to my plans, I should have given up photography forever in 1963, after my big exposition at the Bibliothèque Nationale. They even presented me with an award, as though I were already dead. I shall always love photography, and sometimes I suffer from not doing more these days. But I have taken many photographs in my life and published relatively few books, so now I prefer to travel in the universe of my photographs and make them better known. I think working on this is more important than taking new photographs.

You are often described as the Henry Miller of photography. What is your reaction to this?
Right, as far as my photographs of the Paris underworld are concerned. Miller rediscovered in them everything he loved about that city. Also, many of his books have been illustrated by my photographs. He wrote a sort of essay on me called "L'Oeil de Paris" ("The Eye of Paris") in 1934, at the same time that he was writing *Tropic of Cancer.* But my other interests cannot be classified as such.

What are your current artistic plans?
I have had no time for sculpture for a very long period. But I hope to return to Carrara soon, where I would like to once again carve out a few large pieces.

And your clichés-verre?
I became interested in these around 1935, and twelve of the prints appeared in my album *Transmutations.* Unlike the great masters Corot and Delacroix, I was not interested in engraving in the gelatin of a virginal plate. What intrigued me were plates that already had images, particularly nudes. I then shaped these as if I were working on a piece of sculpture.

Are you doing any writing at the moment?
Yes, more and more. As you know, I have already published texts in *Labyrinthe, Graffiti, Paris secret des années 30, Conversations avec Picasso* (which has been translated into many languages), and *Henry Miller: Grandeur Nature.* I have recently finished collecting the writings that I describe as "photographic" in a book called *Paroles en l'air,* which has just been published; then there is *l'Histoire de Marie,* originally written in 1949, *Bistro-Tabac,* and so on. I am working on other books, but I don't wish to talk about them ahead of time. All these writings are "seen" by the ear in the spirit of photography.

April 1974

BOOKS OF BRASSAÏ PHOTOGRAPHS

Brassaï. Essay by Sean Adhemar. Paris: Bibliothèque Nationale, 1963.
Brassaï. Introduction by Lawrence Durrell. New York: Museum of Modern Art, 1968.
Brassaï. Introduction by Henry Miller. Paris: Editions Neuf, 1952.
Camera in Paris. New York: Focal Press, 1949.
Paris de Nuit. Paris: Edition Arts et Métiers Graphique, 1933.
Henry Miller: Grandeur Nature. Paris: Gallimard, 1975.
Picasso & Company. Preface by Henry Miller; introduction by Roland Penrose. New York: Doubleday, 1966.
The Secret Paris of the '30's. New York: Pantheon Books, 1976.

André Kertész

(BORN 1894 / AMERICAN,
BORN IN HUNGARY)

Alain Jullien

Do you remember the first photograph you ever took?
Maybe as early as 1900, when I was very young, at a family
gathering. I had discovered a charming old illustrated magazine in our attic which moved me very much; I felt its warmth
and spontaneity, and I decided that I wanted to express my
own impressions in the same way.

What kind of camera did you use?
It was a small box camera called an ICA, which later became

an Ikon. It had twelve negatives, 4.5 x 6 cm. glass plates inside. At this time, professional photographers used a big camera and a tripod as standard equipment, but I wanted to move around and I knew it would be difficult with a big camera. So I bought a small one. Lighting and exposure were real mysteries; first I would push down, move the holder to the right, the negative would fall down and automatically the next would come up. That was really very clever indeed. I didn't have to hold the plates, everything was in the camera itself. After the first twelve exposures were finished, though, I had to learn to develop. It was the same old story: I had absolutely no instruction, only what I read. Red light, darkness, developer—there was nothing written on these. At the beginning, I made ridiculous mistakes—the room was not dark enough, the time was not long enough—but slowly I discovered how the process worked, and after my family went to bed at night, I would go to work. It was not very *agréable*, because I had to be quiet, but I learned how to develop. I began shooting what I saw and what I liked, and that is what I am still doing today.

When did you begin to photograph seriously?
I bought my first camera in 1912. The photograph "The Sleeping Boy," taken in Budapest in 1912, is one of the earliest things that I did.

Was your work shown in Hungary?
Yes. We had a very good illustrated paper in Hungary then, called *Érdekes Ujság*, which means Interesting Newspaper. There were many very good and intelligent Hungarian photographers, although the only one who became famous was Munkacsi. Perhaps it was because our culture was a cross between East and West. We had an absolutely special spirit in Hungary, especially in Budapest, and this was expressed in our photography.

You established your own style in Paris very quickly, a style that became almost uniquely your own—photo-reportage. Was this a conscious decision?
Absolutely not. I only did what I felt, for my own satisfaction.

Did you know Chagall and Mondrian then?
Yes, Chagall was an acquaintance. I would see him often in Montparnasse, and I photographed him for *Vu*. Mondrian was a good friend, and he liked my pictures very much.

When did you come to America, and why?
I came over to stay for one year in 1936. I had never wanted to come here, I was at home in Paris and I was never interested in America. But, for a whole year, there were people after me to come over. Every month a telephone call would come to the Keystone Agency in Paris from their office in New York asking them to send me over. Finally, after a full year of this, the New York director came to Paris to see me. Before I left to have lunch with him, my wife warned me that if I agreed to go to New York, she would divorce me. And now—just two or three days ago—we have been here forty long years. It was impossible to go back once I was here. And later the war came, and by then I was an enemy alien, fingerprinted. They thought I was a spy if I walked in the streets with my camera.

But, in the beginning, I was sure I would be gone for only one year. I thought of it as my sabbatical. Just before I left, an official came to see me from the French State Department and offered me French citizenship on the basis of artistic merit. You can imagine how I felt, it was the most important honor I could receive. It meant that the French had accepted me as an artist and as a French citizen. I promised I would come back to Paris.

When I arrived in New York, the Curator of Photography at the Museum of Modern Art came to see me at my hotel and told me that he wanted my material for an international exhibition at the museum. He selected four or five pictures— one was a distortion—on the condition that I cut out the sex. He told me: "If it's with sex, it's pornography; without sex, it's art." *Bienvenue* to America! In the end, I gave in, I was too green. The director had everything in his hand, he made my reputation, but he had absolutely no idea of what he had. In all those years, the director never asked me to do a one-man show. He was concerned with perfecting and sharpening technique. If a little boy learns to write his ABC's perfectly, that is beautiful calligraphy, but it is worthless unless he can express himself well and use technique for his own art. You should feel what you are doing! Even if you are imitating, you must feel. Technique is only the minimum in photography. It's what one must start with. I believe that you should be a perfect technician in order to express yourself as you wish, and then you can forget about the technique. When I went to *Life* magazine, they told me they liked my photographs, but I was talking in them too much! They wanted documents, technique, not expressive photographs.

When do you feel that you gained the formal quality of your vision, your sense of composition?
There is no explanation, I was born with these instincts. A year after I did my "Entrants de Mondrian," a critical essay was published about one of these photographs. The writer had discovered exactly why this picture was slanted, he had never seen a picture cut in the middle before, with the design and the light balanced. But I had done the picture without knowing, very naturally. Years later, John Szarkowski exhibited the photograph and used it in the MOMA calendar. Szarkowski was the first one who had an eye and who understood my work.

Could you talk about your relationship with Brassaï and Cartier-Bresson? It seems to me that you really started both of them on photography.
Brassaï was a fantastically talented man—an excellent painter, excellent sculptor, excellent caricaturist, and a writer, too. He had his own special philosophy, but he also had the normal problem of an artist—money. I told him he could remedy this by making photographs and selling them, and I took him with me on many of my reportages, explaining everything that I was doing—interpretation, technique, including the night-photograph technique, everything for my friend. Cartier-Bresson is much younger than I. He is absolutely honest and very nice.

Could you tell us about your experience with the Julien Levy Gallery?
There isn't very much to tell. I met Levy in the early thirties,

at the Café Dôme in Paris. He bought over thirty photographs. He was the first American who was interested in the new photography.

Your work has often been associated with the Surrealists, hasn't it?
I am not a Surrealist, I am absolutely a realist.

Did you know the work of Eugène Atget?
Yes. I saw his photographs for the first time at a photographic exhibition in 1929, at the Salon de l'Escalier in the Théâtre de Champs-Elysées, the very first time the modern group exhibited. But I never knew him, he died before I even saw his photographs.

What was your relationship with Condé Nast?
I had been working for them in Paris as a freelancer, using my personal material and doing fashion photography outside. When I came to New York, I worked for a while with Condé Nast publications, but after a time I left. It was not the kind of photography I wanted to do.

Very early in your career, you developed a camera vision, a way of using the camera, with the vantage point looking down.
Yes, I did. I liked it very much. If you have an angle, not too high, you see everything. The European magazine *Du* did a special issue on New York in February, and they asked me for photographs—"looking out of my window." When I did my book *Washington Square*, one critic wrote: "Washington Square is nice only if you are Kertész looking down on it."

There is an intuitive sense in your photographs. Do you see that?
The moment always dictates in my work. What I feel, I do. This is the most important thing for me. Everybody can look, but they don't necessarily see. I never calculate or consider; I see a situation and I know that it's right, even if I have to go back to get the proper lighting.

All through your life you've maintained an ideal. It seems almost as though you've been an artist in spite of yourself. The only explanation is that I was born this way. I sacrificed a great deal over the years—mostly American money. But I have been responsible for myself and my work. I am not a rich man, but I am happy. Do you know I was given recognition by Mayor Beame of New York? After all these years, and now they discover me! The presentation reads: "For arts and culture. To André Kertész, photographer, who has never grown old. In his ninth decade he continues to take a likeness of his beloved city."

April 1977

BOOKS OF KERTÉSZ PHOTOGRAPHS

André Kertész. Aperture History of Photography Series, Number 6. Millerton, New York, 1977.
André Kertész: Photographer. Introduction by John Szarkowski. New York: Museum of Modern Art, 1963.
André Kertész: Sixty Years of Photography. New York: Grossman, 1972.
Day of Paris. Edited by George Davis. New York: J. J. Augustin, 1945.
Distortions. Introduction by Hilton Kramer. New York: Alfred A. Knopf, 1976.
J'aime Paris: Photographs Since the Twenties. New York: Grossman, 1974.
Of New York. New York: Alfred A. Knopf, 1976.
On Reading. New York: Grossman, 1971.
Washington Square. Introduction by Brendan Gill. New York: Grossman, 1975.

George Rodger

(BORN 1908 / BRITISH)

Jonathan Rodger

Quite early on in your life you developed a wanderlust. Could you tell us how this urge to travel and explore came about?
It was probably inbred. Most of my ancestors were travelers and I think I just inherited it from my father, my grandfather, and my great-grandfather. They were merchants and they dealt all over the world—in Egypt, in South America, in China.

What sort of education did you have?
Education! Me? I was never educated.

Was that on purpose?
Yes. I was sent to English public schools—ghastly kinds of institutions—and I just didn't like it. I didn't like the restrictions. But I didn't actually run away—I just didn't go back. When I turned seventeen, I went to sea with the Merchant Marine.

Where did you sail?
From Liverpool to Calcutta—that was my first trip. I was an apprentice on the ship and I did just about everything. I studied navigation (to be an officer) and I eventually got my navigation certificate as third mate. But I didn't stay very long. I was about two years at sea, and I went twice around the world before I was nineteen.

We used to get a little time ashore, being on a cargo boat. It would take about three weeks to unload and load again, and this gave me a chance to travel and see something of each country. I had a little camera with me and I used to take pictures, but, unfortunately, I haven't any of those negatives left.

Were those your first pictures?
Yes, very much so. When you're that age, you take the pictures to show your parents and your sisters where you've been, as a way of augmenting what you tell them.

How did you come to photography?
Right from the beginning I wanted to document what I was seeing. I didn't know why, I hadn't a clue. But I just had an urge to do that. I have one or two of my old diaries and I find that I'd taken photographs to illustrate what I was living through. But it wasn't any deeper than that, unfortunately.

What happened after the Merchant Marine?
I went to America and did all kinds of odd jobs. Before that, I was tea-planting in Assam, northern India.

Did you take photographs in India?
Only when I was traveling around. I went to America just when the Depression started in 1929.

How old were you?
I'd have been twenty-one then.

Where did you go in the States?
I lived in Boston for about five years. I was there during the Depression, and every time I got a job, the firm packed up, so I had to keep changing my professions. I really learned quite a lot.

Why did you go to America?
I'd been there several times when I was working on the ships, and I liked it; I thought I'd like to see more of it. But I found it was a little more difficult than I'd expected when the Depression set in—difficult to get around and difficult just to keep body and soul together.

Did you take pictures when you were in the States?
Yes, I did. Always travelogue sorts of things.

Did you see any photographers' work?
No, unfortunately not. I wasn't really interested in photography as photography at all then. I was only using photography as a kind of mechanical way of expressing what I felt and what I thought. I think that's the only way—I can't presume to any early inclinations toward photography.

You hadn't seen any of the Farm Security Administration photographs?
No, nothing at all.

Were you supporting yourself doing odd jobs?
More or less. I became a professional wool-sorter. I can still sort fleeces of wool even now. And I was making lenses for spectacles in an optical company. I was with the American Can Company, working on the automatic lathes. That's only three of the jobs—there must have been about a dozen in all.

How long were you in the States?
Seven years altogether. I spent five years in Boston and two

in upper New York State, near Seneca Lake. I was managing a fruit farm there, which was very nice. I enjoyed that.

Was it the Depression that brought you back to England?
Yes, absolutely. I was stone broke, and I hadn't been home for a long time, so I thought I'd better come back.

What happened when you returned?
I wasn't altogether welcome. When the only son goes away to make his living, the rest of the world is expecting him to make good somewhere, which I failed to do. So I left home (which was in Cheshire then) right away and came down to London. I got my first photographic job, which was with the BBC, on the strength of six prints which I had made in the bathroom of my place in New York State.

Pictures of Lake Seneca?
Yes, of Lake Seneca, and one or two other things. For some reason they seemed to like them at the BBC and they gave me the job, which was probably about the luckiest stroke I've had!

Why did you choose a career in photography?
There were very few jobs going, and one applied for everything, whether one could do it or not. This job was advertised and no one was more surprised than I when I got it. It was a way of earning something so I could eat—nothing to do with photography. In fact, I didn't know anything about photography then.

How did you handle the job?
Very cunningly. I had as an assistant a young girl I called Esmeralda, who came from what was then the Bloomsbury School of Photography. She'd just graduated and we used to stay late in the evening to figure things out—time, temperatures, and that sort of basic stuff—so we couldn't go wrong. I learned all my basic photography from her—how to use studio cameras and lights and so on—I didn't even know then how to load a dark slide!

You were using a plate camera then?
Yes, a great big half-plate studio camera. I'd never seen one
before, let alone used one!

What kind of things did you photograph?
I photographed all the prominent people who came to speak
at the BBC, for publication in *The Listener*. I had to do
portraits of all these people. For instance, I did the Prince of
Wales, who later became King Edward VIII.

Did you enjoy doing studio work?
No.

Did you meet any other photographers at the time?
No, none at all.

So you were more or less isolated.
Yes. Photography was merely a way of making a living, to
earn some money, that was all.

How long did you stay with the BBC?
I was with them for two years. After about a year I went up
to Alexandra Palace, where the BBC was starting television,
and I documented all the early programs. Then photography
started to become interesting.

Did you work with a plate camera then?
No. I insisted that on the set I wanted something that was
faster, and I finally persuaded them to buy me a Leica.

Was that your first Leica?
Yes, that's right. It was about 1937.

Were these pictures published?
They were held as records, and also used in BBC publications
like *Radio Times*. When I did the printing, I always kept a
print for myself, which of course I shouldn't have done. I had
a wonderful stock of all the first television programs—a complete documentation. When the war started, the BBC sent all

their negatives, prints, and everything else to some safe place which got a direct hit. So they lost everything. Later, during the war, when I was away with *Life* as a war correspondent, I had nowhere to put my prints, so I threw the whole lot in the dustbin. There's no record of those times anywhere now. They would have been worth a packet today if I could have kept them!

So, basically, you worked for the BBC until 1938. Then what happened?
I really got an urge to take photographs. I wanted a job where I could get around, so I freelanced for a year with the Black Star Agency.

Could you tell us something about that agency? It had just started then, hadn't it?
Yes, it really was rather an infant. I didn't get on very well. I only did a year with them.

Where did your pictures sell?
To *The Tatler, Sketch,* and *Bystander.* Garden parties—you know. Lady So-and-so opening a charity affair—I did that kind of work.

Did you see anybody's work that interested you?
I can't honestly say that I did, apart from *Picture Post* people, especially Kurt Hutton. I was more interested in the pictures and the stories, and the approach, than in the photographers themselves. I suppose I just adapted myself to the kind of presentation they were using in *Picture Post.*

This was when Stefan Lorant was there?
Yes. That was very early. I think it was November 1938 that *Picture Post* started.

How did you get the job with Life?
That happened rather fortuitously. (Actually, I had a lot of good luck in those days.) I did a story on the river Thames during wartime, through Black Star, and it ran in *Life.* Then

they called me into the *Life* office and asked me if I really thought it worthwhile losing 50 percent when I could work for them directly and have it all for myself. I didn't see anything wrong with that argument, so I said okay, and that's how it happened. That would be in 1939. I know that's right because I'd tried to enlist in the R.A.F. and the War Office wouldn't have me because I was in a "reserved occupation" as a photographer.

What does that mean?
When war breaks out, you can't give everybody a job in the army, and so they discriminate and classify various professions "reserved," so that if you are of that profession, you are not likely to be called up.

Was it important for you to be a photojournalist?
That was almost an inherent instinct I had from way back, from when I was at sea, writing letters home and sending snapshots to illustrate them.

When you say Life *called you in, was it Henry Luce himself?*
No, no. It wasn't on that level. Luce called me in later. No, this was the London office. When they gave me the job, I went straight from earning about £5 a week to £75 a week!

You were based in London?
I was based in London and I covered the blitz for *Life* in the early days. That was very inspiring. It was the only time I enjoyed living in London. It was great.

Because of the freedom the job gave you to move around?
Yes. And the fact that all those who couldn't take the bombing had left the city.

Were you working with anyone in particular then?
One was Bill Vandivert, and there was Hans Wild; he joined about the same time, I think. He was a conscientious objector and he never became a war correspondent or anything. Then,

during the war years, there were people like Bob Landry, Dave Scherman, and Frank Scherschel. People would drift in from the States for short periods of time.

How did they publish your work?
On a picture-story basis.

Did you have any say in what happened?
Yes, I wrote captions from the very beginning. I'd been doing that with Black Star. I was also writing little stories that went with my pictures.

What kind of assignments did you have during those first years with Life?
They were all connected with war activities. I did the "running of the gauntlet" through the Channel with MacDonald Hastings, the writer. He was then on *Picture Post*. I did the submarine bases up in Scotland, and of course, the nightly blitz. I went with the R.A.F. Bomber Command, Fighter Command, and that sort of thing.

Did you meet Bill Brandt, who was also photographing the blitz then?
I didn't run into Bill until much later.

You seem to have moved around a great deal during the war.
Yes, I did. I think *Life* billed me at one time as their most traveled photographer and probably I was then. My first assignment abroad was when I joined the Free French. I'd been working with de Gaulle's headquarters in London and then I went out to the Cameroons to join Colonel Leclerc, who was leading the Free French. That was a rather adventurous and lengthy journey. It was supposed to take about six weeks, but I finally ended up in China two years later—and I still hadn't been home!

I think there were something like forty or fifty countries that I'd been through, and photographed in, during that time. I know *Life* ran an eight-page article on me when I eventually got back to New York in 1942. They called it "75,000 Miles to War."

Were you and Robert Capa the premier photographers at that time?
Not at *that* time. He was, because he was already established, but I wasn't.

Did you know him?
No, I didn't meet him until later.

What happened when you were in New York?
It was absolute hell. It was the worst campaign I ever went through. Henry Luce invited me to dinner and there was a party for about one hundred prominent people. I sat on his right-hand side and he introduced me as his guest speaker! I can't speak, anyway, I hate it, and I'd had no idea about this. He said: "You can talk about your experiences for half an hour." Once I got started, I didn't stop for an hour and a half! It went down quite well, though. Then Luce sent me on a lecture tour around the States.

Did you meet any photographers then?
No, none at all. I just met people who were likely to buy advertising in *Life*. When I caught on to this, I was *very* annoyed. I was reading the accounts of the war in the American papers and I knew very well that the R.A.F. were bombing Germany night after night, and they were hardly mentioned in the American press. The people getting the kudos were the pilots of the Flying Fortresses. At that time, they didn't fly at night and they didn't even go over the borders of Germany. I was mad as hell! Once, in Detroit, I started telling people about it in my lecture, and the man from *Life*, who was sitting beside me, kept stamping on my foot. I didn't like that. I was asked several questions and I answered them very straight. I said that United States planes hadn't managed to drop a bomb on Germany yet. The man from *Life* immediately got up and announced that the meeting was over. It turned out that the man questioning me was the president of the Boeing Aircraft Company—and that ended my speaking career!

What happened then?
I wasn't very well at all and I spent about six months con-
valescing. Then I got married. This was about six months
before I went to North Africa. I did the Sicily landing, the
Salerno landing, the Anzio landing, and I finally came back to
D day in Normandy.

Were you with Capa then?
Yes. I first met him in North Africa.

Did you get along well together?
We got along fine. I felt quite small in his presence because
he was *the* "star" photographer. I was just plodding along.

Did he act it?
Sure he did, but we got along very well and we were together
quite a bit—in North Africa, Sicily, Italy, and then later in
Germany. We became very good friends.

You must have been in most of the European campaigns?
I think I was in every one this side of China. But I didn't go
to the Pacific at all.

*You must have seen more than your fair share of slaughter and
brutality. How did it affect you and your work, because there
seems to be a sense of gentleness in your photographs?*
I think there may be something in that. I wasn't particularly
interested in photographing the horror of war. I didn't care
for it at all—the blood and spilled guts, and everything. One
doesn't think at the time about the effects it might be having
on you. But very gradually it built up, and the climax came
at the Belsen concentration camp. I didn't know until then—
despite over five years of war—what effect the war had had
on me personally, and I said: "This is where I quit." Fortunately, the war ended soon after. There wasn't any more war
to photograph—and I never went back to another one. Capa,
unfortunately, did.

It wasn't even a matter of what I was photographing, as
what had happened to me in the process. When I discovered
that I could look at the horror of Belsen—the 4,000 dead and

starving lying around—and think only of a nice photographic composition, I knew something had happened to me, and it had to stop. I felt I was like the people running the camp—it didn't mean a thing.

What did you do about it?
I stopped. I never went back. I did the surrender at Lüneburg, and fortunately for me, that was the end of the war.

Did you wonder, when you were working like that, why you were doing it?
No, one doesn't. You've got a job to do. I mean, everyone was involved in the war, civilians being killed, people starving to death in concentration camps, and we were also getting shot up ourselves. The mortality rate for war correspondents was the highest of the war. You don't think about those things.

What purpose did you see the photographs serving in terms of the war effort?
I felt I did a great service, because I was a Britisher on the staff of *Life*, and the British needed supplies and ammunition; we needed money, we needed everything America had in order to fight the war. I was able to show the American people, all of Henry Luce's however-many-million readers, what was happening to their money and why we needed it. I really felt that I was doing a much better job with my camera than I could ever have done wih a bombsight or a rifle or a tank.

What happened after the German surrender?
I disappeared. I went straight to Denmark from Lüneburg. Denmark was the last occupied country and it was very interesting. The German communications had collapsed completely, and even fifty miles from Lüneburg they'd no idea that the surrender had been signed. I found myself driving alone in my jeep right into German territory and the soldiers had no idea that the war was over. All the German troops had massed in Schleswig-Holstein, and they were all going north to get out of the way—to regroup or something like that—and

they were out of fuel. They had one truck towing about four other trucks, all laden with German soldiers, and I came along with my little jeep. Peep! Peep! I had the Union Jack flying, and they were so amazed they didn't do anything except salute. I got waves and whistles—it was the most fantastic thing I'd ever lived through. I lost my way in Flensburg, which was the headquarters of the S.S., and I had to ask the way. An S.S. soldier turned his gun on me and marched me off to headquarters, which, although I didn't know this at the time, was actually Himmler's! I was taken before five S.S. colonels and they asked me how I got there. They asked: "Do you realize where you are?" I said: "Yes, sure, but nobody stopped me." I had a photostat copy of the surrender and I showed it to them. I said: "The war's over!" But they wouldn't believe it. They asked me to sit down and they all went out of the room. After half an hour they came back and very Germanically leaped to attention, clicked their heels, saluted, and said that I was perfectly right, and they asked me if there was anything they could do to help me. I said: "Yes, I'd like an escort to the Danish border." There were roadblocks there and I wanted to get through, fast. A couple of the colonels got into a big black staff car, a Mercedes, and they escorted me the whole way to the Danish border. My reception was so great. I remained incommunicado from everything, *Life* magazine included, for three weeks. I got my wife flown in by the R.A.F. We had a wonderful time.

Did you document the end of the war?
I didn't document anything. My main problem was to remain sober! I had a terrific time. *Life* ran one picture that I took at the palace in Copenhagen of King Christian IX and General Montgomery.

What did you decide to do after you had recuperated a bit?
It got to be more and more difficult because, during the war, you were literally your own boss. My territory was Morocco to China, and I knew where to go and what was happening. Editors in New York didn't know and they had enough sense

to realize that. But when it was possible for them to start traveling again and to get over there themselves, with preconceived ideas which we had to illustrate, it became intolerable. I decided to get fired.

What did you do to get fired?
Nothing! That's the best way to get fired. I did nothing for a whole year, waiting anxiously for my severance pay. When it finally came, I financed my first African trip with it.

What made you decide to go to Africa?
When I joined Leclerc in 1940—my first assignment—I drove thousands of miles with him. Then, when he'd taken the ex-French colonial territories and they'd all joined up with de Gaulle, there was no longer any war going on there. The next one was on the other side of Africa in Ethiopia. So I got into my Chevrolet pickup and drove across Africa to Ethiopia, and I covered that one. By that time I was getting into trouble with the British War Office. My "reserved occupation" status had been withdrawn and I was liable for call-up. *Life* was doing what they could to influence the War Office in London, but they were insisting that I come back and be drafted. So, whenever I got to any British headquarters, I had to talk my way out of arrest and transport home under escort.

Were you in Ethiopia when it was liberated? Was that when you photographed Haile Selassie?
Not the first time. The first time I was in Eritrea. It was the second time, when I joined the Indian Army, that we put Haile Selassie back on his throne. Mine was one of the first pictures of him taken after he was reinstated.

Was Alfred Eisenstaedt, the Life *photographer, there at the time?*
I didn't see him, but I think he was there very shortly afterward.

When the Life *money gave you the chance to go back to Africa, was there any particular place you felt you wanted to go to?*
No. I just wanted to travel and see the whole continent. My

wife and I went down to Capetown, bought vehicles, and organized a safari. We spent two years driving from Capetown to Cairo. It was on that trip that I did the Kordofan story, which is the best story I've ever done. It is still being used today.

How did that story come about?
I heard about the Nubas of Kordofan when we were in Juba on the Upper Nile and I was determined to find them. We drove for two weeks cross-country before reaching their isolated territory. But, on arrival, our welcome was great.

By that time, of course, Magnum was well established—it was 1949—so we shipped film from Khartoum, and our New York office handled the distribution.

How did Magnum start?
First of all, there were five founder photographers—Bob Capa, David "Chim" Seymour, Henri Cartier-Bresson, myself, and Bill Vandivert. Bill was the fifth, but he dropped out early on.

I was a founder member but I cannot claim any credit for the actual establishment of Magnum. All the planning and the donkeywork was done by Capa, Chim, and Marie Eisner, who had already had agency experience in Paris. I was away in the Middle East at the time but had agreed to join Capa if he could ever get our dream going.

Had you talked about it before?
Oh, yes—with Capa. I didn't know Henri and Chim. I think it was a couple of years before I met Henri. But I had talked it over a lot with Capa, and we knew what we wanted.

What did you want to do with Magnum?
We wanted to form some kind of a business association through which we could market our own material—an office to handle all administration, selling, and billing, so we would be free to travel and take pictures. I was covering the abandoned battlefields of North Africa for *Illustrated* while Capa was talking with the others, and when I reached Cyprus, I received a cable welcoming me to our newborn organization.

How did the name Magnum come about?
That was Capa. I don't know whether it had anything to do with champagne, but it was a very good excuse to have a bottle every time we had a meeting.

What was your first story for Magnum?
That was for the *Ladies' Home Journal.* They did a series called "People Are People the World Over."

To get back to Africa, how did you, a white man, fit into Nuban life?
My wife, Jinx, calls me a chameleon because I can always become part of my environment. I think that held true even then.

Did you speak their language?
Good gracious me, no.

How long did you stay with them?
I should say it was about six weeks.

Did you take photographs every day?
I used to take photographs every time something happened. I think the whole of our African travels really came to a peak there, and I was definitely feeling I was into something. But it was also stopped short because, sadly, my first wife died and I didn't go back.

You have said that something happened when you photographed the Nubas?
I felt an affinity with primitive people. Maybe there's something primitive about myself, I don't know. I really felt that my best work would have been there, with the tribes. If only I'd been able to go back, but somehow I couldn't.

Did you know the work of Laurens van der Post, the writer?
Yes, I was with him in Ethiopia. We campaigned together and I respected him highly. He is a very interesting character.

Did you ever have a hankering to see Albert Schweitzer?
I saw him and stayed with him on a later trip to Africa.

Did you photograph him?
Yes. He was a fascinating subject.

*His way of understanding the primitive people seems slightly
different from yours, though.*
Oh, yes—in a way. But neither of us underestimated the primitive people. I didn't find it easy to talk to him, as my French
isn't any too good and I have no German. I found his guttural
Alsatian French extremely difficult to understand. But he had
a fantastic sense of humor. Every word had a double meaning
and I found it very difficult to decipher what he was saying.
I certainly think he was a great humanitarian. He sacrificed
much of his life trying to better the lot of the African people.
I did nothing like that—no sacrifice.

It seems he changed them, though.
No, he didn't. His hospital was just the same as a native
village. He said he could have had millions of dollars to build
the most modern hospital, but what was the point? They'd
never have come to it. He said: "If we are to do good for
these people, we'll have to run the hospital like their own
village."

Did you do a story on Schweitzer?
I did a story which was published all over the place. It wasn't
as deep as Eugene Smith's; he did it much better and stayed
longer. We didn't have much time with Schweitzer. I was with
Jinx then and we were working for the Marshall Plan trying
to find out what the French had done with the dollar loans.
We sneaked away for a week or so in order to stay with
Schweitzer while we were reporting on the building of the
Gabon road. We couldn't really spend much time at Lambaréné.

How did the Delpire book on the Nubas come about?
That was part of a series. Henri Cartier-Bresson was part of it.
He did his book on Bali and Robert Doisneau did one on Paris.

Did you edit your book at all?
No, no. I just gave the pictures to Delpire; I thought he did a very good presentation.

What happened after Africa?
After 1949 I got back on my feet, which took some time. Magnum then was not like Magnum today. Magnum was definitely a family unit and I'm certainly very grateful to them for the way they looked after me as far as work was concerned. Work was diversion then and I don't really remember the first jobs that I did. There was an essay in Haiti, and one in Jamaica.

What was the work like for the "People Are People" series, which Capa originated?
Interesting. I did the "Egyptian Family," the "Sudan Family," and I left my wife in Cairo while I went to India to do the "Indian Family." It was the first time there had ever been a worldwide approach to a subject like that. It was Capa's idea.

It seems that Steichen took the idea and later turned it into the "Family of Man" exhibition.
Yes, it was probably based on Capa's idea. I'm sure it was.

How did the Magnum people feel about the "Family of Man" show?
We had an awful lot to do with compiling the whole thing.

You became involved with National Geographic *around then?*
Yes. Jinx and I did two big essays for them. We did "The Sahara." Then we did elephants in East Africa, which was a good story. The Sahara story was an entirely speculative job. We built it up and then Magnum submitted it to the *National Geographic*, who loved it. They gave us great billing, and the next thing we did was "Elephants Have Right of Way."

You were creating your own market.
That's true.

It seems that with the deaths of Capa and Chim Seymour you had a lot of work to do to keep Magnum solvent?
Yes. I think Magnum as a business probably suffered more from the death of Chim than from Capa's. Capa was the fellow who had all the inspirations and Chim was the businessman who was able to hold Capa down. He would tell him not to be quite so ambitious and say: "You can't have things if you don't have the money for them." So, as a business, we really felt the loss of Chim.

Magnum seemed to change after that. Did you find the change for the better?
I think it was inevitable. I wouldn't say it was for better, or for worse, because that's relative. But we couldn't go on being a happy family like we were, especially after Chim and Capa had gone. Then we had the younger people who hadn't been through what we'd been through. They didn't see things in the same light; maybe they looked at Magnum more commercially than we did. Gradually the whole thing changed. But I think it was inevitable.

Did the founders see Magnum primarily as a commercial possibility, or was it a possibility for something else?
The *founders* very definitely did not see it as a commercial proposition at all. It was a means to an end.

What was the end?
To make our own lives easier so that we could operate, each in his own field. As I said earlier, an organization to hold us all together and to do the administrative work. It was never supposed to be profit-making.

It seems that the concept of the "concerned photographer" emerged through the development of Magnum. What does this term mean to you?
I'm afraid it doesn't mean as much to me as it does to a lot of people.

With the decline of the illustrated magazines, it seems Magnum began to accept industrial patronage to create work. Is that correct?
Yes, as a matter of necessity, but I was never very good at it.

Did you ever find this turn of events slightly paradoxical?
Indeed. I thought that after doing a few annual reports, I could then spend the rest of the year doing what I liked. But, unfortunately, I wasn't very good at doing annual reports, so I didn't get very far.

How did you view the decline of picture feature magazines?
I viewed it as a tragedy, because I'd never really been interested in, or able to do, anything else. For me it was really a body blow.

Wasn't photojournalism communicating any more?
It was communicating, but there was less outlet for it and you saw less of it.

It was a matter of market availability, then, rather than a lack of effectiveness?
Absolutely.

What do you believe constitutes the documentary?
It's one of the best ways of expression. It should be articulate, very visual (on the pictorial side), and a reflection of thoughts on the writing side. The combination of the two should then be very powerful.

Did you find that there came a time when you felt you no longer wanted, or needed, to travel?
I thought I probably might, but I've never lost the urge to travel. I'm torn just now between two things: my very great attachment to Kent, where I live, and my family, but still this damn thing keeps creeping in—my itchy feet—and I want to go places.

You seem to have directed your vision in a particular way.
I think I aimed my camera at a definite composition of differ-

ent things; a very simple, uncomplicated, pictorial approach, which is maybe one that is my own. I don't know. I've never tried to analyze it.

Your pictures seem to reflect an attitude about humanity that's pretty special.
Maybe, but it isn't in the form of a definite crusade, where I've got to go and produce pictures of "downtrodden man" to try to better his situation. That is not my approach to photography.

Could you describe your own approach?
I like to create something—it sounds terribly smug—which gives me pleasure to look at. Could that be possible? I don't know. I've never thought about it. I like creating something which I find interesting or pleasing, and if other people like it, well, that's fine. Then I really feel I've achieved something! If they don't like it, I don't give a damn!

Does photographic education interest you?
No, not in the least!

Are you skeptical?
Yes. I don't think you can really teach something which is *in* you. I never had a lesson in photography in my life, except from Esmeralda, in the early days. She showed me how to load the dark slides, but never anything deeper than that. I do think that there is a kind of photography in which I'm interested, and it's a creative kind of photography which can't really be taught. You can be helped with the mechanical side of it. If you are going to become a fashion photographer, a wedding photographer, an industrial photographer, there're lots of things you can go to school and learn about, but this is not the case with the kind of photography which has concerned me all my life.

Could you talk about what you mean by "creative"?
Define the word "creative?" A factual reproduction of something that is in your own mind, I suppose. You're asking

questions that I have never thought about before, so I have to search around for words—but I think that is acceptable.

Do you consider the photograph, then, as a "window on the world"?
Yes. It's a view of "what's out there," reproduced in a form that's interesting and pleasing to look at. But the form comes from within you—from inside your head, or your heart.

Do you see yourself participating in photography as a fine art?
Some people have said that my pictures are a form of fine art, which absolutely amazes me. I can't go any further than that.

Did it insult you?
No! I'm honored by this criticism, but I really haven't considered my pictures a form of fine art.

You were given an Arts Council of Great Britain grant in 1977. Has this caused any difficulties for you?
The problems are entirely individualistic. I got my grant to do what I wanted to do. There was so much I wanted to do which I couldn't afford to do—primarily to go back to Africa and see what it's like now, compared to what it was when I felt myself part of it. And of course, I got back there and found I wasn't a part of it at all! I was a complete outsider who had absolutely nothing in common with it. I wasn't even allowed to use my camera freely, and I felt the frustration, which was terrible. I went to Kenya because we'd always used Nairobi as a base and gravitated out from there, but I didn't expect I'd come back with any great pictures. I really looked at it as a sort of reconnaissance period. I wanted to go down and see what it was like and see what I could do; and in that I was very successful. I found out what I could do—which was nothing—and so now I've got to think again. Think of a different territory and making different approaches.

Will the territory be African?
Yes. It's got to be African.

70 / George Rodger

Why does it have to be African?
Because I've always felt this affinity with Africa and things African. I've been to China, to India, to Australia, and felt absolutely nothing about them at all. But with Africa, there's something that seems to draw me. Maybe it's just a coincidence. My first impression of a foreign land wasn't Africa, it was India, but India didn't have the same impact for me. The first time in Africa I felt really close to it. But I've found that there is nothing to get close to any more. I've done some wildlife in color to restock the Magnum files, but I'm also doing some black and white for my own satisfaction, from which I hope there will be an exhibition in the end. What it's going to prove, or what angle it's going to take, I've absolutely no idea, because I'm a new boy in Africa now. I joined Magnum as the African expert and now I'm the new boy. I don't know the place any more.

We had it so good before and we just didn't realize it. It's like that with life all the way through. Actually, you should never, never go back. I would never go back to Nuba territory because that would be just too hard.

Are there any photographers working now who you feel are working with the kind of vision you respect?
Yes. The people I feel a sympathy, or an affinity, with are the people doing the same kind of thing that I used to do. Marc Riboud, who is still making a very good living out of photojournalism, and Ian Berry. Definitely Bruno Barbey. These are all Magnum people, because I know them best. Living here in Kent, I'm miles away from even London photographers. Naturally, the people I know best are my partners in Magnum. They are people who are still carrying on the old tradition.

Is Magnum still important to you?
Very definitely. After all, we bred the damn thing; naturally I'm still interested in it. I feel very close to it, even now.

Is there anything that you'd like to see Magnum do?
No, I don't think so. There are young people there now—let them take over.

What photographs do you like to see?
When I see somebody producing a set of pictures without distortion, without gimmickry, it makes me very happy.

Does the idea of "straight photography" mean anything to you?
Isn't it just a matter of evolution? If you look back to a Royal Photographic Society annual exhibition of twenty years ago, there's naturally a tremendous difference, but isn't it just a matter of development?

Has it never developed toward what might be called "realism"?
No. I think the early pictures were more realistic than they are today.

Would you be willing to talk about what contribution you think you have made to photography?
To be very brief, I don't think I have contributed very much— other than an honest documentation of people and places over the past forty years. I've pleased myself, which again sounds smug, but I don't know that I've really contributed anything toward the development of photography as an art.

As a communications medium?
Using my pictures to influence thought is really past. In my wartime work I felt that I was contributing something.

What about the Nubas?
The Nubas did something which was extremely difficult to define. Communication with nature, between myself and something absolutely unspoiled, unsullied by civilization, if you like. There was no crime, no corruption, and this is a sort of idyllic existence that you are so amazed to find. I think they have something wonderful there that I want to record and be part of. I think it's something very special, even unique. I don't think it's universal at all.

If you could start again, would you still be a photographer?
It would be a lot more difficult now, but I'd still want to be

one. It's the best way for me to express myself and record those things that interest me in life.

December 1977

BOOKS OF RODGER PHOTOGRAPHS

Desert Journey. London: Cresset Press, 1944.
George Rodger. Introduction by Inge Bondi. London: Gordon Fraser, 1975.
Le Village des Nubas. Paris: Robert Delpire, 1955.
Red Moon Rising. London: Cresset Press, 1943.

Henri Cartier-Bresson

(BORN 1908 / FRENCH)

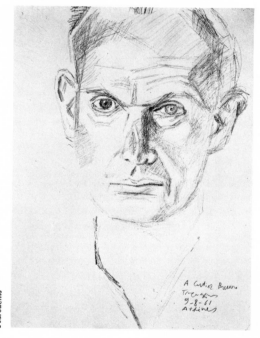

Tsarouchis

Did your family have any artistic inclinations?
My father drew very well; his younger brother was a good painter with a great deal of promise, but he was killed at the beginning of World War I. I started to paint with one of his friends at the age of thirteen or fourteen. Then, for two years, 1927 and 1928, I worked in the studio of André Lhote, a Cubist painter and an excellent teacher. I finally left, because I was afraid if I stayed there much longer, all my paintings

would resemble Lhote paintings. I did not return to painting until 1943, when I escaped from a P.O.W. camp and I took up gouaches. In 1973 I began to draw actively again. My major concern has always been the plastic arts, and photography is only one aspect of that. After my return from Africa in 1932, I discovered—thanks to that rapid and unobtrusive apparatus, the Leica—this method of drawing that carves and shapes reality in an instant. I often think of what Françoise Cachin wrote in her book on Degas monotypes: "What must have intrigued Degas the most about the monotype technique was its rapidity and the element of surprise. In this work, Degas behaves more like a photographer, because of a certain respect for reality that comes through, than like a painter, who merely re-creates reality."

In my opinion, there is a common point of departure for both drawing and photography: the act of looking. But from then on they diverge; drawing is an elaboration on reality, whereas photography, for me, is a supreme moment captured with a single shot. The first photograph that truly overwhelmed me and still does, because of its palpitating life and rigor of composition, is one of Munkacsi's in which three black children are running toward the waves.

What role did Surrealism play in your development?
I have been influenced by Surrealism as a concept, as an attitude to life, but I have great reservations about Surrealist painting, which seems too literary for me. The only aspect of the phenomenon of photography that fascinates me, and will always interest me, is the intuitive capture through the camera of what is seen. This is exactly how Breton defined objective chance (*le hasard objectif*) in his *Entretiens*. My own statement is the preface to my last book, published by Aperture, which I shall read to you:

Photography has not changed since its origin except in its technical aspects, which for me are not a major concern.
Photography appears to be an easy activity; in fact, it is a varied and ambiguous process in which the only common denominator among its practitioners is their instrument.

What emerges from this recording machine does not escape the economic constraints of a world of waste, of tensions that become increasingly intense and of insane ecological consequences.

"Manufactured" or staged photography does not concern me. And if I make a judgment, it can only be on a psychological or sociological level. There are those who go out to discover the image and seize it. For me, the camera is a sketch book, an instrument of intuition and spontaneity, the master of the instant which—in visual terms—questions and decides simultaneously. In order to "give a meaning" to the world, one has to feel oneself involved in what one frames through the viewfinder. This attitude requires concentration, a discipline of mind, sensitivity, and a sense of geometry. It is by great economy of means that one arrives at simplicity of expression. One must always take photos with the greatest respect for the subject and for oneself.

To take photographs is to hold one's breath when all faculties converge in the face of fleeing reality. It is at that moment that mastering an image becomes a great physical and intellectual joy.

To take photographs means to recognize—simultaneously and within a fraction of a second—both the fact itself and the rigorous organization of visually perceived forms that give it meaning. It is putting one's head, one's eye and one's heart on the same axis.

As far as I am concerned, taking photographs is a means of understanding which cannot be separated from other means of visual expression. It is a way of shouting, of freeing oneself, not of proving or asserting one's own originality. It is a way of life.*

Why have you never allowed yourself to be photographed?
In order to observe, one must be unobtrusive and able to pass by unnoticed. That is the only reason.

---

* *This text was first published as the preface for Volume I in the* Aperture History of Photography Series, *copyright © 1976 by Henri Cartier-Bresson, Aperture, Inc., and Robert Delpire.*

What have you found are the aesthetic differences between taking photographs and making films?
In 1935, when I was in the United States, I learned the rudiments and techniques of filmmaking from Paul Strand. That year, I did not take any photographs at all. I owe a great deal to Jean Renoir, as well, for whom I worked as a second assistant director. What I enjoyed most was working on the dialogue. I never had anything to do with camera work or lighting. But I felt I had no gift for feature films. I have made four documentary films. In my opinion, there is no relation between the still photograph and the cinematic image. In cinema, the photograph is fleeting, like a word in a speech. In photography, it is closer to monotype, lithography, drawing.

What qualities do you try to achieve in your prints?
I used to do my own printing, which meant I knew exactly what I could get from my negatives. But I have not made my own prints for many years now. I much prefer to take more time to look, and I am only able to do this because I know several printers whose work I supervise. I simply ask them to respect the values and their equilibrium. We understand each other very well, and I am extremely grateful to them, for now I don't have to work in a darkroom, which is a craft in itself.

Do you have any thoughts about what should constitute an education in photography?
There should be a *visual* education emphasized from the very beginning in all schools. It should be introduced just like the study of literature, history, or mathematics. With a language, everyone learns the grammar first. In photography, one must learn a visual grammar. What reinforces the content of a photograph is the sense of rhythm, the relationship between shapes and values. To quote Victor Hugo: "Form is the essence brought to the surface."

What do you think of the aesthetic of art direction in magazines, books, and exhibitions?
My intuitive approach to photography and my constant pre-

occupation with the single image makes me a poor designer. I find it difficult to create a harmony among different photos. I leave this to my publisher friends, to art directors and curators, with whom I always discuss the layout. I don't look at many photographs as a rule. What interests me are those that arouse feelings of rivalry in me. On the other hand, I spend much time looking at paintings and drawings, both old and contemporary.

Was it you who took the last photograph of Stieglitz? Had he proposed an exhibition for you?

I took a photograph of Stieglitz a week before his death, but I have no idea if any other photographs were taken after mine. We did not speak of an exhibition. In fact, my first exhibit had been organized in 1932 by Julien Levy in New York. I owe him a great deal; as well as Nancy and Beaumont Newhall and Monroe Wheeler, curators of the Museum of Modern Art in New York; not to mention Lincoln Kirstein. These were the people who made my work known in the United States. Many other friends promoted my work in other countries afterwards.

Some of my best photos were taken in those first days with my Leica. But, at that time, my general standard was extremely low; I destroyed all my mediocre negatives just before the war. Exceptional photographs continue to be rare, even though my general standard has improved. In all my photo essays I am always looking for a unique photo, the exceptional one that could be looked at for more than a few seconds. It takes a great deal of milk to make a little cream.

Why are you interested in ecology?

Ecology is concerned with the relations between man and his environment, and the ecologists warn of the dangers which menace the equilibrium of life on earth. Tensions and contradictions increase daily. Ecology makes people conscious of the imminent danger that contemporary societies are bringing us to. The agronomist, René Dumont, poses this dilemma in his book, *Utopia or Else.*

What do you think the future of documentary photography will be?
I have never been interested in the documentary aspect of photography except as a poetic expression. Only the photograph that springs from life is of interest to me. The joy of looking, sensitivity, sensuality, imagination, all that one takes to heart, come together in the viewfinder of a camera. That joy will exist for me forever.

November 1977

BOOKS OF CARTIER-BRESSON PHOTOGRAPHS

About Russia. New York: Viking Press, 1974.
Cartier-Bresson's France. New York: Viking Press, 1970.
Coup d'oeil Americain. Text by Lincoln Kirstein. Lucerne, Switzerland: *Camera* magazine, July 1976.
The Decisive Moment. New York: Simon and Schuster, 1952.
The Europeans. New York: Simon and Schuster, 1955.
From One China to Another. Preface by Jean-Paul Sartre; text by Han Suyin. New York: Universe Books, 1956.
Henri Cartier-Bresson. Aperture History of Photography Series, Number 1. Millerton, New York: Aperture, 1976.
Man and Machine. New York: Viking Press, 1971.
People of Moscow. New York: Simon and Schuster, 1955.
Photographs by Cartier-Bresson. Introduction by Lincoln Kirstein and Beaumont Newhall. New York: Grossman, 1963.
The Photographs of Henri Cartier-Bresson. Introduction by Lincoln Kirstein and Beaumont Newhall. New York: Museum of Modern Art, 1947.
The World of Henri Cartier-Bresson. New York: Viking Press, 1970.

Robert Doisneau

(B O R N   1 9 1 2 / F R E N C H)

Very simply, what were your beginnings?

I began taking pictures because I was interested in my surroundings. I had already seen a few pictures by Brassaï, to
whom I still owe a debt of gratitude. That man showed me
that one could make very moving pictures from surroundings
that are scorned and that so-called cultivated people would
not even look at. For me it was the kind of locale I had always
encountered. It was my life. So, instead of grieving over my
surroundings and saying, "Oh, dear, this universe is so sad
and rotten and sinister," I realized that this was the very
environment which filled Brassaï and Kertész with wonder and
I too could work within it.

Did you know Brassaï and Kertész?
No, no, no. I didn't have any reason to know them. I didn't
even have a way to meet them.

You knew their work, though?
Brassaï was doing *Paris de nuit* in 1933 and a few photos from
it were published. I found them absolutely marvelous! They
transported me from my art-history course at school, where
we were being shown pictures of an art that was *completely*
academic. Suddenly, Brassaï's pictures showed me that my
need to be filled with wonder could find stimulation in the
photographing of everyday life in Paris. A little later, when
I thought I had learned the rudiments of photography—by
reading what there was in boxes of film plates—I was taken
on as a camera operator by a man whose name was André
Vigneau. Little is now known of him. He was probably influenced by the current Bauhaus thought of the time.

*Would you speak briefly about your family background and
your education? How did you come to do lithography and
then photography?*
I was born in Gentilly, a suburb of Paris that was particularly
ugly—though no more ugly than the other Parisian suburbs!
It's on land that was built on the course of the river Bièvre.
I am still a little sentimental about it, though now it's a place
for sewage disposal. It was filthy then too, so very filthy. The
Bièvre began its course in the Chevreuse valley and then
passed through Arcueil Cachan. In Arcueil there were laundry
works, and the river was polluted by the water from these
places. At Gentilly there were also many tanning factories.
The tanning process smells very, very bad and makes the
water so filthy that it really becomes a kind of thick paste.
That was the state of the river where we lived. That is the
setting of Gentilly, my home.
   At school, around 1925, my eyes were opened concerning
functional things. People wanted art to be functional, houses
to be functional, life to be functional. I hated Gentilly because
of its "unfunctional" nooks and crannies, because of the
absurdity of its little, irrelevant craft trades and odd jobs.

But now Gentilly is functional. There are no more nooks and crannies, there is no more unused land. It's worse than before! It's horrible! But what seemed to happen there was that this suburb served as a foil for human beings. What I mean is that when a human being passed through that setting, say someone who was young and in love, he was a thousand times more active than he would be in a pastoral setting or a romantic one. There was this continual opposition between the setting, which was so hard, so absurd, so stupid, so ugly, and its people. Now, big business has made the place much larger and harder than before, and the young of this period couldn't transform their setting or they would be called outlaws.

So there I was in this absurd little universe. My father worked in a roofing and plumbing firm, and he wanted me to have a sedentary job. He thought that by putting me in a school for the book trade I would find a profession that would make me what might be called a semi-executive, in a profession that would be stable, sedentary, and without problems. But it turned out that, after being enclosed for a while in the discipline of that school, I escaped for a trade that is the least stable, the most adventurous, and the least guaranteed by security! I escaped for photography!

I have a need for liberty that must be greater than that of my contemporaries. I can't stand to be held back by people or things. I was miserable when I was in that school because the discipline was very strict. I was miserable when I was in the military service. I was miserable when I was in the Renault factory for five years because you had to clock in and out and the number of people working there was so large. I've always aimed for that solitude, that liberty, and that desire to play.

In the end, it was school that made you feel the importance of liberty?
School made me feel constraint, and constraint has one fine aspect to it. It's like a kettle in which steam is enclosed. When there is a real need to explode, there is an explosion! I even feel this from time to time when I am asked to work on an advertising or commercial job. I get so fed up with it after

a very short time that I just explode. Automatically then, I find my way back toward the street, toward liberty again. The *street* is something that I need right now.

Do you regret the discipline you received in school, or the kind of precision and discipline that there is in photography?
No, I became a professional! It's true that the discipline, the extraordinary amount of patience that is needed to become a photographer, is instilled. You know, they always say that a photographer is "a hunter of images." That is a flattering image, the idea of a hunter; it's virile, acquired power. Actually, though, it isn't that. We are really fishermen with hooks and lines! Happily, man is still the most important part of the picture-making process. This is an idea that is still not well established in people's minds. They think that, thanks to this potential for repetition, in photography an extraordinary picture will be found every time—but this just isn't so. The best photos, the ones that are remembered, are the ones that have first passed through the person's mind before being restored by the camera.

When you went to Vigneau, did you go as an assistant to earn a living, or did you go for art training and study?
To earn a living. I was introduced to Vigneau by a friend. Vigneau was a sculptor and he understood the science of light. He knew very well how to light a subject by extremely simple means. He did two fine books on Egyptian art, one at the Louvre and one at the Museum of Cairo. He had a sculptor's training that gave him the patience to really look. Vigneau needed a camera operator. I was rather unconscious of everything at the time, because I didn't know much, but Vigneau hired me anyway. He was a fine, kind man who, over lunch, loaned me some books to learn photographic technique. Every day at lunch, I studied technique. He wanted to push technical perfection to the maximum—that is to say, give to emulsions the best bath for the print. It was perfection. It was the Weston manner, which isn't really fashionable at the moment. But it was the technique of a man whose fundamental ideas were very sound.

I stayed on with him and started doing architectural and fashion pictures because he was involved in so many different things: advertising, fashion, industrial advertising, etc. But he always photographed with the spirit that the object was primary and that the beauty, say the beauty of a tire, was something really marvelous. It was a sound training, and I was very fortunate to work for him. He also deterred me from a few false paths at the beginning. But afterward, because of my natural curiosity, I branched off on a few false paths of my own.

Is it at this period that you also worked for newspapers?
Yes. Saturdays and Sundays I took pictures in the streets with very bad equipment. I worked with a tripod and an old wooden camera. I did a reportage on the flea market. Not many people were doing reportage then. It seems that one day Vigneau showed these pictures of the flea market to the director of *Excelsior*, who said: "This is very amusing. We'll publish it!" This was the first time my work was published. That was in 1932—"The Flea Market." Afterward, there was "The Birds," then "The Quais." Finally, after leaving school, I dared to open my eyes to real living people! When you're looking under magnifying glasses all day, you do not dare look at such people. And then, all of a sudden, photography allowed me to look at these people! I still didn't dare talk to them. Years passed before I could do that. Now, I am not intimidated by anyone. I realize that the people I photograph are like me. I don't see them as case studies. I am one of them and they understand this very well. I take my pictures first in order not to destroy the spontaneity of contact with a person, but then I almost always speak. I also keep up relationships with these people either by letter or through visits. I give away many, many pictures this way. And I always do follow-ups. It slows me down a little in my work, but it allows me to get to know a little of the world in which I've lived. If there is one thing that I hate, it is tourists that are here one second and gone the next. I am not a tourist myself. I really do partake of my contemporaries and of my environment.

When you began working for Excelsior, *you took pictures on Saturdays and Sundays. Did you still continue to work for Vigneau, or did you work full time for magazines?*
No, it isn't that simple. I was doing reportage for myself in the streets. This was a kind of affirmation of working on my own—to know what I could do with my own work—no longer being the chick of a rooster like Vigneau. But then there was that ridiculous interruption of military service. I had to go and play the fool as a soldier. When I returned from military service, Vigneau had completely changed his activities, and the firm had faded away. He was involved in the cinema, so I didn't have any more work with him. I then found a spot as an industrial photographer with the Renault factories at Billancourt, and for years I took pictures of machines, car parts, trucks, bodies, motors, with materials and equipment that were out of date. I did this for five years, but I knew it wasn't my life's goal! I was married, though, and I had to make a living.

At what age were you married?
Very young, twenty-one years old and just out of military service. I had to assume the responsibility of my new home, so I joined Renault. Naturally, I still took pictures for myself, but not as many as I wanted to do. I was then starting to take pictures of the Paris suburbs. Much later these pictures resulted in the book with Blaise Cendrars. This is still one of the happy friendships of my life.

For five years I took industrial photographs at the Renault factories. I began work at 8:00 a.m. and finished at 6:00 p.m., so I couldn't have too much to do with the outside world of photography. It was a solitary and very long time for me. Once again, I learned patience, because I never despaired that one day I'd be able to work again for myself. I was fired from the Renault factories in June 1939. It was about that time that I met Charles Rado, founder of the Agence Rapho, who told me: "Well, I guess I'll try to sell your photos." He represented Brassaï, Ergy Landau, and many other recognized photographers.

Why were you fired from Renault?
For being late so much! It was an exciting but very difficult
time for me. I didn't have any support and had no relations
whatsoever. But in the month of June 1939, I was back in the
street AT LONG LAST! Naturally, 1939 was a badly chosen year,
because something else was happening. My new-found freedom ended very quickly because of the events of September
1939. But it was only another deception. Once again, patience
was needed.

*At the beginning, when you worked for Agence Rapho, what
kind of photos were requested of you?*
Well, the first work that Charles Rado recommended was on
canoeing. He knew that I used to do a lot of canoeing. One
time we went down the Dordogne River in a canoe and it
ended up as a shipwreck. I photographed the whole adventure
and he actually published it after all!

Was it a commissioned work?
Yes, he had had a request for pictures of leisure activities.
Canoeing was a way to spend one's vacations—very spectacular and intelligent, and with the beauty of French rivers
that were, at that time, without dams. That was the first job
he asked of me, so I was as proud as can be. At the same time,
he asked me to do a reportage about ancient caves and
prehistory. I was off working inside one of these wonderful
caves when I learned about the Declaration of War. It was
awful. I was fifteen thousand years in the past when, abruptly,
the war put a stop to my involvement with the Prehistoric
Era. I have always regretted that, because it was an extremely
interesting time. The war period was not pleasant. It leaves
me with bad memories.

What did you do during the war?
I was a private. I was at war but you could say that I missed
it. I was a front-line infantryman. It's not interesting for the
non-specialist. In February 1940, I became sick. The cold
hit me. I wasn't made for the cold, I don't like it. I was sent
home for three months to recuperate on a temporary sick-

leave discharge from the service. Those three months extended themselves slightly, and when the end of the war came, I was still at home, still in a bad state.

Now I was back home in Paris, but I didn't have work. I was sick. I had a strange feeling of having left my friends. It was a very, very curious and unhappy period. Afterward, there were four complex years, when I had to live despite everything.

What did you do during this period?
I did lots of things. I took pictures of jewelry, things like that. At the end of the war I worked for something called Ministère des Sports et de la Jeunesse, where I photographed high jumpers, runners, and so forth. Things were not going too badly. Then I met Maximillien Vox and he asked me to do a book on French science. I worked in scientific laboratories, ranging from astronomy to medicine. That was a good job. Then there were a few women who were trying to found a newspaper called *Vrai*, which was a social paper, and I began taking pictures for them.

At last, with the Liberation of Paris, there was unquestionably an explosion of liberty! The streets that I had been prevented from knowing during the five years at Renault and the four years of war were handed back to me!

During the war, was it dangerous to take pictures in the streets?
Yes, but I took some, not many. Even so, I have a few of that time—people on bicycles, transportation, things like that.

Evidently, during this period, you made postcards?
Yes, I did. They were about the life of Napoleon for the Musée de l'Armée. They were reproductions of canvases, twenty paintings of Napoleon, twenty paintings representing Napoleon's life, beginning with his house of birth in Ajaccio up until Austerlitz or Waterloo. We lived with Napoleon for two years!

Did you know Cartier-Bresson during this time?
I knew him after the war. Henri was a P.O.W.

You used your skills to forge passports and ID cards for the Resistance, didn't you?
Yes, but it's a small anecdote, irrelevant. I hid many Jewish friends who had to be helped out. I made false papers for them as well, because I had once been a printer. Afterward, there were escaped prisoners, then the Communists and so forth, who all needed papers too. So, with means that were completely rudimentary, I made them. But I tell you, it is a little bothersome to talk about it, because it gives the impression of me being an old veteran—a war hero—and I am not one.

Did you develop a strong social-political consciousness at this time?
I had already formed it at Renault, where the working conditions were distressing. Naturally, you can never forget the worker! I hate factories, and when I see one I make a great detour around it just so that I don't have to go inside. But I will never forget the conditions that existed before 1936. In the Renault factory, people couldn't wash themselves. Bicycles were stacked in bulk in front of the door of the factory because there were no garages, and there were searches of the workers as they left! Lots of humiliating incidents. It cannot be forgotten.

During the war did you ever take pictures of subjects that might be categorized as political?
No, no, that was not possible. The only action on my part, the only one that was a commitment, was to help people. It was a political commitment. I sincerely believe in the character of someone who extends a sense, not necessarily of generosity, but rather one of welcome, of hospitality! The moment you receive someone, it is an engagement, a meshing, a position that has a hold on you. You become a partisan.

Did all this translate itself at some time into photographs?
Yes! It made me wish to go deeply into things. From all this arose my desire for a full-hearted political option for action.

Was there a turning point in your understanding of this option, or was it realized gradually?
It was gradual. It came from the 1936 strike. I was married in 1934, a young husband—the canoe, happiness, youth, liberty! I mean relative liberty, of course. People struggled for the improvement of factory life and for paid vacations, and later, in 1938, there was more pressure and militants were chased from the factories. Then there was the war in 1939, then the Occupation, so naturally the progression toward a real option was slow.

Besides, I believe that it is the role of the photographer to look on as a privileged observer, one who can penetrate everywhere. The photographer sees very well. Even now, people who are here in this town still don't know about the working conditions of those who are in the north, or in the Pas-de-Calais, or in regions where life is difficult.

I was recently asked a question: "In your opinion, who is a hero?" Heroes, for me, are trade-union militants. They do work that won't bring them glory, yet they are propelled by feelings of justice and aspirations for a better world. Every day they continue their political action. They are really extraordinary people.

In the past, you have occasionally mentioned what you call the "visionary sense." Would you talk about that?
I find that the profession of photography gives a certain sharpness to visual observation. It gives one a clearer visionary sense than that of the average person, whose perception is generally somewhat dulled by watching too much television. This visionary sense, plus one's own sensibility, go hand in hand, of course, to create a kind of visual ecology. I think that this kind of ecological balance can help disentangle us from the immense influence of the media, which is so very powerful. Photography is really a return to the visual source. I think that when someone who is humble looks at things made by his own eye, the primordial tool, he understands them. The eye is the instrument of the poor. Photography is akin to this. The eye is something one has at birth. If you use it well, you can struggle against the maleficent powers that pollute the media. I think

this is very important. Maybe this is why I am so grateful to be able to practice the profession of photography.

So, when the war was finished, you went back to the streets?
Yes, it was especially marvelous, because at the same time there was that extraordinary feeling of liberty. Charles Rado had left for America, so the agency was now in New York. Here in Paris I was visited by Raymond Grosset, who told me: "I would like to restore the Agence Rapho in Paris. Would you like to be part of it?" Now, I'm not too intelligent, and I'm not very organized, but I said to Raymond: "I'll try to see if we can do something together."

I took a series of photos that he was able to publish immediately. At that time there was a lot of work. (The people who photographed the Liberation of Paris numbered no more than maybe fifteen or twenty. In May 1968, during the Paris riots, there were two thousand people who took pictures!) I started with Grosset and I'm still with him. Raymond supports me, because I'm still undisciplined. I bring an idea to Raymond and say: "Raymond, I have an idea that I think is good because we can do something with it." And he says: "Be careful, be careful . . ." I'm not always wrong—I'm wrong two out of three times, but that is right enough!

To come back to the postwar period . . .
There were many, many magazines at the time. First of all, the appearance of American magazines in French—*Life*, for example. I worked a lot at that time for French magazines too: women's magazines, making pictures that weren't always interesting to do—for instance, how to replace your bicycle tire with a hose, things of that sort! On the one hand, there was that, and on the other, there were all the reportages on the first vote for women. There was so much work to do and I had a formidable desire to work! And I really did *work* at that time.

At that time magazines published large photo stories, didn't they?
Exactly. There was a lot of space. Six pages could be taken

up by a pair of ballet slippers! It was unbelievable. Picture stories were done to take up space. When you now see photographs published by papers such as *Le Point, L'Observateur,* they are only as big as postage stamps! It's sad.

Your sequence work from that period seems to forerun that of Elliott Erwitt and Duane Michals.
Yes, that might be true.

You seemed to develop an idea about the use of the sequence in time.
That's right. I did that because I wanted to make films. Fortunately, I was never able to. I say "fortunately" because later on I was confronted with the problems of filmmaking and I realized that, working with a team, you really have to be very persuasive to animate and direct people. And that I'm not, because I always doubt myself.

You're a solitary individual?
I am very solitary. I am troubled when I work with people around me. It is not, however, the people in the street that impede me. There I don't care at all—that doesn't bother me in the slightest. But to have technicians around me that are paid by the hour—it's a little bit like taking a taxi when you don't have much money. You just can't take your eyes off the meter that ticks and ticks and ticks. And I have something of this feeling for the team. It scares me.

What are your feelings about film?
I prefer my hesitations, my false paths, my stammering, to a preconceived idea. With photography one's time doesn't matter. And the material doesn't add up to too much, although it must be said that cameras are expensive and so is film. But it's nothing like moviemaking, where as soon as you release the shutter, immediately large sums of money fly past.

I'm not that sure of myself. I start off with a story. I wait for the moment that fills me with wonder. Or I wait for some kind of miracle that will always happen. But you need only *wait.* When I am in the same place for three hours, lots of things happen to me. A man who stands still in a town in which everything else moves has to be an attraction after a while. People come and ask me the most dumbfounding things. One person asks you for a screwdriver, another asks you the best way to get to the Porte de Clignancourt, one of the suburbs of Paris. They take me for a spy. It's true. The person who stands still is not a contemporary.

To try to come back to the sequencing for a moment, you did this because you liked the cinema?
Right. Because I thought I could translate, with a succession of images, a kind of small film onto fixed images. That was it. And now let's go further ahead.

I would like to talk about the isolated image. There are pictures that may not only possess an astonishing graphic presence, due to some uncommon element or strange composition, but that may also radiate a unique atmosphere of their own, one that stays with you and that leaves an important imprint in your mind. I think of photos by Edouard Boubat, by Brassaï, Cartier-Bresson. These all have an extraordinary power and are stamped in the mind, my mind. They all touch an extremely sensitive chord. But how are they made? There isn't any law to describe them. *This, however, is what I'd like to aim for now: an isolated image whose contents possess the magic power of remembrance or memorialization.* This does not happen just by saying that there is an encounter with the setting, a meeting with the people. There is light too. These images are pictures that, for me, have a kind of perfume. They stay near like a little tune that annoys you because you whistle it all the time. You can't disentangle yourself from them. This isolated image has an evocative power that is far greater than that of the series. I can't remember who said that "to describe is to kill, to suggest is to give life." This, I think, is the key.

You have to let the person who will look at the picture— provided that he isn't an ass—always walk along that visual path for himself. We must always remember that a picture is also made up of the person who looks at it. This is very, very important. Maybe this is the reason behind these photos that haunt me and that haunt many other people as well. It is about that walk that one takes with the picture when experiencing it. I think that this is what counts. One must let the viewer extricate himself, free himself for the journey. You offer the seed, and then the viewer grows it inside himself. For a long time I thought that I had to give the entire story to my audience. I was wrong.

Is it when making a picture that you are, in a way, connected with the expression of this "inward" voyage?
Yes, although the verbal expression of this is most difficult and awkward, and that is annoying. You see, I'm always trying to understand the individual that I am. But there is the continual constraint of living everyday life to deal with. A kind of fury grows as a result because we are not really free. Then there comes a sort of slow boiling up inside so that finally we explode. Then, abruptly, there is that exasperation that at one moment translates itself into a need to be filled with wonder, a need for a kind of happiness of the eye, and a need to look with intensity and with courage, and a need, perhaps, to move inward.

Finally, there is that moment when we are truly visionary. There, everything works tremendously well. But all this is only a part of that great game that puts us into a trance, into a state of receptivity. This trance doesn't last long, however, because life always calls you back to its commands. There are always contingencies. But somehow, despite it all, the effect does last. I think that it could be classed as a feeling. For me it is a kind of "religion of looking."

But when you have to photograph high-society ladies, or someone who is artificially self-important and full of himself, you don't want to surpass yourself. To give something in that situation you work automatically just because of your job, and that's all. But Cendrars, Prévert, Picasso, and many more, they were different. One fellow who I liked a lot was Ardelet. He is dead now, but as a writer he is beginning to be known. With people like this, you want to do something good, because doing a mediocre thing would be to behave with coarseness and vulgarity. One doesn't ever want to be vulgar with such people!

Did your pictures inspire them in turn?
I don't know. I know that with Cendrars something happened. I knew Cendrars in Aix-en-Provence. I had been sent to take pictures of him. I stayed two days in Aix, and he pleased me tremendously. Afterward he asked me: "May I have some of those pictures?" We'd really enjoyed ourselves at the photo sessions. We went into the streets, we went to pubs. I sent him some pictures. And, as we had talked of the café Kremlin-Bicêtre, he said, "Oh, I went to the Kremlin-Bicêtre often with Fernand Léger." So I sent him a few pictures of the café, and by return mail he asked me: "Do you have many pictures like this of the suburbs?" So once again, I wrote a letter saying: "Yes, I have many because I have photographed what's around me for quite a long time." "Send me what you have." I sent many photos to Cendrars. I've still kept the letter saying: "The package arrived split open but there are sixty-four photos. You may have put more in. I intend to do a book on them. Now you have to show me the arrival of the train at the train station, St.-Lazare. You have to show people in buses, etc." So I put myself to work, happy this time to have found an accomplice!

So it was a collaboration, then?
In a way. He was the one who propelled me to do the work. I brought him the first pictures because it was my world—the world where I was born, where I was married, where I still lived with my children, where I lived with my children who are now married. It was a very, very pleasant exchange.

This is what the people that I like have in common—Cendrars, Prévert, Ciro, Ardelet—when they enter a café they take possession of the place! They talk to everyone! After a half hour we have *friends*. Everyone pays for the other's drink.

What is terrifying in a town now is that people tend to establish blocks of specialization saying: Here there will be young executives, here there will be the miserably poor, etc. It makes towns *very* annoying. So the café was, for me, the reunion of people from different milieus, all of whom brought together their own ideas. With the excitement of a little wine, these people talked without holding back, without fear of being ridiculous. And what happened was that they really gave of themselves. I discovered this well after the war, because I didn't go to the cafés before.

And did Prévert, Cendrars, and the rest speak to you of your pictures? Did they tell you what they saw?
Maybe not. Because it was a kind of silent complicity. They didn't describe what they found.

Was it at this time that you met Cartier-Bresson?
No, I met Henri afterward. The first time was immediately after the war. At that time there was an agency that was founded as a workers' cooperative, and we both participated in it.

What was it called?
Alliance Photo. It became "Adet." We were all a little swindled by them. Henri left quickly, *very* quickly. The other photographers also left little by little. I was one of the last to leave since I didn't have much of a sense for practical matters. I left at the time when Grosset told me that he had reopened Rapho in Paris. That's where I met Henri.

What was your conception of Magnum, what did it represent?
Smashing, terrific photography! There was "Chim" Seymour, Capa, and Henri! They were three impressive individuals. And there was a woman who managed it all. Later on, Henri even asked me to participate in Magnum. However, I had found Grosset once again, and basically, Rapho suited me better than Magnum, so I said no thank you. Magnum was an agency that took big trips. I thought that I too was a traveler. I didn't understand then that I wasn't really made for that kind of travel work. However, I've remained close friends with all those people, with Henri especially, whom I like and admire a great deal. I liked Chim too. There was also the Swiss photog-

rapher, the one who died in the Andes, Werner Bischof—he was such a charming fellow.

Did you travel for Rapho during this period?
Yes. They made me travel. They even sent me to America, and then, ten years ago, to Canada. In America I worked in New York and afterward in Palm Springs. That was another rather amusing break in my life. *Vogue* asked me to work for them and so I was a society photographer for two years. Grosset negotiated with them. He released me for two years and I was appointed to *Vogue*. It was a completely false course. It was there I met the society people I photographed.

Did you also take pictures for yourself during this time?
No.

Did you know the editor-in-chief of Vogue, *Edmonde de Charles-Roux?*
Yes, and there was de Brunoff before her. He was a charming man. Charles-Roux was a very funny, and a very good, journalist. Whenever we saw each other, we were really happy. I was working on "Life in Paris" and was doing fashion like a pig. I didn't know anything about it and I didn't give a damn!

You were doing fashion in the studio?
Yes, and I didn't know anything about it, either. I took the job because it offered a certain working security at last, but I regret it a little today because of all the pictures that I was unable to take at the time. I kept only ten negatives from that time. The rest, little dresses—I don't give a damn! I also did some "trick photography" in the lab—solarizations, etc.—and some literary illustrations as well. All were complete mistakes.

Which were the Vogue *years?*
1950 and 1951.

Did you have contact with other photographers in the United States during that time?
At *Vogue* there was Irving Penn, who was very kind to me.

He was the number-one photographer at *Vogue*. He was the great master. What he did was splendid. But the other photographers were a little jealous of me because of differences of character, and because I took some work from them.

Do you think that the atmosphere at Vogue *had an influence on your own work, on what you saw?*
Oh, yes, it played a part, as Renault did. I had a tremendous desire to go back into the streets! The guaranteed contracts at *Vogue* were marvelous security after the war, especially since I had had a difficult time.

Did you have contacts with any photographers apart from Penn?
Beaton. I knew him, but only from a great distance.

Around this time, you began developing a humorous side to your pictures, didn't you?
I find that when I am witnessing an extremely tender and intimate sight—in order to excuse myself for having been witness and voyeur to such a tender, deeply moving moment— I take refuge. The refuge I take has been in humor. I seek humor so that the moment will not be such a solemn declaration. Humor is a way to hide yourself a little bit. But even when the situation is impossible, I make fun of myself as well! I don't take myself seriously at all. One just can't.

Do you think about how pictures should look?
I just say: "This is what I think today." I don't maintain that I know the truth. One does, however, need a few convictions when one works in conditions that are troubling. In the street you are always working with living things. There, you have to have a few convictions. Something else is important, too. It is that the form of a picture is only perceptible when that form corresponds to the graphic training we have all had since our childhood. From time to time, I even believe that a composition that looks a little like a letter of the alphabet is more easily perceived by people than one that is not, since we are

trained from childhood to recognize a certain graphic form
of things.

*If a sign is utilized, is it because there was a learned graphic
sense which allowed it to be easily remembered?*
Yes, there's the triangle, the circle, and even letters, because
they're quickly learned, too.

*Are you suggesting the foundations of a populist aesthetic
where a maximum number of people might understand and
appreciate images?*
No! I think that one cannot ever yield to demagogy, producing
art which merely pleases people! There is an extremely delicate line between facility and vulgarity. If you wish, the
fellow that tells a rude story will have an acquired public. Of
course, if it is very fine smut, people will laugh. But I think
that, again, one should not yield to it. It displeases me enormously, because the more I like laughing, the more scatologi-
cal stories displease me. I am not as accommodating as all
that, not at all.

*To come back to a previous question about Parisian person-
alities—did you know Atget, or see his work? Did it mean
anything to you?*
I knew him when he was very old. Atget was a fellow in whose
spirit I very often find myself. Atget did a body of work that
is tremendously important, like the people who did picture
postcards of the period. These people did an important job
of documenting how people dressed, how they traveled, what
the setting was. I believe in the importance of these unknown
people, much more so than in the aesthetics of the photographers from the old French Society of Photography!

Did you have large-format cameras at the time?
Yes, of course. I had a Lorillion 8 x 10 inch camera (it had
to be turned upside down to be used vertically), with double
dark slide, tripod, dark cloth. I was champion of the shutter
because I wore a beret and I managed 1/25th of a second

with that beret covering the lens! It was very difficult to do. Around 1932 I bought a Rolleiflex because I was photographing the flea market and had to use an English 9 x 12 cm. view camera with a tripod and a dark cloth. I got the first Rolleireflex, which is a model with six exposures and a Tessar 3.5 lens. It's a camera that you hold in your hands, and there was the magic of that little mirror in which you could see a smaller version of a marvelous scene. I stayed with the 6 x 6 cm. for a long time, but now I work with the 24 x 36 mm. (35 mm.) because there are longer and shorter lenses, which are much more luminous, and much greater film latitude, too. Someone as logical as Henri immediately understood all this: what kind of material is needed without having the bulk. Henri really has an economy of means. This is always a priority for the artist. Henri is really a very methodical, very intelligent man.

What happened after Vogue?
I worked a lot for magazines such as *Life* and the English magazine *Picture Post*. The big classics were good magazines, but they all disappeared. I continued to work for a labor union review and a weekly, *"La Vie Ouvrière,"* which brought me into contact with the people I am at ease with. But the press has completely changed. There is something else that exists now—the tremendous infatuation of the younger generation with photography and for reportage. They still seem to believe that they'll find freedom, money, travel, visits to important people. Of course, this is all a hoax. It's fool's money! But it has brought a great many new people to photography. Since these are younger people, ready to travel at a moment's notice and physically strong, it's only normal for them to take those kinds of jobs. It's something that I am no longer able to do— and I no longer want to.

This raises the question of commissions and livelihood, doesn't it?
Sometimes you can amuse yourself very well while doing commissions. It forces you to penetrate places that you wouldn't go to yourself, i.e., my "Front de Seine." It's not useless, I do it, I obey, and it suits me fine but it isn't what

I'd choose to do. You have to remain contemporary, though. You can't simply dream or withdraw, or do the work of a Carthusian monk going off to the provinces to take pictures. That is not my domain. At Rapho there is a photographer named Hans Silvester, who lives in the provinces, but who can really work! He is a marvelous photographer, and will not yield to easy images—to that well-known blue sky!

Why is most of your work done in Paris?
This is extremely simple for me. I've traveled enough—to Siberia, the Pacific. These are stories that are to be told after dinner. But, basically, I didn't do anything worthwhile in those places. In Paris, I know the town. I always need a lot of time, I have to be very familiar with a place, to feel I'm part of it. Here, I am part of the environment of Paris. I can be seen with my old cap pressed down around my ears when it's cold. I am part of the setting. I know it. Everywhere. I know places where I can stop if I'm tired. I have a friend who's a printer, another who's a leather gilder, another who's a cabinetmaker. I go to see them. I know that it is city life, but I like it. When I go off to another country, I begin looking and feeling like a tourist.

Very often in Paris I say to myself: But that's stupid, it is this that I should have shown, and I turn around and go back. You can't do that in a foreign place. If I go to Siberia to photograph people, once I am gone I can't come back. Nor can I wait around. In Paris, on the other hand, I can wait. I can wait hours and hours.

I think that the fundamental reason I like to stay in Paris is that I refuse to accept brutal disappearance. I like to think that the universe I have liked will continue on a little bit longer, and then will dissolve slowly, gently, after I die. Fading in and out, like in the cinema, where we are accustomed to a fade-out at the end. I accept a fade-out. But what I cannot conceive of is a "click" at the end. In the case of people that I have liked who have passed away, we continue to read their books, we continue to look at their drawings, their photos. It seems to me that in this way they continue to walk a bit of the way with us. And it is perhaps for this reason that I have photographed the old Paris that I liked so much when I was twenty or thirty years old.

Paris seems to be a city of lost time.
Yes, it was true, but not any more. For economic reasons, Paris was emptied of its living essence, the workmen. Like skimming milk, people were chased outside Paris. The result has been that these people are so preoccupied with their displacement that they no longer have the time to stop at a corner, to look at a window, or to sing. In the past, these people would stop at a street corner and make a circle around a fellow who played music, and then they all sang together. Nowadays we can't even imagine that this was possible. Fortunately, the tradition now continues in front of the new Pompidou Center. Now, in order to reanimate this city, groups are being created once again to do spectacles, which are so-called spontaneous animations. It's hilarious! It's crazy! These traditions were driven away. Now they are once again being encouraged by giving groups subsidies to help them exist. This all used to happen of itself. It is so ironic.

What is special about Paris for you?
It is a city for pedestrians. That is very special. In Paris the center of interest is still rather small. You can very easily go by foot from Notre Dame to Etoile, whereas in London you cannot even conceive of crossing by foot.

Don't you think that there is a certain historical value in your pictures?
Well, if this is correct, it is despite me, it wasn't a conscious aim of mine. But if my work is of historical interest, so much the better. My idea was much more egotistic, it was to hold the world that I loved! I liked Brassaï's book *Paris de nuit*, because that world too is now destroyed. There are no more streets left with that kind of lighting, that kind of feeling.

You just said that your photographic purpose was egotistic. Was that a conscious intent?
"Intent" is often unconscious. It is the game of seizing and

delaying! There is something in Prévert that is wonderful—the "small second of eternity." Nothing is more beautiful than this expression for me. It appears in a poem called "Jardin" in *Parc Montsouris*:

> *The bench of the Montsouris park*
> *Where you kissed me and I kissed you*
> *In the Montsouris park in Paris*
> *On the earth that is astral and that is all*
> *And this small second of eternity.*

And this is it! This "small second of eternity" that we are lucky enough to be able to find! The understanding of this is not yet visible for all people. But when a tiny bit of this "small second" is captured by photography, when it is put in a rectangle that has a form accepted by culture or scholastic training, then people look and say, "Oh, yes!" Maybe it would be ideal to think that, afterward, these same people would want to go out and see for themselves. That would really be success! But I don't think it will happen. I believe that the more time goes by, the more people will use substitute experts. People will delegate their eyes to the eye specialists! It is easier and more comfortable to let specialists be accountable for filtering our responses to life than to face them ourselves. Already, people seem willing to delegate *all* their senses to specialists.

All your life you have worked alone. Is there an existentialist attitude that permeates the way you have worked? Or is it, perhaps, that the idea of solitude is an idea that is somewhat romantic?
I do not know if it's existentialist or romantic, it's only that the presence of someone at my side physically hinders me. I'm a little ashamed of my illogical steps, my gesticulations. I take three steps to this side, four to that side, I come back, I leave again, I think, I come back, then all of a sudden I get the hell out of the place, then I come back. People would think I'm insane. The way I work is so illogical, and my movements are so unfunctional that I really must do it all alone.

You were suggesting a while ago that you would like people to take photographs and photographers more seriously.
I hate collectors, the ones who take something just for themselves. Me, I like to give. I like to discover something and show it. I'm the village idiot who goes off to the forest and comes back with a bird in his hat and walks around everywhere saying, "Look and see what I've unearthed!" And this bird of an unknown species immediately bothers notable people simply because they don't know how to categorize it. They never saw that kind of bird before, so they say: "Yes, it's amusing. Now go play elsewhere and let us be, because we're talking about serious things." This is a bit like the photographer's role now.

I do pictures as gifts for my friends. They are the people who are my accomplices, and I am very happy to tell them: "Here, just look at what I've unearthed!" I am happy that it might make them chuckle a little bit, like the way I chuckled inside when I took the picture. Or maybe it's an emotion more delicate than chuckling. I want to give, *always* to give.

There are certain things that you seek, situations that you wait for?
I am not interested in refined culture, but rather in instinctive things. I wait for surprise, to be surprised, I do not ever want to have a preconceived idea, or to bring back mere pictorial souvenirs.

Often, you find a scene, a scene that already is evoking something—either stupidity, or pretentiousness, or, perhaps, charm. So you have a little theater. Well, all you have to do is wait there in front of this little theater for the actors to present themselves. I often operate in this way. Here I have my setting and I wait. What I am waiting for, I don't know exactly. I can stay half a day in the same place. And it's very rare that I come home with a completely empty bag.

Have you ever given a photography course?
In 1968, the professionals were summoned by the students of l'Ecole de Photo de Vaugirard, and all of us talked a lot of nonsense. I just don't know what should be done to teach

photography. This isn't my role. I have enough work as it is without getting on my own hobby horse. The days are too short! I'm amusing myself well enough by *doing* the work, but I would be utterly incapable of *teaching* it because I'm not sure of myself. I assert nothing, whereas to be a professor you have to assert. You have to have convictions. I have a few convictions, but I would never try to assert them.

You have, nonetheless, your own experience and some counsel to give?
I do have my convictions, but I don't want to impose them. I say what I believe, but I don't insist that I possess the truth.

Don't you think that a young photographer can be helped enormously, or can grow much faster, with external aid?
Yes, of course this is true. Of course we have to be grateful to those who have helped us—a fellow like Brassaï animated and excited me a lot.

Are there some photographers or painters that made you realize certain things about your work?
There is a person of merit who I consider to be a genius of our times—Georges La Faille. I knew him when he was giving puppet shows. Three months ago in the Pompidou Center he did a twenty-minute cartoon to show the diversity of pictures in the collections of the Pompidou Center. It was an astounding spectacle—wonderful! He is a fellow who animates you, propels you. He makes you want to work. There are so many images that make you want to make images, and there are some that completely discourage you. It's not a question of plagiarism. It is not a sport or a competition. Fortunately, there is still no grading system!

You have said that taking pictures is like decorating a hat with flowers.
That is true. No work is more extraordinary. I have a lot of admiration not only for people who decorate hats but also for the women who make the hats' bouquets. That, for me, is an extraordinary feat. You see a big fat lady who hasn't learned a thing about pictorial composition or the Japanese art of

flower arrangement and she will make you up a marvelous bouquet in three whisks of the wand! It is marvelous, balanced, beautiful. It is like a popular song. Why did Piaf sing so well even though she was not very sophisticated? It's some kind of a mysterious gift that cannot be learned anywhere.

It would be marvelous if photographers were able to live from what they made.
Yes, it is not forbidden to dream of the type of ideal life where people would do things only for their joy. It has happened. Basically, people who used to express themselves in an art such as literature or painting had a means of support either through the church or royalty or the bourgeoisie. There were always patrons. But I haven't found many patrons in photography.

There are now more and more foundations and grants, at least.
I am happy to see that certain collectors buy—and not always in a spirit of speculation—very expensive pictures. I agree with this, but only on condition that I, as the photographer, am not limited in the quantity of prints that I may wish to sell. I totally disagree with editions, I do multiples. Editions go against my idea of giving. But it causes the whole question of collecting to be a little confused in my head. These isolated purchases of photos may one day allow us to be rid of these self-imposed tasks of drudgery in which we are obliged to photograph a toothbrush, or do an annoying cover, or to get into fashion when we don't want to, just so we can eat! One day these purchases may even give us economic independence. But this is utopian. For the time being, most of the galleries are set up for speculation and nothing more. A situation like that caters only to "distinguished" people—and that's death! Still, the photographer certainly has the possibility of surviving.

You do a lot of the printing yourself?
I work a lot in the darkroom because it gives me economic independence. It is, of course, a little stupid to work too much in the darkroom, because during this time you're not on the streets. But if you give your work to a lab that will do it well,

you have to pay, and to pay the debt, you will have to take mercenary work.

Do you think that the beauty of the print adds something?
Oh, yes, surely!

Do you consider yourself a "concerned photographer"?
I'm a little afraid of declarations of this type. It's a little bit like the chorus of an opera that shouts, "Let us walk, let us walk!" and then stays put! If you begin talking too much about doing things, it is usually because you don't really know how to go about doing it at all. To be labeled as a "concerned photographer" seems impudent. I don't like it at all. But I do know photographers who discuss these things for hours on end, and their pictures are very good. Take the case of the cooperative French photo agency, Viva, which I like very much. Le Querrec, Dityvon, Kalvar—they are all excellent photographers who have brought new things to this profession since 1968. But they have one fault, which may be a sickness of youth: they want to be heroic and they talk about photography too much. I don't think that this is very important. However, I too can be reproached for having acted without much consciousness of the importance of my photos. Henri, for example, fought hard to ensure that the captions of photos would be protected and that the framing would be protected too, because if it isn't, you can change a photograph's basic meaning. He is right, of course, but I am not as serious a man. I realize, though, that he did the profession a great service by being so rigorous.

The photographer should be a filter between the mysterious unknown and the reception of this world. It is possible that the photographer has a "psyphoto" side. . . . But when you say this you seem crazy—"the poor fellow, he must be exhausted!" But I believe in this to a certain extent. There is a language in photography that is somewhat mysterious, which isn't a vocabulary, which isn't an alphabet, which isn't a science, or even art as a "cultural phenomenon," which may be, as a fellow said, "in direct contact with the unconscious." This may be possible in relation to photography.

Do you relate this to poetry?
There is nothing closer! It is tremendous! The poetic language of people, like Ronsard, is extraordinary. The choice of words, the bouquet of words without logical construction, is the same as that within a photo. Poetry and photography are much closer together than photography and painting. It is wonderful! You touch the exact thing, the unconscious side of this thing! And again, it is here that the poetry of Prévert was very close to photography. It is taking, within language, the used and worn-out expressions and setting them into a kind of ring so that they shine. This is marvelous. It is true poetry, not studied, not Lamartine. Oh, he can be so boring, Lamartine. Baudelaire, Rimbaud, Ronsard, Rabelais, and Cendrars —they used images, and they didn't mince their words. They were ruthless! They exaggerated a little but they were right. They were not speaking in halftones and subtleties.

Do you think you approach the procedure with which the poets . . .
I was never a poet.

Is it important for you to touch people through your work?
Oh, of course! That is why I do it. I am delighted when there's a reaction—whether it's favorable or unfavorable. People are not too nasty with me on the whole. When we live, we occupy a certain space, and I try to make my space as small as possible. I weigh 110 pounds, am five foot four, and I have a small car. I like people who are "concentrated." But even though you take care not to take up too much space, not to impede others, some people may have something against you by the mere fact that you're alive. It is possible that I exasperate some people.

Isn't it a virtue in certain photographers that they are here to see everything and at the same time impose themselves?
Yes, of course, like the Americans who arrived in France after the Liberation. They had so much material. They couldn't work without having three flashes. But life passed them by in front of their very eyes. Naturally, they only photographed the "accepted" things. Whereas someone like Henri understood

very quickly that you had to have a small, quiet camera, and that freedom helped him produce wonderful new pictures.

On the other hand, we have the example of someone like Atget. That's completely different because at that time the photographer was a kind of mountebank who took his time. People ended up either forgetting him or placing themselves comfortably in front of him.

What is important is that you take pictures of people who are part of the town you are a part of.
I have a center. My center is my friends, my accomplices. Is this evidence of a lack of an adventurous spirit? Perhaps it is a lack of confidence in myself to go and conquer the world. I am rather lost in a foreign land. I don't speak languages, and I hate not being able to communicate with people. Then, there is this idea I have of being the overbearing tourist, which I'm ashamed of. I once found myself in Portugal, with many children asking me for money because I was having my coffee outside. I was really ashamed. So I don't do my traveling this way. If I have to take cover behind the picturesque or the exotic in order to do something, my images are of no value. The first photos of palm trees were striking. The thirtieth picture of palm trees or the thirtieth carnival of Rio—God, it is boring to see! We just don't give a damn after a while. Why should I have to photograph in a foreign place when people there do it very well themselves?

Photography is very subjective. Photography is not a document on which a report can be made. It is a *subjective* document. Photography is a false witness, a lie. People want to prove the universe is there. It is a physical image that contains a certain amount of documentation, which is fine, but it isn't evidence, a testimony upon which a general philosophy can be based. People can say, "Here is a fellow who has seen such and such facets of life, but not the whole."

If it is not about reality, what does photography mean to you?
It might involve the principle of the committed photographer who thinks of himself as socially responsible. There may be

something there that is important. You may choose to report on a socially deprived area. Most people would not take their cameras to these places. But the committed photographer may reveal a certain aspect of the condition of people's lives there. Photographers have done this, and I find that this is one of the great merits of photography. Beforehand, apart from the few paintings, there were no documents of the actual social environment. The people of Viva who took pictures of low-income-housing projects did work that was very interesting. Whether it is reality or not, it is, nevertheless, the penetration of an environment that had never been seen in a picture before. The fact that the photographer may have this social responsibility is very important because he will be showing something that most people may hold in contempt, that they may want to hide.

You take a certain type of picture—how do you relate this to your political ideology?
I am not militant. The photography profession doesn't permit me to be militant. When you're militant you really have to spend a lot of time at it. You really have to found your life on it. Whereas my militancy is photographic and *all* my life, if I can, if I have enough will, if I am not overwhelmed by paperwork and red tape, I spend taking pictures. Thus, I do have convictions that are, if you like, political. My photos are not pictures that say, "Here is good and evil, right and wrong." If my work speaks, it does so by being a little less serious, a little less solemn, and by its lightness it helps people to live. I think that this is a social role that isn't negligible. I don't say that it is important, but just that it isn't negligible. I would rather *help* people through photography than produce "symbolic images" for propaganda purposes. I work more in everyday chronicles and with "smallness." I would not be at ease doing violent or "heavy" things.

In your photos we do not find people who are in extremely private emotional conditions or physical circumstances.
True, because these are what I call "secret gardens." It bothers me to trample on these aspects of life and to show them. It is

probably useful to show this, but it isn't my way, just as it isn't my way to be a political leader, or an orator, or a teacher.

I'm afraid of taking too much of people's time, too much space, by imposing myself with solemnity. I am a little like the poor Martin who dug his own grave in order not to bother the gravedigger. It is a little bit like my grandfather. He would excuse himself all the time. He always sat on the edge of a chair. I am a little like this. I am not pushy and it has hindered my development. I guess I should have been more egotistical. But I'm not, and that's life! And I am glad!

November 1977

BOOKS OF DOISNEAU PHOTOGRAPHS

Le Paris de Robert Doisneau et Max-Pol Fouchet. Text by Max-Pol Fouchet. Paris: Editions Français Réunis, 1974.
Les Parisiennes tels qu'ils sont. Paris: Robert Delpire, 1954.
My Paris. Text by Maurice Chevalier; afterword by M. F. K. Fisher. New York: Macmillan, 1972.
1, 2, 3, 4, 5. Lausanne, Switzerland: Editions Claire Fontaine, 1955.

Herbert Bayer

(B O R N   1 9 0 0 / A M E R I C A N ,
B O R N   I N   A U S T R I A)

Jonathan Bayer

Did you get involved with art when you were a youngster?
I started to paint in my teens.

Was there any art background in your family?
No. My mother was the one person who understood that I was
artistically inclined and that I had talent. She told me: "Do
what you like to do and what you can accomplish by yourself." There was no chance of getting any financial help to

study art. My father had died and I was supposed to take a job as a clerk in my hometown of Linz. I tried it for half a day, but I was so depressed that when I came home for lunch I told my mother I didn't know whether I could stick it out. She said she understood and I could stay home and do something else. Then I started to work freelance, and I got some small jobs in graphic design and other design areas.

Did you naturally gravitate toward design?
Yes. I left Austria at the end of 1918 and went to Germany to become an apprentice to an architect in the artists' colony in Darmstadt. I stayed there for a year or so. Then I heard of the Bauhaus. I was active in a youth movement, and we had a reading circle, where we read a book once a week. One of the books was Kandinsky's *Concerning the Spiritual in Art,* which excited me very much. I assumed that Kandinsky was already at the Bauhaus, although I was mistaken—he came after I joined. At the same time, I saw the first manifesto of the Bauhaus, with the famous woodcut of the "Cathedral of Socialism" on the cover. Both of these things had such an effect on me that I just left Darmstadt and went to the Bauhaus.

Who did the woodcut?
Lyonel Feininger.

This was after World War I?
Yes.

Did you do military service?
I joined the army in 1917. We arrived at the Italian front just as the war ended there, so we returned home. But I was in uniform for some time with a group of volunteer soldiers, to keep order in Linz. The troops of the Austrian monarchy were made up of Slavic soldiers who had come back to Austria on captured trains, which they ran themselves. They mounted machine guns on the roofs of the carriages and would shoot as they rode along. Our group of volunteers had the task of disarming them. They were our own troops, but they had separated themselves from the Austro-Hungarian monarchy.

Was it while you were in Darmstadt that you first became interested in graphic design and typography?
No, that started while I was still in Austria. The influence of the Viennese workshops was very strong in Austria, but it was more arts and crafts than design. Industrial design, as we know it today, was really born later, during the Bauhaus years. I was very interested in it, partly because I wanted to go to an academy in Vienna to study art. There was no money to pay for it though, so I turned toward something that I could make a living with.

You have said that you were influenced by Concerning the Spiritual in Art, *which is considered to be esoteric and romantic, yet you went to the Bauhaus, which had quite a practical emphasis.*
You have to look at the history of the Bauhaus. As its manifesto will tell you, at the beginning it was rather romantically oriented. The manifesto called for artists to unite, in the same way in which the medieval craftsmen were united—a true collaboration for the task of building the big cathedrals and other large works of art. The manifesto asked the artists to unite so they could become craftsmen again. They should not only understand their own craft but have an understanding of all related areas. If they were really talented, they would develop into what you might call superior craftsmen, who would be considered artists.

Was there any selection process before you entered the Bauhaus?
Oh, yes. There was an acceptance committee which consisted in my case of Walter Gropius and Paul Klee. You were accepted, and then you went through a basic course, on probation, for a year or half a year.

Who ran the preliminary course?
At that time it was run by Johannes Itten, who invented the Bauhaus concept of teaching. After the basic course, the student exhibited his work, and if he was found acceptable and sufficiently talented, he was expected to make a legal contract

as an apprentice in one of the crafts. For instance, Marcel Breuer, who was interested in interior design and furniture, apprenticed in the wood workshop, which meant he studied to be a carpenter or a cabinetmaker. I joined the wall-painting class, so I am now an experienced house painter. Of course, it was a different kind of house painting than what one expects a house painter to do today. It was rather thorough and complex. They asked a great deal from us, and it was hard to pass the examination. There were no age or education requirements for entering the Bauhaus. Nobody asked for a degree, only the quality of work and personality counted. Even in the first years at the Bauhaus, no degrees were given. One could only acquire documents stating that the student had successfully completed his apprenticeship. Degrees came later, when students asked for them.

How long did the apprenticeship last?
It lasted three years, three and a half years; in some cases, four years.

When you were at the Bauhaus in the early twenties, how significant was their involvement in photography?
There was practically no photographic involvement at that time. We were in Weimar until 1925, and then left for Dessau because of political difficulties. The interest in photography actually started in Dessau, where it was introduced by Moholy-Nagy.

How did you become a teacher?
I had left the Bauhaus late in 1923, after we had had an exhibition of our work. We felt that it was necessary to show the world exactly what the Bauhaus was and had accomplished. After that, I went with my painter friend Josef Maltan on a long hike through Italy and Sicily—the centuries-old "urge toward the sun" that all North Europeans have. I did odd jobs and sold some watercolors. I returned to the Bauhaus when Gropius asked me to become a Master of the Graphic Design Workshop and the Printing Workshop. Gropius thought there should be some teachers from the ranks of people who

went through the Bauhaus training, people like Josef Albers, Breuer, and myself. There were also old Masters, artists who had been asked to come to the Bauhaus as teachers—Johannes Itten, Paul Klee, Oskar Schlemmer, and, later, Kandinsky, Moholy-Nagy.

Were you and Albers students together?
No. Albers wasn't much of a student! He never attended a course. He started in the glass workshop and was experimenting on his own. There were often exceptions to the rules, since there was no rigid structure.

How did you pay for tuition and facilities?
I attended for free, because I didn't have anything to pay with.

How was the Bauhaus funded?
Art schools in Germany were all supported by the state and by individual municipalities. The tuition fees were very small, and the teachers were paid a salary by the state or city.

Even an experimental place like the Bauhaus?
Yes, but you must remember its history. Gropius had been the director of an established arts and crafts school immediately after the war, and it was this school in Weimar that he turned very quickly into the Bauhaus. The state and the officials were dubious about the school. We were generally unaccepted and looked upon as dangerous liberals.

Were you forced to move from Weimar?
We were not forced. We decided that the atmosphere was intolerable and therefore we wouldn't stay. The Nazi Party was gaining strength and they made things difficult for us, by accusing us of being Communists. Our troubles became known during our first exhibition and a week of cultural performances. Among others, Stravinsky was there with his "L'Histoire d'un soldat"; there was an exhibition of modern art. All this made a great impression, and an organization, the Friends of the Bauhaus, was founded; it consisted of prominent people who stood up for the Bauhaus. When we announced that we couldn't

continue in Weimar, there were three cities that were interested in getting us. We accepted the offer from Dessau, because it included an invitation to build a new Bauhaus building and a few houses for the Masters.

Was Moholy-Nagy teaching at the Bauhaus when you were a student?
No, he came in 1923, just about the time of this first Bauhaus exhibition. Kandinsky came a little earlier. Moholy really started to teach when the Bauhaus was in Dessau.

Was his photographic work known to the students at that time?
I am not certain.

Did it interest you?
Yes, and I was also inspired by it. It made me feel that photography was an interesting medium and that I should try it.

What aspects of Moholy-Nagy's work interested you?
I was very interested in his photo-montages and his conventional photography, but not so much in his photograms. I felt they were too formalistic.

Were you doing any photography yourself then?
Yes. I was married, and my first wife was studying photography in Leipzig, which was close to Dessau. We were interested in photography for media communication, particularly advertising, and we also did some experimentation. This was the beginning of my photographic work. I also traveled, and I was constantly looking with the eyes of the camera.

Had you seen the work by Christian Schad, the manipulations, or Coburn's Vortographs?
No. I don't think so.

Were you influenced by the "New Objectivity" (Neue Sachlichkeit), which was gaining strength in Germany then?
No. This was something entirely different from our orientation.

What did you think of it?
As much as we did of German Expressionism, which was also something that just was not considered to be in our area of interest.

Was there any involvement between members of the Bauhaus and the German Expressionists?
I am certain there were acquaintanceships there, particularly with Kandinsky and Klee, who had lived in Munich. Some of the early works of Kandinsky are, in some ways, related to the Expressionist landscape painting that was being done at the time. But all the teachers at the Bauhaus were individuals. Moholy-Nagy was constructivist, Schlemmer was very classical, Klee was on his own, and Kandinsky, with his abstractions, was again different; so was Itten. When Gropius founded the Bauhaus and decided that he wanted painters as teachers, he could have admitted the Expressionists. They were at the height of their fame; it was *the* art in Germany at the time. But I cannot imagine the Bauhaus with Expressionists as teachers. The painters called to the Bauhaus were all very much related to architecture, which you couldn't say about the Expressionists. It would have been impossible to admit Expressionists as teachers once the Bauhaus changed from the early romantic orientation to a more rational way of thinking and working. One of the statements that the Bauhaus made was that the artist should accept the machine as a tool and should think in terms of mass production.

Did this make it possible for the Bauhaus to accept the camera as a tool for vision?
I believe so. It is a mechanical instrument, which you operate in order to make photographs, and all such media interested us. Machine aesthetics were very powerful then and we were romantic about them.

Did you involve photography in your teaching at Dessau?
No. I was the Master of the Graphic Design Department, which was, in fact, a printing shop. In the old Bauhaus in Weimar there was a printing shop where artists' prints—

lithographs, etchings, and woodcuts—were printed. This again underlines the switch from the *romantic* to the *rational*, to the machine age. I said: "If I am to be running this workshop, then I don't want a printing shop that makes artists' prints. I want a typographic shop where we have movable type, where we set the type, and where we are printing from type."

Did you come into contact with the work of Lissitzky and Malevich?
I met Lissitzky two or three times when he came to the Bauhaus for short visits. As far as I know, Malevich came once, but I didn't meet him.

Did you see any of Lissitzky's photo-montages then?
I knew some of Lissitzky's work. My interest in him was mostly typographical, though. He used cut-out photographs and pasted them together with typefaces. He later used this method in exhibition designs. This kind of montage was also practiced by the Dadaists, particularly Kurt Schwitters, who often came to the Bauhaus. We were friends and had fun together. Nothing was taken very seriously; this was not an intellectual activity, it was all rather intuitive.

Did you see the photo-montages of Heartfield and Grosz?
I may have seen some of their political montages. I do not remember if they had any influence at the Bauhaus.

How large was the photographic involvement in Dessau under Moholy-Nagy?
Moholy-Nagy never taught photography, he practiced photography. His wife, Lucia, was a professional photographer and she taught for a while at the Bauhaus. The photographic department was officially established shortly before Gropius left, but it became more important when the new director, Hannes Meyer, took over. I can't tell you how large it was because I had left by then.

It seems that you and Moholy-Nagy arrived at certain visual conclusions more or less at the same time.
Certain things happened simultaneously, as our interests were

similar. There is one photograph—"The Pont Transbordeur, 1928"—that we both took from exactly the same point of view. Mine was a year before Moholy's. This iron bridge spanning the port of Marseilles was a marvelous structure, we were all enthusiastic about it and went to photograph it from many angles. Sadly, it was destroyed during World War II.

Were you conscious of discovering a new way of seeing through the camera?
We simply found possibilities there. Looking at things from above, below, foreshortened—these were new discoveries.

What did you show at the "Film und Foto" exhibition at Stuttgart in the late twenties?
I believe they were conventional photographs of subjects which I thought were interesting. At that time, my photographic orientation was directly related to typography. We worked exclusively with movable type. But then came the time when we decided we needed images to enforce communication! And when it came to images, we only thought in terms of photography, because that was seen as an impartial medium without the subjective and personal character of hand-drawn illustrations. We wanted images that could be used as objective information.

Did you get involved with the Bauhaus magazine?
I assumed the editorship for one issue and I did the cover.

How often did the magazine come out?
Four times a year, or something like that. A few of the Masters edited issues. Moholy did some issues. For the one issue I did, I wanted to have a photographic cover. Geometric forms were dominant at the Bauhaus, and I thought a group of symbols—with the cone and the sphere—would make an interesting design.

When was this?
The first issue was in 1928, so this was in 1927. This was perhaps one of my first montages, although it was technically

different from my later ones—I made the montage and then photographed it.

How did you go about constructing your montages?
There were two ways. Either I would actually make the plastic objects which were photographed, or I would photograph a background with holes in it, then montage something in the back of the holes, as though you were looking through it. Sometimes I would paint clouds over it, or air-brush clouds; other times, I would make false shadows or highlights. Then, the entire paste-up would be photographed again on one negative, from which prints were made.

What about fotoplastiken?
These were mostly montages also. Some of them were montages that had been staged before being photographed. I called them *fotoplastiken* because of the three-dimensional character of the subject.

Was anybody else working this way?
Not that I knew of. Of course, the medium of collage was used a great deal for things like birthday greetings or dance posters.

What prompted you to leave the Bauhaus?
There were two reasons. One was that a few of the teachers—mostly Gropius, Breuer, and myself—decided to translate our theories into practice. The other was that I felt I was too young to be a teacher. I thought it was wrong to be a student at the school and then just turn around and teach there. One has to be mature to be a teacher and one has to rub against the world before one can tell others what to do.

How old were you then?
I was twenty-eight.

And you had been teaching there for three years?
Yes. It was teaching with very little theory, though. We printed all the forms and posters for the Bauhaus, which kept the shop busy. You see, the students learned by doing.

Were there any academic lectures at all?
There were some lectures and some theory. Klee and Kandinsky had art courses. Klee analyzed paintings from his sketchbooks. Kandinsky's course was in composition and abstraction. Itten and Kandinsky also taught color courses. As I've said, Itten was the one who founded the now famous basic course, in which students would experiment and play with materials. This was later taken over, expanded, and enriched by Albers and, in part, by Moholy-Nagy.

Was there any political trouble when you were at Dessau?
Not when Gropius was still director. But, under the directorship of Hannes Meyer, trouble started, because there was a Communist cell at the Bauhaus. Once the city authorities found out about it, Hannes Meyer had to go. This was the only time when there was real political activity at the Bauhaus.

Were the Nazis giving you problems?
Oh, yes. They called us "Cultural Bolsheviks," and we were *persona non grata*. They made our life difficult and unpleasant. Finally, the Bauhaus decided to leave Dessau and move to Berlin. There, at the time of Mies van der Rohe's directorship, the Gestapo came with trucks and soldiers and closed it down.

Were the students working politically in Berlin?
I don't think so. I am not familiar with what went on while the Bauhaus was in Berlin. But I do not think that Mies van der Rohe would have accepted this.

So, essentially, the Bauhaus was apolitical?
Yes. This was a subject that was discussed quite often in the early days under Gropius. It was always emphasized that artists should not be political. We could not be political as a school.

Can you explain why?
The rationale behind it was simply that if you become political as an artist, then you must devote your work to your convictions. And we know what has happened in Russia.

Are you saying that work devoted to a political cause then ceases to be art?
Yes, that can happen. Think of the early attempts by the constructivists in Russia to create art for the masses: they were never able to achieve it, nor were they ever able to influence industry. But you must not forget that the Bauhaus concept was a social concept: with mass production, people could gain access to good things. The Bauhaus-designed buildings have so often been criticized for being drab, but that was largely because we wanted inexpensive housing.

Were you sad to leave the Bauhaus?
No. I was looking forward to practicing independently. Although it was not easy at the time, I managed, and I was successful in Berlin. I had ten good years there. It was a very interesting place at the time, it was *the world city*. Everything was happening there, in architecture, film, theater, design. I had my own studio and was art director of *Vogue* for a short while. My studio was affiliated with an advertising agency, so I had a base on which to build my practice.

Were you attracted to the idea of working in advertising because of your Bauhaus experience?
Yes.

The concept of mass advertising and mass art and design must have been relatively innovative at that time?
If you paint a painting and a private collector buys it, it's hidden away. But when you design a poster, you have the satisfaction of seeing it in the streets and you can influence many people. If you do it well, this is a great satisfaction, because it's both artistic *and* functional.

Did you feel any sort of moral dilemma in using your art in advertising—to get people to buy things that, perhaps, they didn't really need?
In my work, I had relatively little to do with advertising consumer goods. I did a great deal for exhibitions—exhibitions for education, for office machinery, flowers, radios, etc.

This was an area which was more interesting to me than straightforward consumer advertising.

Did you commission any photographers for your work with Vogue?
No. I had a photographer under my supervision in my studio. We never had to commission fashion photographs for *Vogue*, because we would get them directly from Paris.

Who were the photographers that you met then?
There were those who became well known—like Kertész, Munkacsi, and Eisenstaedt. I met Eisenstein a few times, when he came from Russia to visit Moholy-Nagy. There were exchanges of skills and ideas among artists, photographers, and filmmakers. Photographers had been accepted and were considered to be artists. However, except for some close friends, I was rather isolated during the Bauhaus years. I was only aware or concerned with what was happening at the Bauhaus. I was shy, and this perhaps accounts for the fact that I did not meet many of the famous visitors. Also, I did not know what was going on in art in Paris. Of course, I knew about Cubism, but I only became aware of Surrealism later on, through a Belgian magazine, where I saw the work of René Magritte. Belgian Surrealism was quite a strong movement then. Their magazine published one of my paintings while I was at the Bauhaus.

You saw the rise of the new illustrated magazines. Did they interest you?
Yes, definitely. I saw that the photograph was becoming more and more important in communication. I also saw that the camera was a marvelous instrument with which one could catch moments of life which otherwise would be lost.

Did you ever discuss the conventional versus the manipulated use of photography?
No, not even with Moholy. You simply did what was needed by whatever means.

Was it just the excitement of image-making?
Yes, but it was more the excitement of a new *way* of image-
making that made us experiment. As far as I remember, there
wasn't any analysis or discussion. It was just done that way.

Why did you move to America?
I stayed in Germany longer than most of my friends, because
I did not think that the mad political regime could last. But
I was wrong. After a few years, I thought about going to
England, or to Switzerland or Italy, but then I decided that
America would be the place to go. So I came to America in
1937 with Breuer, who had already received an invitation to
go to Harvard, as Gropius had. I went back to Germany, but
only briefly, because otherwise I would have been drafted. I
escaped from Germany by luck.

*Before you left, were there any political restrictions on your
work?*
This was a curious situation. Don't forget that I was a for-
eigner, an Austrian. Interestingly enough, I had three paintings in an exhibition of so-called degenerate art that was being
shown in Berlin while I was still there. Yet the Nazis did not
connect my work in this exhibition with my design practice
in Berlin! I had many Jewish clients; I stuck with them as
long as they were there, but they gradually disappeared—
emigrated or disappeared, we didn't know which. We just did
not know what was happening. This was the curious thing.
The Nazis let me work and I had a great many commissions
when I decided to leave for America. But nothing I did was
political. I never went to the Propaganda Ministry and I never
said "Heil Hitler!"

Whom did you work for when you first went to America?
I came to the States with a commission from the Museum of
Modern Art to put on a Bauhaus exhibition. That had already
been decided when I had been here on my first visit in 1937.
I went back to Germany to collect material, which made me
very nervous, because collecting the work of the Bauhaus was

dangerous. I got away with it, though. I put on the show at the Museum of Modern Art in 1938.

My first job from industry came from the Container Corporation of America. They had begun to do some interesting advertisements which were based more on visual concepts than on a text. The requirement was that no more than fifteen words could be used. I was affiliated with the Container Corporation for a long time and later became chairman of their art department.

Did you meet Beaumont Newhall at MOMA?
I met him when I was putting on the "Road to Victory" exhibition. I saw him quite often. He took photographs of the installation.

Did you stay in New York?
I was supposed to go to Chicago and teach at the New Bauhaus, which later became the Institute of Design, but I didn't want to teach. So I stayed in New York and worked as a freelance designer.

Did you work much with Steichen during this period?
Yes, I worked with him on the "Road to Victory" exhibition and we got along extremely well. He asked me constantly for my opinion. We always spread photographs on the floor to look at them and he always became sentimental about American things. I also met Ansel Adams at MOMA. He popped in a few times while we were working.

Alfred Stieglitz was one of the primary forces working in photography in New York at this time. Did you meet him?
I met him once, just briefly.

When you first came to America, did you see any photographic work that interested you?
Yes. Walker Evans's photographs were very interesting to me. Also Paul Strand's. Evans interested me because he brought to my attention subjects I had not known about before. You see, I hadn't traveled through America, and I didn't know

those wooden buildings that he photographed. I met him quite a few times. I knew Ben Shahn very well. We commissioned him to do some works for the Container Corporation, and I saw him intermittently.

What photographers did you commission yourself at that time?
I'll have to think very hard. Herbert Maher, Wynn Bullock, Art Kane, Jerry Uelsmann, and Man Ray did a page for us.

Referring back a moment: the "Road to Victory" show was primarily a photographic exhibition?
Exclusively.

Could you mention how you designed it? Did its design influence the "Family of Man" exhibition?
I believe so. And I am surprised that Steichen didn't come to me to do the "Family of Man," although I had moved away to Aspen by then. The "Road to Victory" was done exclusively with photographs, as I said. I had developed some theories about exhibition design: one of the important elements was the necessity of guiding the visitor clearly through all that he has to see. There has to be a floor plan which he can follow logically, and which shows him the work progressively. I had also worked out a theory of extending the vision by including the floor and also the ceiling, when it was possible. And raising the visitor on a ramp so he could overlook the floor, walls, and ceiling in an enlarged field of vision. The third concept was to do an exhibition in such a way that you see and use few structural elements. In the "Road to Victory" exhibition I accomplished all three ideas. The photographs were on panels just off the wall, so that they appeared to be floating. The floor was painted white, as were the walls and ceiling. One looked down on the panels which were presented vertically and at different angles.

You were in total control of this?
I was in total control. We used only black-and-white photographs, and black-and-white type, no color. It was a completely

black-and-white show. I thought it was one of the best shows I did.

Did you get any comments?
Not to speak of. I only heard one, indirectly, from my wife, who was then married to Julien Levy, the art dealer. He had shown the exhibition to Salvador Dali, who said: "It's all wrong, it should have been done completely differently!" And that's the only comment I've ever heard about the show.

Did you worry about it being considered propaganda?
Of course, exhibitions can be used for propaganda purposes, but this exhibition was simply to show the national sentiment during wartime. There was no propaganda. It showed a ship being built, a mother with pies, the churches, people at work on a common task.

When you saw the "Family of Man" show, did you feel it was retrogressive?
Yes. There were many very sentimental pictures. It was a little pompous, too. But this was Steichen's outlook.

Why did you move to Aspen, Colorado?
I was not very happy in New York. I'm not a city boy, and we were trying to move out. Then Walter Paepcke, president of the Container Corporation, came along. We became friends through my association with his company. He owned a ranch near Aspen, and he thought it was such a beautiful place one should do something with it. His first idea was for a sort of colony of friends, but it soon developed much further into the idea of creating a new community, and he asked me to come and help him.

In what way did he want you to help him?
There were many architectural problems—the old houses had to be remodeled and modernized. It was all very primitive, a sort of ghost town. There had to be advertising, then skiing was developed and ski lifts were built. It was quite a big

project, all very interesting and exciting. We went there in 1945 and decided to stay.

Can you talk a bit about the conception of the community?
We thought we could create a better community in which one could live in peace and with more dignity than in the city, in a beautiful climate, with sports, culture, music, and nature. And it all happened. It was marvelous and exciting for the first fifteen years. But as soon as it became known, the speculators moved in on us. Walter Paepcke did not have all that much money and didn't know how to raise it to buy more real estate to protect us from the speculators. They now dominate what has become a resort town and they've pushed up prices enormously. The developers have also built many condominiums of cheap quality. But we have tried to guide the development through planning commissions. It could have been much worse. In the meantime, we have founded the Aspen Institute for Humanistic Studies, which has become important worldwide. I created a special environment for it and did all the buildings, but the character of the community has changed from what we thought it should be. We were naïve and idealistic, we never thought of what would happen if it became successful. But it has. Aspen is much bigger, its quality has changed. I moved away two years ago because I had trouble with my heart. The doctors say I shouldn't live at that altitude all year round.

Which is your favorite kind of photography—the straight approach, fotoplastiken, *or photo-montage?*
I always thought that photo-montage was more artistic than straight-image photography, simply because in a montage there has to be an idea, a concept, and it needs special skill to express it and make it into something meaningful. Today, I feel it's easier to take the camera and shoot a good picture than to create a montage, because for montage you need more than looking and seeing. In straightforward photography no purpose or function is involved; it's like painting, it's a piece of art as it is. I wouldn't make any judgment about whether

photography is art or not art, or whether painting is more art than photography. This seems unnecessary. It's simply a question of quality. It's like a good chair is better than a mediocre painting.

Did you get involved with photography at Aspen?
Yes. We started a photographer's conference there in 1948, because Aspen in its fall colors is particularly beautiful. It was quite a good conference; we had excellent people attending—Ansel Adams, Minor White, Berenice Abbott, Frederick Sommer, Eliot Porter. We hoped they would organize themselves to repeat the conference every fall, but they didn't. However, there was a design conference that started a year later and has been meeting ever since. It's grown into an enormous international conference with many participants each year.

Have you any comments on contemporary photography?
A great deal is happening. There are many technical improvements and a lot of experimentation. But there is also much repetition. God, how many things happen simultaneously, artists not knowing each other and doing very similar things. Being different is becoming increasingly difficult.

You seem to have been able to overcome a sense of alienation that a lot of artists have felt toward industry by working with and in it as an artist.
There is always this question of support for the artist, and I've never believed in that. Society needs the artist as much as the artist needs society. Industry needs the artist today as much as the artist needs industry. Industry has found out that they have to give the consumer aesthetically valuable things. They have to use the artist for their corporate image. I don't like the attitude: "Poor fellow, he needs some money to keep him alive." I think there should be an equal relationship. I have never expected anything from the government. In America they still seem to distinguish between born Americans and naturalized Americans. Perhaps in smaller countries

it is better. In Switzerland or in Holland the governments seem to be intelligent supporters of public art.

Art should go to the people. It should not just be produced as merchandise to disappear into some rich man's apartment as an investment. I believe that artists should be drawn more into the forces of life. They should be just as important as the banker or businessman. An artist should be taking part in all the big issues because he is the one person who is capable of adding the value of aesthetics. Nobody else can do that. When it comes to building a highway, he should be called in, and the same when it comes to planning a new city. Instead, he's always called in as an afterthought.

I have been fortunate in that, in recent years, I have found a company—Atlantic Richfield—which is very receptive to my ideas. They believe in me, and it's always a great pleasure to work with them. There are more and more industries and banks who use the artist well. But the artist has to be trained properly to fill commissions of a public character.

Have you been involved in recent years in any photographic work yourself?

No, I haven't used photography for quite some time, although I do collect photographs (which I occasionally take) for future use in montages.

How do you view the renewed interest in your photographic work?

It's quite curious, but also understandable, because photography wasn't really recognized as an artistic medium when I started. Its time had to come. Perhaps it is also that anything that hasn't been evident before is seen as something new, and this enlivens the scene. There was a great renaissance in the making of artists' prints that has subsided again. It was exploited too much and was cheapened, and so the market is now saturated. I hope this doesn't happen with photography.

There are other kinds of work I am more interested in now than photography. To photograph again, I would have to concentrate on it much more—you can't do something like that "on the side."

In what order of importance would you place your various artistic activities?
I would put my independent, creative work first. Then, commissions and larger environmental pieces, because they are out in the street, so to speak.

Have you any thoughts on art education?
It has to start very early. One must be exposed to art as much as possible. It's like music; unless you are exposed to music you will never understand it, it will never become part of you. It is this way with the visual arts, too. But, now, art education has gone back again to the academic approach for the most part. You still have people who go and teach *how* to paint a painting. In art schools they seem merely concerned with what is going on within the picture frame. I am quite surprised that this academic concept is still alive, because this is what we turned against at the Bauhaus some fifty years ago. But, in my opinion, you cannot teach a person to be an artist anyway.

November 1977

SELECTED BIBLIOGRAPHY

Bauhaus 1912–1928. Edited by Herbert Bayer, Walter Gropius, and Ise Gropius. Museum of Modern Art; distributed by New York Graphic Society, Boston; 1959.
Herbert Bayer (catalogue). Introduction by Ludwig Grote. London: Marlborough Fine Art, Ltd., 1968.
Herbert Bayer: Photographic Works. Introduction by Leland Rice; essay by Beaumont Newhall. Los Angeles: Atlantic Richfield Company, ARCO Center for Visual Art, 1977.
Herbert Bayer: Printer, Designer, Architect. New York: Reinhold Book Division, 1967.
The Way Beyond "Art": The Work of Herbert Bayer, by Alexander Dorner. New York: Wittenborn, Schult, Inc., 1947.

Henry Holmes Smith

(BORN 1909 / AMERICAN)

Paul Hill

How did you first get into image-making?

I suppose that I was given some crayons by somebody in the
family when I was a fairly young child, around six or seven
years old. At the time of World War I, my main activity was
drawing pictures in which Uncle Sam was kicking the Kaiser.
In my fiftieth anniversary show, there was a drawing of an
Eskimo and an igloo and the aurora borealis, and on the
Eskimo there was a little cotton coat that was meant to repre-

sent a fur coat. I drew that when I was in the second grade, so I suppose that there is evidence that my image-making began fairly young.

Is there any art background in your family?
My father aspired to become a violinist and he practiced a great deal. But he found that there was more to be gained, as far as income was concerned, by playing drums in a band for beer parties.

You were very interested in cartoons at an early age. How did this develop into an interest in photography?
I wouldn't say that they were linked with one another directly. I got the idea of drawing cartoons from the advertisements in magazines for applying to cartoon schools: "Draw this little figure" or little face, or whatever, and send it in. You could subscribe to lessons for twenty-five dollars. There were two schools in those days and I actually did subscribe to one.

What's more important for my later work, I think, than the fact that I began to make these cartoons is the sensibility revealed in the cartoons. It seems to me that the evidence is there in a cartoon I did of a hat that has just been bought by a man: it blows off his head as he leaves the store and it's run over by a truck. A sense of injustice, of damage, of accident— somehow I tried to come to grips with that in later life. And the other thing that seemed to show up in those early cartoons was the sensibility associated with longing and frustration. I suspect that these two elements are evident in the very first drawings and are evident in some of the photographs I've made as recently as a week ago.

You mention longing and frustration, how does this relate to your work?
As a young person I would fall quite deeply in love with one of the girls at school all the time, and I would be very shy about it. I suppose this is a standard experience. I would go and look at the apartment where she lived, for hours, in the evening. I would walk behind her as she went home. That's both longing and frustration, it's a good example of what I'm talking about.

Can you remember the first photograph that meant anything to you?
That would have been travel photographs: archaeological wonders, scenes from Europe, and so on.

How did you come to take your first photographs?
I had an acquaintance in high school who I thought looked a little bit like me. We struck up a friendship, and one day in 1923 he announced that he had a camera which he'd won as a prize for selling magazines. He didn't want it any longer and I bought it for a dollar. It was a Connolly fixed-focus 2¼ x 3¼ roll-film camera with a miniscus lens, one shutter speed, and several f-stop settings. That's how I began. I shot a couple of rolls of film and took them to the drugstore to finish. There would have been a day or two delay between the time I sent the rolls and the time I got them back, but it seemed terribly important to me not to wait that long. So I went to another drugstore and bought a little developing kit, and of course I messed up the first roll! But after that I mastered the skill enough so that I didn't go to the photo-finisher for a couple of years.

Considering the work you're best known for, the multiple-color dye-transfer process for creating abstract forms in color, how great is your interest now in camera-made photographs?
I would say that I have used the camera from 1923 right up until today. There's been no abandonment of that, but it's a matter of convenience now. In those days it was a matter of necessity.

Did you study photography when you were in college?
Just what I did by myself. It wasn't studied in those days. I enrolled in an art program which was taught by a young person who was a "chalk and talk" lecturer. He taught dogmatically, with a profound lack of culture and an envy of talent, not good qualities to have in a teacher. He introduced us to Helen Gardner's *Art Through the Ages* and *Drawing from the Cast*, and we did totally irrelevant perspective exercises. At the same time, though, through the good fortune of being adventurous, or rather, of having an adventurous friend

named Leo Zaluka, I was submitting all kinds of material to magazines. By the time I went to college in 1927, I had sold an idea for a cartoon to *The New Yorker* magazine. That made my head as dizzy as wine does now! So I continued to send these things out, though with more seriousness, and *Colliers* magazine bought a couple of ideas. There was a magazine newly started in Chicago called *The Chicagoan*, doing its best to be an imitation of *The New Yorker*. I sent the rejects from *The New Yorker* to *The Chicagoan*, and after looking at the very first batch, the editor of *The Chicagoan* wrote back and said: "We like some of these ideas. May we see the drawings?" And so I began to actually make the cartoons, and by 1928 they were being accepted by *The New Yorker*.

How did you become aware of photography?
The New Yorker used all kinds of things, including photographs, in its ads. One of my favorites was a still life of three saucy little male figures dressed in suits. They were called the Fabric Group, after a selection of men's clothes. Every week they had a picture of these three doll cut-outs in some sort of preposterous circumstance. They always had some sort of wisecrack concerning their predicament. After seeing them I tried to do photo-cartoons.

The other influence was the sort of pictures that were published in *Theatre Arts* magazine, and in *Creative Arts*, which was a magazine devoted to art but occasionally had an article on a photographer. One I saw in those days dealt with Edward Weston's *Daybooks* and his pictures, mostly from Mexico. The article must have been connected with some exhibition he had in New York, because at the same time *Theatre Arts* magazine published four pictures of his. One was the dry-bone jaw of some animal, the other was "The Egg Slicer." I can't remember the third one, but the fourth was the famous "Pepper." I think that photograph meant more than any other picture I saw, and the first chance I had I bought one. I still have it.

Another major photographer who meant a great deal to me in the twenties was Francis Bruguière, whose work was also being exhibited in New York. He made pictures that were dynamically lighted paper cut-outs. They were actually abtract sculpture, light-play. I remember trying to do something with the idea of close-ups of plants, but I botched it!

Would you say that your affinity at that time was more toward Weston or Bruguière?
Funnily enough, it was toward Steichen. I subscribed to *Vanity Fair*, where Steichen's work was appearing every month, and I kept trying to imitate his picture of the George Washington Bridge—all upward angles and diagonal composition. I would go around the campus in 1930/31 photographing, looking up at the buildings and up at the chimneys. Steichen was a very important influence at that time.

I was also very susceptible to theatricalism. I loved the theater. I would do things like read about the way Gordon Craig designed a set and then try to design a set that would be for a play I knew. I remember cutting *Macbeth* to the length of a puppet play and designing the sets and the characters for it. I was well known in my own little community for my skill in lighting, so they invited me to light their stage plays. I was interested in typography too, as well as cartooning, editing, writing—everything.

Did you show your work much?
No. You didn't do that then. There were only camera clubs. It's very strange to think of those days in terms of today. The local paper didn't even have its own cameraman. In 1925, for example, our paper would hire the local photoengraver to take the pictures they needed for stories. Since it was a nuisance job, they let me do those jobs for nothing. I would go out to photograph people sitting on a swing at the inauguration of a little park and the guy in the local team who pitched a no-hitter. That was the way my pictures were seen—to send them to exhibitions was beyond conception, even as late as 1932. I was trying to think of how to make money with this stuff, rather than gain recognition from it.

Were there any other incidents that happened in your college career that had a profound effect on your artistic life?
Yes, I left my little teachers college in Illinois in 1929 and

went to the Chicago Art Institute for a couple of semesters. It was a very unsatisfying experience, as all the teaching was done by rote. When I came back, I rediscovered the Illinois landscape and I began painting watercolors. I also began to make fantasy drawings which I think are an important key to the work I do now with syrup refraction. That would be the psychological link with frustration, aspiration, and that sort of human experience.

And, when I went to Ohio State University to finish school, I worked with Felix Payant, who was in charge of the design program and was publishing a magazine called *Design*. I did a lot of assemblages and cut-paper cartoons for him, hoping they'd be cover designs. He did publish some of them in *Design*, and that was the way my work began to be seen.

Was there anything that you read at that time that had meaning for you—Moholy-Nagy's The New Vision *for example?*
Yes, I did read that. I was always walking into secondhand book stalls, new book stalls, secondhand magazine stalls. Every month I would go to get the issues of *Theatre Arts* that had portfolios of photographs. I'd find ones by Weston and ones by Bruguière—I still have the tear sheets from those magazines because they meant so much to me—but one time I went into a bookstore and asked: "Do you have any books on photography?" And the girl behind the counter said: "No, but we have this book that has lots of photographs in it." She pointed to *The New Vision* which was lying open at a page on which there was a wrinkled apple and the wrinkled face of an old man. I knew I had to have that book—there was something special about those two pictures being juxtaposed with each other. Felix Payant ordered it for me. It was a three- or four-dollar book, and in 1933 that was a significant sum of money. I took it as a kind of payment for all the things he'd published of mine without any financial compensation. It was a key book for me, and apparently it was a book of great impact for many people at that time. There was nothing like it. The book had proposals for life, and it had proposals for ways of artistic behavior. It introduced me to certain possibilities, and I promptly went to work; on my own I tried to practice some

of these things—doing them ineptly, but doing them. I didn't
have any job at this time and I was living with an aunt.

Which of Moholy-Nagy's concepts excited you the most?
The idea that man, the human being, the individual, needs a
balanced outlet of his capacity. One must have psychological
as well as physical release. There must be satisfaction, perhaps some frustrations, and some goals, reasonable goals. All
the potential that one has should be let out, not forced. There
has to be a balance between the various aspects of a living
form, and I think this is pretty self-evident now. In my life
I have felt a tremendous amount of truncation, a cutting off,
frustration in various ways that I didn't know how to deal
with symbolically. The Bauhaus was something I didn't even
dream of entering, and while I didn't know it was closed, I
knew that I couldn't get there. Economically I was stuck in
the Middle West and I didn't know how to get out of that
particular trap. It was a difficult financial time; I was imposing
on everyone and I felt very self-conscious about it.

But Moholy-Nagy presented a proposal that gave importance
to human potential which had been totally ignored by the
culture; I think this was the most inspiring and also frustrating, thing: the constant awareness of possibilities and the
awareness that one didn't have the strategy to deal with the
possibilities. I never dreamed that I'd even know Moholy-
Nagy. I wrote him a fan letter in 1934 and I sent it to an
address in *Photo Eye*.

Was it after reading The New Vision *that you felt a growing
commitment to the "photographic experience"?*
No. I wish I could be very clear about this. You can't ascribe
to photography the thing I'm trying to talk about. It is a
necessity that is over and beyond any of the media.

A basic cultural imperative?
It's a need within the individual, and I think every human
being has it. I don't know if they know what to do with it,
and I certainly was having trouble finding out what to do
with it.

When you left college, what did you find yourself doing?
Once again my aunt helped. She was an editor with the American Ceramic Society. They published three periodicals and I worked on them: I did routine editorial work and finally got to the point where I did some of the typography. I worked there from 1934 until they fired me in 1936. Then I tried some freelance designing and a little commercial photography, but I messed up all of it. I'm gratified today by reports that many people who eventually amount to something are commercially inept! So, being defeated, I left that community, sold my house, and went home to Illinois to my parents' home. I set up a little darkroom there and tried to do some photo-finishing, and I kept looking in the want ads for positions. A Chicago paper had an ad for a darkroom assistant at Marshall Field's, which was opening a new photography studio. I applied for the job and got it, and that's why I was in Chicago when Moholy-Nagy arrived. I didn't know he'd be there—it was a complete surprise.

How did you eventually make his acquaintance?
I read in the newspaper that he was going to open a New Bauhaus school in the old Marshall Field mansion, and he was going to give a lecture at the Knickerbocker Hotel. Also, this fellow who had employed me as a darkroom assistant in his portrait studio gave me a copy of the *Penrose Annual*, in which was an article by Moholy discussing new horizons in color photography. I had some ideas that supplemented what he had written about, so I wrote him a letter and offered him my technical collaboration. The next thing I knew he came to the darkroom where I was working and asked me to help him plan his school's photography area.

You got involved with teaching for the first time then?
No, I was teaching before that, but informally. I began to teach photography in Columbus, Ohio, in 1933.

What were you teaching?
It was a small group of people who didn't know anything about photography. One of the things I did was use an exer-

cise based on Bruguière's ideas and the Bauhaus ideas: cut a piece of paper and make it into a three-dimensional object, then put it into the light and photograph it. People could not understand why we did it. That was the first time I applied the Bruguière modulated principle.

What photographic images were you making at this time?
Even then I was trying to do experimental things in photography. I got a Hipwell Synchronizer with the idea of trying to do flash photography of action subjects. That was very new in 1931 and I was determined I was going to get some basketball shots for the college annual. I got some special Wratten-Wainwright plates from England, which were the highest-speed plates available, and I took flash pictures with an open flash. I stopped the action with the flash because I couldn't really do it with the shutter. You synchronized the darn thing with an actuated shutter from a plunger. The plunger went up and passed the contact point, which flashed the bulbs on the way to actuating the shutter. I got an RB Auto Graflex in 1932, and in 1934 I bought a Leica. Then I began to take a whole different kind of picture—close-ups of people, street scenes, that kind of thing.

What photographs were you seeing in exhibitions at that time?
One of the most important exhibitions I saw then was the show in Columbus of Anton Bruehl's "Mexico Photographs." He'd published them in a collotype book. That was one of the most impressive shows I saw at that time. I was also interested in advertising. The photographers in advertising were on display like popular entertainers on television are now. They were the most visible of the artists. One had trouble seeing Weston's work, and Stieglitz's was not readily accessible, either.

Did you know of it?
I did not know Stieglitz's work. I might have known his name.

On what terms did Moholy-Nagy employ you at the New Bauhaus?
He offered me seven dollars to teach one day a week, and I

had a big fight with my employer at Marshall Field's because it had to be a Thursday and I had to make that time up somehow. But I said I'd quit rather than give up this chance. That's how much it meant to me. But within a short time I was fired anyway.

What did you teach and how did you teach it?
Moholy wanted his people taught all day long, from maybe nine in the morning until ten or eleven at night. There were seventeen or eighteen students. He provided one camera, I provided my Auto Graflex, my Deardorf 5 x 7 and my Leica. I also provided the enlargers—an Ellwood 5 x 7 and two Leitz enlargers. That was the basic equipment, because they ran out of money by the time they got down to our floor. Photography was in the basement!

Did you and Moholy ever teach together?
He came in and gave lectures. But I team-taught with Gyorgy Kepes. We had a joint task in the photography room.

Who was in charge of the school?
Moholy was in charge of the education and Norman Staley was in charge of the operating budget. It was a kind of mixed command, and that was one of its fatal blunders. I was just there to help, I wasn't a policy-maker.

What was your impression of the Bauhaus tradition, as it was applied to the American scene?
I was a disciple and I looked at it with totally uncritical eyes. As I look back on it, I think the difficulty was not with the school but with the culture.

That's an extraordinary statement. What do you mean?
I think it's a destructive culture here.

Do you mean the specific American culture?
I'm talking about Western European culture, but it came to America via the Spaniards. They destroyed Stone Age culture after Stone Age culture. They destroyed the vestiges of their

Henry Holmes Smith / 141

own heritage, and the twenties inherited the problem that the White Anglo-Saxon Protestants introduced into our culture. My head, and my tendencies, were somewhere else and I knew there was something terribly wrong with all these "no-nos." I didn't know how to do anything about them, and they created a great burden for me. As far back as I could go in my art, I was aware of injustice as a problem, and it is still a problem for me. I don't understand how to cope with it, and being reduced to tears is not any solution. So I felt that the book *The New Vision* had tremendous promise, but I didn't know how to implement this promise. The school had its problems with the egos of the students more than anything. It had an enormous task which it couldn't accomplish, unfunded, in a short time. It had to have continuity and it had to have people who were more interested in developing as human beings than in being freaks.

The people who ran the New Bauhaus expected the school to function as a quick-term supplier of designers—the way you'd send somebody to a business college and get a typist out in ninety days. And it didn't work like that, it couldn't work like that, the school wasn't meant to work like that. Strangely enough, that first group of students turned into artists, but to expect them to become journeyman designers for Sears, Roebuck, or whoever, was a preposterous thing.

When you were working at the New Bauhaus, what images were you making?
Camera images, but very few of those. It was a troubled time for me and I had enormous drains on my energy. The main one was the intense effort that I put in to try to cope with the logistic problems in the school. I taught several days a week and I often would be there till late at night. And Chicago's always been a town that drains my energy; it's almost like it turns a tap on and leaves it on. I just couldn't cope with all that, so I didn't do a great deal of photography then.

Were you making color images then?
I began color photography in 1936, while I was in Columbus. I made a darkroom out of the kitchen and I did color separa-

tion negatives and color prints—chromotone prints first (three layers of stripping film were put on top of one another and you got your color picture that way). But shortly after the dye transfer, the wash-off relief transfer process came out, and I began working with that. I went to Illinois in 1937, and there I began to make color pictures with the dye-transfer method; those were the things I took to Chicago which helped me get the job at the New Bauhaus. It didn't have anything to do with the job; it was just one of those little extras that made Moholy pay attention to me.

You continued working with Moholy until when?
The summer of 1938. The school closed for that year and we had all been assured we would have jobs waiting for us later on, so I went home for the time being. While I was there, a letter came from a secretary, not from Moholy, saying: "I don't believe you should count on this job or coming back to the school because it's going to close for lack of funds." And that was the only word I had. That was another great disappointment. I'd had many rejection slips, but this was like a big rejection slip. Some people know how to cope with these things better than others.

What did you do as a result of this?
I decided I was going to write. In the early part of 1939 Moholy recommended me to the editor of *Minicam* magazine to write an article on solarization. Later, in 1940, I was hired by them as an associate editor, and I stayed there until I was drafted into the army in 1942.

While you were an editor of Minicam, *was your primary contribution the selection of articles or the actual writing of articles?*
I had all the duties that the editor didn't want! I was probably not a very good editor, though. I had a chance to edit one issue, but it was typical hack work: an article on photographing presidential candidates from Wilson to Willkie, on how to take football action pictures, all this crap. I can't speak very proudly of it. I was probably a rotten editor.

Henry Holmes Smith / 143

What happened to you when you were drafted? Did you go into photographic work?
No. That's an interesting thing. I wound up in public relations, tied to an Intelligence office in Hawaii. I had said that I could do cartooning and I started drawing cartoons on mimeograph stencils. I did that for over a year; I can't say they were very funny, and I can't say it was very important.

During this time (from 1940 till the end of the war) did you have any contact with any other photographers that proved to have an influence on your work?
I was not up to my ears in photography. I did some photography when I was with *Minicam*, but not very much and not very well. It was a time of considerable frustration and "duty work." "Duty work" is work you do because someone else pays you to do it. When it comes to "duty work," I can become dreary—my work is dreary and my product is dreary. Occasionally something will happen to spring me out of the "duty work," and then I come to life and the things that are generated are lovely and it becomes a more beautiful experience to be alive. You could say my life operates in those two ways—from the peaks of delight to the valleys of "duty work."

What else happened to you during the war?
I didn't prove to be a very helpful Intelligence aid, and lacking other things to do with me, they decided to draw on my photographic skills. They set up an informal photographic laboratory—totally illegal—with scraps, so that an Army Intelligence officer could have his pictures photo-finished. They were largely pictures of the natives, as he was going to write a book on his experiences in that part of the world. After the war I went into the printing office of a friend who paid me seventy-five cents an hour to do certain types of letterpress jobs—some typography and some designs. In 1946 I got my enlarger and began to experiment with the ideas that I'd proposed to Moholy in 1937—the ideas about the supplementary ways of releasing color photography from the burden of the camera, from the burden of representation.
One of the great problems was that trying to replicate the colors of nature was very burdensome, and there had to be

many ways in which you could explore the possibilities of color without having to link it to, say the green of grass, or things of that sort. The photography of colored objects was in stages, and at that time one of the simplest ways to get from a colored object to the color record, which you were then going to resynthesize, was through the separation negative method. This meant that you took an aspect of the colored object and put it in a monochrome record and then reconstituted it by changing the monochrome record to a positive. This recorded the negative aspect of the color of the filter and gave you the tones you then put in its opposite color; and you then made a matrix from it and transferred it back. There was no reason why you couldn't just use arbitrary monochromes which you then took to the next step and put back in to color. That's what I was working on.

Was there anybody else involved in this kind of work?
I did see a frontispiece in one of the issues of *Minicam* which had a color photogram by Nicholas Ház. I think that might have been the same kind of thing and it might have come from Moholy showing Nicholas, who was also Hungarian, the letter that I had written. I have no evidence for this, but it was a color photogram, and I think it was done the same way. But it is done throughout publishing—any time you put a duotone together you're doing the same thing.

You are well known for the syrup and watercolor images on glass, made with the use of refraction. How did this come about?
I suppose it started at a very early age with my response to a Christmas tree—to light and its beauties, the dazzle of the candles. I remember later in life sitting in Moholy's apartment, with his little girls and his wife, and the sun streaming in through the window. There was a tumbler and I turned it, letting the moisture interact with the light. I remember sharing this delight with Moholy, who was always responsive.

Then I went to Indiana University, in the fall of 1947, to teach. On the bus ride there I had formulated a whole course of study. Among the things I was going to teach the first year were light principles, in terms of refraction and reflection.

They were mechanically feasible and economical. I wasn't going to use defraction. During that time one of the students brought in some corn syrup and it was a beautiful refracting medium. It held still and you could put it into any shape. It would hold a while, it would wash off easier than oil, and it was inexpensive—you couldn't ask for more. I began doing that purposefully some time in 1949, and I've been at it ever since. At the same time, I was having my students make photographs with water with little speckles of dust in it. They got small star-shaped refraction elements, and I just loved all this stuff. I remember one time going into the darkroom and working with these various things and then, on an impulse, just taking some syrup on the end of my finger and flicking it at the glass and then printing it. That's when I got my picture "Battles and Games," which was a reference to the Trojan War. I'd been reading about the ancient Greeks and their habits of combat.

But the basic way that you do it is to have a fairly clean piece of glass; then you pour a not-too-heavy gesture of syrup on the glass, and then you either print it, or throw some water on it and print it. Some distance from the glass there will be a light source which gives a very clean kind of light that casts crisp shadows. The glass may be three or four inches or more from the paper, and the light is in such a position that the shadows and the refracting elements from the syrup and water will print on the paper. Then you turn the light on and give it an exposure that is appropriate in length, and you develop it just like a piece of normal photographic paper. Now you've got your key element in the process, and from that point on, you can do anything you want with it. You can leave it alone, you can copy it on a negative, you can make a positive from it, you can print it on matrix film with different degrees of density, and you can dye them, then transfer them in any combination you care to in multiple printing. I guess that's it.

Is your image-making with syrup and refraction controlled in any way?
It's going to sound pretentious, but I've always loved to draw in a spontaneous way. And after you've done that for a great

many years, and I have now done this since the twenties, you feel at ease with the gesture you make. If you combine this with the conception that Herrigel introduces people to in *Zen in the Art of Archery*, you'll come close to what I'm talking about. It is a concept that is a little difficult for the Western world—which thinks that the head controls everything, which, of course, is nonsense.

The Abstract Expressionists thought in the same way, didn't they?
They existed before I did this, but I didn't know them. It may sound kind of dumb but I didn't connect that with my work then.

So what you are saying is that there is an intuitive control?
I think control is the wrong word. I would put it this way. You see a lovely girl across a crowded room and you walk toward her with hope in your mind. That's the way these pictures are made.

What is the source for your inspiration?
I'm a person who is fond of the past but doesn't wish to relive it. I long for my family, and of course, the family is bigger than I am, and it's been going for a long time, and barring the kind of stupidities we now face, it could go on a while longer. In that context I think it's really reasonable to say the family, and the earth family, are my major concerns. By the earth family, I mean mankind; but man, because of his strange imagination, has created for himself a series of superior beings, superior powers, superior forces, and they enter into my family, too. And that is about all I think I should tell you.

Do you consider these images visual metaphors?
Yes. For instance, "The Giant," which was the first important one, the one Steichen put in that first show and kept, is a father image. You know, "Fatherhood," "Motherhood," "Family" (yours and mine), that kind of thing. "Mother Nature," "God the Father." These figures of speech are in the Western

European and related cultures. They are also in the religion of the Stone Age cultures, of which there are still remnants in this country. I'm very much of the opinion that Western Europe did its greatest disservice when it destroyed the Stone Age culture it found in the North and South American continents. I think it lost sight of where it came from by the compulsion to civilize people it had no business touching. They wound up forgetting what their own early resources were. It isn't that this is going to matter to a great many people today, but I think it's a tremendously important thing for people to know about.

Does the word "visionary" mean anything to you in terms of your work?
I don't reject it, but I don't think that would be the word that describes what I am involved with. One of photography's problems, that the other arts don't have, is that something has to be in front of the camera. That's a very limiting thing; and so, if you photograph a crusader, or if you're going to photograph the people who stoned the woman who was found in sin—as Billy Graham might put it—you have problems. Not only the problem of finding someone who might look like them, but the problem of putting the right clothes on them, and so on. So if my work is devoted to what I am really concerned with, it has to face the problem of finding a way of doing things without resorting to a dramatic charade or tableau. I like the theatrical effect, but I don't want a cast of human beings if I'm talking about something else. If I'm dealing with an idea that's bigger, like Stone Age man's conception of natural forces, I'm constantly returning to this form of figurative work. It is figurative, not abstract. It's quite depictive in its own special way, and it uses light to convey the message. I'll take what *it* refers to rather than what I want *it* to refer to.

Do you see light as more than just a basically material substance?
I think we are totally light-dependent, but we hardly know

it—like we are air-dependent. It's like a fish being water-dependent. There is evidence that if you get away from light, a personality distortion of a very serious kind occurs. We are, in a dumb way, creatures of light. We are fed by light; it's an incredible resource. We hardly know what we are doing to ourselves when we mess with light, and of course, too much of it is as bad as too little. Plants feed the animals, and we eat the plants and the animals. Neither one could exist without the nourishment that the plant generates out of the light resource. We are just full of it.

Are your photographs full of it?
Well, it comes two ways. The negative of the photograph presents light as dark, and if you do that, you have a strange kind of light that most people don't understand, except X-ray interpreters. But once you turn it back around, it's full of light. In the colored ones you have to remind people the light is there. But I have a feeling that they both serve a function—that light is dark and light is light.

During your experiments with light refraction, have you continued to take pictures in a more conventional way?
Yes, what you might call mundane pictures. I did camera pictures up until the end of the fifties. I feel that it's the right of a human being to express what he really means and not something that somebody else thinks he should mean. So in good conscience I'll use the camera to copy anything I need a copy of.

You mention that the camera used in its conventional sense has many limitations. Are you interested in the conventional photographic print?
In general, I love other people's camera photographs. I own and admire the well-known Ansel Adams pictures of Yosemite. When I knew that cataracts were going to diminish my ability to see the world, I bought them from Ansel so I could have them to look at in my last years of sight. I have some of Weston's pictures, I have some of Aaron Siskind's, and I have

some Minor White pictures. I'm not insensitive to camera photographs, but what I'm dealing with doesn't necessarily require me to use a camera. It's a burden.

Did any of your university colleagues become interested in your work?
Many of the artists in the art department at Indiana University were supportive. I'm not convinced that painters or print-makers, with exceptions, are ready to let photography enter their world. I'm not in touch with enough of those people.

In the beginning, how did photographers react to your experimental work?
I can only think it was with indifference. They certainly didn't write me fan letters, although I have occasional testimony that some people were enchanted with them.

In 1960, Steichen organized a show called "A Sense of Abstraction." I was invited to participate; as were Minor White, Nathan Lyons, Fred Sommer (with some pictures on cellophane) and Lotte Jacobi, whose work was hung right beside mine. I have great admiration for her work; I think she's a genius, although unrecognized, as is Fred Sommer. No one really praised my work. It might have been that I was too excited to hear tributes if they were said, and it might have been that the work wasn't impressive enough. It was mounted on black mats, on a black wall, which didn't do too much for it; they were kind of soaked up. When I'm around these people, I don't get euphoric statements about what the work's doing for them. Maybe they don't talk that way.

How did you meet Steichen at that time?
I just saw him once. I wanted to introduce a course in the history of photography in the spring of 1948, the second semester I was at Indiana, and I got a small grant and went East. Steichen was at the Museum of Modern Art, and I just went to talk to him about his own work and life for my history course. Later, in 1951, he chose two of my pictures for an abstract-photography exhibition.

Your work has not been seen very often. Is there any reason for this?

I'm going to give you a cynical answer to that question: it's hard for me to believe that it was to anybody's advantage to show it. Steichen was beyond attaining fame by showing anybody else's work. And it might be that I interfered with certain moments when it might have been shown. In the 1960's there were many shows I turned down, but I didn't have a large body of work then, and my eyes were failing after 1963. I also wasn't convinced that most people took care of photographs, either on the wall or in transit.

During this time you were a teacher of photography at Indiana University?

That's the only place I've been officially employed for any length of time. I was employed there from 1947 until I retired in 1976.

It must have been one of the first colleges to have a major commitment toward the study of photography as a creative endeavor?

No, there were several. Van Deren Coke has written a brief history of photography and higher education, and I think Ohio University was probably the place that started the first program, outside of Columbia, where apparently Stieglitz had a course sometime before World War I. But it really started after World War II, when the major universities began to do something with it. Some of the larger universities, the ones with the greatest standing, seemed to be the most reluctant to introduce photography. It's an unfashionable subject and it's confused in the minds of scholars because of the indignity of having a mass audience. These things are pretty rough obstacles in academia! How many courses in the appreciation of the comic strip do you know about in art history? Mass culture maybe, but when is that going to get into art history? Of course, the snobs would ask why.

What prompted you to help found the Society for Photographic Education?

For several years before the actual founding, I'd been hoping that photographers who were trying to teach photography could join together and exchange whatever kind of help they were willing to exchange with one another—and I wasn't the only one. There were a number of people across the nation who felt this need. But it really wasn't to form an organization that was going to be a scholarly group and do all the stupid things that scholarly groups do. It was to solve problems that were particularly important to teachers of photography. Photography probably occupied a position in the universities such as physics may have occupied in 1810, when the philosophers had hold of it. And also it was a relatively new art with no tradition, very few master practitioners, and so little published history that you had to scour the market to find enough material on some people to do anything about them.

In 1956 I had a workshop in Indiana University on interpreting photographs, and I invited Minor White to come and present his theories and Aaron Siskind to come and present his material. We got together quite an interesting group of twenty people who sat through miserably hot days in a darkened room with no ventilation, while Minor showed his slides and expounded on his then current theory of "Romanticism and Classicism in Photography." Aaron Siskind took the students on field trips. It was those events in 1956 that made me feel that it was a very important thing for photographers to get together. Van Deren Coke and Ralph Eugene Meatyard both came to that workshop as participants, and Ralph Hattersley was also there. In 1962 I organized another workshop on teaching and invited a group of teachers; among them were Art Sinsabaugh, Nathan Lyons, Jerry Uelsmann, Oscar Bailey, Gerry Stephanie, and Robert Fichter. It was a rather exciting group, and among the things we discussed was the possibility of organizing a group of people interested in teaching. Then Nathan Lyons invited me to participate in his 1962 conference at George Eastman House, at which there was the proposal by Clarence White, Walter Servadi, Walter Rosenblum, and me to organize this group. We were appointed to a steering committee, which included Nathan Lyons, Aaron Siskind, and several others. The following year, in Chicago, we brought out a report and a society was formed. I remember having the sense that if it went wrong it would go wrong because of egos. People would decide to use it in ways that were inappropriate to group action, and that, I felt, would be the one difficulty that I wouldn't know how to solve. I don't think anyone knows how to solve it. I think, perhaps, that some of that has now come about.

You're renowned as one of the best teachers of photography in America. Would you prefer to be better known as a teacher or as an artist?
I prefer to be better paid as a teacher. I don't know how this culture can pay its artists.

What are your thoughts on photographic education today?
I think it's excessive. I think people all over the country are busy teaching people things they don't need to know. They are incapable of teaching students things they need to know, and if they taught them things the student needed to know, the culture would see that it was quickly extirpated.

So how do you see the future of photographic education?
I would like to see it less institutionalized, less victimized by manufacturers, and less addicted to routine and redundant imagery.

What do you mean by redundant photographic imagery?
The kind of pictures that come out of 99 percent of the 35 mm. cameras and 2¼-square cameras has very little to do with creating and the sense of humanity which could unite individuals. People are competing to win at a game that is a loser's game. The game is to have better routine images than somebody else's routine images. If you want a prescription for routine images, you just have to go through any student's portfolio.

At a certain point, human beings creating art no longer need to be told what they're supposed to do. They may need to be told what they're going to get paid to do, but that's different from being told what they're supposed to do. The predicament of photographic education in this country seems to revolve around false rewards. It doesn't create a bunch of free people; it creates a bunch of people with a terrible burden on their back, like the Old Man and the Sea or Sinbad the Sailor, and it's a cultural commitment to an unrewarded activity. The rewards are at best nominal. Somebody said recently that the best thing a student could do was get in some shows and publish a book; but nothing about becoming a human being, nothing about having important feelings or concepts of humanity. That's the sort of thing that is bad education. I'd say be a human being first, and if you happen to wind up using photography, that's good for photography.

How do you tell students that their rewards are only nominal?
I do it by telling them at the beginning. I try to persuade them not to get involved in the program. In art school, for instance, it takes $9,000–$12,000 to get through four years, and in graduate school it may be another $8,000–$12,000, plus a considerable burden of psychological grief. Maybe they'd best spend it on becoming a human being and not bother with our program. That's why I'm leaving the education profession, that's why I'm abandoning my career—I'm nearly at the end of it anyway—because it's a false career. I don't mean I was a Judas sheep, and people do say that I help them clarify their goals. But I don't want to lead them down the garden path any more—the garden path to nothing, where there are too many masters of fine arts and not enough human beings. It isn't like getting a medical degree, or even a registered nurse's training. Photography students are getting a so-called academic program with no place for them in society.

Why has it taken you twenty-five years to come to this conclusion?
I don't believe that it is a new conclusion. I think it's a little easier to utter these things at the end of one's career than at the beginning, because of economics—maintaining one's family. Considerations of this sort urge discretion early in one's

life. One's life is controlled by certain kinds of behavior—not to work against the grain with too much eagerness. I do feel an artificiality in education, and I'm not going to single out photography, because that's not only unfair, it's untrue. Higher education as it now stands in America is about 60 percent off the point. And I think it would be far better if people were taught how to avoid the cheater, how to avoid the rotten manufacturer, the bad merchant, how to avoid the charlatan in medicine, how to avoid the food that kills rather than nourishes. If you could learn that kind of thing, it would, in the long run, be better by far than learning about the humanities as they are now constructed. I don't want this to sound as though I'm against the humanities. I think they are tremendously important, but I think they should come after you know how much DDT you're being assigned unwittingly by agriculturalists and chemists, and how much you can tolerate. Because a dead humanist is a very useless humanist! A lot of education today is time-occupying rather than life-enhancing, and time-occupying is a very bad reason to spend all that money for students or for parents.

A large part of your teaching has been aimed at the encouragement of photographic scholarship, hasn't it?
That all began in the fifties, when, as far as I could see, it didn't exist, and it still doesn't exist much today. There's an awful lot of bad scholarship and it won't be corrected until fine minds get into the field, not just careerists. One hopes that eventually someday there will be a corrective in this field as Bronowski was in his field. You need people with sensibilities and intellectual rigor, and we just haven't attracted very many to our field. So the ones that do publish get away with an awful lot, and I must include myself.

If you were given a limitless amount of money, how would you like to construct an ideal teaching situation?
Once, I had a small group of students and I gave them the problem of having an unlimited amount of money and setting up an ideal museum. Very few of them coped with it seriously.

Some of them made a joke of it. I don't suppose I have the brains to set up a formal structure which would be worthy of that money. But I could call in people like Robert Forth (of the California College of Arts and Crafts), who could do it, or would know how to get the help. All it takes is money—the brains are everywhere.

Who would you say have been the major influences on your work?
Instead of naming people, I think I'd have to name photographs. I would say Weston's "Pepper" of 1930. Edward Weston's sensual nudes would also be included. Pictures that remind me of my own senses, and my own sense responses.

What has been your major philosophical concern?
The idea that there are overwhelming forces that dwarf man, but which have some interrelationship with him and without which he can't possibly operate. I'm thinking of things like the sun, the great winds, the great bodies of water, the vapor clouds that bring rain, those forces that make plants root and prosper.

Do you see your work as an affirmation of life?
It deals with those forces. I just can't bring myself to claim for my work more than other people will consent to. But that is what they are about for me. If they don't mean that to others, that doesn't deny what I'm trying to do, but it does limit what I am trying to do as far as others are concerned.

What has the creative process meant to you?
I have nothing but respect for the creative process. I think it's central to man's experience. I've always admired the great inventors and I consider them the growing edge of the creative process. Of course, great artists are among those inventors.

I've aspired to be an honorable man, whatever I've wound up being. When somebody was paying me by the month, or by the year, to do something for other people, then I did it as best I could. There's only so much energy and so much life a person has, and if you're really involved with the development of young people, you spend a lot of time with them, thinking about how to deal with their particular personal problems of creativity. That takes away an enormous amount of the energy, effort, and concentration I need to do my own work.

I don't think you have to be around a student all the time. I think that if you see him once every thirty or sixty days it might be enough. Then you should see him maybe for an hour or two. In my particular discipline, I think the whole idea of having classes, and things like that, is nonsense, and I would prefer not to be involved with it.

What contribution do you think your work has made?
That's a loaded question. My work is not really visible yet. I think the activities of my students are probably my greatest contribution.

A young man took one course in photography with me and he went on to be a school administrator, carrying with him a knowledge that photography mattered. As an administrator he could dispose of funds and he gave another young man $30,000 to establish secondary-education photography in a large area. Now, that's the sort of complex satisfaction that I get, which is much more than having guys teaching photography all over the world.

What kind of projects do you run for students beginning photography?
I try to have them look closely at their experiences to realize what they are trying to show in their pictures. They go around the world looking at it and there are things they find themselves paying attention to, repeatedly. There is a certain feeling that they link with the thing that they pay attention to. This is nothing to do with whether they make a picture out of it or not; the linkage of the feeling with what they saw is the best clue I know of. If that happens enough and you are not photographing it, you're ignoring your subject. If the two events do not coincide, maybe photography is not your medium. The thing is to try to help them find out what their subject really is. Now, the subject is not the object out there in the world; it is the object, plus how it looks under a par-

ticular circumstance, how they feel about it, and what they link with it in their memory. If they eventually arrive at a point where they can have enough memory of what they felt when this event occurred, they can make a much truer appraisal of the picture than anybody else in the world.

The trouble with a great many students, and this is what really frustrates me, is that their subject is frequently culturally unacceptable. It's something that they need to deal with, however, so you find concealed subjects which can only be revealed by some sort of indirect approach. It's like a fellow who praises someone and looks at another person and winks. This sort of thing occurs in photographs and it accounts for the weakness of photographs where the subject is true but the feeling about the subject is false. It's these problems of contradiction, where the culture is telling you to do one thing and your heart, your mind, or your psychological stance is telling you to do another thing, that creates a tremendous amount of problems. You can not, however, solve it in the context of a university structure—you have to be in a freer situation to do that.

Years ago, when it was forbidden to take explicit sexual pictures in this country, Jack Welpott told me about somebody in one of his classes who photographed himself and his girl in the nude. He had a magnificent erection and she was astride him. I thought at the time, What a marvelous male picture, you know, in terms of how males really feel about that moment and how unpicturable it is. Well, there must be lots of this kind of unpicturable material to be dealt with. Back in the 1950's and 1960's, when you could not photograph explicit sexual activity, my students would go out and photograph healing tree-trunk wounds, that type of thing!

The feelings associated with the visual experience, that is the link. You can have an intense visual experience for which you have been prepared by maybe hundreds of photographs, but the feeling at that point is almost nil because it cannot be sustained all the time. I cannot feel about Weston's "Pepper" the way I did when I first saw it. I have to look at it sparingly.

March 1975

SELECTED BIBLIOGRAPHY

Henry Holmes Smith: Selected Critical Writings. Tucson: Center for Creative Photography, University of Arizona, October 1977.
Henry Holmes Smith's Art: Fifty Years in Retrospect (catalogue). Bloomington: The University of Indiana Art Museum, 1973.

Helmut Gernsheim

(B O R N   1 9 1 3 / B R I T I S H ,
B O R N   I N   G E R M A N Y)

Paul Hill

How did you first get involved with photography?
Through the history of art. I began wondering in 1934 whether
I could complete the five-year art-history course at the university before being drafted into Hitler's army (I was unable
to emigrate). My goal was London, where my older brother,
also an art historian, had just opened an art gallery. Not that
I wanted to join him in business, but English was the only
foreign language I spoke, having had a classical education.

My brother advised, "As an art historian you won't be able to make a living in England. You need a practical profession. Why don't you study photography? It is vital to every art historian, and was to me for illustrating my Ph.D. thesis. With a knowledge of photography your ties with the art world will become stronger." Fortunately, the leading school of photography in Germany was in Munich. So, in September 1934 I started my studies at the Bavarian State School of Photography, and in July 1936 I left with a first-class diploma.

Was this school a creative photography school?
I would say it was the most creative in Germany, and practical at the same time, for its purpose was to train you in practically every branch of photography so that you could afterward find a job, or as a freelancer earn your bread. With the purely creative training you used to receive at the Bauhaus—by then already defunct—most students were at a loss how to apply their ideas of art to everyday life. So Munich never lost touch with the practical requirements of life. In the first year you obtained a thorough training in technique in practically every branch of photography, from studio portraits to industrial and scientific applications, such as photomicrographs. In the second year your eye was trained in the essentials of art: composition and form. By frequent analysis of your own prints and those of your fellow students, you became aware that some students had solved the problem more successfully than others, and why. I can assure you that having your work dissected in front of the class by students and teachers sharpened the creative faculty better than any theoretical art discussion, and I applied the same method many years later in my own creative photography class at Franklin College. Apart from this practical training, we received instruction and had to pass exams in a number of theoretical subjects: chemistry, electricity, accounting, art history, and law—as far as it applied to photography. Then there was the art class, which comprised in the first year drawing, retouching, and spotting, and in the second typography, layout, and poster design. In fact, I doubt that there is another college that provides such a thorough grounding. In a third-year course, which was not obligatory, you could learn

gum biochromate, bromoil, and other pictorial printing processes much in vogue at the turn of the century, but they did
not interest me in the least. I had been brought up in the spirit
of the *Neue Sachlichkeit* and had a distaste for the manipulated print. So I skipped that to employ my time more usefully
in learning the Uvachrome process of color photography. For,
meanwhile, the Institute of British Photographers had persuaded the British government to admit into Britain no more
professional black-and-white photographers from abroad. This
happened just as I finished my studies in 1936.

What areas of art history were you taught in Munich?
Chiefly European architecture and sculpture of all periods. We
had to be conversant with their evolution from the Greek
period to contemporary styles, be aware of the cultural background and identifying features of each style; for it was rightly
considered that a photographer can grasp the essentials of a
building or sculpture only when he understands the spirit of
the time in which they were created. This was, in fact, a con-
tinuation of my interrupted studies and proved of immense
value in my war work for the Warburg Institute of Art. But
art and art history had been my main interests since the age
of fifteen and they still are.

Is there any family reason for this particular interest?
Partly, perhaps, because my father was a historian of literature
and both my older brothers became historians, of art and
economics respectively.

*While you were at college studying photography, did you see
any photographic image that really moved you?*
I do not remember one, but I was also far too busy taking
photographs to look at picture magazines, all of which were
thoroughly Nazified by that time and full of lies and propaganda. I think only a superb news or reportage picture could
move me. Other photographs may leave a strong impression
on me, but they don't move me. There was a high-class magazine called *Die Dame* which published fine creative photographs, I am told. I only saw a couple of cuttings a friend sent

me. One was an excellent shot of some birds in flight by Martin Munkacsi, the other was to be my first introduction to the work of a great nineteenth-century British photographer, Charles Clifford—very picturesque and impressive architectural and landscape studies of the Spanish summer palace Capricho, taken around 1855. The name of the collector and author of the article in *Die Dame* meant nothing to me at the time, but in 1952 we were to collaborate on the World Exhibition of Photography—Dr. Erich Stenger.

Did the work of any particular photographer influence you while you were at college?
No, but indirectly all the great photographers and photo editors of the past ten years had left their mark. Being Jews or political opponents of the regime, they had either emigrated or were lying low. Their names were tabu: Salomon, Man, Eisenstaedt, Heartfield, Moholy-Nagy, Bayer, Renger-Patzsch, Lerski, Sander; the editors of the Munich and Berlin *Illustrierte* —Stefan Lorant and Kurt Korff; Ludwig Ullstein, owner of the largest German newspaper concern and publisher of the *Berliner Illustrierte, Die Dame,* and ten other leading daily and weekly papers; Kurt Safranski, an editor at Ullstein, and numerous others. No teacher would have dared refer to them. It was a hot iron no one wanted to touch for fear of a political discussion leading to his dismissal. I don't think anyone who has not experienced the workings of a totalitarian state can possibly visualize conditions of life under it. All these men had shaped German photography in the thirties; their work had been absorbed. The college was very progressive and modern. There were no restrictions on personal expression and creative ideas in pictures. The surface texture of an object had to be brought out, and a clear, sharp, glossy bromide print was the accepted standard.

Did you see any exhibitions?
Not of photography, but I did see an unforgettable exhibition, "Decadent Art," in which every great contemporary painter and sculptor found himself represented. Altogether, 16,500 works had been confiscated from German museums.

Helmut Gernsheim / 163

Were you acquainted with the work of Renger-Patzsch, Sander, or the Bauhaus while you were in Munich?
Not then. I bought some of their books secondhand in London during the war. The majority I acquired only in the late 1950's. It was then that I began to realize fully the outstanding contribution Germany had made in the 1920's and 1930's, and I made a point of visiting the pioneers of the new photography, their widows or descendants, to round off my researches.

When did you leave Germany?
In July 1937. As part of my diploma work, I had made a fairly extensive reportage on the Munich puppet theater and had become friendly with the director. He knew that I was half-Jewish and waiting for an opportunity to leave Germany, and he was aware that my call-up papers for military service in October would prove a great obstacle in the execution of my intention. In May he informed me that his company had been invited to give a number of guest performances at the World's Fair in Paris, which the Ministry of Propaganda had endorsed. He said to me: "I intend to exhibit your photographs in Paris and would like you to hang them in mid-July." Thus, I was able to leave Germany on official business. When work was concluded, I continued the journey to London with an order from my former employers, Uvachrome in Munich, to reproduce a number of paintings at the National Gallery. This collaboration continued until the war put a stop to it.

Was there much demand for color photography in Britain?
It was quite a new venture in most countries, except Germany, and on account of the great expense and relatively poor color reproductions by most printers, the demand was restricted to a few art publishers, art galleries, advertising firms, and large industrial concerns. I received orders from all of them, but worked chiefly for the P & O shipping line. My photographs were used in brochures of new liners and summer cruises, of new Rolls-Royce models, in *The Studio* magazine, etc. One dealer in Old Masters used to send my 13 x 18 cm. color transparencies to interested clients abroad. In 1937–39 there were only two professional color photographers in Britain, and for

both of us business was fairly brisk. Dr. A. C. Spencer produced large color prints by his Vivex process, which was, I believe, a wash-off relief method, whereas Uvachrome was a dye-transfer process. Both were based on three separation negatives produced with a one-shot camera or a repeating back attached to an ordinary plate camera.

Did you exhibit your work?
I had two exhibitions at my brother's gallery at Stratford Place, London. The first, in the autumn of 1937, consisted entirely of work I had brought with me from Germany: portraits, landscapes, architecture, still lifes, close-ups of flowers and puppets. The second, the following year, was of black-and-white pictures I had taken for my own pleasure in Britain. Portraits of well-known personalities, country houses, life in London, friends. I showed no color work, which circumstances had forced on me, and which would not have been appropriate in my brother's gallery of Old Master drawings.

What was the reaction to your exhibitions among English photographers?
I don't think I had the pleasure of meeting one, apart from Lucia Moholy, but they heard of my existence when the editor of *Photography* published a two-page article on my work a few months later.

Did you also meet Moholy-Nagy?
They had separated a few years before. László was then active at the New Bauhaus in Chicago. Lucia had a portrait studio in London.

What did you think of her work?
She was a highly competent photographer and her Penguin book *A Hundred Years of Photography* is a fine piece of research and writing which was never reprinted. It is a pity that her photographic work is so little known. After the war she took up her original work in scientific documentation again. Five years ago she published *Marginalia*, in which she corrects several misconceptions about László's position at the Bauhaus

and his photographic work. I think she did the printing of all the photographs and may well have taken some of the experimental photograms credited to him. Lucia could probably have made more of herself, but she was one of those clever women who live in the shadow of a clever and assertive husband with public position and influence. El Lissitzky expressed very strong criticism of Moholy's method of taking—he says stealing—ideas from others in a letter of September 1925. He also confirms what Man Ray had told me, but Lucia denies, that the idea of making photograms came to him only *after* Tristan Tzara had shown him some rayographs published in *Champs délicieux* in 1922. Lissitzky, by the way, credits Hans Richter with the invention of the abstract film.

What sort of photographic work was going on in Britain before the war?
With the exception of a few independent spirits such as Hoppé, Beaton, Brandt, Nürnberg and other foreigners, I had not seen such antiquated, fuzzy, sentimental, sugary work before. This applies in particular to portraiture and the pictorial work shown at the Royal Photographic Society and at the London Salon, triumphs of sweetness and cosiness. It was an artificial world one associates with chocolate and soap boxes, completely novel to me. So were the manipulated prints, executed in historic processes introduced around the turn of the century. I didn't know whether to laugh or to cry. Tradition has its advantages and handicaps.

How do you account for this backwardness?
The British are not a visually minded nation. They love literature and music. Refinement of taste was an aristocratic requirement, and some became great connoisseurs of art, which they amassed in their country houses, partly out of love, but mostly for prestige reasons. With the industrial revolution a decline in taste set in. The new monied class were the manufacturers and speculators, who often rose from humble origins. Their taste too was of a much lower order, as had been the case in the seventeenth century in Holland, when rich burghers became the patrons of art. In the mid-nineteenth century art

developed into an industry in England, and the Royal Academy turned into a market for the manufacturers in art. Academic art, surrounded by the social trappings of the annual picture show, acquired chic, insularity, and inbreeding. The pictorialists of the R.P.S. and the Salon are the academicians of photography and proud of upholding the pictorial tradition of the older art. In *Photograms of the Year* you have an official record of their ineptitude over the past seventy-five years.

What were your relations with the R.P.S.?
My "new-fangled, modernistic views," as J. Dudley Johnston used to say, fitted ill into their retrogressive system. Yet they were broadminded enough to recognize quality, even if the contents were not to their taste. They conferred on me the associateship in 1940 and the fellowship two years later. Despite my completely different outlook, I was frequently asked by the R.P.S. and associated societies in the country to be on the exhibition jury. They knew I could do no harm, because I was always outvoted by the old fogies. It was a diplomatic trick to have me in and out at the same time. Yet to the uninitiated the mere fact of my sitting on the jury at all seemed the acme of fairness. Once, before a fellowship committee meeting, Dudley Johnston took me aside and handed me some superb pictures of sand dunes—rippling sand in strong light, divided by deep shadows, very graphic. I immediately recognized the master eye of Edward Weston. He said: "How do you feel about this work?" "We should be honored to have the great man in our company," I replied. Then D.J. pointed at the shadows and muttered: "No details whatsoever. I don't think he will get an exhibition." And of course he didn't. After fourteen years of this sort of game, I resigned, in 1952. It was impossible to modernize the R.P.S. as I had hoped, but equally unrealistic to remain a member while fighting with the progressives against their antiquated outlook.

Do you feel conditions changed later?
Yes, a great deal in the last seven years, but not before. Dis-

satisfaction with the state of affairs just described became quite apparent after the publication of *New Photo Vision* in 1942. Lots of photographers wrote to me expressing agreement with my criticism, but nothing could be done until the end of the war. In March 1945 I was invited to assist in the launching of the Combined Societies at Cheltenham, a secession from the R.P.S. of the photographic societies of Bristol, Hereford, and Wolverhampton. E. O. Hoppé joined forces with me and Hugo van Wadenoyen was the third council member. Our purpose was the promotion of contemporary photography with annual exhibitions to be shown in turn in these three cities. We also met for discussions and lectures. Many young photographers from other societies joined later, and for fifteen years or more the Combined Societies lived up to the foundation ideals. However, owing to pressure of work, I had to withdraw from the organization a few years later. The Institute of Contemporary Arts could also be occasionally enticed to show the work of promising modern photographers, and in 1963 we had the formation of the Creative Photography group in London, which took its name from my book, published shortly before. All these efforts and the short-lived *Album* magazine helped to pave the way, but they lacked both money and official support to make much impact with their gallant efforts to modernize the British scene. The three main events which were to revolutionize and revitalize photography are of recent origin. The establishment of the Photographers' Gallery in London in 1971 was entirely due to private enterprise—the imaginative and energetic Sue Davies. The second was the Arts Council's reversal of its previous policy by recognizing photography as one of the arts, thus making it eligible for financial grants. The third was the creation of a national collection at the National Portrait Gallery.

To return to 1939, what happened to you when war broke out?
With the declaration of war my activity came to a standstill. All German nationals were declared enemy aliens. Those who had come to Britain for racial or political reasons were classified as friendly enemy aliens and free, provided they could support themselves or show affidavits confirming the assistance

of friends or organizations. Being without work, I offered my services to a number of non-combatant organizations on the home front appealing for volunteers, but was rejected in each case on account of my former nationality. I had become stateless in surrendering my passport to the German embassy when I refused to return to the "fatherland." Like every other refugee, I waited for a government decision, which came at the end of May 1940, after the fall of Dunkirk. With the German Army standing across the Channel, an early invasion of Britain seemed likely, and every able-bodied enemy alien between the ages of sixteen and sixty was to be "interned for his own protection." In fact, the British government was scared that there might be quislings among the refugees, while the known Nazi sympathizers among the British were still at large.

Where were you interned?
Early in July 1940 came the expected roundup in St. John's Wood district, where I was living, and after spending a night at Kempton Park race course, I was transferred with others to the internment camp at Huyton near Liverpool. There I found myself sharing a tent with (Sir) Nikolaus Pevsner, whose art lectures at the Courtauld Institute and at Birkbeck College had been a tremendous inspiration to me. Huyton was only an improvised transit camp. We assumed we would be transferred to the Isle of Man, like my brother and thousands of others before, when a Home Office official advised us to volunteer for Canada, where we would be free. He needed two thousand men, and the ship would be sailing in a couple of days. We knew that British children and women were being evacuated to Canada, and as the High Commissioner, later Governor-General of Canada, Vincent Massey, had been my main sponsor in England, I decided to seek asylum in Canada, despite the fact that only the previous week the *Arandora Star* liner with 2,700 Italian and German internees on board had been torpedoed and sunk in the Irish Sea.

The voyage was a nightmare. We were crowded into the hold of the troopship *Dunera* and treated as prisoners of war, against the international convention. All exits to the deck had been fenced off with barbed wire and were guarded by tom-mies with fixed bayonets. Our suitcases were taken from us and never seen again. Unfortunately, our dream of being rid of this "Nazi" prison ship in five days' time did not materialize. Early on the morning of July 12, we heard a sharp metallic scraping sound along the hull of the ship and a few seconds later a loud explosion. We were warned to keep calm during "practice shooting" and learned the truth only after our arrival in Sydney, Australia, two months later. Two torpedoes had been fired at us: one slid off the hull due to our zigzag movement; the other hit another vessel accompanying us, with children and women on board. Two days later, west of the Outer Hebrides and in the Atlantic Ocean, we were apparently out of the danger zone and for the first time allowed on deck. This fresh-air break of ten minutes once a day was all we had until we arrived at Sydney fifty-eight days later. The rest of the time we were down in the hold of the ship and never saw daylight. A few days later we noticed from the position of the sun that we had changed course. Instead of going west, we had turned south and we were perplexed. The intelligence officer, asked for our destination, claimed he didn't know. We were running short of food and other essentials when we eventually reached Freetown in Sierra Leone on July 24. Unable to take on supplies owing to a large British convoy and warships being in the harbor, we docked three days later at Takoradi on the Gold Coast, now Ghana. Early in August we took on more supplies at Cape Town, and our hopes of disembarkation were finally dashed. The voyage through the Indian Ocean was uneventful except for one incident. During exercise a man suddenly jumped overboard and was lost. We heard that he had been desperate because his visa to the Argentine, where his mother lived, had expired that day.

What happened to you when you finally got to Australia?
At Freemantle, Australian health and customs officials inspected the ship. They did not know our destination, but complained about our state of health to the captain. At the next port, Melbourne, over five hundred men who had been rescued from the *Arandora Star* were disembarked, and our turn came

soon after at Sydney. However, this was not the journey's end. An eighteen-hour train journey to Hay, five hundred miles from Sydney followed. Hay is the terminus of the New South Wales railway line and the soldiers warned us that Hay and hell were synonymous in Australia. Hay lay at the edge of the desert and marked the end of civilization, excruciatingly hot in summer with plenty of sandstorms. We were very depressed when we saw the two concentration camps built for German prisoners of war, each enclosed by three four-meter-high barbed-wire fences at a distance of five meters from one another, and every hundred meters a manned watchtower with searchlight and a machine gun pointing at us. We couldn't believe our eyes. We protested that we had not left Nazi Germany to receive such treatment from our friends. We appointed a delegation to see the camp commandant. He knew that we were not prisoners of war, but there was nothing he could do. "The camps were built for the British government and it is their territory. We are only your guardians while you are here. You must lodge an official complaint with the governor-general for improper treatment as internees. Write down all the indignities that happened to you on the way out, that you look like ragged beggars because your suitcases were stolen. The whole business is British responsibility, as is your confinement in this godforsaken place. About your treatment here, you won't have any complaints. You are our guests and will get food, much better in fact than if you had stayed in England. We'll do our best to make you feel content until the British can think of a better solution for you. Meanwhile, you can transfer your British bank accounts to the camp and do mail-order shopping with any firm you wish. I'll see to it that you get some catalogues. You may also order any newspapers and magazines. For those who like to get some exercise, there will be work parties on new agricultural land we are trying to create. All others are free to spend their time as they wish."

Didn't you do some lecturing during this time?
We felt we would go mad if we didn't do something to occupy our minds. I can, of course, only speak of the camp I lived in. We had no contact with the other. Both were identical in

structure. Each had twenty-five huts and each hut held forty men sleeping in double bunks. There were, in addition, huts for eating, entertainment, administration, etc. Cleaning was done on a voluntary basis, that of the sleeping quarters by the inmates of the hut in rotation. A choir was soon formed and a theatrical group, as well as a small university. We had specialists in practically every field, especially in languages. I had gathered on the *Dunera* a small group keen to discuss the aesthetics of photography and to hear of my experiences in Britain and in Germany. Few of the sixty thousand refugees in Britain ever had a working permit, and the difference in taste was an intriguing subject. Friends in the United States kept me supplied with photographic magazines and sent me Stenger's *History of Photography*, an English translation of which had recently been published. Someone lent me his copy of Lucia Moholy's Penguin book, which I had read in England. Both these books stimulated my interest in the history of photography and provided me with basic information for our reconvened group meetings. They also extended the scope of our discussions.

An unforeseen practical experience came my way when the camp commandant called me to his office one day and asked me whether I would take a number of passport photographs for visa applications to other countries. He handed me a Kodak roll-film camera and a tripod and ordered a soldier to take me to the chemist in Hay to buy the film I needed. A plain background was soon found, and I rigged up a primitive studio in the visitors' hut. Developing and printing were done by the local chemist and the work turned out satisfactorily, yet proved in vain. The various consuls pointed out that release from internment was a prior condition to emigration.

How did London react on this matter?
After months of waiting, some people did in fact get their release papers, but then the Australian government stated that it could not grant freedom to people it had not interned and who had not immigrated in the normal way. A release paper, they stated, merely entitled the holder to return to England if he wished, when shipping space was available. A de facto

release and emigration to another country could only take place from Britain, the country of origin. Some weeks later a Home Office official confirmed the Australian attitude, but he also brought new proposals with him. We would soon be transferred to more suitable camps. The government granted compensation for all stolen property. Anyone over sixty or under sixteen at the time of internment was automatically free to return to England, because their internment had been a mistake. The same applied to married men, who had been promised reunion with their wives. In addition, the British government would sympathetically consider release of any applicant falling into one or other of the following categories: (1) acceptance by and emigration to another country; (2) joining the British Army; (3) any civilian occupation of importance to the war effort. The rest would stay interned for the time being, but might be released later on, if willing to join the Australian Pioneer Corps for services of a noncombatant nature in Australia.

On what grounds did you obtain your release?
I fell under two categories and plugged both. American friends sponsored me and secured me a position as curator of the Museum at Santa Fe, New Mexico. Friends in London informed me of the recent establishment of the National Buildings Record to secure photographs of buildings and monuments of national importance in danger of destruction by bombing. After the loss already sustained, this matter was now considered urgent and regarded as equivalent to war service. However, my release papers did not come through until the end of September 1941. Meanwhile, we had changed camps twice, each transfer constituting a great improvement in amenities. The heat of the summer at Hay, with the thermometer rising to 45 °C. in the shade, had sent many people to the hospital with heart trouble. The climate was simply unfit for Central Europeans. When it became cooler in May, the Australian autumn, we were transferred to Orange in the Blue Mountains, where a camp had been prepared for Japanese prisoners of war, none of whom had been captured yet. We had hardly had time to get acclimatized to the winter and

snow in this lovely mountain resort when some of us were moved again in July, this time to Tatura in the state of Victoria. This small camp, originally housing some five hundred Italian internees and German refugees picked up from the *Arandora Star* disaster was beautifully situated on hilly ground among meadows and eucalyptus trees, around five hundred miles north of Melbourne. I was lucky in that I had to wait only a fortnight in camp after release. The first group had waited for several months before sailing. I was in the second transport going to England with forty-four others released for special qualifications and ninety joining the army. Among the specials was Peter Stadlen, the pianist, and Hein Heckroth, designer of the postwar films *The Red Shoes* and *Tales of Hoffmann*. We also had on board the *Stirling Castle* a contingent of Australian, and later on, New Zealand, forces. We were free on board ship, which sailed October 13 for Auckland, but when we docked there for nine days to take on supplies for Britain, we were not allowed to disembark. A delegation of the Jewish community commiserated with us by sending presents. Their application to have us as guests had been turned down by the New Zealand government. After a brief call at Wellington, we continued on a southerly course, as if to round Cape Horn before turning northward to the Panama Canal. This detour was necessary, we heard, to avoid possible Japanese raiders prowling around the direct route. The four days in the Canal Zone were the most fascinating of the voyage. After Colón we passed Puerto Rico and then steamed north to Nova Scotia before making a dash for Britain. We approached Liverpool through the North Channel, as we had left the previous year, but this time under the protection of air patrols. It was on November 28, 1941, that we docked, after only forty-six days at sea. My enforced trip around the world without a camera had taken one year and four and a half months. From the immigration office I received some cash for a meal and a ticket to London. I now was de facto free. My former apartment in London stood empty. It had been cleared during my absence and the furniture stored due to my inability to pay the rent.

How soon afterward did you start working?
Not until three months later. Sir John Summerson, director of the National Buildings Record, advised me to contact the Warburg Institute, London University, which had offered to collaborate in the work and were looking for someone for the London area. Before they could hire me, special permits were required entitling me to have and use photographic equipment and a security pass. I also needed the collaboration of the Ministry of Labour and the good will of military, naval, and church authorities. All this took time. For me this was a convenient moment to polish up and enlarge my Australian lecture notes, which were published as *New Photo Vision* in October of that year.

What sort of work did you do for the Warburg Institute?
I was hired to make photographic surveys of the most important historic buildings and monuments in the Greater London area: Westminster Abbey, the Prime Minister's residence, the architecture and monuments of St. Paul's Cathedral and a number of other Wren churches, the British Museum, Chatham House, St. James's Palace, Ashburnham House, Chiswick House, Brooks Club, Hampton Court Palace and Greenwich Palace, better known as the Royal Naval College, and much else besides. The work was directed by the art historian Dr. Rudolf Wittkower, who selected each building and gave me a general outline of the pictures required. The rest was up to me.

What was your working method?
I started with the monuments in Westminster Abbey. Most of the windows had been blown out during the blitz; some were blocked up. I had to rely entirely on my three 500-watt floodlights. Some of the monuments were so high that I had to work from the platform of a 15-foot-high heathman which had a floodlight fixed to it. One assistant had to wheel me into position and place the floodlights on the ground according to my direction. The other had to look after the cables and mend any fuses I blew—which was not infrequent. The first thing I

noticed was a ten-year-old layer of dust covering the monuments and showing up strongly under my lights. The Ministry of Labour agreed that each monument should be cleaned before I took my photographs—usually the entire monument and several detail shots. I worked with a 9 x 12 cm. plate camera, and the setup for a picture usually took me about an hour. Neither I nor the Warburg Institute was interested in the mere production of records. I tried to re-create with light the sculptor's intention to instill life and action in the stone. The dean watched me sometimes in amazement, saying: "I have never seen what you are creating here. What a pity we can't keep your lights installed permanently." My working hours were rather restricted by the morning and afternoon services, which slowed down production. It took me over six months to photograph all the important monuments. A few had been protected by sandbags and had to be left out. The medieval bronze figures of kings and queens had been moved to safety and those pictures were taken on Lord Rosebery's estate in Hertfordshire.

What did you do at 10 Downing Street?
I photographed the historic cabinet room with Churchill's study leading out of it, the wrought-iron staircase, and various details from the bedroom on the top floor to the fortified cellar, where the Allied heads of Europe had their consultative meetings with him. I had a strange experience, finding myself at the nerve center of the war against Hitler so soon after my internment. I had not yet finished my work when Churchill returned from one of his meetings with Roosevelt. Seeing me in the hall, he asked: "What are you doing here?" I replied, "Taking photographs for the National Buildings Record." Next question: "Where do you come from?" "Well," I replied, "the last place of residence was Australia." "But you are not an Australian, are you?" "No, sir, I'm not. I am a refugee from Germany, volunteered to go to Canada and found myself in Australia instead." "Ah," he said, "I remember. That matter caused us a lot of trouble. But we brought you back. I hope everything is all right now," whereupon the great man vanished into his study. In 1954, when I was working on my book

Churchill, His Life in Photographs for his eightieth birthday, I met at Randolph's house several other members of the family, including his grandson Winston, then at Eton.

Did you come into contact with Sir Kenneth Clark at this time?
Not until June 1944, I believe, when the National Buildings Record held a big exhibition of its work at the National Gallery. The largest single contribution came from me. But prior to this, Lady Clark had paid me a visit and selected a prewar picture of mine of Potsdam as a birthday present for her husband. She also invited me to have a one-man show at the Churchill Club in November 1943 of my Westminster Abbey monuments, about which Sir Kenneth, director of the National Gallery, had written a few months earlier a long and effusive article in *The Architectural Review*. He said that they were "the first step in a new valuation of English art" and that I had "achieved nothing short of a rediscovery of the Baroque monuments."

Were your photographs much publicized in print and in other exhibitions?
Sir Nikolaus Pevsner, for many years joint editor of *The Architectural Review*, frequently published articles on my photographs and so did the *Illustrated London News, Country Life, The Architects' Journal,* and several others. Reviewing the National Buildings Record exhibition I have just mentioned, *The Statesman and Nation* wrote that my photographs had "set a standard of excellence by which it would be unfair to judge the other exhibits," and *The Times* expressed similar views. As to exhibitions, I had at least half a dozen one-man shows at the Churchill Club before the end of the war, two at the Courtauld Institute of Art, and in 1948 a one-man show at the Royal Photographic Society. My photographs also made up a large part of the traveling shows sent abroad by the British Council and the Ministry of Information respectively. After the war I published selections of my wartime work, supplemented by new photographs, in my books *Focus on Architecture and Sculpture* (1949), and in *Beautiful London* (1950).

How did the public react to New Photo Vision?
Critics of the national and weekly papers considered my credo
on photography very timely, if not overdue. To them it was
no secret that photographers in Britain needed a radical change
of mentality fit for the 1940's, and obvious that it was as
anachronistic to produce pictures in the style of 1914 as it
would have been to fight the war with the planes and tanks
of World War I. Yet to the mentally blind nothing is obvious.
There's still a group in Britain today claiming that the world
is a flat disc and not a globe. No amount of facts and arguments will convince them. A few photographic papers agreed
that I had a case, others were critical of my challenge, saying
that British photography has its own national idiom and cannot be judged from a German point of view. I was bold enough
to cite the work of a number of leading German cameramen
in comparison. Lastly, I had been ridiculing the overim-
portance attached by most amateurs to equipment and technique and had been calling for a discriminating eye and a
constructive mind. I think my essay is as readable and lively
today as it was thirty-five years ago—though most of my
opinions are now generally accepted. It was illustrated with
thirty-two of my photographs, all taken between 1935–38. A
storm in a teacup was very much what the Fountain Press had
expected, even hoped for. After the war they signed contracts
with me for four further titles, all on the same day. I'd call
this great enthusiasm, wouldn't you? The books were: *The
Man Behind the Camera, Julia Margaret Cameron, Focus on
Architecture and Sculpture*, and *The History of Photography*.

Would you say that New Photo Vision *launched you on a new
career?*
It did become a turning point in my life a few years later
through circumstances impossible to foresee in 1942. No doubt
it had aroused my interest in writing and research and led me
to abandon professional photography almost completely in
1947. Yet all this might not have happened if my essay had
not become instrumental in my starting a photo-historical
collection.

We were not aware of this. Could you explain in what way?
It occurred to me to send a copy to Beaumont Newhall at the
Museum of Modern Art—as a first contact. I promptly heard
from Nancy that Beaumont was with the U.S. Army photo
group stationed in southern Italy and that she would be sending me a copy of his *Short Critical History*, then known to me
only from hearsay. Soon afterward Beaumont informed me
that he had bought a copy of my book while on leave in Cairo.
He wrote: "I have read your thesis with satisfaction, as it is
so in agreement with my own philosophy of photography.
There has been so little genuine criticism of photography as
an independent art form that it is a real pleasure to make the
acquaintance of a fellow critic." He expressed the hope that
our paths might cross. This was not to happen until December
1944, when Hitler's secret weapon, the rockets, blasted London. We soon found that we had many interests in common
besides art and photography, and spent many evenings together, either at my home near Regent's Park or at the
American Club. Alison, my British-born wife (we had married
in April 1942), was impressed by the gallant officer who
praised her coffee and helped with the washing up. He told
us of his search for old photographs and photographically
illustrated books in the Charing Cross Road, his finds and
disappointments. One day he said: "Helmut, I admire your
zeal to reform British photography, but that will happen anyhow. So why don't you first rescue what's left of the historical
material we both find so fascinating? England is full of it, but
due to lack of appreciation, it is fast disappearing. Today I saw
a nice daguerreotype case, but on opening it, found it empty.
The shopkeeper said: 'You surely don't want somebody else's
grandmother?' I told him I did, but the picture had been
thrown away. Saving photographs from destruction is an important mission, too. Some of the vandals are the G.I.'s;
they are buying the empty cases to put their own portraits in
and send them to their folks at home. I was luckier yesterday
when I picked up a copy of Emerson's *Life and Landscape on
the Norfolk Broads*, which is illustrated with forty platinum
prints. A great rarity for only two pounds." "That's all very
sad," I replied, "but I can't start collecting yet another field.

I'm interested in African art and German Expressionist wood-cuts, of which I have built up quite a nice collection in the last two and a half years. On the salary I'm making, I simply can't afford more." Beaumont countered: "Very well, then give up collecting them for a time. You'll find them later on. But for how long will there be photographs to collect?"

I was working at Hampton Court at that time, and walking from the station to the palace, I must have passed the same antique shop at least a hundred times. Yet it was only after this conversation that I noticed in the window a bundle of stereograms. It contained quite a number of American views and I bought them with the intention of presenting them to Beaumont as a little parting gift. He had brought us so many delicacies from the G.I. canteen. When we met again, Beaumont glanced through them, then handed them back to me with the remark: "No, I won't take them from you. Let them form the basis of your own collection." I was dumbfounded. "This is not my field." "Then make it your field. You'll be doing a good job for the country." What was I to do? In bed that night, I thought, it can't do any harm to try, and on the following Saturday I went out to see what I could find. That's how I began collecting in January 1945.

Could you give us some details of what you were looking for?
The majority of the dealers did not know the difference between a daguerreotype and an ambrotype, but when I described them and the little red morocco cases, their faces suddenly brightened and they would find me one in a drawer or ask me to come back. They would collect them for me. It was easier when I had one of each to show as a sample. Often I was offered an empty case, as Beaumont had said. I combed through London, district by district, visiting antique and junk shops alike. I also called on secondhand booksellers at the same time and usually returned home with a full load of manuals, odd journals, and photographic albums. In this way I established many valuable contacts, but it was time-wasting to go from place to place like a peddler. And I never found the large exhibition prints I was dreaming of. On inquiry I learned of the existence of a trade journal read by all the

antiquarian booksellers in Britain, and by advertising my *desiderata* I soon established a nationwide network of suppliers who were only too happy to know of a client willing to take their unsalable photographic material. Before long I received at least one catalogue daily to scan through, and ever so many offers. I also advertised in the Personal column of *The Times.*

Once bitten by the collector's bug, you can't leave off. Having been an inveterate collector in other art fields, I applied the same criteria to photography. I only bought what appealed to me, yet with the connoisseur's critical eye for quality. There were no books to guide me and no public collections. I had to pioneer the field myself. Knowledge was gradually acquired, but if you bought by intuition, you could not go wrong. Fakes did not exist. I made it an iron rule never to buy anything in poor condition, and never to acquire mediocre work, however cheap. A collection stands by its quality, not by its quantity. The second- and third-rate only encumber a collector looking for top quality, quite apart from the problem of storage. This and the limited means at my disposal made me very selective. While knowledge and money may be acquired, discernment and taste are gifts which some people have and others lack. All four are prerequisites for a good collection.

When you gave up working for the N.B.R. at the end of the war, could you then give your entire time to collecting and research?

I never achieved this ideal condition. I had to earn my living first, and until the beginning of 1947, and occasionally even after, I spent part of my time on freelance photography for publishers, *The Architectural Review, Country Life,* an advertising agency, and several sculptors. In later years I had to make reproductions of pictures in the collection for our and other people's articles and books. It was always an irksome interruption, but provided useful income for new acquisitions. My first postwar job was to take photographs of twelfth-century wall paintings in two Sussex churches. They had recently been uncovered from the overpainted whitewash layer and were of considerable importance from the historical point of view. The difficulties connected with my work were also considerable, for in both churches the erection of scaffolding and a builder's platform were necessary, in addition to the installation of a dynamo to provide electric light. Clive Bell was the art historian responsible for the text of the book, and I met him a number of times. One day he asked me: "Have you ever heard of Julia Margaret Cameron?" "I have indeed," was my reply. "I know many of her portraits and studies, though mainly from reproductions." "Well, in this case you'll no doubt be interested to see my wife's collection. She's a great-niece of Mrs. Cameron." I did not at that time know the book Virginia Woolf (Vanessa Bell's sister) had published in 1926 with Roger Fry in a limited edition of four hundred copies. It was based on this by no means outstanding collection, which had been sold at Sotheby's. During lunch Vanessa Bell told me that her sister had written a play on Mrs. Cameron, which I naturally wanted to read. She said: "Oh, no, I'm afraid you cannot. Too many family matters come into that play and I keep it under lock and key. It is not for publication." When I prepared the new edition of my monograph on Julia Cameron some years ago, I asked Quentin Bell, executor of the estate and co-author with me of *Those Impossible English*, whether he would let me publish it, but meanwhile, the University of Sussex had become the owner.

I think you state in your book that you owned over two hundred of Mrs. Cameron's finest photographs. Where did you find them?

I acquired them gradually over a period of many years. In addition, an album with over sixty prints and three volumes of her illustrations to Tennyson's *Idylls of the King*, which Mrs. Cameron had presented to Anne, Thackeray's daughter, were passed on to me as a gift by his granddaughter. The first Camerons I more or less found by accident. At a shop where I sometimes bought Japanese prints and Pre-Columbian art, I inquired one day whether they knew of a dealer selling old photographs. "As a matter of fact," said the lady, "I believe we still have a few Cameron portraits. But I don't know where my husband has put them. He wanted to use them for packing because of their stout cardboard. I stopped him and asked him to keep them. I was sure somebody would pay good money one day for such fine portraits of the great Victorians, although they are not fashionable today. Could you call back another day?" When I did, she produced superb prints of Herschel, Carlyle, Darwin, and the famous profile of Mrs. Duckworth. I was excited and probably asked far too quickly how much she wanted for them. "Five guineas each." I said that I had never before paid such a high price for a photograph, which was true, and that it seemed to me a gross overvaluation of something originally destined as packing material. Thinking it over, the lady replied: "They are fine, aren't they? The only one which I could let you have cheaper is Mrs. Duckworth. I've never heard of her. You can have her for three guineas." Not knowing when I would come across these great portraits again, I wrote out a check while she packed them up. When the parcel was under my arm, I said: "By the way, Julia Duckworth was the mother of Virginia Woolf and Vanessa Bell by her second husband, Leslie Stephen, editor of the *Dictionary of National Biography*. In case you should find any others of her, please keep them for me." She nearly fainted. I then walked into the antiquarian bookseller next door to her shop—and found the other pictures myself in a collection of at least fifty prints which had once belonged to Mrs. Cameron's nephew, the artist Val Prinsep. I bought the majority at one or two guineas a print. In 1947 I had the pick of the G. F. Watts collection at Oxford.

What sort of prices did you have to pay when you started collecting?
They were pretty much the same for daguerreotypes and ambrotypes. The average was five to ten shillings, depending on the size, the beauty of the case, and whether colored or not. Studies by Mrs. Cameron cost one guinea, her portraits two to five guineas, according to the fame of sitter. Hill-Adamson calotypes could only be found in Scotland, and Craig Annan charged me two guineas per picture in 1946. For Fenton and MacPherson prints I used to pay one guinea, and this was the standard price for prints by most other photographers. Pictures by Samuel Bourne and Frith were in plentiful supply

and could be had for ten shillings and less. Le Gray's sea-scapes were rare and I was charged the equivalent of five pounds even in Paris. Paper stereograms and *carte-de-visite* pictures of famous sitters were one shilling each, Silvy's one and sixpence. Known rarities in books and photographs had no ceiling, but there was only one specialist dealer in this field: Dr. Ernst Weil. He was a scientist buying mainly for American scientific institutions. His catalogues usually had a section on early photography, a veritable treasure trove of rare books, fine autograph letters, and pictures not to be found anywhere else in the world. His prices ranged accordingly. I paid him ten guineas each for letters by Talbot and Daguerre and twenty guineas each for superb Talbotypes, uncut and in mint condition, which had been found in a box at Lacock Abbey. This was the largest amount I ever had to pay for a single photograph, and it was a lot in 1947/8. After our Festival of Britain exhibition in 1951, masterpieces of Victorian photography increased considerably in value, and I was quoted higher prices again after the publication of our *History of Photography* four years later. All the same, it was still possible for me to obtain Talbot's *Pencil of Nature* at Sotheby's in January 1958 for 90 pounds! It was a world auction record price for this very rare incunabulum, complete and in excellent condition, and formerly belonging to the Marquis of Northampton, president of the Royal Society when Talbot announced his invention.

You mentioned Craig Annan before. Did you find much in Scotland?

I shall never forget my shopping trip to Scotland in 1946. The previous year I had written to J. Craig Annan and inquired whether T. & R. Annan had any carbon prints left of the set they had produced from Adamson's negatives in 1880 for the intended publication of Dr. Andrew Elliott's on D. O. Hill. Alternatively, were there still any photographs he had made in 1904 for *Camera Work*? Soon afterward I received two complete sets, his own, which he wrote were the last, each for five guineas. He also sent me a history of their production, and the reasons for the many delays in the publication of the

Elliott volume until 1928. Enticing me to visit, he mentioned that he still had quite a number of the original calotypes from which I could make a selection. Annan was eighty-two when I saw him, and full of the most interesting reminiscences of his father, a friend of Hill and portrayed by him in the "Deed of Demission" painting. When Hill moved to Newington in 1869, Thomas Annan took over Rock House and found in the darkroom a large number of Adamson's calotype negatives and prints, the printing frames, cameras and lenses, all apparently untouched since Adamson's death in 1848. This was the origin of the Annan collection of their negatives and prints. The lenses and reflecting mirrors were later presented by Craig Annan to the R.P.S. Heinrich Schwarz had acquired, during a visit in 1930, a number of prints for the Albertina in Vienna, but some thirty mounted prints were still left and I bought ten.

Both in Glasgow and Edinburgh I found a number of books and journals, daguerreotypes and ambrotypes, and when after a fortnight's collecting and sightseeing my two suitcases were full, I took the train back to London. There was a long queue at King's Cross station for taxis, so I carried my suitcases into the street hoping to be able to hail a cruising taxi. The street lights had not yet been repaired and the blackout was still in force in London. It was difficult to make out a taxi from a private car, and so I made a few steps into the road, got a taxi—but my suitcases were gone. Vanished from the earth in a few seconds. Well, that was a terrible shock. I reported the theft to the police immediately. When I told them the contents had nothing of salable value, they assured me that I would get them back. For months I tried my luck at lost property offices, and at stations for unclaimed luggage, but there was no trace of them. Perhaps they were dumped in the Thames. I felt particularly embarrassed because Craig Annan had lent me a number of personal mementos I had wanted to reproduce and now could not return. He was extremely nice about it. That summer my wife and I took our holidays at Ballachulish and on the way paid Annan a farewell visit. He was ill in bed and delighted to see us. Talking had become difficult for him and he died shortly afterward.

What were your most important finds in the first years?
They were so manifold that my bank account was permanently
in the red, my overdraft increasing to alarming proportions.
One day the bank manager told me point-blank that I was
living beyond my means. I knew it. Luckily my wife inherited
a few thousand pounds soon afterward and generously put
them into my account. She believed in my assertion that I
needed a collection and a library before I could start writing.
A milestone for the latter arrived one day by post. The unknown sender was the owner of an East German university
bookshop enclosing Johann Heinrich Schulze's rarissimi dis-
sertations on his experiments with carbonate of silver, fundamental to all further experimentation with light drawing on
paper. The first was contained in a thick volume of the Im-
perial Academy at Nürnberg, 1727, the other in his post-
humously published *Chemische Versuche* of 1745. How the
sender had heard of me is an enigma, but the world is small
and news travels fast. All he asked for in exchange was a new
winter coat, size 50!

On my regular rounds of the leading antiquarian booksellers
in London's West End, I was offered the first volume of
Gardner's Photographic Sketch Book of the War (1865), with
the fifty albumen prints in superb condition. This is a much
coveted work in the United States, never seen in the English
sale rooms, and I was delighted. Some weeks later the same
dealer in rare books showed me an album supposedly containing seventy photographs by Lewis Carroll—children and
well-known personalities, each with their autograph signature.
Lewis Carroll's hobby was then completely unknown to me,
as it was to all the biographers I consulted. There was no
evidence of any name except that of the last owner, Charlotte
Young. The bookseller assured me that he had had the album
for fifteen years. "So why didn't you show it to me before?" I
asked. "It only just surfaced again when an assistant shifted
books in the cellar." It all sounded rather improbable, but
turning the pages once more, I noticed a handwritten index
of sitters in purple ink. This struck me as very odd and an
idea occurred to me that it might prove a clue to the author-
ship. I reserved the album. The next day I took Alison to the

shop to have another look at it. She then went to the British Museum manuscript room to study Lewis Carroll's handwriting and the ink he used. After an hour or two, she rang me up: "It's okay, they're identical." This acquisition cost me £25 in 1947. Soon I was able to trace other albums and Lewis Carroll's diaries, and I was in a position to document the long-forgotten chief hobby of the author of the Alice books in *Lewis Carroll—Photographer.*

Let me give you one more example, and this will be my last. In 1946 I had made the acquaintance of Felix H. Man, who had just started collecting lithographs. Like me, he was an avid reader of booksellers' catalogues and we often exchanged information. One morning he rang me to inquire whether I had received the catalogue of a leading bookshop in Edinburgh. Though I knew the firm, I hadn't. He then mentioned that they offered a calotype album by D. O. Hill containing one hundred pictures, price £100. I immediately phoned them. The album was still for sale. Its condition was stated to be very fine and the prints unfaded. As it was too heavy to be sent by post on approval, I decided to give a firm order. I was amazed by the quality of the album and prints when it arrived. I had never seen anything like it before. There was a painted frontispiece by Hill, and the calotypes contained the cream of their photographic activity, each signed by Hill and Adamson. It was dated October 1845, and was their first presentation album. The recipient was the marine painter Clarkson Stanfield. This unbelievable piece of luck compensated me for the loss of the Craig Annan prints the previous year.

Was Julia Margaret Cameron *the first photo-historical monograph?*

In many ways it was, for my book was the result of thorough research on her life and work, her technique and the opinions of her contemporaries, my own aesthetic appreciation, and a rough classification of her work. Julia's personality, her social standing, and her friendships with Tennyson, Watts, and other giants of the Victorian age, they were all sharply drawn, as they should be in a monograph. Heinrich Schwarz did none of these things in his monograph *David Octavius Hill,* which precedes mine by sixteen years. He merely published an album of eighty plates with a brief introduction, but failed to expand the generally known information on Hill's life and his collaboration with Adamson. It was I in fact who first linked their names and moved Adamson's contribution into its proper light, and I think the few pages on their work in our *History* are considerably more informative than Schwarz's volume. Instead of doing research, he padded the book with lengthy biographies of the Scottish personalities represented in the plates which anyone interested could look up in a biographical dictionary. Since then we have had several picture albums on Hill and Adamson by David Bruce, Roy Strong, and Colin Ford, but we still lack a proper study of Hill's life, his paintings and graphic art, though I handed my research notes to Kate Michaelson eight years ago. Nigel Gosling's recent monograph on Nadar follows this facile trend of publishing picture albums with stupid biographies of the sitters. Only in this case Jean Prinet and Antoinette Dilaccer had painstakingly researched and published Nadar's life and work in an unpretentious paperback in 1966. In recent years far too many people with no prior knowledge of or interest in the history of photography have swamped the market with hastily compiled, and frequently badly produced, coffee-table books which fill the shelves but are worthless to the photo-historian.

Why did you consider it essential to build up a reference library of your own when the British Museum and the R.P.S. libraries were available to you?

Digging in uncharted fields is no easy task. Pioneering a new field confronts one daily with new problems, and unless you can constantly refer to the manuals, journals, and exhibition catalogues, you waste a tremendous amount of time in journeys and waiting. In the first postwar years, lack of staff obliged the British Museum to restrict readers to six books per day, and you had to wait two hours for delivery. We used the R.P.S. too on occasion, but Alison could not go there alone as she wasn't a member. So I decided to have my own reference library and gradually amassed nearly four thousand volumes, from sixteenth-century treatises on optics and chemistry in

Latin—the prehistory of photography—to publications of our time. Whenever we were abroad, I called on the leading antiquarian booksellers. The *Comptes Rendus* of the French Academy of Science is a very important source for early photography in France, but nowhere was it to be found. The British Museum set had been lost in the bombing. Hopefully we set out for Paris in 1948. But it was not in any shop, except in a long run of two hundred volumes or more costing a fortune. We gave up. But one day, crossing over from the Louvre to the left bank of the Seine on the Pont-Neuf, I noticed on the rue des Grands-Augustins a house with a large signboard and the name Gauthier-Villars. "Aren't they the publishers of the *Comptes Rendus*?" I asked Alison. "I believe so" was her reply. Upon reflection I said: "But it is madness to think they would still have the volumes of 1839–45 we need. They will laugh at us." "Then let them, but trying does not cost us a penny." And so we entered and inquired, but instead of laughing the assistant replied with a straight face that they were still available in sheets and would have to be bound for me. Each year consisted of two half-yearly volumes, each with 1,200–1,500 pages! Boldened by this good fortune, I then asked whether they still had some of Professor Marey's books or photographic manuals. He reached for a catalogue and said, "Anything listed here is still in stock." The catalogue was two years old and the books had been published between 1875 and 1938!

What part did your wife play in your various activities?
Knowing shorthand and typing, German, French, and some Latin, Alison played ,a most important part in research. She was fast and efficient and much more in her element at the British Museum reading room than in the kitchen. I did the shopping and cooking while she typed for me or catalogued the continuous flow of books and photographs I brought home. Until March 1947 she was private secretary to a Member of Parliament, a friend of ours, and dealing with his correspondence at the House of Commons. But after I had signed four book contracts in one go, I said to her: "Now the time has come for you to quit your job and work full time for me.

At last I can afford to drop photography and give my time entirely to writing and research. We will now start folders for each important photographer, for photographic processes, exhibitions, apparatus, and other subjects. Whatever we read that might become useful one day will have to be typed out and the sheet put into its subject folder. We can't possibly remember where we have read what." So we systematically started folder upon folder with stored information. If we owned the original book or journal, a reference to it sufficed. Occasionally Alison would sort the notes and retype them, and by the time we started work on the *History of Photography*, we had a wonderful supply of information to draw on. It was a perfect system. Many folder titles became chapter headings in our *History*, and it is only a pity that much available material had to be dropped to conform to the requirements of Oxford University Press. The folders must contain some three to four million words. They are still in existence. The published material is with my collection at Austin. The folders with unpublished manuscripts, largely biographies, our bibliography, and research for other books, I have kept for the time being.

Did you train your wife in photographic research?
Alison knew nothing about photography when I first met her and her husband in August 1938. However, we both started research almost together. She knew the problems involved from my experience and I had only to indicate what information I needed and the most likely source. An intelligent woman will soon learn to adapt herself to almost anything, provided she wants to. She collaborated with me on every book. While I was going through our notes prior to dictation, she would scan one of the numerous general-interest journals to see what they had to say about photography. I would regularly check her brief abstracts before they went onto the different information sheets. Some points I might delete, others I wanted enlarged or even in full. On some books we divided our labors. Alison was strong on British history and she enjoyed working on the biographies of Queen Victoria and Edward VII while I was busy at Windsor Castle selecting and

reproducing the illustrations. She also rewrote most of A. L. Coburn's autobiography and might have published more than one book, *Fashion and Reality*, if she had not been constantly engrossed in my projects.

What was her background, and when did you marry?
After passing through Hampstead High School and a finishing school in Paris, she married the chief accountant of the De Havilland aircraft manufacturers. Her father was a director of Spicer Brothers, the paper manufacturers. She was granted her divorce in March 1942, and the following month we set up house together. So that she would not lose her British citizenship, we did not legally marry until the end of the war. I thought one enemy alien in the family was quite enough! My naturalization papers came through in 1946.

Your most important discovery was the world's first camera picture by Niepce. How did this happen?
This is a long, involved story which I recently published in considerable detail in the *History of Photography* quarterly and in the Italian magazine *Bolaffi-Arte*. I think we would be wasting time and printing space on a repetition.

How did your fellow historians react to your find?
The only two photo-historians in existence then were Erich Stenger and Beaumont Newhall, and both were delighted and amazed when they saw it. The picture is so well documented that not the slightest doubt ever arose. Recently it has been suggested, however, that it dates from spring 1827 rather than from 1826, and that the position it was taken from is more likely below the window I had indicated. Both points are feasible, but neither has been conclusively proved. The existence of this foundation stone in America has led a few French ninnies to propagate another photograph as the first. It is a still life on glass which was smashed early in this century. Nothing whatsoever is known about it. It may have been taken by Daguerre in 1829, trying out his partner's heliographic process. It certainly wasn't taken by Niepce or prior to 1829.

Until a few years ago the Arts Council was not prepared to support photography. How did you obtain their agreement to back your exhibition in 1951?

"Masterpieces of Victorian Photography" was not a photographic exhibition per se, but formed part of a general plan to celebrate the centenary of the Great Exhibition in 1851 with a number of retrospective shows on the Victorian Age. In 1949 I reminded the Arts Council that it would be fitting to include photography in this scheme, as it had formed part of the original Crystal Palace exhibition. I also mentioned that Alison and I could arrange it from our collection. One day Sir Kenneth Clark came to have a look at it, and he was surprised by the scope and beauty of the material. He paid us several more visits and each time his enthusiasm rose. Victorian photography was a revelation to him. Eventually the Arts Council confirmed the acceptance of my suggestion and informed me that the Victoria and Albert Museum had offered their acquisition hall on the ground floor for the exhibition. I was asked to state my requirements and ideas in the way of decoration. We agreed on a suitable Victorian setting, and they provided two final-year students from the Royal College of Art as designers. We had great fun selecting Victorian wallpaper for the screens, Victorian lettering, a sofa of the period, red and black velvets, and plenty of palms and aspidistras to evoke the right atmosphere. Lastly, the designers found some stuffed pheasants and peacocks to place on the screens. A week before the opening Leigh Ashton, then the director, made an inspection tour and was flabbergasted by the transformation of the hall. He told the designers: "I'm not going to have this exhibition unless that sofa and this feathery stuff go out. This is not a Victorian parlor but a great art museum." The Arts Council backed the designers. The catalogue was printed. There was nowhere else to go. We were in despair. Luckily, Lady Rothermere, a friend of the director, came in one morning with him and exclaimed: "How delightful, Leigh. This is splendid. Where on earth did you find these lovely birds? It's the best period setting imaginable." Smiling, he turned to the designers, saying: "Continue with your work. Everything is okay." Our exhibition proved extremely successful with the public. It lasted over five months and acted as an eye-opener to many who had previously pooh-poohed photography.

When did you conceive the idea of a National Collection of Photography?

Before this exhibition. In the foreword to the catalogue I mentioned that the 520 exhibits were only a small selection from over five thousand photographs, besides a large collection of books, apparatus, and associated items, "which it is hoped may one day form the nucleus of a National Museum of Photography." In a long memorandum to *The Times* the following March, we expanded our ideas on the need for a national collection, the functions we envisaged and the contents of our collection, which we stated we were willing to present provided suitable accommodations could be found and a sufficient grant obtained to provide a center. The letter was also signed by Clive Bell, Tom Hopkinson, Sir Gerald Kelly, Nikolaus Pevsner, J. B. Priestley, and a few others.

And Sir Kenneth Clark?

Strangely, he did not want to be associated with it, nor did Cecil Beaton. Though the urgent need for such a center was generally recognized, opinions differed as to its functions. Some correspondents went rather far from the original plan of a limited objective which would have been realizable. The R.P.S. reminded the public that they too had a fine collection which should be on public view; the British Film Institute put forward the idea of a museum of photography and film. In the end, the ever-increasing demands only confused the public, and the practical result was nil.

Did you drop your campaign?

Never. Between 1952 and 1963 we had discussions about it with no fewer than thirty-four organizations, museums, town councils, foundations, and photographic manufacturers. Wherever our exhibition "One Hundred Years of Photography" was shown abroad—and we received far more invitations than we could accept—it received immense publicity and had a record number of visitors. This enticed museum and town officials to invite us to talk. We were always ready to present our collection, provided our program, as outlined in *The Times*, could be realized. But it never could for lack of a building or funds. In Stockholm they found us a building which we accepted, and we were waiting for funds. In Cologne Dr. Adenauer made both available and we drafted a contract, when at the last minute some town councilors objected to the creation of a new museum before all the existing ones had been rebuilt. Not an unreasonable demand. Perhaps my estimated value of the gift we would bring seemed to some town councils too low in proportion to the estimated running costs. Lord Rothermere had warned me in 1952 that business and town executives looked on gift horses with suspicion and advised me to put a higher value on the collection to attract attention. Yet, how could I do this without proof? Photographic auctions did not exist. The first was held in Geneva in 1961 and this served me later as a guideline. Of all the photographic manufacturers, the only one promising financial assistance was Gevaert of Antwerp, on condition that at least one manufacturer in the country where the museum was to be established would do the same. They never did.

In 1955 you and Alison were invited to attend a UNESCO conference on photography and film in Paris. What was its intention?
The conference had been initiated by French cultural and manufacturing interests in the hope of creating an international photographic center under the auspices of UNESCO. We were the only British representatives, and over luncheon with Sir Julian Huxley, the secretary-general, discussed our museum plan. In the committee meetings and at the full sessions a great variety of problems were raised, and in due course I was called upon to put forward my suggestion of an international museum in France, to which we would present our collection. At the same time, I expressed the hope that the French Society of Photography might add theirs, which was then still in storage. Many delegates, including Jean Adhemar of the Bibliothèque Nationale, and Edward Steichen, the American representative, gave strong support. However,

the Egyptian delegate pleaded for UNESCO's financial assistance in shifting Abu Simbel. This was a matter of the highest interest to all the civilized world. It should have priority. A photographic center was no doubt desirable too, but shelving it for a little while could do no harm, while the temple of Abu Simbel would be flooded if the world failed to re-erect it on higher ground. It was a perfectly sensible argument, but hardly a legitimate one for a photographic conference. Abu Simbel was saved, and the international center of photography was never heard of again. The French lost their opportunity of getting our collection.

The year 1955 also saw the publication of your monumental History of Photography. *How long had you been working on it?*
This has quite a history of its own. It was one of the books I had originally contracted for with the Fountain Press in January 1947. The British scene, unrecorded so far, had been grossly neglected in the previous histories of Eder, Stenger, Newhall, and Lecuyer. My specific interests in photography as an art medium also strengthened my intention for an entirely new approach. Eder and Stenger had overstressed the technical and chemical aspects of photography, completely overlooking its great contribution to the aesthetics of nineteenth-century picture-making by the novel way of image recording. This was Newhall's forte, but his history was more in the nature of a doctoral thesis. It was not a reference book.

It was foolish of me to think that I could deliver my *History* and three other titles within fourteen months of signing the contracts. I was inexperienced and too conscientious to let anything out of my hand that I felt could be improved by maturing. This became quite clear when we started working on the *History*. In the contract I had limited myself to the early period 1839–70, which had appeared to me then in most urgent need of revision, because we had so far concentrated our research on it. Yet the longer and deeper we delved into events in Britain, the greater appeared to me the necessity for extending the scope of the work to 1914. No new developments occurred during World War I, but by the mid-1920's modern photography started to manifest itself in Germany and the United States. The year 1914 seemed a natural break. The new publisher of the Fountain Press only reluctantly agreed to the much larger volume I now envisaged and was annoyed by the long delay in delivery. In 1952 he lost interest altogether when I informed him that I had still not written a word, though our folders were bulging with stored information. He failed to see that the original advance of sixty pounds was totally inadequate for the great work I now felt ready to write, and so we agreed to cancel the contract.

Thereupon, I was able to interest the Oxford University Press in the project, and in August of that year we signed a contract limiting the work to a maximum of 120,000 words. To enable us to live during the twelve months I felt we required for writing, the publisher generously suggested an advance of £1,000 in monthly installments—a quite unheard-of amount for a non-fiction book twenty-five years ago. Actually, it took us fourteen months to complete the *History*. When it was discovered that I had exceeded the limit by 63,000 words, the typescript was returned with the request to make cuts. Unable to follow the instruction except by omitting whole chapters and mutilating the work, neither in the publisher's interest nor in our own, we settled on two arbitrators, known to both of us, and agreed to abide by their judgment. One was the president of Trinity College, Oxford; the other Charles Gibbs-Smith of the Victoria and Albert Museum. After a delay of six months, they both gave their verdict in my favor. Production took another year.

What sort of public response did you have?
The national newspapers and weekly journals of the intelligentsia were effusive in their praise and accorded it—as usual with our books—long reviews. So did the American press. Newhall called it "a milestone in the history of photography" and an "encyclopaedic work" in *Popular Photography*, which gave him twelve pages for his review. Others spoke of "the photographers' bible," "a monument to photography." I was pleased to be acclaimed as the Berenson of photography. Only a small section of the British photographic press was cagy,

reluctant to acknowledge our achievement, and fault-finding. Instead of saying, "Thanks to the Gernsheims' research of ten years, we now have the first history recording the great British contribution to this field," they wondered why we had omitted cinematography, accused us of blackening Talbot's image, and were dissatisfied with the size of the 390 illustrations. But despite their criticisms, the *History* immediately established itself as the standard reference work of scholars and teachers wherever people knew English. An enlarged edition appeared in 1969, and I am working on a new edition in two volumes.

How would you compare your history with Newhall's?
It is invidious to make a comparison, because both works are so different in conception and intention. I set out to write a general history in which British photography plays a central part, as it did in the last century. Nonetheless, all the photographers, inventions, or processes of importance in the evolution of photography, of whatever nationality, get their due. Though limited by my exclusion of the modern period after World War I, its 600 pages are a mine of information. Beaumont, on the other hand, limited himself to the aesthetics of the photographic image throughout its history, and his fine treatise of 215 pages is hardly a reference work. It could only be compared to my 314-page *Concise History*, published in 1965, which includes the modern era and has proved a popular introduction for the general reader in several languages.

Is there a difference in approach between a European historian of photography and an American?
There should not be any. Each one is bound to have more information about his own country than any other; that lies in the nature of the source material available to him. But unless he limits the scope to writing a national history, he should assimilate the main events and leading artists of other countries. Photography is an international language and its history can be traced today on a supranational level. I corrected several articles in the *Encyclopaedia Britannica*, because they had been written too narrowly from an American point of view and were one-sided. Generally speaking, Britain

and France made the chief contribution to the technical and aesthetic development of photography in the nineteenth century, America and Germany in the twentieth.

Which photographers do you feel have had the greatest influence on the aesthetic history of the medium?
Each decade in photography has brought forth particularly gifted people who had a strong influence on style. The effect may not have become apparent immediately, for up to about 1870 the means of communication were slow. There must be many candidates for that honor in the last 150 years. And yet, curiously, some of the greatest artists like Hill or Mrs. Cameron left no mark. Their work was not known outside a small circle or not considered worth imitating, because it was not appreciated. Robinson's pictorialism and Emerson's naturalism were influences in the later decades of the nineteenth century. Those in the twentieth century are much easier to define: Stieglitz, Strand, Steichen, Atget, Man Ray, Moholy-Nagy, Renger-Patzsch, Salomon, Weston, Cartier-Bresson, the Farm Security People, Steinert, Fieger, Siskind, and Fontana would all warrant inclusion. Your question would need careful consideration, for you specified "greatest," not just "great" influence.

What qualities should a photo-historian have?
University-level education, capability, reliability, sound judgment, wide knowledge, aesthetic appreciation, patience, endurance, and ability to write. These are probably the most essential qualifications.

You said that basically there are only two historians today: yourself and Newhall. Aren't you a bit restrictive?
I spoke of a period up to five years ago when this was a plain fact to anyone. It is fashionable nowadays to style yourself a photo-historian, particularly in Europe, though little attempt is being made to widen existing knowledge by investigating new aspects through time-consuming research. What has been known for the last twenty-five years is chewed over and over again, popularized for an ever-increasing readership. The

many newcomers to the field in the last few years are merely exploiters of the boom, their research confined to my *History*. New historians are not produced so quickly, but I have met several assistant curators who would have the capacity, if they were freed from other chores. Recently I have been traveling extensively in the United States, visiting the chief centers of photographic education and collecting, meeting with museum and university curators, dealers and auctioneers, and seeing the great private collections. I was gratified to discover that wherever I went, my *History* was cited as an indispensable sourcebook. A few first-class monographs have been written based on original research, those on Brady, Muybridge, Riis, Nègre, Daguerre, or *Art and Photography* by Scharf. Yet just as one sunny day does not make a summer, writing one good book doesn't necessarily turn you into a historian. As a young man I used to play the piano quite well. Do you think this would have entitled me to call myself a pianist?

You mentioned Aaron Scharf just now. What do you think of his books?

His first book, *Creative Photography*, apart from trying to cash in on the success of my book by adopting the same title, was a facile compilation, hastily put together and shoddily produced. His second, *Art and Photography*, on the other hand, is based on sound research and is an excellent work. I know something about the subject, for the relationship of painting and photography had intrigued me even before I had started collecting. In October 1955 I gave the first lecture on this theme in Europe, at the Victoria and Albert. I made my comparisons with two projectors and 118 slides. In the following years I gave this lecture at a number of European and American universities and art museums. It was a novel subject and a matter of great interest to all art historians. Scharf was at my lecture in London and telephoned me a few days later wondering whether we could collaborate on a book. He was then still a student at the Courtauld Institute, and told me of his great interest. I informed him that I had been collecting material for such a publication for ten years and was neither in a hurry to publish nor intending to share my research

material with anyone else. Every year I discovered new facts
that strengthened the documentary evidence. At last in 1967
I felt ready to sign a contract with Thames & Hudson, and I
was in the middle of working on *Painting and Photography*
when twelve months later Scharf's treatise anticipated mine.
My intention had been to go back in the history of art to
Egyptian, Greek, and Roman art, van Eyck and the Dutch
seventeenth century, for long before photography was invented
there were long periods of "photographic" realism in art.
From 1840 to our time I would naturally have covered the
same ground with frequently the same illustrations Scharf
used, or rather, I had used in my lectures before Scharf's book.
Van Deren Coke, in largely specializing in the American
situation past and present, has made a valuable contribution
in extending Scharf's thesis. The latter's recent publication,
Pioneers of Photography, is lightweight television fare. A
souvenir for those who followed the television show, nothing
more.

Do you think there is a lot left to be discovered?
I don't think there are any major photographers to be discovered. The technical evolution has also been researched
extensively, but there is much scope for critical analysis, old
photographs seen under new aspects, national histories of the
Scandinavian and East European countries, and much better
monographs than we have had of late. Too many writers with
nothing to say compile picture books which do not convey
any meaning, either.

*Have you any thoughts on how the Royal Photographic
Society, with its great collections, has coped with its responsibilities to the photographic world?*
The R.P.S. has consistently shirked its responsibilities in the
last hundred years. In the early decades of photography, it
was a learned society. Now it has degenerated into a social
club with two meaningless titles to sell. Several times it has
been on the verge of passing away, but as the corpse provides
a dignified platform for the managers of photographic industry, the obstruction impeding the progress of photography has
remained. I acknowledge with gratitude the use of its fine

library in the early stages of my photo-historical research. I also know from personal experience that rarely could anything I wanted to see in its collection be found. It probably was too much work to untie the parcels. Never to my knowledge were any historic photographs exhibited, with the exception of Niepce's heliographs on loan to the Science Museum. I once put a similar question to the then-curator Dudley Johnston. He replied that, since the R.P.S. was a private society, it had no obligations toward anyone except its members. And as the vast majority of them showed not the slightest interest in the collection, storage was the least expensive. Now I learn that the collection is to be on public view at the Pump Room at Bath and to be commercially exploited at very high reproduction fees. Colin Ford's very sensible suggestion that the collection be bought for the nation and be used in the national interest rather than a private one found little response, I gather. The trust which members, presenting historic items or their own work, had placed in the society has been badly abused.

Presumably you had been in touch with the National Trust?
I had, indeed, for they own plenty of properties with empty top floors, carriage houses, and barns. The trouble is that the majority are situated in inaccessible places and closed to the public for half the year. Lacock Abbey would have provided a fine historic setting for photography, but I rejected it when I heard that the house was not to be used. The barn did not provide enough space for our activities. When I asked for something nearer London, I had the choice of several properties and selected Osterley House, which is not far from the Underground. The entire top floor was free, but its availability depended on the good will of the Victoria and Albert administrators of the house and of the historic rooms on the ground floor. In November 1958 I had a meeting with the then-director Trenchard Cox and Charles Gibbs-Smith, curator of the museum extensions. I was told it would not work. Even if I first presented the collection to the museum, Alison and I would still remain outsiders, not museum staff. This seemed to me to be quite an incredible excuse, and so I was informed that photography did not come within the terms of reference

of the Victoria and Albert and that they saw no reason for changing. Whereupon I could not help remarking that Victoria and Albert would turn over in their graves if they knew of this outrage against their own intentions. A couple of months ago Dr. Roy Strong changed the terms, and today there is a photographic department, nineteen years after my original conversations. The minds of civil servants work slowly.

The Victorian Society offered us two buildings they did not possess but hoped to save from demolition through a preservation order, if we could have put them to use without altering the construction. One was the Coal Exchange in the City, for which the City Corporation had other plans; the other was the old Alexandra Palace, which was a white elephant, and I said no.

Did you offer the collection to an English university or college?
There would have been no sense in that, for they are themselves handicapped with space. Unlike American colleges, British universities do not have museums or exhibition places attached to them.

Was the public appeal on BBC television timed for any special event?
When we were at our tether's end and prepared to accept Cologne's offer, the national press was full of our leaving Britain. That was in November 1961. Thereupon the BBC approached me with the splendid idea of making a film on our collection and the cramped storage space in our home. It was a ten-minute film, shown at the best time in the *Tonight* program. It was an appeal in the national interest, not a personal one. Macdonald Hastings was the speaker. My wife and I also appeared briefly. Drawers and cupboards were opened in every room, the kitchen, the loft—everywhere photographs. Friends rang me up and told me that to any businessman the publicity would have been worth £10,000.

And the result?
We all assumed there would be a nationwide response. All the BBC-TV received were two pathetic letters from schoolboys

offering to take some of the photographs, if the Gernsheims could no longer cope with the quantity! No one in the country had the slightest intention of moving a finger. Few people in Britain realized the uniqueness of the Gernsheim collection. One was Lord Snowdon.

Did you have a discussion with Lord Snowdon?
At his request a meeting was arranged at the art critic Nigel Gosling's place. Lord Snowdon told me that he had watched the BBC film and that he had been greatly impressed. He thought that something should be done to keep the collection in Britain. He mentioned that he knew the property developer Charles Clore, who was then in the news in connection with the rebuilding of Piccadilly Circus. Clore might perhaps be prepared to provide Snowdon with a freehold house for a Photography Center. This, he outlined, should have a modern department and a historical one, the whole under his direction. On the top floor there should be a restaurant, and in the basement darkrooms that could be let to amateurs by the hour. "Darkrooms," I queried, "that could be hired by the hour? I'm afraid that idea would never work. They would constantly be in use—but not for photography. And as to a restaurant, don't you think there are more than enough in the neighborhood? I should be very happy to have your collaboration in running the center, but since I was the originator of the whole scheme, it could only be in equal partnership. Apart from the building, do you think you could raise an annual grant of £10,000 for running the exhibitions, to pay for the staff, and for acquisitions?" He thought he could, but I never heard another word, and as you know, the plans for the redevelopment of Piccadilly Circus have not been accepted to this day.

And what happened subsequently?
In May 1962 the chancellor of the University of Texas, having no doubt read about all this in an interview I gave to an American journalist, sent a representative with the following offer: permanent archival space for the Gernsheim collection at Austin in a newly created photographic department, with very attractive salaries for me as director and Alison as

curator; other staff to assist us; possibility of my lecturing on history; exhibitions at the university museum in rotation with other departments. Alternatively, outright purchase of the collection. No price was discussed, as we were not considering this possibility. In fact, I was still asking for permanent exhibition space. If that had been granted, we would have gone to Austin. But after a few months I was informed that for reasons of cost this request was not feasible.

Did you then accept the purchase offer?
I left the door open, for meanwhile I received, quite out of the blue, a telegram from a businesswoman in Detroit saying that she had read that we were looking for a building with sufficient space to establish a museum of photography and to have regular exhibitions. She could offer the required 10,000 square feet and even double that amount. A friend of hers would come to London to discuss the matter with me, and was empowered to draw up a contract. Soon after, we learned that Mrs. X and a partner had acquired a former Chrysler office building with 230,000 square feet of floor space. It still needed modernizing alterations before we could move in. The ground floor was to be used as a display center for the building industry and the products of about five hundred manufacturing companies. Conference rooms, a film library of products, marketing research, and other services were planned for this and a nationwide network of thirty other display centers. It was a new concept backed, apparently, by leading names in the business world, and it sounded good. We were to provide the cultural background to attract the public with exhibitions. They were to be the focal point, and we were assured complete freedom in our activity. A Gernsheim Museum of Photography Foundation was registered in Detroit in October, and the following January we flew over with a large slice of our exhibition material. The mayor of Detroit received us and made us honorary citizens. We had a grand apartment in one of the leading hotels, with a car at our service to keep us content while waiting for the modernization, which was supposed to begin any moment. We waited for Godot from week to week and month to month. The mysterious Godot was cash from

Texas oil wells that didn't gush. In March we were looking for alternative exhibition possibilities and were invited to participate in the Detroit Arts Festival the following month, lasting until the middle of May. None of the cultural institutions could provide space for the exhibition as a whole, and a very sensible division was arrived at by showing Victorian photography at Wayne State University, which also printed the catalogue; modern photography at the Detroit Institute of Arts; books and albums at the public library; and apparatus at the Historical Museum. All four places lie within a few minutes' walking distance from one another. "Creative Photography, 1826 to the Present" remains to this day the largest retrospective photographic exhibition ever arranged. It comprised over one thousand items. It was a great success.

Did you pursue any alternative possibilities for your collection?
We had talks with the university and the Institute of Arts, but they soon petered out for lack of funds and space. Despite the great pioneer work done by George Eastman House and the Museum of Modern Art, I soon realized that the situation in the United States was pretty much the same as in Europe. There was plenty of money for art, but none for photography. That was the sort of thing you expected to be donated. The Museum of Modern Art paid ten dollars for a modern photograph (if it wasn't presented), but had no difficulty in finding donors spending one hundred thousand on a painting. We were invited to have talks with officials of the Library of Congress and the Smithsonian Institution in Washington. Both were interested in the acquisition for archival purposes. The former needed an act of Congress for the $500,000 I was asking; the latter vainly chased a possible donor who was traveling in Europe. Two household names in greeting cards and soft drinks respectively also showed interest for publicity purposes, but we had no intention of becoming a traveling circus by courtesy of X or Y. After this lesson I saw the Texas offer in a new light; it showed great vision and I contacted them again. We were undecided, however, whether to go with the collection or to sell, and in sounding out all my American friends, I found that they were unanimous in their advice to

sell. They felt that we, used to the culture of the European continent, would not be happy there, and that the climate wouldn't suit us. Mentioning this to the university's representative, he said: "Don't worry. During the hot summer months you will be free to tour with an exhibition or to do research for a new book in Europe. Whatever you do will be in the interests of the university. You will enjoy much freedom." All the same, we decided to sell and live in Switzerland.

Did you previously offer the collection to the Museum of Modern Art or George Eastman House?
I did. Both John Szarkowski and Beaumont Newhall came to see the Detroit exhibitions. John thought that MOMA would not be interested "because they are primarily purchasing contemporary art, and the strength of your collection lies largely in the historical material." He was right. MOMA for years had refused to spend $30,000 on acquiring the unique Atget collection of Berenice Abbott and Julian Levy. Beaumont also said, "No, Helmut. We've got too much of the same Victorian photography." As a flashback, I might mention that in 1953 Steichen asked me in London whether I would be willing to join forces with Beaumont. As a trustee of George Eastman House, he thought he could arrange it. But I didn't think there was any point in having two queens in one hive. Nor did we relish the idea of being penned up for life in an industrial place like Rochester.

What was your next move?
While still in Detroit debating what to do, we received a letter from the Swedish Minister of Culture inviting us to come to Stockholm to start a photomuseum as part of the Museum of Modern Art. We had had discussions in Stockholm in 1957 while exhibiting at the Nordisk Museum. Meanwhile, the plans had matured to a decision, but the offer came too late. We were worn out with discussions and had come to an agreement with Texas. In the end, the Swedish state bought all my duplicates in the collection, and this was, and is, the foundation of their photomuseum. During the six-month stay in the United States, I broke the long waiting periods with lectures at various

museums and universities until my lawyers advised us to leave
the country, as we would otherwise become liable to United
States tax. Before returning to England, we toured Canada
for a while. At the end of August, I sent a cable to Texas
accepting their offer of purchase.

For how much?
I am not sure whether I am free to mention the figure. It was
considerably less than the half million dollars I had asked for.
As there had been no photographic auction since 1961, no
one had any means of assessing the value. Now the collection
would probably fetch $4–5 million at auction, but no institu-
tion could afford to spend such an amount, and I would never
have considered breaking up the collection to make more.
I had not collected for speculation. The collection continues
to exist under the name of its founder, is being used and
enlarged, and is free to any visitor. I'm happy with the way
things have turned out in the end.

Why did you decide to leave Britain and move to Switzerland?
We had wanted to live in or near Lugano ever since we first
discovered this beautiful spot in 1947, but my work and future
was bound up with London. It was not until I had severed the
ties with our collection that we could think of buying an apartment in this lovely, subtropical climate. Thirty-three thousand
photographs and 4,000 books had become too much for two
people to cope with, and too costly in insurance. I don't think
any outsider can imagine the constant pressure of work that
forced us to keep a fourteen-hour timetable for eighteen years.
Five people are engaged at Texas to do the work we formerly
did alone, and they don't collect the way I did, they don't
arrange an exhibition every year; neither do they write the
books and articles on which my income depended.

What have you been doing since you moved to Switzerland?
I am as busy as ever preparing enlarged and revised editions
of a number of books. I write articles, lecture, and have an
enormous correspondence to deal with, all typed by myself

since Alison's death in 1969. For the last ten years I have been advisor to the editor of the *Encyclopaedia Britannica*. For a year I was lecturer on African art and the history of photography at an American university college. I'm also a trustee of the Swiss Foundation of Photography.

Are you working on any particular projects at the moment?
Next year a new edition of *Alvin Langdon Coburn, Photographer* will appear. At the moment I'm up to my eyes in work preparing *A Bibliography of British Photographic Literature* and *A Bibliography of British Books Illustrated with Original Photographs*, both for the period 1839–75. For twenty years no publisher showed any interest in these bibliographies—and I must have asked at least as many. Yet all of a sudden three publishers want it, and one of them, I'm pleased to say, is Derby Lonsdale College. After this, a Swiss publisher wants to bring out an enlarged edition of my big *History* in two volumes, in English and German. I have also been invited by the Universities of Texas, Georgia, and Jerusalem to teach for a semester as a Distinguished Visiting Professor. I really don't have to worry about ever being idle.

Where do you think the medium may go in the future?
I am following contemporary trends very closely, but I doubt that any of them have any staying power. At the moment, many young European photographers ape the Americans, whether good or bad, mostly bad, I'm afraid, although we in Europe can offer the United States productions on a much higher intellectual level. Unfortunately, they do not receive any publicity in *Camera* magazine, which is edited with the intent of popularizing American trends and completely disregarding European photography. Hence, the excellent European work is not known across the Atlantic and many critics falsely assume that it does not exist. They had not been aware of the pioneers of new objectivity, of photojournalism, fotoform, and subjective photography, either, until I exhibited them in 1963. We in Europe do not employ the same export methods. We have a number of other magazines, of course, but of these only *Creative Camera*, being in English, is seen in the United

States. To mention but a few names of contemporary European photographers I have in mind: Paul Almassy, Pierre Cordier, Lucien Clergue, Pino dal Gal, Jean Dieuzaide, Erwin Fieger, Franco Fontana, Robert Häusser, Victor Gianella, Niggi Messerli, Jean Mohr, Raymond Moore, Floris Neusüss, Hans Silvester, Jean P. Sudre, André Cros. Some work in reportage, others make abstractions from nature, and a few experiment in conceptual photography. All of them still have something new to add to photographic image-making and beat hollow any recent American work I have seen publicized in *Camera*. There are also some excellent Czech and Polish photographers.

How would you detail your criticism of the young American photographers?
Most of it lacks form and content, the essential ingredients of any art. Some is vulgar and tasteless, reflecting on the producer. Westerns, cheap crime and sex films, and commercial television have debased American standards and have also led to a marked deterioration in European standards in the last twenty years. You can notice this not only in film and photography but in all fields of contemporary life. There are too many snapshooters today clicking the shutter on utter banalities. This is, I think, my main criticism, this fetish of brainless snapshooting—in Westerns it is brainless, senseless shooting— or glorified banality, images that belong in, and any critical mind would consign to, the wastepaper basket. Every American teenager considers himself the producer of masterpieces worthy of an exhibition or a portfolio. And if you don't agree with them, they persuade themselves that you, the critic, are an old fogey. That was often enough the case in the past in art and photography, but it is too facile an excuse for expecting recognition of rubbish. These youngsters are not only uncritical but also arrogant. Apart from the snapshot and banality fetish, there is another American trend which we see a good deal in Europe. It is this so-called art photography, which is artificial picture-making in modern dress, frequently undress, and in worse taste than anything the H. P. Robinson pictorial school ever committed to paper. Lastly, we have sequences that are not sequences in a picture-story sense but

multiple repetitions of the same boring subject with meaningless variations.

Maybe, when everyone is thoroughly sick of all this pop photography, a creative mind will emerge again. America was rich in great photographers between 1925 and 1965, but much of what parades at the moment under creative photography is not worth serious consideration.

May 1977

S E L E C T E D   B I B L I O G R A P H Y

Alvin Langdon Coburn: Photographer. Edited by Helmut and Alison Gernsheim. New York: Praeger, 1966.
A Concise History of Photography, by Helmut and Alison Gernsheim. New York: Grosset and Dunlap, 1968.
Creative Photography: Aesthetic Trends 1839–1960, by Helmut Gernsheim. London: Faber and Faber, 1962.
The History of Photography: From the Camera Obscura to the Beginning of the Modern Era, by Helmut and Alison Gernsheim. New York: McGraw-Hill, 1969.
Julia Margaret Cameron: Her Life and Photographic Work, by Helmut Gernsheim. Millerton, New York: Aperture, 1975.
L. J. M. Daguerre: The History of the Diorama and the Daguerreotype, by Helmut and Alison Gernsheim. New York: Dover, 1968.
Lewis Carroll: Photographer, by Helmut Gernsheim. New York: Dover, 1969.
Masterpieces of Victorian Photography, by Helmut Gernsheim, with a foreword by C. H. Gibbs-Smith. London: Phaidon Press, 1951.
The New Photo Vision, by Helmut Gernsheim. London: Fountain Press, 1942.
Roger Fenton: Photographer of the Crimean War, by Helmut and Alison Gernsheim. New York: Arno Press, 1973.

Brett Weston

(BORN 1 9 1 1 / AMERICAN)

Paul Hill

How did you become involved with photography?
Well, of course, through my father, who I was very close to.
I appreciated his work and I loved it. Then, when we went to
Mexico in 1925, when I was about twelve years old, he showed
me how to use his 3¼ x 4¼ inch Graflex. He put it on a
tripod and gave me some idea of exposure (in those days
we had no meters). I looked into the camera, at the back in
the ground glass—it was tremendously exciting. I've never

been the same since. But he left me very much alone; he never tried to steer me intellectually.

Did you have some hard times in Mexico?
Oh, yes, my father was struggling. I was used to that, all my life. It was nothing new. In fact, I still live a spartan life.

Did meeting any of the great revolutionary artists in Mexico influence you?
It had a big impact on me. It was a very formative period in my life. I knew Orozco, Diego Rivera, and Charlot. I got my education through these people.

Did they see any of your work?
No. They were more involved with my father. I was only a child, you know, though fairly mature in some areas.

What happened when you came back to America?
We went back to Los Angeles. Dad had a studio in Glendale, and we lived together during that period, the late twenties.

When was your first show?
Actually, the first show was a joint show with my dad when I was fifteen. Barbara Morgan arranged it before she married Herb Morgan of Morgan and Morgan. She was a lovely young woman, a teacher in the art department at the University of Southern California. Then I had an exhibition in Stuttgart about 1928 or 1929.

Was that the "Film und Foto" show?
I believe so.

How old were you?
I was about seventeen. They used things that I did when I was thirteen or fourteen.

What sort of work did you show?
Mostly, they were fairly simple arrangements—abstractions,

I was doing them even then. I was also in a photo publication in Germany, I forget the name of it.

Was that Photo Eye?
I think so.

Was it about this time that you met Eisenstein?
Oh, that was a strange thing. I was about nineteen and living in an old house in Hollywood. A friend of mine and my father, Seymour Stern, a young Communist who worked in one of the Hollywood studios, asked me if I wanted to photograph Eisenstein. I had seen his films, and I admired his work very much. After I had photographed him, he looked at a few of my prints. I'd done one of an ear and three fingers, and he said, "I want that!" He just made off with it! One of the greatest compliments of my life.

What brought about the move from Hollywood to Carmel?
My father had a friend named Johan Hagemeyer, who lived in Carmel, and he rented a studio from him. Eventually they split up, and their friendship came to an end over something trivial. Johan was jealous because he always thought that he was the great Western photographer. He was a charming, brilliant man, Dutch, very debonair. He and Dad were very close, particularly during World War I.

How did they discover Point Lobos?
In 1915, Dad and Johan hitchhiked from Los Angeles to San Francisco and Carmel. Dad saw Lobos for the first time then. But we both worked there in 1929, when we drove out together.

What was it like living in that art colony on the West Coast?
It wasn't really a big art colony, but it had always been a center for writers and painters. Robinson Jeffers, the great poet, was there, and many others.

Did they have any effect on your work?
Of course.

You had a show about that time, didn't you?
I had a show at a gallery in Carmel in 1930, one of my first shows. Then later, a more important show, in 1932, at the de Young Museum, San Francisco. That was my first big one-man show.

How many prints were in that?
I've forgotten, about fifty.

It covered your work up to that time?
Yes. From 1925 to 1930, which was not a very long time. But in those days a year was a long time. Today the years go by much too fast.

How did you get involved with Group f/64?
I was in Santa Barbara at that time, and Ansel Adams, my father, Willard Van Dyke, and a few others formed this organization. I was never a member, but they invited me to participate in their first show, and that's how I got involved.

Had you moved away from your father by then?
Yes, we broke up in the early thirties. I spread my wings. He gave me the car, fifty dollars, and a camera—which was a lot in those days.

How were you earning your living at that time?
Taking portraits.

You were a commercial photographer?
Yes, but a very bad businessman! I had no real studio, so I did home portraits. At the beginning of the Depression, I was barely eking out a living—portraits for ten dollars plus three prints.

What was it like to be a young photographer in the Depression?
It was rough going, but food was cheap. You could buy a lot of lettuce for a penny, an avocado for a nickel, a pound of cottage cheese for ten cents.

Did you ever get involved with any of the public-works photographic projects?
Yes, I was with the W.P.A. for a couple of years, and was actually a supervisor for one of the projects, but I used to disappear and go off photographing. I'm not much of a joiner or an organizer. I did the same in the Army.

When did you start sculpting?
About 1929. I do sculpture with a lump of wood and tools, it's in my blood. My grandfather was a shipbuilder and a carpenter, and my brother's a fine cabinetmaker. I love tools and machines, but it goes beyond that.

Did your photography influence your sculpture?
Very much, back and forth. I've shown some and sold some, but I'm primarily a photographer.

Has the quality of light been important in your work?
That's the most important thing of all, I think. If you've no sense of light, you might as well forget about it.

Does it mean any particular thing to you?
Photographically, yes, of course. It's throughout my work: a sense of light, a feeling for it, a love for it.

You say that you're interested in machines?
I photograph man-made things a great deal. It's true, I am a modern man in many ways. I love modern architecture, modern machines and tools.

The natural landscape?
I love that also—I don't limit myself. I hope I'm not too stylized or too much in a rut. I use various types of cameras and photograph anything, anytime. It could be something modern or an ancient rock, it doesn't matter. But, unless a landscape is invested with a sense of mystery, it is no better than a postcard.

Would you agree that in your father's work there was a sensuous, almost an erotic, quality, and in yours the concerns are more graphic and formalistic?
I suppose so. I've never thrashed this out intellectually with myself, but there is an enormous difference. There is an influence—way back especially—but our work is so different.

What do you feel to be the basic difference between your work and your father's?
Oh, God, it's hard to verbalize it. My work is, perhaps, more graphic, but at times it is more sensual. I don't know. I can't do it. You'll have to look at his work and look at mine. The difference is enormous, that's all.

What was it like, living very close to a person who was almost a legend in his own lifetime?
It was a fabulous experience. He was such a big person, he would say that I had influenced him. We were very close, we traveled and worked together for years, we even chased the same girls often. He called me his brother—we were great friends. He would say that I was his best audience. I loved his work and had a real appreciation of it.

Apart from your father, who would you say have been the major influences on you?
There have been many people, women and men. But I was never a follower, consciously, of any tradition other than perhaps the big-view camera. I now use the small cameras a great deal, however.

What moved you to go toward the really big-view camera, the 11 x 14 inch?
Just for a change of pace. That is why I went to the Rollei, the Mamiyaflex, the RB67, and also the single-lens Rollei. For a change of pace. You get in a rut. Basically I still love the big-view camera. It's pretty hard to beat that quality. It's a different tool, that's all. You can't do with that what you can do with your 35 mm. There's no way.

What did you do during World War II?
They made me a truck driver. They knew about my photography and they wanted to make me an instructor in New York, but I didn't want to do that.

Instruct what?
Photography. But after I'd had truck-driver training, I finally got sent to a photographic school, where they thought I would like to teach, but I didn't want to at all, I really wanted to photograph New York. I didn't feel I would be a good teacher.

So what work were you doing at that time in New York?
Photographing with the 11 x 14 and the 8 x 10.

What was it like, going through the streets of New York with an 11 x 14 camera?
Well, in those days there was less congestion. I think I even had my little car there and I used to be able to park everywhere and anywhere.

Did you ever meet Stieglitz or any of the people from An American Place?
Yes, I met Stieglitz very casually just before he died. Nancy Newhall took me over, and he was very friendly and warm. I'd heard all these hair-raising stories about old Stieglitz. Dad had seen him many years earlier, and Willard Van Dyke had seen him and couldn't stand him. I saw him just that one time, but I saw a great deal of Paul Strand and Nancy Newhall.

How did Strand feel about your work?
I'm not sure. One night Nancy had a party. Cartier-Bresson was there with his Oriental wife, and Paul Strand and his new wife were also there—people I knew about but hadn't met. Nancy asked me to show some prints. It didn't bother me at all who I showed them to. I was fairly arrogant—I guess I'm even more so now! I don't know, but it seems to me if you're in love with your work, you've got to be. An artist is just that way. Anyway, I showed my work and Strand's wife said:

"Paul, let's buy some of Brett's prints." He didn't say a word, not a word—so that's the answer!

What did Cartier-Bresson think about them?
Not much. But this was a long time ago. But then I don't think he ever cared for my father's work, either.

What opinions did your father have of the Stieglitz circle?
Dad was very stimulated by Stieglitz. They corresponded for twenty years. Dad let me read the letters and he'd also read them aloud to me. I think Stieglitz was interested in my father, but Dad didn't become a follower. He was moved, stimulated, by Stieglitz, but he was not influenced deeply. When Dad became famous, I think probably Stieglitz resented the fact that he didn't pay tribute to him. Yet, I think Dad did in his way. I don't admire Stieglitz's work, but he was a stepping-stone, he helped us all.

We were talking about influences a moment ago . . .
I think I've been moved deeply by two different wives. My first wife was a magnificent woman, Elinore, and then later Dody, who was a fine photographer. She was my father's protégée, and we eventually married. She was a fine influence. Johan Hagemeyer was another influence. Similarly Beaumont Newhall and his late wife, Nancy. Things rub off from all these people. I never consciously followed anybody. I was self-assured and direct when I was a child and a young man, and I've always been that way.

How did you make a living after World War II?
Back to my bread-and-butter—portraits.

Where did you live at that time?
I had a house in Santa Monica. We eventually came to Carmel and bought a place. My dad's health was failing, and Cole and I sold our respective houses in Santa Monica and moved to Carmel. We bought a ranch together and I took my daughter Erica up there with me. I was also trying to work in color, which I did very badly. I had an occasional job for

Holiday magazine. I was trying, but my heart wasn't in it. It was depressing. My father was very frail, but he still retained his sense of humor. It was a tragic time for all of us, though. We'd see him constantly, and Dody was there during that period. He was in love with her, but he was an old man and she was a young woman, it just didn't work. That was in the late forties and early fifties.

How did the 1952 portfolio of your father's work come about?
As I recall, Dody proposed it and I was all for it, so we put it up to my father. The very thought of such an amount of work was staggering. I said: "Dad, we'll do it. You just direct it, you choose the negatives and we'll do it." We had to twist his arm a bit, but he was frail and he gave in.

You printed all the work?
I did the basic printing, but my brother Cole helped briefly. Dody helped a great deal, and our close friends Morley and Frances Baer also helped. It was a real labor of love. We did 105 portfolios. Dad would approve the first master print; then he would say: "Duplicate that." We made nearly 150 prints to get 105 faultless ones. It was very difficult work. The printing lasted for two weeks. The portfolios cost $100 apiece, but we couldn't sell them. Now they are worth $6,000 each. Of course, we were not promoters, we Westons, let's face it. Dad had only $300 in the bank at the end, that's all he had. But gradually the portfolios started to sell. We raised the price to $200 and people balked at that, but we finally sold them. Now, people scream for them, and one print from the portfolio could sell for $500–$800.

How did your father feel about the publication of your book Brett Weston Photographs, *in 1956?*
He was delighted.

How did you feel about it?
I was very thrilled, very honored.

How did the book come about?

Through Merle Armitage, who was a close family friend. He was a promoter of opera and theater, and he published books as a hobby. He was the first person to do a book of my father's work and the first person to do a book on me.

How was it received?
I don't know. It was a long time ago, I've forgotten. I don't pay much attention to the write-ups, anyway. I've had reviews over the past forty-five years, and they're mostly worthless. What they say is often distorted, badly written, and misquoted, right down the line.

What interests do you have outside photography?
I read a great deal and I get very involved with women. I'm a chip off the old block!

How many times have you been married?
Four. I've avoided various other invitations to marriage. Once they think they have you nailed, they change, you know.

Are you married at the moment?
No, no. Four times is enough. You never know, though!

Any other interests?
My whole life is photography, but I love music. I have dear friends who are musicians and writers as well as photographers. I also love traveling.

What impels you to travel?
New imagery. It's exciting. We Americans are wanderers.

Do you think being a Westerner has had an effect on you?
Sure. I'm very much a Westerner in many ways, although I've spent a great deal of time in Europe as well as in the United States.

Have you received any grants?
Yes, I had a Guggenheim many years ago, and I had a National Endowment of the Arts grant to go to Alaska.

Why did you go to Alaska?
Just the lure of adventure. I was out there when I was a kid and I had always wanted to go back. It's fabulous country, immense. You can put Texas in one corner of Alaska, or half of Europe.

What sort of work did you find you were doing in Alaska?
It's a very black-and-white country; intense black shadows, and whites. Snow, ice, and glaciers.

Have you ever been tempted to go into teaching?
No, no. I've been invited by universities to teach, which amuses me because I never went to college. I never went beyond sixth grade. I'm not really a teacher, I'm too self-centered in my work, but I've conducted a few workshops on a very informal basis, for money, or just for a change of pace.

Do you see the photographs from your travels as part of books?
When I photograph, I don't have anything in mind except the photograph. I don't think in terms of magazines, books, or promotions. I photograph for the love and the excitement. It's just a self-centered, dedicated thing.

How often do you exhibit?
Sometimes I've had four shows running simultaneously. I've had more than 100 one-man shows. But it's bread-and-butter, you know—if I didn't show my work, I wouldn't eat! For the last thirty years I've existed on the sale of my personal creative work, which is rare in our times. But when I photograph, I don't photograph with the idea of selling. I don't have this in mind at all.

Have you made a lot of money from photography?
Oh, no—my God! But last year I had a great number of large sales, as much as I've had in the last ten years combined. I guess it's a sudden awareness of photography, perhaps also personal recognition. People are starting to collect photographs. I've had three different sales, over $10,000 apiece, which is incredible for me, considering my simple way of life.

My father never had that in his whole life. The biggest amount he made from a sale was probably a thousand dollars. He had a rough time. As you can read in the *Daybooks*, he was always worrying about money. When he made a ten-dollar sale, he was thrilled to death!

What future projects do you have in mind?
I'm doing a new edition of the *White Sands Portfolio* and I'm in the middle of an Oregon portfolio.

Looking at your fifty-year retrospective, is there a major concern that seems evident in all your work?
No, I don't analyze my work in those terms.

Do you look at your work closely?
Oh, I do. I tear it to shreds. I'm very hard on myself.

Is it an intuitive process?
Yes, I think it is largely.

What are you looking for?
You're trying to pin me down! I'm not a verbal person. Look at my work and decide for yourself. It's hard to put it into words.

Do you have any kind of general philosophy?
Yes, a dedication to photography and freedom. That's all I want. I don't want a lot of money. Freedom is the paramount thing—the freedom to work. It's very hard in our times, with all the material abundance around us, to have it. We're distracted—we want this and we want that.

Materialistic considerations have never been terribly important to you, then?
Well, up to a point, they are. I have to buy film! I'm concerned about money, but that's not my goal. I want to have enough money to be free—this is the ultimate wealth. People like Paul Strand and Stieglitz had money. I don't know how much, but enough to be free.

Do you feel you have enough freedom?
More than ever, and for the first time in my life. Last year I had the freedom to travel, and I had the equipment I wanted, and the kind of car I wanted.

Is there anything that you are trying to show people through your photographs?
No. I don't photograph for other people. I love an audience, mind you. Once I've got them there, then I love an audience. Not a big audience, though. I'd rather please ten people I respect than ten million I don't. But I don't play to an audience, I do it for myself.

March 1975

BOOKS OF WESTON PHOTOGRAPHS

Brett Weston. Aperture, Volume 7, Number 4. Millerton, New York: Aperture, 1960.

Brett Weston: Photographs. Text by Merle Armitage. New York: E. Weyhe, 1956.

Brett Weston: Photographs. Introduction by Nancy Newhall. Fort Worth, Texas: Amon Carter Museum of Western Art, 1966.

Brett Weston: Voyage of the Eye. Afterword by Beaumont Newhall. Millerton, New York: Aperture, 1975.

Manuel Alvarez Bravo

(B O R N   1 9 0 4 / M E X I C A N)

Paul Hill

How long have you been taking pictures?
More or less from 1922, not seriously to start with, though.

Did you get involved with photography as a child?
No, not really. I started when I was twenty years old.

Was there an art background in your family?
My grandfather was a painter who loved photography, and my father made portraits.

What was your father's job?
He was a teacher in a secondary school in Mexico City.

What effect did the revolution in Mexico have on your life as a boy?
The aspect of death had a great influence on me. During the revolution I was in a boarding school, and sometimes on my way to school I would hear rifle shots. During peaceful periods we used to go to a little hill outside the village, and sometimes we would find a dead body.

In Mexico City?
Yes. In a suburb called Tlalpan.

What effect did seeing death have on you as a young boy?
One does not exactly know how one's own sensibility and mentality are formed. It undoubtedly had an influence on me. I was also interested in the ceremony of November 12—the Ceremony of All Dead, which is also a celebration. On this occasion they used to sell children toys representing death—skulls made of sugar which we would eat. I think this is where the real feeling of Mexican duality comes from—the duality of life and death.

Did the revolution start your interest in the arts or was it your family's influence?
It was more my family's influence.

Why did you decide to study accountancy and not one of the arts?
Those days were very difficult and it was important to study something profitable, something that would help the family economically.

Where did you work?
I started with commercial companies and stayed with them for some time. A rather important year was 1916, which was when I started to work for the National Treasury.

Why did you study art subjects in the evenings?
The reason was the restlessness of my age. It was something different, something immediately practical, something that could satisfy another part of me. I studied literature at the Central School of Classic Art, then some painting as well. But when I was given the camera, it gave me more independence and enjoyment.

Personal fulfillment?
It was a very pleasant fulfillment, but I didn't consider it very significant until later, around 1925.

How did you become a professional photographer?
When Tina Modotti left Mexico in 1930, I took over her job, which was photographing paintings. I was working as an accountant for the Mexican government at the time.

What was your relationship with Tina Modotti? Was she an important person to you?
Yes, she was an excellent friend of mine. She used to show me her photographs and also those that Edward Weston was sending her. Although she and Weston were not living together any more, they had remained very good friends.

How did you first meet her?
I used to buy magazines. There I saw her photographs, and through one of the magazines I got hold of her address and telephone number and gave her a ring.

Was it her photographs, her art, or her political views that first fascinated you?
It was mainly her art. But all the *inteligencia* of Mexico were left-wing, so her political views were not unusual.

How did she and painters like Diego Rivera, Orozco, and Siqueiros react to your work?
Very positively. But also I had direct criticism, especially from Diego Rivera. I think that Diego also had a great influence on Tina and Weston. When he was criticizing my work, or a

young painter's work, he criticized the substance of the work, rather than the sentiments behind it.

Why did you send your photographs to Edward Weston?
Tina once told me that he was collecting photographs for an exhibition in Germany, *"Film und Foto."*

Did you ever meet Weston?
No. My photographs also arrived too late for the exhibition!

Did his comments about your work influence you?
The correspondence I had with him would have had more importance for me if I hadn't my own problems. And writing letters was always difficult for me.

What did you think of Weston's Mexican work?
I think it had no more importance than the work he did when he returned to the States, but he was certainly influenced by the muralists in Mexico.

Did you like his work?
Yes. I liked the neatness, the purity of the conception, and the realization.

Did anyone else outside Mexico see your work?
Henri Cartier-Bresson and Paul Strand. My photographs did not go out of Mexico until much later. The first time I sent them outside Mexico City was for a touring exhibition with Cartier-Bresson. It was, in fact, the same exhibition we had together in the Palacio de Bellas Artes in Mexico, which was also when I first met Bresson.

The Museum of Modern Art, New York, first acquired some of your work in 1931. How did this come about?
I didn't sell them to MOMA. I sold them to a Mr. Kaufman, who then donated them to the museum.

You were earning your living at that time as a professional photographer?
I started to work professionally around 1928.

How did you become involved with teaching?
I did not have much work with the painters, so I gave lectures at the Academy of San Carlos. I was teaching *and* learning about photography at the same time.

What was your approach to teaching then?
It was partly based on discussions which were not directly connected with photography. I divided my lectures into two approaches—discussions about literature, music, painting, and so on; and then practical work.

What part did you enjoy teaching most?
The first one, because it was more flexible.

This was the early thirties and a very political time in Mexico. How were you involved?
The whole intellectual world was left-wing—but I never joined the Party. I did belong to a league which was called LEAR (The Revolutionary League of Writers and Artists), but at the same time I was friends with some artists who were not left-wing. I always believed that talent and sensibility had nothing to do with politics.

At this time your great friend Tina Modotti was deported for her political views. Did you get involved?
I was the only person to take her to the train station, and I waited with her until the train left.

Were you alone because other artists were frightened to be seen with her?
People who belonged to the Party were not frightened, but they were not provocative, either. They preferred to work peacefully.

Did the government put pressure on you because of your association with her?
Absolutely not.

Did you know the work of the Farm Security Administration in the United States?
Not at the time. I learned about it later when the Anna Sokolow Dancing Group came to Mexico. Then I realized that the F.S.A. was helping artists. But during the Depression, my own life was difficult enough.

How was your 1935 exhibition with Cartier-Bresson received?
Photography was not very popular in Mexico. People were interested in painters and writers, but not in photographers. The only thing I can say is that there was a great interest in Cartier-Bresson's work.

Did you go abroad?
Yes, I visited Chicago, probably in 1935.

What did you think of America and the photography you saw there?
I did not see any photographs on that visit.

Why did you go to Chicago?
I had two exhibitions in Chicago. One at the Almer Coe Optical Company, and the other at Hull House, which was open to all artists. This exhibition was organized by a very good American friend of mine, Emily Edwards. Originally I did not bring photographs to exhibit there but just to show them to people I knew.

How did you meet Emily Edwards?
I met her in Mexico. She was a very good friend of Diego Rivera. Diego taught her how to analyze paintings by using photography.

What did she think of your work?
She found my work very calm, and liked the way I used and composed to the *golden rule*. We were very good friends indeed. Afterward we worked on a book called *The Painted Walls of Mexico*.

In 1934 you had an exhibition at the Julien Levy Gallery in
New York with Walker Evans and Cartier-Bresson. Did this
have great meaning for you?
Yes. The pleasure of communication, the pleasure of doing
what one likes, the pleasure of seeing.

André Breton, the leader of the Surrealists, came to Mexico.
How did he meet you?
Breton was living in Diego Rivera's house, and it was at
Diego's that we met.

What did he say about your photographs?
He liked them very much.

Did he feel there was a surrealistic element in them?
I don't think so. Breton had a great ability to recognize the
authentic. He would, for example, immediately notice a painter
who falsely tried to be surrealistic. Art for him, if not surrealist, had to have dimensions of the fantastic.

How many of your photographs did he publish in his maga-
zine?
I am not quite sure, eight or ten perhaps. He arranged an
exhibition in Paris at Renou en Colle, called "Mexico." I
had a few photographs in that exhibition.

What was the main thing that Breton saw in your work?
Probably the relationship of the photographic values to the
content, although he also talked about photographic quality
and photographic realization. He was, however, most impressed by the content.

By the content, do you mean the subject matter or do you
mean the way the subject matter is used?
I mean the way the subject matter is used.

Did Surrealism have an effect on you then?
Probably not. I knew about it, through some French maga-

zines; and I might have produced some work under its influence.

What commissioned work did you do at this time?
There was never much photographic work in Mexico, but I did lots of portraiture.

How did you exist?
I taught photography, and I knew lots of painters who gave me jobs. But it was very difficult.

In 1933 you first met Paul Strand. What was the consequence of this meeting?
I was really unaware of the importance these meetings with authors, photographers, and painters had for me.

Did Strand interest you in film?
Yes. I knew his film *The Wave.* Interestingly, while Strand was working on his film by the river in Vera Cruz, I produced my photograph "The Assassinated Worker" quite nearby.

There was a great deal of interest in Eisenstein's work in Mexico. Did you ever talk to him while he was in the country?
Very little—he didn't speak Spanish, and I didn't have a translator.

In 1942 the Photo League in New York had an exhibition of your pictures. How did you become associated with them?
Through the Anna Sokolow group. I was a friend of one of the girls of the group, Sasha, who told her husband, Henry Rothman, about me. He invited me to exhibit in New York.

At this time you got involved in teaching at a school where they taught filmmaking, didn't you?
I worked for the Mexican film industry from 1943 to 1959. During those years I taught photography, *not* cinematography, at the Film Institute in Mexico City. I taught it as a creative medium, but at that time lots of people were only interested in the technical aspects of photography.

Why did you leave the job in 1959?
Because in 1959 the Fondo Editorial de la Plástica Mexicana was started, and I joined it as a member of the technical committee.

Did you exhibit much?
For sixteen years I did very little personal work and had only one exhibition, in 1957, at the National Institute of Art.

Your new job was chief photographer at the foundation. What did you do?
To be a member of the technical committee meant making photographs and promoting Mexican art around the country and abroad.

How did you do this—through exhibitions or books?
Through books.

How did you come to be in an exhibition in 1945 at the Museum of Modern Art in Moscow?
They collected photographs in Mexico for Moscow, so I gave my photographs; and I never saw them again. They were not meant for any exhibition, they were just photographs to be given away.

In 1955 Edward Steichen invited you to participate in the "Family of Man" exhibition, in which you showed two photographs. What was your opinion of the exhibition?
I think that the "Family of Man" was one of the most important exhibitions ever made—not so much as a photographic exhibition, but as a concept.

Was it seen widely in Mexico?
Not really. It was not put up well. It was held in a building which had been an embassy.

How did you come to know Edward Steichen?
I did not meet Steichen. Since MOMA had a small collection of my photographs, he knew about me. They had a circular

which they sent to photographers asking them to send photographs to the museum.

Was there a growing philosophical concern that was becoming evident in your work at this time?
I think that a visual artist's philosophy develops much more freely than a writer's or a thinker's philosophy. It is not so disciplined. The photographer works with both his eyes and his mind.

You have traveled in Europe. Do you feel that your work has more affinity to European rather than to American photography?
I think it consists of both. It's rather difficult to separate the traditions, which are a series of mutual influences. I think that my work is more related to Mexican art and Mexican life than to photographic traditions.

It has been said that your work deals with a kind of cultural documentation, even spiritual documentation.
The most immediate form of traveling and getting away from the places where one is constantly living—a kind of escapism, I suppose—is in your own countryside. It is the closest thing you have, the most direct thing as well; I was always interested in the native life of my country.

Why do you title your photographs?
When you put an exhibition up, you aim for two things, one of which—the most difficult one—is good titles. Usually the titles are rather obvious and absurd, with no objectivity— that's when you put the title just to distinguish one photograph from the other. There is no doubt at all that the title which is invented and not obvious is the most real one—the one which most accurately defines the photograph.

Your work seems so full of personal symbolism. Do you see yourself working in a symbolist tradition?
I think that the symbols one can find in my photographs

essentially refer to life and death. But naturally there are symbols which do refer not to these two aspects but to Freudian symbolism, where the symbol occurs regularly. You, therefore, produce an exterior symbol, a symbol which is there and might, for example, refer to your constant preoccupations. It is true that any work can have symbols which have been produced unintentionally, but it is dangerous for these to be studied too seriously.

You seem to deal with a kind of sexuality in your nudes. You ask the viewer to look and understand a whole new reference point. Is it something that you do purposely?
I think that a great part of it is conscious. For example, the lying nude portrays *life*—woman—but shows also the danger of this life.

Do the bandages in some of the nudes have any special significance?
The bandages most certainly originate from a visual experience. I found the relationship very recently. I used to watch the Anna Sokolow group, and the girls used to bandage their feet for the rehearsals.

The cactus along the side of the woman, and the way she is bandaged—it seems highly ritualistic and also strangely religious.
I do not think so. But it might be possible that it deals with sacrifice. Since people have been insisting on reading and interpreting my photographs and establishing things that influenced my work, I thought about it myself, and I came to the conclusion that Rousseau's "Bohemia" had a great influence on me.

It seems in your pictures that sometimes the light not so much gives life as oppresses it in a way.
I think that light and shadow have exactly the same duality that exists between life and death. In a certain way the shadow, the absence of light, is the negation of the light.

Have you pursued any constant philosophical concern in your work?
No. I believe in experience through all the senses—through literature, music, friendship, art, etc. All of them produce in a person a series of experiences which accumulate, and these accumulated experiences form a philosophy—not a closed, but an open, one. The artist always works with his eyes.

Your work has only recently been widely recognized. What do you feel about this?
I do not think an artist should change once he becomes widely recognized. It is a pleasure to see that what one does has a significance, communicates with other people, produces an interest and pleasure. This does not mean searching for recognition—it happens. I think one's work should always be a form of research, examination, inspection. It is like a stone thrown in the water—it makes ripples that go outward. From the beginning you get acknowledgment in your small, immediate environment. Then the orbit grows larger until it transcends itself. It would not be possible to produce work without being able to communicate.

What have you been trying to communicate?
My human experiences.

Your work echoes with solitude.
I think solitude is idiosyncratic in Spain and Latin America. Latin American baroque literature deals very much with solitude. One can find in it two parallel aspects—solitude and dream.

Do you see your work as beginning to realize the collective dream, or the collective myth, of Mexico?
No, it is a repercussion. One can wake up from a dream, and escape from solitude.

Is there anyone working in the medium that you really admire?
I have great admiration for many photographers, all for different reasons. For instance, Ansel Adams is extraordinary.

A great academic who produces emotion through his mastery of the technicalities. One also thinks of close friends that one admires—Cartier-Bresson, Paul Strand, Bill Brandt . . .

Are there any young photographers emerging in Mexico?
There is a great interest in photography courses in Mexico, and there are young talents.

Is there anything you would like to see happen with Mexican photography in the future?
I would like to see in Mexico publications similar to *Contrejour* and *Afterimage*. Fewer words, more reproductions, better printing quality.

As a teacher of photography, how do you see the rise of photographic education today? Does it mean anything to you?
There is no other art with as great a democratic capacity as photography. Teaching is of vital importance for photography.

What advice would you give to the young photographers of today?
I think that to be able to acquire personal expression one has to be economically independent or have parallel work to support oneself. Often, photographers cannot live just from their own creative work, and unfortunately, noble ideals are often sacrificed in order to become a big commercial name.

May 1976

BOOKS OF BRAVO PHOTOGRAPHS

Manuel Alvarez Bravo. Text by Fred Parker. Pasadena, California: Pasadena Art Museum, 1971.
Manuel Alvarez Bravo. Text by Denis Roche. Paris: La Photo Galerie, 1976.
Manuel Alvarez Bravo: 400 Photographs. Mexico: Instituto Nacional de Bellas Artes, 1972.
Manuel Alvarez Bravo: Photographs, 1928–1968. Mexico: Organizing Committee of the Games of XIX Olympiad, 1968.
Painted Walls of Mexico: From Prehistoric Times until Today. Foreword by Jean Charlot; text by Emily Edwards. Austin: University of Texas Press, 1966.

Eliot Porter

(B O R N   1 9 0 1 / A M E R I C A N)

Paul Hill

How did you get involved with photography?
I started even before I went to college. I was interested in
photography in general, but mostly bird photography. After
I got through medical school and was connected with a
bacteriological department doing research, I learned about the
Leica 35-mm. camera. I was shown the results of 35-mm.
photography by a friend of mine who was working in the same
department. I thought the camera was very versatile and could

do a lot of things I'd never thought of doing before. So I got myself a Leica camera and as an avocation I would take pictures—nothing to do with medicine at all. I took all kinds of subjects. It was these Leica photographs that I showed to Stieglitz and to Ansel Adams once in Massachusetts.

What year would that be?
Probably around 1931 or 1932. I was invited to meet Ansel Adams in Boston, because the people who invited me knew that I was interested in photography. They asked me to bring some of my photographs and they said that this other California photographer would be there with some photographs too. I was asked to show mine first. They were 8 x 10 inch enlargements, perhaps some larger, made from 35 mm.—they were details of nature, and things of that sort. Ansel Adams looked at them and offered some criticism. Then he showed some of his pictures and I wished I'd never shown mine! Some of his famous pictures were in that group. At that time he was preparing for a show at An American Place. Stieglitz had a very high regard for Ansel Adams, who he thought an extraordinary technician and perceptive photographer. This probably had more influence on me than any other experience. I was then introduced to Stieglitz through my brother, who was a painter and who knew him. Stieglitz let me show him my work and he criticized it.

What year was that?
Perhaps 1935 or 1936. This was while I was still teaching in the bacteriology department at Harvard. I would go back to New York every now and then with a bunch of photographs and show them to him. He would look at them and say: "Oh, these are all woolly—it's not a matter of sharpness. Photography is a lot of work, and you've just got to keep working harder." He was always very nice, and was never rough on me. He never said, "You're just wasting your time," or "This is trash." But he considered them all carefully. Then one summer I went to Switzerland and Austria. As a result of his criticism, I bought myself a 9 x 12 cm. Linhof, and started taking larger pictures; and I took this camera with me to Europe. When I came back and made some prints of the

pictures I'd taken in the Tyrol and other places, including bird pictures, I showed them to Stieglitz. He looked them over very carefully, and he looked them all over a second time, and he said, "I want to show these." Just like that. I wasn't expecting that. Well, it was sort of a blow on the head in a sense, but a very pleasant one.

What was Georgia O'Keeffe's response?
She was very helpful. I spent a whole afternoon in their apartment and we went over them. She discussed them all. Then I made better prints of some of them for the exhibition.

What kind of work was in the 1939 show?
There was this group from Austria, and there were a few pictures taken at Bonaventure Island in Canada and pictures from Maine.

What was the subject matter?
Trees, nature, pictures of flowers, rocks, and so forth.

Any color?
No, this was all black and white. I wasn't even thinking of color then. There were one or two bird pictures, a dying seagull, a skeleton of a seagull, birds' nests, rocks, sea, landscapes from Maine.

Had you exhibited previously?
I had had a small exhibit before that at a place called the Delphic Gallery. Stieglitz recognized some of the pictures. He said: "These have been shown before, or some of them." I'd almost forgotten about that at the time and I was rather embarrassed. I had to admit that this was the case, but he didn't mind really. After that show I decided that my talents would be better directed toward photography than bacteriology.

Was it basically the encouragement of Stieglitz and the American Place exhibition?
It was as a result of that exhibition that I gave up medical research for photography—a direct result.

What was the public reaction to the work?
I sold a good many pictures from his gallery. The reaction
was favorable. Stieglitz thought they were worth exhibiting
but he didn't try to sell any—he never did. He would offer
them to the public to look at, and if people wanted to buy
them, that was all right. I have one wonderful letter somewhere from Stieglitz.

Would you read it for us?
"I have been wanting to write to you, but I have been swamped
with people and things, and I am far from being physically
equal to the demands I make upon myself. I think I know how
you feel about me. Men don't really have to thank each other.
Still, I must thank you for having given me the opportunity
to live with your spirit in the form of these photographs, that
for three weeks were on our walls, and 'our' includes 'you.'
   "Some of your photographs are the first I have ever seen
which made me feel: 'There is my own spirit.' Quite an unbelievable experience for one like myself. I wonder, am I
clear? Probably not. As for your prints, Mr. McAlpin decided
to take seven originals, so you'll have to make no duplicates.
I enclose a check for 400 dollars. I have marked the catalogue
telling you which is what as to purchases. You cannot put
a better use to the money than acquiring a Protar [lens]. Once
more my deepest thanks to you and Mrs. Porter, also the same
from O'Keeffe." And he signs it: "Your own, Alfred Stieglitz."
   That made me feel very pleased.
   I went off after that to New Mexico, because we could live
anywhere, we didn't have to stay in Boston. We came here for
one winter, to try it out. Then the war came and interrupted
everything, and it wasn't until 1946 that we came back for
good.

*What was the response to your 1939 show from members of
the Stieglitz circle?*
I don't know whether there was any at all. I never had any
word from other photographers.
   I soon took up color photography, although I continued in
black and white. I took up color photography because I was

told by an editor that it was necessary to photograph birds in color in those days to publish anything—they couldn't be identified in black and white. I got as much information as I could from the Eastman Kodak Company and went to work on bird photography using a flash technique. I knew I had to learn how to make prints too if I was going to photograph birds in color. I learned how to do what was called "wash-off relief" printing methods, the precursor of the dye-transfer technique. I took them back to the editor and he said: "Oh, these are very fine, but we can't publish them—they're too expensive!" Anyway, I was young enough not to be discouraged by this and I went on. As I worked in color with birds, I began to see other things in color, and as a result, a lot of my work has been in color. I've never been able to persuade the traditionalist photographers—Ansel Adams, Minor White—I don't know about Strand, I've never talked to him about it—but Brett Weston, any of these—that color is really a valid medium for expressing your ideas in photography. They always have taken a very negative attitude toward color photography.

Why?
Well, Ansel says that it is too literal—there's not enough room for personal interpretation.

How do you feel about it?
I really shouldn't get into this; it's a long-drawn-out argument and sometimes it's been acrimonious. I do it, so naturally I don't feel that way. I know from the color process itself that it is not necessarily literal, nor does it restrict interpretation. You have a tremendous range for freedom, for interpretation, in making color prints. You can do just as much as in black and white, as a matter of fact, maybe more.

Do you consider that color photography has its own aesthetic?
I think it's entirely different from black and white. When photographing subjects like rocks, the approach is entirely different, because in black and white you see the forms much more than you do in color.

I've never said that color invalidates black and white, and I don't think that people who do black and white should say that black and white invalidates color—I take exception to that.

You must look for color rather than form?
You don't have to look for it—you see it. When Ansel Adams photographs something, he sees it as a black-and-white image right away, and so he photographs it that way. I see it as a color image right away—not always, because I still do take some black and white. Some of the pictures I take in color could just as well have been done in black and white. But others, like the "Rose Petals on the Beach," I just don't think that would be anything in black and white.

Would it be through your medical studies that you got interested in delving deeply into the mysteries of nature?
No. I don't think it was my medical studies that had anything to do with that. I think it came from my father's influence when I was a child—his interest in nature and the camping trips we went on. My preoccupation as a child in school was with the outdoors. Instead of doing sports, I always used to go out into the swamps, woods, and places like that.

Was there anything in your background that led you to photography?
I suppose there is a conditioning that takes place in a family because of the interests of your parents. My father was an architect and a scientist. He later had to go into business, but he was always talking about scientific matters and theories of science. He liked camping and took us to the Canadian Rockies and then took us to Maine in the summer. My father liked to get away—he introduced us to this preoccupation with the outdoors and nature. My brother took up painting about that time, too. This was when I was thirteen.

Are you a very strong advocate of conservation?
Yes, but it didn't happen immediately. I guess I was prepared for it. All my life I was prepared to be an advocate of nature,

but I didn't think about the *necessity* of becoming an advocate. It wasn't until the Sierra Club published my first book, *In Wildness*, that I realized what could be done along those lines —the influence that book could exert toward protecting the environment, preventing industrialization destroying things, and so forth.

You selected the accompanying Thoreau writings yourself?
I did.

Do you see any relationship between your selections of Thoreau and your own philosophical view of nature?
Yes. Particularly what Thoreau said about the influence that nature had on him and his perception of nature. This was an eye-opener for me. I didn't get into it without a struggle, though! It was my wife who suggested that I do a book on Thoreau when she saw the kind of photographs I was taking. So then I read *Walden* and I found it difficult, and then I found other things a bit difficult, until after a while I began to realize that this was the way I felt about things, too.

About what year was this?
Well, the book was published in 1962, and it was probably started about ten years earlier. Before that I had tried to do a book in black and white on the islands in Maine where we went. I had a group of pictures and I wrote a short text which I sent to *National Geographic*. They paid me an honorarium of $200 and filed it away—that was the last I heard of that! I worked on the book quite intensively, at the same time as I was doing other kinds of photographs. I would take Thoreau's journals with me when I went off photographing birds and read them in my spare time. I would mark passages that I thought I could find subjects for, or that I thought fitted together with subjects that I already had. I gathered it all together in a dummy which I peddled around to a number of publishers but none of them would take it. Finally the Sierra Club did.

At the time, I was having an exhibition called "The Seasons" at George Eastman House. I got talking to Nancy

Newhall about my book at the opening of the exhibition and she said: "Oh, I think the Sierra Club would be interested in it." So we called up David Brower and he said: "Yes, I would. Send me the dummy." After a while he was able to publish by getting some money to support it.

How did World War II affect your photographic work?
It brought it to an abrupt end! I got a job at the M.I.T. radiation laboratory, where they were developing radar from the original investigations that were done in England.

Did you work on the Manhattan project—on the atomic bomb?
No. Somebody got that idea and they published it. It was the M.I.T. project that I worked on—not as an electronics engineer, but just in the machine shop as an expediter.

And that took you through the whole war?
It took me into the summer of 1944. I left the radiation laboratory—I got so I couldn't take it any longer. I was relieved, allowed to quit, and we moved back to Illinois for that winter.

What did you do at the end of the war?
I continued photography as much as I could at the time. In the winter of 1944, I learned how to make dye-transfer prints. I spent all my time doing that because I couldn't go out and photograph, since there was no gasoline.

When you were at M.I.T., did you ever have any contact with Dr. Land and his people working on Polaroid film?
Not directly with Dr. Land—I've never met him—but with some of the people he employed. I was given some color film to try out, but I never liked the results, so I gave it up.

What did you do at the end of the war to earn a living?
I was fortunate in that I had enough means not to have to actually earn a living, but I could continue to work on what I had. My principal project was to try to get various books

published. At that time things were cheaper than they are now and living was easier, so I made out. I did sell photographs to magazines, so I had some income from my work.

What books were you involved with at that time?
There was *Living Birds of the World*, a little book called *Land Birds of America*, *Living Insects of the World*, *The Lower Animals*, a whole series. I had pictures in all of those.

What equipment were you using at that time for your bird photography?
I was using electronic flash equipment that I had had made by a company called Strobo Research. This took the place of flashbulbs, which when used with an open-and-shut shutter only give you an exposure as long as the calibrated shutter exposure. This was much too slow to stop the action—two-hundredth of a second wouldn't stop action. Using an electronic flash, the exposure was determined by the duration of the flash, which is something like 1/5000th of a second. The exposure during the rest of the time the shutter was open was negligible because of the poor light.

What camera were you using?
I was using a view camera.

Didn't that necessitate a great deal of preparation?
Yes, it did. Most of the time was spent finding the birds, finding the birds' nests; then after that, it was setting it up. I was practically the only person who did it that way. There was a man named Sam Grimes from Jacksonville, Florida, who also did some work like that, but not very much.

At this time were you also taking photographs of the natural landscape?
I was doing both these things at the same time, though I was preoccupied with bird photography during the nesting season. After that was over, I would devote most of my time to other kinds of photography—not birds.

What was it that you found in Thoreau that attracted you so much?
What he saw and felt about nature, his appreciation of it. When he's speaking of the brown water that comes out of the ground when the snow melts, and when he speaks of his subjective feelings in the woods, which are not descriptive at all. This appealed to me, but I have no philosophy in the sense that I have to interpret my feelings of nature in terms of light or anything like that. I just think that nature is so enormous and varied—it fascinates me because of its complexity. I don't understand this mystification that people feel. I think the light is there, and that's what you see.

Do you think that the process of seeing is a thing that you advance through?
I don't think you advance through it, it's something that you advance *into*. You learn to *see* things by practice. It's just like playing tennis, you get better the more you play. The more you look around at things, the more you *see*. The more you photograph, the more you realize what can be photographed and what can't be photographed. You just have to keep doing it.

I get requests from young men who want to go in for color printing, and they say: "I'd like to come and have you teach me how to make color prints." I tell them that the way to make color prints is to get the materials and start making them. It's all adequately written out by Eastman Kodak. They don't really need any more guidance than that. But they want a short cut. They want to have instant success. I've noticed that over and over again, and it's a rather disturbing thing. You know, it's laziness in a sense. Here they are in their twenties, they have plenty of time, their lives are ahead of them, so they can learn to master a process if they are diligent and work on it. But they don't want to do this, they think there is something mysterious about it.

When I started doing it, during the end of the war period, there wasn't anybody to consult about anything. There were just a few directions given with the products that I bought, and some articles on color reproduction in the journal of the

Optical Society of America, which suggested ways of doing it, but nothing else. Why not set to work and learn something? That's what I can't understand.

Did being a research scientist help you?
Yes, I'm sure it did. I understood what a characteristic curve was, I understood logarithms. But even so, the directions given by Kodak simplified all that.

Has your research in color printing been taken up by Kodak or any other company?
No, because I've just modified some of the techniques, that's all. I haven't made any original discoveries. I haven't been interested in developing a color-printing process; I've only been interested in using it to its maximum advantage.

No mystique?
No, no. People think I have a secret. Sometimes they come to watch me make a color print, or watch my assistant make a color print. But it's nothing, I don't try to hide anything. I'm not running a school, though.

Some people can't believe the quality of the color in your print. Is it a manipulated thing?
I don't quite know what you mean by manipulated. I spoke before about the control that you have, and about interpretation. Now, interpretation in color photography means that, in making the final print, you can accentuate—increase the contrast—if you want. You can make it more brilliant, or less brilliant. It's the same in black and white. But the colors are there. People say: "Oh, that's not true color; that's not really there; there's nothing like that; I never saw anything like that." All I can say is that they're not looking. They don't *see*.

Have you ever thought of teaching advanced photography students?
I've thought of it, and I've thought of having people come from time to time, but then I have so much I want to do that this would limit my own activities. It would mean that I

would have to give up doing things that I want to do for myself. Maybe that's a very selfish point of view, but there are a lot of things I still want to do.

What are your thoughts on the state of photographic education as you observe it from the outside?
Now, that's very interesting, because it bothers me a good deal—what I see coming out of the workshops. I don't understand it. I understand least of all the feelings of some teachers, like Minor White, that you have to mix up the various ways of expressing yourself. For instance, Minor White would say you have to be able to verbalize your feelings about a photograph in order to understand the photograph. I more or less reject that. I don't think it's necessary to put your feelings about photography in words. I've read things that photographers have written, for exhibitions and so forth, about their subjective feelings about photography, and mostly I think it's disturbing. I think they're fooling themselves very often. They're just talking, they're not *saying* anything. I don't like that.

Does being a scientist lead you to have this opinion?
Yes, maybe it does. I have to look at things very directly and in a detached way. I think my nature photographs are detached pictures: I think there's very little subjectivity in them. I think, "That's just what was there, but I've made a selection."

Do you find them contemplative objects then?
There is enough mystery in nature if you just present it straight on, in a perfectly detached way. There's still plenty there that is not understood.

This seems very much akin to the conclusion Edward Weston came to about his work: no more interpretation, just presentation.
Yes, maybe, although I'm not as tremendous an admirer of Weston as Ansel Adams is. I have a couple of his photographs and he influenced me at a time when I was doing just black and white. I think that probably I have reached a stage where some-

body's going to come along and do something on nature entirely different from the way I do it. Mine will be just old-hat stuff.

Does that excite you?
Well, I don't know quite how they're going to do it!

Who have been your major influences?
The photographers that have influenced me most are Ansel Adams, whom I quarrel with easily! And Weston, to a certain extent.

What part of Weston's work?
Some of his pictures around Death Valley, the seashore, and Point Lobos. Not so much his portraits. I don't take portraits, except of my own children and one or two other people. I'm not a portrait photographer. I don't like Ansel Adams's portraits. I don't think he's a good portrait photographer. I think Imogen Cunningham is superb in this respect, and I think Dorothea Lange was wonderful; Stieglitz was good too, and Strand. I like his pictures of people almost better than I do his landscapes. He did a book on Scotland and there were some landscapes in there that I thought were second-rate, but I think his pictures of people are marvelous. I don't know how he did it.

Is there something about photographing people that you just don't like?
Why should I try to do the human condition and the social situation of this country? Why should I go and photograph in cities the way Bruce Davidson does? Why should I do that when my emotions, instincts, and interests are all with nature? I stick to what I can do.

Do you see your nature work dealing with something fundamental within the human condition as well?
I don't see how we can live without it. Walker Evans said: "Color is vulgar, beauty is unimportant, and nature is trivial."

What do you think of that remark?
I think it's stupid, and I also think it's very blind.

What has influenced you outside photography?
A lot of nature books, like *The Twelve Seasons, The Roots of Heaven, Silent Spring, Road to Survival.*

Have you ever thought of collaborating with a writer?
Very often, but it hasn't worked out yet.

You seem to travel abroad a great deal. What impels you to do this?
You know, it's a small world and there is a lot of it I haven't seen; so before I die I'd like to see as much as possible. I went to Iceland because I'd heard that this was a great place for lichens, and it was indeed. But in every other respect it is a beautiful country also. That gave me an interest in northern parts of the world, which is why I was so glad to have the opportunity to go to Antarctica, which is even more stunning than Iceland. I did a portfolio on Iceland. I tried to sell it, but I can't seem to get it going because no one has any money these days.

Who did you do the Antarctic project for?
The National Science Foundation.

Is there anyone who you think is doing exciting work in nature photography at the moment?
Paul Caponigro—I like his things very much. Also Bill Clift, who did a portfolio on the old Boston City Hall. He has moved up here now, and has a Guggenheim to photograph New Mexico. He and Caponigro are friends. Arthur Lazar, a young man, who studied under Minor White, teaching now in Albuquerque.

Minor White is a photographer whose work I admire very much, but I don't admire some of the ways he uses it. I don't understand it, that's probably why I don't admire it. I don't understand his sequential pictures. They don't seem to be meaningful, because they're so personal. It can mean something only to him, I feel.

What has been your main concern as a photographer?
Originally, one of my main concerns was to get people to look at my pictures, to get some kind of recognition that color photography was a valid medium. Now I don't need to worry about that because I think there are enough people around who appreciate color photography. If you work in a vacuum, it's very hard to keep going. You have to have great determination and persistence. Once you have got a little recognition, it's very stimulating, and you immediately become more productive. I've noticed that with myself and with other people. Once they've been able to get a little acclaim that they are artists, that they have some perception, then it enhances their perception, and then I think they are much more creative. I think it's helped me that way, because once *In Wildness* was published I was able to see things more clearly. I was more daring after that, not so inhibited. I didn't say to myself: Oh, this isn't worthwhile doing, nobody will care about it. Although it's not quite enough to say: Well, I was only doing it for myself. Because you're not really doing it for yourself, you're doing it for an audience somewhere, at some time.

I am trying to show the audience what I think is important in nature—these are the things that I see, and this is what I think is important. This is what we have around us, and if we're going to have a good life, if the human race is going to survive, to have a static, steady state here, so that we are not continually going downhill, then these are the things that we should preserve, these are the things we should value. You can't preserve something if you don't like it; and that's the trouble with a lot of our official preservation—things are being preserved for people who don't really care about it. People will value nature by seeing what it is and by experiencing it for themselves. I also feel that perhaps they can get some of this experience, vicariously, through my photographs in books.

March 1975

American Birds. New York: McGraw-Hill, 1953.

Appalachian Wilderness: The Great Smokey Mountains. New York: Dutton, 1973.

Baja California and the Geography of Hope. Text by Joseph Wood Krutch. San Francisco: Sierra Club, 1967.

Down the Colorado. New York: Dutton, 1969.

Forever Wild: The Adirondacks. New York: Adirondack Museum and Harper and Row, 1966.

Galápagos: The Flow of Wilderness. San Francisco: Sierra Club, 1966.

In Wilderness Is the Preservation of the World. Text by Henry David Thoreau. San Francisco: Sierra Club, 1962.

The Place No One Knows: Glen Canyon on the Colorado. San Francisco: Sierra Club, 1963.

Summer Islands: Penobscot Country. San Francisco: Sierra Club, 1966.

The Tree Where Man Was Born. Text by Peter Matthiessen. New York: Dutton, 1972.

W. Eugene Smith

(1 9 1 8 – 1 9 7 8 / A M E R I C A N)

How did photography become interesting to you?
Oddly enough, I started out wanting to be an aircraft designer,
because the fascination of the sky and flying is something that
intrigued me very much. I still have that love of the sky—
not in an airliner, but in a small plane, a soaring plane when
there's just me and the elements. I was living in Wichita,
Kansas, and there was a lot of aviation activity there. I
started trying to talk news photographers in the city into

giving me prints of the planes they photographed in national races and time trials. I hounded one local news photographer not just to give me photographs but to let me go along with him on assignments—especially those that involved aircraft. In a short time I had purchased a camera from him, and finally I became more interested in photography than in becoming an aircraft designer, which is to the benefit of the aviation world, because my supersonic plane probably would have been noisier than the Concorde! Within six months I was taking pictures for the local paper.

How old were you then?
Fourteen.

Who was the photographer who helped you?
His name was Frank Noel, "Pappy" Noel. He won a Pulitzer Prize later on with a minor picture, but he was a good guy.

So, at fourteen you decided to devote yourself to photography?
It became my main interest and it became very important to me, but it was not my only interest.

You have said that literature, music, and philosophy were perhaps your greatest influences. At what point did you become involved with these studies?
When I was about ten years old I started reading serious books. I had been in an accident and they said that I would never walk again. I had to spend six months in bed and I read about fifteen volumes of history. This had much to do with my early thinking and, perhaps, early seriousness. The other thing that affected me a great deal when I was growing up was seeing my family go down in the Kansas Dust Bowl period. I photographed the Dust Bowl at that time. I also photographed sports, which gave me a sense of timing that still comes in handy. But I think my involvement with humanity, seriousness, and compassion began back in those early days. I matured very quickly.

Were there any photographers, other than "Pappy" Noel, who affected you?

The only photography I really knew was news photography, and a lot of that was dull or sensational. It wasn't until I was around seventeen that I saw some photographs by a Hungarian photographer named Martin Munkacsi. His name doesn't mean much to people now, which is too bad. For the first time I realized how tremendously deep, rhythmic, and powerful photography could be. It was this simple revelation by Munkacsi—that photography offered a great deal more than I had seen—that affected me greatly.

How did the Depression in the Dust Bowl affect you? Did you see any of the F.S.A. work?

I don't know whether I had even heard of the F.S.A. But I did have permission to leave school any time I saw a dust storm coming up so I could photograph it. I had an arrangement that, as long as I kept up with my lessons, I could be absent when I wanted to. I somehow managed to have a car and I would go out into the dust storm. I would photograph cattle herds that were dying of thirst. One year we had a grasshopper plague that killed off much of our crops. My family dealt in grain, and we were destroyed. We lost everything we had, and my father committed suicide. I was photographing for the paper that reported his death, and they distorted his suicide to the point where I felt that I just couldn't work in such a profession. When I read the stories, I swore that I could not continue in journalism, but then somebody pointed out a very simple truth, even a cliché—a profession is not intrinsically honest, but the people who practice the profession can be. I've tried to follow that. It's one of the reasons why I'm so temperamental.

Why did you destroy all your early work?

I thought it wasn't any good.

Did you, like Edward Weston, ever regret that?

Yes, in a way. I realized that, no matter how bad my early

work was, it still has a direct lineage to the work I do today. I am continuously trying to refine what I felt in those days. I hope I've learned something, and I always hope the next essay that I do will be my best.

Were you working with a small camera then?
No, I was working with a 4 x 5 inch. I stopped working on the school annual because there was a photographer in town who told the journalism teacher that an 8 x 10 was the only camera for serious photography. I became angry and I wouldn't work, so I taught my best friend to photograph and he did the pictures for the annual. When I started working for *Newsweek* in New York, they were against me using a 2¼ square!

What date was this?
1936, the year following the year that *Life* was first published. I was fired from *Newsweek* because I insisted on using a 2¼ instead of a 4 x 5. But that was fortunate because I went to work for *Life*.

Didn't you receive a photojournalism scholarship to Notre Dame University?
It was not a photojournalism scholarship. I had been in journalism at Notre Dame, but they simply created a photographic scholarship for me, the only one of its kind.

What made you leave college?
They wouldn't give me enough freedom to photograph as I thought I should in those days. Also, I had to be in by eleven o'clock every night; and sometimes to do a proper job of photography—the Senior Prom, for instance—I would have to go on until at least one o'clock. So I would be forbidden to leave the campus and punished for trying to do a good job! The turning point was a ludicrous situation. I failed a history test that I thought I knew very well, especially after my fifteen volumes of history. I was dumbfounded and I went to my teacher and said: "Is it possible that you've made a mistake with this? I know those questions so well that I not only wrote

the answers you expected but I added to them!" The teacher's response was a terrible tongue-lashing, and I walked right out of the classroom into the Western Union office. I sent my mother a telegram saying that I was going to New York. It was an excuse in a way, but I couldn't stand it. Two weeks after I got to New York, my roommate wrote that there had been a mix-up and my grade was 96, which is my lifetime average in history! But I never regretted leaving college. I think it was one of the most fortunate things that I ever did. It might have improved my English to stay there, but I doubt it . . .

How did a young Midwesterner get a job on a big New York magazine?
I had taken some pictures of a medical operation. Operation pictures were still rather unique in those days (incidentally, they were with a 35 mm., which I was later fired for using). But they offered me a chance to go on the staff, which I accepted.

What happened when you left?
I freelanced for a while.

How did you join Life?
I simply took pictures that I thought would interest them, and they gave me a few assignments.

What made you gravitate to photojournalism?
To me, photography was simply news photography, as it had been in the early days, and this was just a refinement of journalism. I was powerfully interested in people and, I suppose, the excitement of different situations

What kind of assignments did you do?
Straight news and feature stories.

At nineteen you started working for Life. *Whom did you work with?*
I never knew the other photographers well. I was a very shy

person and I didn't push myself. But later I grew to like Margaret Bourke-White very much. I think in the very early days I did not have too much respect for her, but the more I knew her, the more I began to respect her, and I finally ended up with a tremendous love for the woman—her courage, and what she tried to do.

Do you believe there is a distinction between photojournalism and documentary photography?
No. I think photojournalism is documentary photography with a purpose. I think the only thing wrong with the word "documentary" is that it can give some people the idea that you can make absolutely dull pictures of the *ingredients* of something instead of the *heart* of something.

What exactly did you do at Life? *How did they react to your work?*
They had me do a lot of theatrical photographs, which I enjoyed, because I was interested in the theater. I think it was also good training, and I still like to do it occasionally. But the thing I couldn't stand was "*Life* Goes to a Party" and things like that. Actually, I joined *Life* the day they ran out of other photographers because Bourke-White, Carl Mydans, and their other aces were running around the world with the U.S. Fleet. Finally, they were at the bottom of the barrel, and they said: "We're just going to have to send that nineteen-year-old out." And eventually, I ended up with a cover and many pages on the inside.

What was the cover?
It was a double training story—one was a naval academy, the other was the Aberdeen proving ground. They told me I was traveling in awfully fast company, and I said I didn't mind!

How long did you work for Life *before you got involved with the war?*
I resigned from *Life* when I was twenty-one. I became disturbed and fed up with assignments such as "Sadie Hawkins'

Day" and the "Butlers' Ball," things like that. So I wrote a long letter to the picture editor of *Life* saying what I wanted out of photography and what I believed in. He wrote back, saying that he, too, once wanted to write the Great American Novel! My contract was coming up for renewal and he asked me whether I was going to renew, and I said: "I'm sorry but I'm not willing to renew the contract." And he said: "I assumed that was going to be your choice. If you want to work for *Colliers, The New York Times*, etc., it's up to you. But thousands of young men would have given their right arm for the opportunity you have had." This was a rather snotty way of putting it.

I said: "I know and I appreciate very much the chance that I've had." Then he added (unnecessarily, I thought): "You know, you'll never have another chance to work for this magazine."

I thought, Why can't I resign quietly without being threatened like this? This was an old habit of the picture editors, this kind of power and punishment, and I did not appreciate it. It's not the way to get the best work out of me. For some reason I thought quickly for a change. I looked at him and said: "Yes, knowing you, Mr. Hicks, I assumed this would be your answer."

Was this Wilson Hicks?
Yes. Wilson later took great credit for allowing me to do my photo essay "The Spanish Village," but he wasn't even on the magazine at the time. I think he knew a great deal about pictures, but he was petty in his treatment of photographers. Later, as a professor, when he didn't have the power any more, he was probably a fine influence upon young photographers. But I have no bitterness about him. I speak grimly about such events in my life, but I don't bear any grudges against the people involved.

I had made a mistake by resigning. I didn't know the war was going to happen. *Life* was really the only outfit to work for if you covered a war. They had the greatest freedom, the greatest power, and the best expense accounts!

Steichen tried to get me into the naval unit that he had

set up. But I had already been in a dynamite explosion, suffering some severe physical injuries, and my eyes were weak. These two things combined made the Navy turn me down. Steichen appealed, but the statement from the hierarchy was: "Although Eugene Smith appears to be a genius in his field, he does not measure up to naval standards." So Steichen managed to arrange with Ziff-Davis publications to send me out as a correspondent. When I came back, *Life* wanted to hire me again and I turned them down three times. I wanted to work for them on the basis that we were intelligent human beings trying to do the best job we could. This was the only way we could cooperate, but they weren't interested.

You went out into actual combat when you were with the Ziff-Davis people?
At first I was mostly on carriers.

Can you relate any of the experiences that happened to you as a war photographer—intellectually, emotionally, philosophically? After all, war photography was still relatively new to the mass public.
The secret of my photography is that I have a great ability to understand how things are going to be before I experience them. So I was never surprised by what I learned in war. Many of those who had gone to the Naval Academy and other war teaching schools suffered shell shock, but I was never surprised. When I was finally injured, I think one of my first reactions was: Well, it's just about the way I expected it to be. This does not mean, however, that I did not look at the world with openness and curiosity. But I suffered no real traumas from any experience, because few of them were beyond the realm of my imagination.

You wrote that you felt the Japanese, as well as the Americans, were your brothers in your family.
Yes. My private thoughts were that I wanted to use my photographs to make an indictment against war. I hoped that I could do it so well that it might influence people in the future and deter other wars.

Do you think that was a little naïve?
Of course it was, but I still believe it. There are some things which you must attempt to do, even though you know you're going to fail. Sometimes, enough can be done in small ways. I know I, at least, changed a concentration camp into something better. Small things . . .

An American concentration camp?
An American concentration camp; only they called it a civilian stockade, which sounded nicer. The Navy had asked me to photograph it after I'd come back and was preparing for the next Pacific landing. They wanted me to photograph it so that *Life* would run a story about how wonderfully well we were treating those who surrendered to us. Then the Navy could drop the magazine on other islands, and on Japan itself, so that more people would surrender.

I said: "It's a terrible place, a stinking hell-hole."

And the admiral said: "I just had a report this morning that conditions are very good there."

So I said: "All right, I'll show you your concentration camp, your stockade." And I went out and I photographed with a great deal of anger, because there were six people dying for every one that should have. Fifteen thousand people had access to only one or two water supplies. They had no plumbing facilities for daily needs. It was just a terrible mess, badly run by our own people. I brought the pictures back and the censors were furious.

Which censors?
The American Navy censors. For once, they became angry at the pictures and not at me. They took it to higher authorities, and the concentration camp was completely changed around. The officials were replaced. It never was a paradise, but at least they brought it up to the minimal standards of human decency.

Recently, when I went to Minamata, I was on television one morning and an ex-P.O.W. saw the show. Before the show had ended, he managed to make his way to the studio to publicly state that I'd saved his life. It was truly rewarding.

It's at times like that that I realize the power to activate people that photographs truly have.

During the two years that you were recuperating from war injuries, you didn't photograph. What did you do during that time?
I had thirty-two operations on my mouth and nose alone. A shell had entered my head over the roof of my mouth— nearly cut off my tongue—and took all the bone structure out of it. Part of the shell is still lodged a fraction of an inch from my spine. I was also hit in the hand, arm, leg, and chest. I really didn't know whether I was ever going to be able to photograph again. My first thought when I was wounded was that I still had music. When I managed to get my eyes open (I didn't know my glasses had exploded into my face and that some glass had gone into my eye), I saw a blurred sky, and I said to myself that I still had photography. The third thing I thought was that I wanted to use a camera and photograph what was happening. Not because it was me, but because it was a picture that was important to me.

I tried to retain consciousness in order to write out instructions for someone to pick up my stashed film, but I couldn't see to write. Then I tried to take a sulphur pill, but I found I had several mouths and I couldn't swallow it.

What was the first photograph that you took after your recuperation?
I wanted to make a good photograph, but I was out of control. I just couldn't do it, and I did not know whether I would ever photograph again. Finally, I decided to try, but it was very difficult. My face was still pouring pus and it was draining into the camera and my nerves were . . . I was not only about to go through the ceiling but through the sky. I decided to try, anyway.

I got the whole family out of the house, except my two children. Then, I took them for a walk. I wanted it to be a good picture, to contradict and contrast with my war pictures, the last photographs that I had taken. So I followed the children, and I saw them stepping into this space as they went along the path. I stopped and clumsily tried to focus, and as they stepped into the space, I made the photograph. I felt that it was fairly good.

How did you come to title it the way you did?
"The Walk to Paradise Garden"? Most people think it has a religious connotation, but it's as much a tribute to music as anything. There is an opera by Delius called *A Village Romeo and Juliet*, and one piece of the music is called "The Walk to Paradise Garden." I've left it with an ambiguous title so that anyone can take from it what they wish. But it's basically my tribute to music and to humanity, because I think it shows hope.

You've always been called a moralist with a camera—
No, I'm a compassionate cynic.

—but in this picture you seem to set up what becomes a constant duality in most of your work, the battle of dark versus light, and in it there is the actual release of the subject into the light.
You've said it all. I don't have to say anything.

Will you talk a bit about that?
I don't know how capable I am of talking exactly. In music I still prefer the minor key, and in printing I like the light coming from the dark. I like pictures that surmount the darkness, and many of my photographs are that way. It is the way that I *see* photographically. For practical reasons, I think it looks better that way in print, too.

"The Walk to Paradise Garden" has become one of the best-known photographs in the world. Do you ever feel that that photograph is a ghost for you?
It's fine with me that it's so popular. I sometimes wonder about it; I find several flaws in it. I don't think it's quite as good as its recognition has been, but I'm glad it's worked as well as it has.

Are you satisfied with the way Steichen used it in the "Family of Man" exhibition?
It was all right.

Shortly afterward, did you start photographing full time again?
I forget how long it took. It must have been half a year or so, because I still had to get my hand under control.

How did you get restarted?
I think the first pictures I made were of the opera *Peter Grimes*, which I took between hospital visits.

Was this for a specific purpose?
Working for *Life*.

So this is the second or third time you went back with Life*?*
I didn't leave them after the injury, so this was the second time I was working for them, around 1947 or 1948. The first important story that I did was "The Country Doctor," then Dr. Schweitzer, and then I went to the University of Notre Dame to do "germ-free" animals. I'm the only man who was ever passionate and compassionate over white rats!

It seems from "The Country Doctor" essay that you began to put a stamp on the medium of magazine photojournalism that has never been erased, a way of seeing that nobody else had been brave enough to follow before. Was this a conscious attempt?
I learned it all from Beethoven.

Which Beethoven piece?
Oh, many of them; but if I had to go on that desert island with one piece of music, it would probably be the String Quartet No. 14 (Opus 131).

You have a special interest in the idea of the healer, don't you?
That's why I now practice medicine all the time. I felt an affinity with the kind of hero you could touch back, who could inspire someone else to change his life. "The Country Doctor"

affected people that way. I cut my hand once on a glass and was in the emergency room, and the guy took about four times as long as he needed to get the glass out of my hand because he wanted to talk to me about whether he should become a country doctor or not. That essay changed people's lives and gave them a feeling of inspiration for good, and compassion.

How does a picture story like that come to be?
Well, let me jump to the essay I did in 1951, "Nurse-Midwife." I first came up with the idea when I was in Britain, where I thought about doing a midwife in Wales because it seemed an interesting idea. When I got to Spain—I was doing "The Spanish Village" then—I thought I would try to incorporate the two. But unfortunately we had to leave the village rather hurriedly because we were worried about the safety of the interpreter, myself, and the film I'd shot. Even though two chances were gone, I kept thinking about it and the idea kept growing in my mind. I finally said: Christ! The best story is in the United States, where we're supposed to be so advanced.

So I went to midwife school and became a midwife. I asked the nurse who taught me if she could put up with me for six weeks, and she turned out to be the greatest human being that I have ever known, as far as having a useful and fulfilled life is concerned. In the back of my mind was the racial problem in the United States. Here I was, doing a story on a black, and a black had never before been the subject of a major serious essay in an American magazine.

There were three things about the midwife story that were important: its medical significance; the fact that it was a story of a great human being; and third, I was fighting racism without ever making racism the point. I had long crusaded against racism, not by hitting people over the head with a hammer, but by compassionate understanding, presenting something that people could learn from, so they could make up their own minds.

How did you talk Life *into doing something that radical?*
They finally agreed to my doing the story. But then, as I often do, I more or less disappeared, because they didn't want

me to spend so much time on a story. They had become used to this by now, but they never found it acceptable to let me take time and do a story the way I wanted to. Just before my "Country Doctor" piece, they put out a memo which stated: "Just as soon as we break the idealism out of Smith, we'll get more mileage out of him as a photographer." But, since "The Spanish Village" was one of their most successful stories, they more or less let me get away with doing "Midwife" my way. They thought they were running it as a prestige piece. They never expected it would have such a response.

How does one gauge such a response?
From letters sent in by readers, from the reaction of the advertisers. By *Life*'s standards, it was commercially one of the best stories they'd ever run. And it served my purpose, too.

Is there a difference between the "picture story" and the "photo essay"?
I think a picture story is a portfolio put together by an editor, while an essay has to be thought out, with each picture in relationship to the others, the same way you would write an essay. Perhaps the writing of a play comes closer. You keep working out the relationships between the people, and you look back at the relationships you have established, and you see whether other relationships must be established or strengthened. There should be a coherence between the pictures, which I don't think you find in the usual publication of a group of pictures which are called picture stories.

It has been said that "The Spanish Village" is the classic photo essay . . .
I think that "Midwife" is better. But the Spanish essay is more poetic perhaps.

Can you say why you think that?
No, I'm not sure that I can. "Midwife" was the story of an individual human being; in "The Spanish Village" it was of many people creating a village. There was not much attention

paid to any one person, so the village itself became the hero of the story.

How did you go about doing "The Spanish Village"?
First of all, I learned as much about Spain as I could. My liking of its music goes back to a love affair I had with a Spanish girl, a flamenco dancer, who first introduced me to music. There were also my feelings about the Spanish Civil War. Spain is one of my favorite places, and I knew quite a lot about it. Actually, I was on a *Life* assignment about the drought, and there was no way I could do a story. So I simply thought I would show the hard times in Spain, the difficulties of life, and the pride of the people.

How long did it take?
About two and a half months. I would have stayed longer, but they were trying to get rid of us. I finally fled the village when the secret police from Madrid started moving in to find out why we were photographing the poor.

Did Life *publish the essay the way you wanted?*
It was a reasonable facsimile. They had just done an editorial, I think, about helping Franco, so I thought that was the end of my story. I sent them rather angry and bitter cablegrams. I said I was going to resign if they didn't lay it out properly, the way I wanted. I only turned in about forty-six pictures— I was afraid that if they had more pictures, they would twist it around and even make a plea on behalf of Franco. But several of the people at *Life* said that if it did not come out the way I wanted it to, they would resign, too. I don't know whether they would have or not, but that was the best backing I ever had for my work.

You did two more essays during this time. They were diverse, but very personal essays; one on your daughter Juanita, the other on Albert Schweitzer. They both have a strange kind of intimacy.
My daughter was easy because I simply kept my cameras around, and much of the story was done when I was testing

film. I just followed her around and photographed her. It didn't bother her because I generally entered her games. When the story came out, she started getting fan mail from all over the world. She even got some presents from Japan.

Schweitzer was much more difficult because I had assumed he would be easy. I first knew Schweitzer because of his music and I had read several of his books. I really thought a rapport with him would be fairly easy to establish, but it turned out quite differently. When I got there, I found many contradictions with what I had expected to see.

You couldn't tell whether it was a zoo, a hospital, or a native village. It seemed to have very few of the standards of medicine that we have more or less grown to expect. I couldn't correlate Schweitzer's attitudes and his ideas of brotherhood, and I didn't know how to photograph them. It wasn't just a question of Smith photographing as Smith always photographs, or how people think I do. With every subject I had to "shade" the pictures accordingly. That's why my pictures from Pittsburgh are mostly rather cold. It's very difficult to feel warm about Pittsburgh. But, with Schweitzer, I was disturbed. I was very much for the idea of brotherhood, but his kind of brotherhood was not mine. I ended up writing about 100,000 or 200,000 words for myself: why I couldn't accept Schweitzer and why I could accept Schweitzer; why Schweitzer's idea of brotherhood was against my idea of brotherhood; where did Schweitzer's sense of brotherhood fit into history. And I had to go through all these thoughts before I began to know how to photograph him.

How did you react to him?
He was friendly enough, but I had a problem with him. He had a vast ego, and like many people of that age, he didn't like to be photographed with his glasses on. He wanted me to tell him every time I was going to make a photograph so that he could take his glasses off. I took a photograph of him picking up a bucket to throw water into the cement, which he was wont to do, and he said: "Oh, if you show that photograph, they'll think the old man is pretending that he works." He kept putting little restrictions on me, saying: "Don't

photograph that—" He would pose for pictures, and I felt that the pictures were getting more and more superficial. Finally, I sat down one night and wrote him a letter. I said: "I must leave Lambaréné because I too search for the truth and you deny me the truth here. You force me into superficiality and to me superficiality is untruth. Therefore, I must leave Lambaréné."

I gave him the letter at lunch the next day. We didn't speak during the meal, although I was sitting opposite him. At the end, he said he wanted to speak to me, and we went over to the side. He put his hand on his forehead and closed his eyes and said: "I want you to remain in Lambaréné. You can photograph whatever you wish." And so I stayed. I found out that he was more honest about himself than anybody else was, because people were building their hopes and making a legend out of him for their own ends. They kept writing and trying to make him better than he was, to the point where it got out of hand. But he was basically very honest with himself. I went there with respect for him and I came back with sympathy as well as respect for the man.

What was the goal you sought when working for mass-circulation magazines?
Magazines such as *Life* were the best vehicles for a photographer's work. Even if you didn't get as much in as you might have wished, it was the best chance of influencing people. When I went to Minamata, I found two people in this little village in Japan who had complete scrapbooks of my work. This is the kind of influence that I think is very important. A book cannot reach that number of people. It may last longer, but "The Country Doctor" has lasted from 1948 on. I think the world is much worse off because some of the fine, and not so fine, magazines have disappeared.

Around 1955 you joined Magnum. Why?
There were many photographers at Magnum who were friends of mine and who I had considerable respect for. I am also very stupid about handling contracts and dealing with people. I was starting to do the Pittsburgh story and the man I was

involved with over the story was a very sharp person. I actually joined Magnum to get protection from him, but they were as foolish as I was. It turned into a rather disastrous situation. In short, the reason I left was that I wanted to stick to my ideals by refusing to work for publications unless I had the right to withdraw a story if it was being distorted. I also wanted to do the layouts—or certainly the work on them— although I never insisted that a magazine use my layout exactly. I would have compromised on some of the details, but not on the distortions of my story. And, as I understand it, some of these magazines were threatening Magnum by saying: "Well, if you can't control Smith, maybe we won't be able to use any Magnum photographers." I thought that I was a bad person for Magnum to have around. I didn't believe there was any reason why anybody else should suffer for my ideals, so I left.

That was while you were still completing the Pittsburgh essay?
I was trying to, yes.

There seems to be a subtle change in tone in the Pittsburgh pictures.
As I said about Schweitzer, I knew beforehand that I could "shade" the photographs. In Pittsburgh I had to take the city as the subject. I did not know the people too well; therefore, I had to try to photograph in such a way that you could know the city if you were there. It was a cold place and I photographed it coldly.

The pictures do seem to allude to the depression in the fifties.
I don't think the photographs reflect a depression. After all, Pittsburgh was proud of itself, for the strides it had made against pollution. That's the reason why I photographed it with all the smoke—because men's miracles are seldom perfect, and they were calling the salvation of Pittsburgh "a miracle."

Robert Frank was coming into prominence about this time. Did you know him?
I knew Bob.

How do you react to his work?
I'm very fond of Bob's pictures. I react to them this way: if I were an editor, I would insist that Bob be given his head to photograph the way he wanted to, no matter how it came out, because the pictures would be valid. I do not call him a journalist, I think he is the Franz Kafka of photography. I think this is perfectly valid, as long as you don't try to twist him into being a journalist. I used to tell *Life*, "Please use these people for their strength, but don't take them and twist them into some other mold."

Can you say why he is not a journalist?
I don't think he gives a damn about being a journalist, or from what I've heard, he doesn't. A journalist has to thoroughly understand the subject, and you have to try to interpret that subject, keeping true to what it is. I think Bob photographed only for himself, regardless of whether he was being exactly fair to his subject or not.

Would you call the position that Robert Frank took that of an artist?
No. He just didn't have the other interest. He's as much an artist as any other photographer, but I think I'm as much an artist as any other photographer, too. When I was about nineteen or twenty, I worried about it a little bit, and I even wrote that there was a constant battle between myself as an artist and as a journalist. But that was when I was young. I no longer have any conflict whatsoever, because for me to be the best journalist that I could possibly be, I have to be the best artist.

You said that one of the reasons that Frank is not a journalist is that he's more true to himself than he is to his subject?
No. He's being true to himself at the expense of the subject.

But don't you think that is the case for any photographer?
I have to consider the subject, and I have to be true to it, and find my own way of presenting the truth to myself as well. I

think it's much tougher to be a journalist-artist than to be the free artist who doesn't have that responsibility.

Robert Frank took that responsibility by producing a book called The Americans, *didn't he?*
It was one man's very opinionated statement about what he saw in America. I think this is fine.

Don't you think you did the same thing with Albert Schweitzer?
Bob would not have written 200,000 words to himself trying to figure out who the hell Schweitzer was. I think one of the vast differences between, say, Diane Arbus and myself is that if we both photographed the same subject, unwittingly, there would be a great difference in the way the people would come out. I think it is necessary to know the people well before I photograph them. But Arbus utilized people for her own ends, and I don't think she really bothered to know them. That is perfectly legitimate, I'm not condemning her for it, but I think they would have looked much more human if I'd photographed them, because I would have seen a different set of values—or perhaps not, I don't know. I think Bob is one of the best photographers there have been.

Have you seen any influence from yourself and Frank on American photography?
I suppose we have had considerable influence. I don't know how good it has been for the people who have succeeded in copying, or trying to emulate, me. As for Bob, I think there are an awful lot of people who try to emulate him. And I'm not certain that Ralph Gibson would have come out if Robert Frank had not made him his "son."

Does Frank represent that anti-hero you have talked about?
To some extent he does. I don't know who would be the best representative. I think Bob just looks at the world in a rather grouchy fashion.

You have been called an "idealistic romantic." How do you react to that description?
I don't know what that means. The people who usually call

me a romantic are so frustrated and cynical in their own lives that they don't believe in anything. And when I continue to believe, they call this romanticism.

What is it you actually believe in?
I believe every human being is capable of bad and good. But I believe that if the right influences can be there in sufficient number, and if a man can believe in them, there is a possibility for humanity to actually make a step forward. I don't think we've made many steps forward. Therefore, I am a compassionate cynic.

This is where I put myself, but I really don't think I'm all that romantic. If you try to stir people's feelings, they call it romanticism. I believe in human emotions very much. I believe that if you stir human emotions, much can come out of it. I don't believe you stand a chance of changing many of the important wrongs in this world unless you reach through the emotions that stir the brain.

In the late fifties you began to teach at the New School for Social Research in New York City. What do you think about teaching?
I think I'm a terrible teacher.

It seems that most good teachers end up saying that at some time.
No. I think to be a good teacher you have to be able to do a lot of talking about portfolios, and one thing or another, and I am simply unable to do this.

Why do you teach, then?
I don't know. So many people ask me to, so I try it every once in a while, and I go through agony. I may be a good teacher for someone living with me, but I can't live with all my students. If I can get them to *think*, get them to *feel*, get them to *see*, then I've done about all that I can as a teacher.

Is there anything special that you do, or require of them?
No, I mainly use myself and my pictures as an example. I can also criticize brutally without stomping on any tender

young sprouting feelings. I use literature, music, and I try to get them to see in small ways by teaching them responsibility. For instance, I had a little bottle that said SCOTCH on it, and I kept ducking behind the desk to pour myself a drink from it. Everyone was wild, taking pictures of me, trying to sneak a picture of me sneaking a drink. After a while I said: "Okay, you've been photographing me drinking from this bottle, so you will distribute pictures to show that I drink while teaching. But you've never asked me what's in the bottle. It's a bottle of cider—you are very bad reporters!" The only other thing I did was carry a bag to classes, until one day somebody asked me: "Why do you carry that bag around?" I said: "I don't know, it's just my thing. It's my bag!" I also said: "Iron-clad rules often rust." And: "I have the courage of my convictions, but I don't like to serve the time." Did you ever hear about my sense of humor in all those stories about me? Bob Frank and I have gotten so depressed that we've ended up roaring with laughter. I'm not so sure that was humor, maybe black humor!

One hears that you have a large book of your work you want to bring out, a magnum opus?
I think I've got over five hundred pictures in it at the moment, and the last time I worked on the dummy must have been about 1958. I still intend to get around to it, but it's awfully difficult for me to do a book—it's so expensive. I want to do the layout, the writing, the printing, everything.

You have a strange reputation for being a great photographer on the one hand and a lousy editor on the other. How much control do you really think photographers are capable of having over their own work? Do you think that most photographers are their own best editors?
I consider myself to be my own best editor. I often annoy photographers by using some pictures smaller than they think would be the best way of displaying a work. I did this with the Pittsburgh essay layout, although it was designed for a *Life*-size page and it was pushed down to *Popular Photography*-size pages. But I will frequently sacrifice what is known as the

display type of layout if I feel that it is making a dispropor-
tionate point on the totality of my essay. In the big book
dummy, you'll find a smallish picture of a man and woman
dancing. It's tucked away down in the corner and I really
don't care if you see it or not, but I want you to *feel* it.

Are there other pictures on the page?
The other picture is a dead man with his rifle stuck out in
front of him, in a shell hole. I don't want to be an obvious
editor. The most successful layouts of mine that have been
published are those which come closest to my way of doing
things. There are also those who say I can't write. But I wrote
most of *Minamata*. My wife, Aileen, wrote some, and you can't
tell the difference. She blended her style very nicely with mine.

*Ansel Adams and Aperture have championed you at one time
or another ...*
Ansel did. I've never known Aperture to champion anyone.
They think I'm a dreadful person at Aperture. I think I'm one
of the easiest persons in the world to get along with, but they
kept wanting to misuse my pictures, and I didn't want that.
Most people who find I'm difficult to work with are those who
want to take my pictures out of context, to use them for their
own purposes.

Did you design your Aperture monograph?
I wrote it and sequenced it. And they fought it like hell.

Can you tell us about your association with Ansel Adams?
We have a mutual admiration society. I like his sense of
humor. I get along very well with Adams.

How did you two meet?
I don't know. I think I called him up one time when I was
near his home. He always had nice things to say about me.
I might not have chosen to take the pictures that he takes,
and he might not want to take the pictures I take, but that
doesn't mean we can't like each other's work.

You were involved in a book and exhibition called "The Concerned Photographer." What does this term mean?
I make no big deal out of "concerned" photography. For me, it means someone who photographs situations in which human beings and confrontations are involved. I suppose in that way I qualify, though I think my concern is deeper. The photographers they published were very fine photographers, and I certainly value being in their company. I think that Robert Frank, in his way, could be called a concerned photographer as well.

Is it an attitude they have toward people?
It's the attitude that they have, yes.

It seems an odd kind of elite—a separatist movement.
I'm a separatist from the separatist movement. I just go my own way. I'm not all that unhappy with the title. I was in the book because Cornell Capa asked me to be.

It seems that the ideas are larger than the photographers.
I don't think there are such things as "feeling" photographers.

In the early 1960's you went to Japan, and that trip may have changed your way of life. It seemed to start an important relationship between you and that country.
It was the first time I'd visited Japan, outside of flying over it in a bomber; I was working for an industrial company. I don't usually accept assignments from companies (I can't imagine accepting one from General Electric!), but Hitachi turned out to be a company that maintained a sense of humanity.

I had a very loose plan then that I hadn't followed very closely. I had photographed a Spanish village, and then Pittsburgh, and I wanted to go to Russia to photograph their Pittsburgh. Then I wanted to go to Japan to photograph a fishing village. When I first thought of this, I didn't think in terms of a village like Minamata, but of various kinds of industrial cities and villages. I had photographed men working, and I also wanted to photograph industries. I wanted to leave an open record of my time. And so Hitachi gave me the opportunity to do the industrial side. As I said, it turned out to be a rather good company, and I became very fond of the people. Japan is the only place I get homesick for.

How long did you stay there?
The first time, a year, and the last time, about three and a half years. That was in Minamata.

There appears to be a humanitarian link between the way that you, Paul Strand, Cartier-Bresson, and Dorothea Lange photograph.
It's called romanticism . . .

In your great exhibition at the Jewish Museum in New York, in 1971, it seems you wanted the pictures to have the power of transcendence. Is that true?
That is a more pompous way than I would have put it.

How would you have put it?
I wanted those who saw the pictures to leave with an experience that carried them across the sidewalk and even into the taxicab. I don't know how many letters I got from the show but there were a great many. Some said they were thinking of suicide until they saw it.

What was the concept behind the show?
I was trying to state everything about life—both its cynicisms and its compassion. I wasn't interested in whether they came out of that saying: "Isn't Smith a great photographer." I didn't give a damn. I wanted them to come out emotionally stunned and moved so that they would think, and think in a good way. It was huge, and obviously there were too many pictures for everybody to see.

How big was it?
640 pictures. I not only wanted the individual pictures to stand up, I wanted them to go deep down inside. I can't stand

W. Eugene Smith / 277

these damn shows on museum walls with neat little frames, where you look at the images as if they were pieces of art. I want them to be pieces of life!

You felt your show came close to this?
The best I could do. Obviously, it had its flaws. But you should have seen this one huge room, no music, just the relentless clip of the slides. It was a strange kind of a cathedral, and people just sat there—they didn't move, they didn't talk, tremendously moved.

You appear to have been trying for a long time to find the best possible way to show your work. What conclusions have you come to?
I think the best possible way is a book, because an exhibition doesn't last very long. Take the book *Let Us Now Praise Famous Men*, by James Agee and Walker Evans. The first edition sold only 400 copies, and yet this has been an influential book. Even if there were still only a few copies around, it would be influential.

Minamata is one of the most important works you have done. How did it come about?
When the Jewish Museum show went to Japan, some Japanese friends came over and asked me what I wanted to photograph, and I said I didn't know. I'd always thought of a fishing village and they had in their minds all the time that they wanted to entice me to Japan to do Minamata. They gave me a book on Minamata. In the early fifties, the Japanese fishing and farming village of Minamata was contaminated by industrial wastes expelled by the factory of the Chisso Corporation. Mercury poisoning, carried in the fish, reached epidemic proportions by 1956. I looked at the book and they talked to me about it, and I said: "Sure, I'll go."

The next day I was married, and I spent my honeymoon in Minamata. We rented a house and started meeting some of the victims. We'd talked to the company so that they could clearly get their side of the argument on record for us. We hoped to overcome all the resistance they had toward journalists who had come in. We slowly got to know the people before we started to photograph them intimately.

We photographed the fishing first, because we knew we needed fishing pictures and it was a safe subject—you didn't need to know the individuals involved intimately. But we began to know the people better and we ate their food. It was such an exciting time, and because I was not working for a magazine, I stayed as long as I wanted to. I didn't know where we were going to get money from, because we had none. However, we were limping along. It was very difficult. At times we were six thousand miles from home with only three dollars, wondering where the hell we were going to get money to go on. But the longer we stayed, the more we became neighbors and friends instead of journalists. This is the way to make your finest photographs.

Was the 1972 publication in Life *the first publication of your Minamata essay?*
I think there had already been several publications in Japan, but it was the first in America.

Did you have any idea at the beginning that you could actually stop the problem?
No. But we plunged in.

Did you set out to make a picture essay on it?
I was thinking in terms of a book, not so much of the smaller publications. Many of my photographs were used while the conflict was going on, many shows on prime-time television in Japan, and they were published in magazines, books, newspapers, etc. I think this is one of the reasons I was attacked. We were being so influential that they wanted to try to stop publication if they could. And it was one of their greatest mistakes, because I'm a kind of a folk hero in Japan for reasons I don't know. When I was attacked, many people in the nation rose up in real fury against the company. The people thought there must be something wrong with the company and they really turned the feelings of the country toward the victims—much more than they had before.

How did the famous picture of the mother washing her daughter come about?
By that process of getting to know the individuals. We looked after the child at times when the parents were on protests. They lived about a ten-minute walk from our house. Every time we went by the house, we would see that someone was always caring for her. I would see the wonderful love that the mother gave. She was always cheerful, and the more I watched, the more it seemed to me that it was a summation of the most beautiful aspects of courage that people were showing in Minamata in fighting the company and the government. Now this is called romanticism. But it was the courage that I was interested in. Courage is romantic, too. I wanted somehow to symbolize the best, the strongest, element of Minamata.

One day, I said to Aileen, my wife, "Let's try to make that photograph." I imagined a picture in which a child was being held by the mother and the love was coming through. I went to the house, tried very clumsily to explain to the mother that I wanted to show a picture in which Tomoko was naked so we could see what had happened to her body. I wanted to show her caring for the child. And she said: "Yes, I'm just about to give Tomoko her bath. Maybe that will help you." She first held the child on the outside of the bath and washed her as the Japanese do; then she put her into the bath. And I could see the picture building into what I was trying to say. I found it emotionally moving, and I found it very difficult to photograph through my tears. However, I made that photograph. It's as romantic as could be.

What has been your most consistent personal philosophical concern?
Humanity. I try to take what voice I have and give it to those who don't have one at all.

Are you going to continue to give this voice new causes?
At least one more. I've been practicing all this time, and I want to do this one right. I don't know what the subject's going to be. I've basically been too ill to photograph, and I've been very near death twice in the last year. They said I wouldn't

live half an hour, but I'm still fighting back. I'm feeling pretty good now and I think I can start photographing again. There are some subjects that I have in mind, but there's not one yet that has come across with that chemistry which immediately makes me say: This is the one that I know I can give my soul to.

April 1977

SELECTED BIBLIOGRAPHY

Photographic essays from *Life* magazine 1944–1972
    "American Battle for Okinawa," June 8, 1945.
    "Chaplin at Work," March 17, 1952.
    "Country Doctor," September 20, 1948.
    "Death Flow from a Pipe," June 2, 1972.
    "Japanese Civilians on Saipon," November 6, 1944.
    "Life Without Germs," September 26, 1949.
    "A Man of Mercy," November 15, 1954.
    "My Daughter Juanita," September 21, 1953.
    "Nurse Midwife," December 3, 1951.
    "The Reign of Chemistry," January 5, 1953.
    "Spanish Village," April 9, 1951.

Hitachi Reminder. Tokyo: Hitachi, Ltd., 1961.
Minamata, by W. Eugene Smith and Aileen M. Smith. New York: Holt, Rinehart & Winston, 1975.
"Pittsburgh," in *Photography Annual 1959.* New York: Ziff-Davis Publishing Co., 1958.
W. Eugene Smith: His Photographs and Notes. Afterword by Lincoln Kirstein. An Aperture Monograph. Millerton, New York: Aperture, 1969.

Laura Gilpin

(BORN 1891 / AMERICAN)

Paul Hill

How did you first become interested in photography?
I think I must have been given a Brownie camera when I was
twelve. But probably what did me more good than anything
else was being with my mother's closest friend, who was blind.
During the St. Louis Exposition, I would go to the fair every
other day and describe the exhibits to her. I think that taught
me observation like nothing else could. I can see those exhibits
now, just as if it was yesterday.

It was not so long after that that a friend of mine, Alfred Curtis, read about the autochrome plate and sent for some. I fell for this hook, line, and sinker. I can show you three prints I made from those plates, the first one in 1910. They were in my recent show. I hadn't thought about doing anything with them for years. They were packed away in a box, and when I got them out, they were in perfect shape and I made color negatives of them and then had some commercial color prints done from them.

Did you do anything with the color process after that?
Yes. I began to do dye-transfer work, but World War I knocked that into a cocked hat. Then I got involved in books and I have not had time to get back to it.

About that time were you aware of the publication Camera Work *or the Photo-Secession Gallery?*
Oh, yes, because I went to the Clarence White school in 1916 or 1917. It's strange how things happen in your life. A friend of my mother's had had some portraits made by Gertrude Käsebier in New York. I must have been fourteen and my brother six. She did some things of all three of us.

The San Francisco Exposition was another steppingstone for me, because Colorado Springs, where I lived, had very little in the way of painting and sculpture. There was music, but not much else. It was my first real encounter with painting, and particularly with sculpture; I wrote to Mrs. Käsebier to ask her where I could study, and she recommended the Clarence White school. Then I went to see her. She was interested that I was from Colorado, because she had lived out there in her early days. I used to send her proofs and she would send me back comments. I got to know her very well.

Was there any art background in your family?
Yes, a great deal. One of my Gilpin ancestors was a painter and there was another who wrote one of the first four books on prints. Benjamin West is on our family tree. My uncle drew very well, though he was an engineer.

What was the family business?
My grandfather was in the food and drug business in Balti-
more, and my father came out to Colorado in 1882. He did
not consider himself a pioneer by any means and I have no
record of the things he did. It's a great pity. He was in the
cattle business for a long time, but that went to pieces, and
then he was in mining; eventually he was drowned. When I
was born, the family came to Colorado Springs for my arrival.

What was the Clarence White school like?
It was wonderful. There were about fifteen to eighteen of us,
and Mr. White was an extraordinary person, an extraordinary
teacher. Nobody ever imitated his work, which I think is the
mark of a real teacher. And there was Paul Anderson, who
was the technical man, and Max Weber who taught art history
and design. Max's lessons were invaluable to me—design is
the foundation for everything, I think.

What would be a typical day?
We were given various kinds of assignments to work on, and
we had a print criticism once a week—they were usually
printing-out proofs. Everybody used a big-view camera, of
course. We would do portraits and groups. Both Mr. White
and Max Weber would give us design problems, like taking
three objects and making one of first importance, one of
second, and one of third. This sounds simple, but it isn't.
White against white, and dark against dark, a problem in
rectangles. During World War II I took a job as a public-
relations photographer at a B-29 plant, which was a real
workout, but I saved my own soul by giving myself similar
problems.

*At that time, did you go to see Alfred Stieglitz at the "291"
gallery?*
I went there once, and he scared the daylights out of me!

How old were you then?
Oh, I must have been twenty-four.

How did he scare the daylights out of you?
That was what he did. I don't think that he or Steichen were
the least bit interested in women photographers. There was
no question about that. They did accept Mrs. Käsebier, but
rather reluctantly, I think.

*When you showed Mrs. Käsebier your work, what kind of
things did she respond to?*
I usually would send her landscapes, Colorado landscapes. I
still have a few of those platinum prints.

Were they soft-focus, pictorial landscapes?
I began with the soft focus, which was just at its height of
popularity in 1916. What "sharpened" me up was when
Brenda Putnam (a sculptor friend) and I went to Europe
in 1922. I had been given a Graflex but had not had time to
try it. We were on board the old *Mauritania*, and I saw something I wanted to shoot. I stood up on a bench to lean over
and the lens board fell out. At that time I was using a Pinkerman Smith soft-focus lens and I felt that was what I had to
have. I hurried off before we sailed to order another one and
it was sent over to me. Then the lens developed a terrible
flare and I lost practically all the work I did in Europe. Of
course, you get less if you stop down, and I think this was
when I realized that the sharp image was what I wanted.

*Did you see the work of Paul Strand, who was using the sharp
image?*
Yes, I saw him when I was living in New York a couple of
times at shows that he had. Then I saw him when he was at
Taos for two or three years.

*Were you aware of similar developments on the West Coast,
like Group f/64?*
No, I was isolated. Maybe it was a good thing, maybe it
wasn't, I don't know. I would see things in magazines, but I
didn't meet Ansel Adams until he was living down here after
the war.

Was the documentary tradition a concern of yours?
No, I don't think it was in my early work, particularly when
I saw it up on the wall—very good for you to see it on a
wall, sometimes a little hard to take, though! I do not think
it was documentary, really.

I was very interested in printing and doing books, and
this stems from two or three wonderful days in the British
Museum when I held original Blakes in my hands. I did a
little booklet on Mesa Verde and one on Colorado; then I
did a lot of school catalogues, and that had to be documentary;
but I did those to earn a living.

When did you start taking photographs of Indians?
Not until 1930. A close friend of mine was a public-health
nurse and we used to come down here by car on vacations.
One year we ended up on a Navaho reservation, where we
ran out of gasoline. I hiked a long distance for help, and
when I came back to the car, she was surrounded by about
eight Indians. My friend was very interested in them and she
was later offered a job as a demonstration field nurse out on a
reservation. I went down to visit her and I did a lot of portraits
there, though I did landscapes, too. She made a marvelous
place for herself with these people and they trusted her utterly,
so anything I wanted to do was accepted. Through her, I
found out how to work with the Indians, because most people
treat them like animals in the zoo. It can make you so
angry!

Had you seen any of the work of Edward Curtis at that time?
Yes, do you know the Canyon de Chelly picture, the one with
the seven horses? Well, my father must have been down here
on a trip in the early 1900's and bought a big print of that.
We had it over our mantelpiece for years. I have an old
autochrome of the living room with that picture on the wall.
I don't know what happened to it; it was one of those things
that disappeared when we were putting things in storage
during the war. But there is no question that this photograph
was a great influence on me.

After you left the Clarence White school, how did you earn a living?

Well, in New York I did quite a lot of portraits, and I worked for several sculptors. I cut my eye teeth on Brenda's sculptures and there is nothing like photographing sculptured heads to learn about portraiture. When I got back to Colorado, I did a great deal of architectural work for a firm in Denver. Then I did fancy family albums. I made hand-coated platinum prints of old album photographs and mounted them on beautiful paper. Several people fell for the idea. There was a newspaperman from Chicago who had twelve grandchildren. I made 1,278 hand-coated platinum prints from old album pictures of his!

Then I took a job at Boeing, which was commercial work. This was where I learned how to make one negative only— simply to save the bother of processing more than one. The kind of thing I had to do was "General Arnold's coming in for an inspection and he wants his pictures printed"—that kind of thing. I had several exciting assignments on that job— I made pilot flights in a B-29, which of course at that time was tremendously exciting. That is where I got air-minded, because now I would rather work from the air than anywhere, I just love it.

Was there any discrimination against you as a woman?

No. I never noticed any.

Did you have any feedback about your work at this time from other photographers and artists?

I used to send things to exhibitions and to salons. Some people were very nice about my earlier things.

When did you first start showing the public your Indian photographs?

I had one big show of Navaho things in New York about four or five years ago. Then, when it was being shipped to Oklahoma City, the crates (with 161 prints, many of them 16 x 20 inches) were stolen from Kennedy Airport, and that was the end of that. I had a big show on my other book—the book of the Rio Grande Valley—in Colorado Springs before I left there.

During the thirties and forties, were you making the photographs of Indians available to the public?
Yes. I had a small portfolio of four photogravures published with two very corny pictures—I hope you haven't seen them. Well, that's best forgotten. It was during the period when you posed things, you know.

In your documentary work are you concerned with the social relevance of the subject matter?
I was interested in the Navaho as a people, and what they were up against. I am not a trained social scientist and I do not like the way the anthropologists go about getting their information. I did a great deal of research for the text on my book *The Vanishing Navaho*, a terrific lot, and I kept running into places where anthropologists would differ with each other on the same thing. I always went back to the Navaho to check everything.

Did you get involved in the work of the Farm Security Administration?
No, Roy Stryker didn't like my angle when I sent some things in to him.

Amazing. Did he ever say why?
They were too posed for him. I think he was right.

Did the Depression alter the way you photographed?
I don't know. During the Depression one of the projects I got involved in was state guidebooks. The New Mexico one included quite a few things of mine. Hastings House wrote to me and wanted to know if I had any other material, and that was what stimulated me to finish that first book. I became very interested in archaeology, and every vacation we would go to a different archaeological site. I suppose I was doing a documentary on it.

Were any of your pictures of Indians published in major magazines, like Life?

No. But I had a beautiful full page in the *Illustrated London News*, in 1933 or 1934. I did not fit *Life*'s pattern. I did not use a 35-mm. camera. It just seemed ridiculous to me to make 999 exposures, and then to choose one!

Why did you use platinum-coated paper?

Because of the beauty of it, and because of its permanence.

Today you are considered to be a master of platinum printing.

That is only because I kept doing it, and other people didn't. But the younger people who are doing it now have not discovered how to do a good black. This is something I want to look into. I think it's the light-sensitizer chemical. I think they have changed it chemically to make it last longer or something, because I have yet to see a good black.

Do you still coat your own paper?

I have done some recently. I had a portrait job to do for two wealthy New York people who come out here every summer. They came to see me and wanted me to do portraits of both of them, and they wanted hand-coated platinum prints. I could not believe it, but I did it. I have not done as much as I would like to, but I am hoping that I will do more.

Did you stay with Boeing after the war?

No. I left in 1945, because the public-relations department had pretty well finished its job, and I went on to New York. I went to see some publishers and suggested a book on the Rio Grande from source to mouth, and they snapped it up. New Mexico was a logical headquarters. I had lost my father and brother during the war and I was alone.

How were you using a view camera for that project? How many negatives do you think you took?

I did not take so many, because film was hard to get in those days. I did the hand things, of course, with a 3¼ x 4¼ inch

Speed Graphic and I had a 5 x 7 inch view camera, too. I took that up to the actual source of the river. Every time my view camera got heavy, I used to think of W. H. Jackson! Incidentally, his second wife was a cousin of my father's. The first series of pictures he did on a Western ranch was done around my father's ranch, so I have quite a series of those. I met him about 1933 or 1934 and we had quite a pow-wow! I was getting together a show of some Navaho prints. I showed those at the American Museum of Natural History in New York and at the Library of Congress. I then got involved in the Navaho book, and I was fifteen years completing that.

That seems to have made waves all across the country.
Well, I am glad if it has. It certainly is not viewed that way in the sales department of the University of Texas Press, with its one little salesman! But it has picked up tremendously.

How did the Indians themselves react?
They liked the book, and this means more to me than anything. Last summer, I was up in de Chelly and I had a Navaho boy driving me. We came upon an old-fashioned horse hay baler, and I stopped it. I saw this one older man and I said: "Could I make a few pictures?" He said: "Yes, if you will give these boys a quarter for soft drinks." When I was through I thanked him, and he said: "You don't have to give these boys a soft drink. I'm the superintendent of the Cottonwood School and instead I'd like to have a copy of your book for the school."

So there was that kind of a reaction. I always take the book with me and I have given a great many away; but people are buying it, and this means quite a bit.

Do you consider the documentary photograph purely as a record, or do you think it has an aesthetic of its own?
You can always make it the best you can. There are certain things in the Navaho book that are pure documentary and do not measure up designwise, simply because it was not there. But you always try to find it.

Is it the design element of photography that interests you?

Absolutely. I have been working on some color abstracts recently. Another sculptor friend of mine was over here the other day and she said: "Your 1974 work is the best work you have done yet." Much of it is 35 mm., I'm ashamed to say. I didn't even own a 35-mm. camera until I started to write this book (on Canyon de Chelly) three years ago, and I did it really to learn my way around the canyons and to get a record of where I would want to return. With the modern techniques you can get extraordinarily good things from a 35-mm. camera, but it changes the picture.

I bought a Kodak Medallist in 1950, when I started on the Navaho book. I have three of them. You need one for black and white, one for color negative, and one for an extra.

Do you have any views on the modern generation of photographers?
They all know how to operate a 35-mm. camera and they think that's all there is to know. I have had several students here and I have tried one or two assistants, but they did not seem to work out very well. They don't know how to see; they don't know what to look for; they are not conscious of design, and that's the fundamental issue as I see it. It's very difficult to see it in a 35-mm. camera. Cartier-Bresson is superb, but then he was a painter first. I think of the 35 mm. as an accessory. I am interested to see that there is now quite a swing back to the larger formats.

What has been a major concern in your work?
I think it's a question of trying to produce a superb design in photography and making a print that is adequate to that aim. There is no creative thing, whether it be writing, art, painting, architecture, or music that does not have structure and design. It just does not stand up without it.

What do you think of the recognition you are finally getting for your work?
Well, right now I am swamped with so many extra things that I am not getting enough work done, and this is worrying me!

March 1975

The Enduring Navaho. Austin: University of Texas Press, 1968.

Laura Gilpin Retrospective: 1901–1974. Text by Anne Noggle. Sante Fe: Museum of New Mexico, 1974.

The Mesa Verde National Park: Reproductions from a Series of Photographs. Cole Spring: Gilpin Publishing Company, 1927.

The Pueblos: A Camera Chronicle. New York: Hastings House, 1941.

The Rio Grande: River of Destiny. New York: Duell, Sloan and Pearce, 1949.

Temples in Yucatan: A Camera Chronicle of Chichen Itza. New York: Hastings House, 1948.

Imogen Cunningham

(1 8 8 3 – 1 9 7 6 / A M E R I C A N)

How did you get started in photography?
Everyone asks me that question. I'm asked it at parties, every-where. Nobody started me, I was self-motivated. But I did see something of Gertrude Käsebier—and that's all I'm going to tell you about what started me off.

Can you remember the first photograph that you actually took, developed, and printed?
The one that I claim to be one of my first might have been me on the University of Washington campus, in the lower part of the woods, stark naked, lying in the grass.

A self-portrait?
Yes. Well, it doesn't show much as I'm in the grass. That was one of the first that I took myself.

Did your family have any involvement with photography?
No, my father considered the photographer "dirty," I'm sure. He said: "Why do you want to go to school if all you're going to turn out to be is a dirty photographer?" He just thought it was a half-job. I remember the only time any of us were photographed was when we were all lined up in front of one of those hack photographers.

Did your father hinder your going into photography?
No, not in the slightest! He made me a darkroom in the wood-shed and he did everything for it, which was quite a chore. He never said a word about it after that. But if he knew that I was now practically making a living out of the image of him in the woodpile, he'd be surprised!

Can you remember the first creative photographer you ever met?
Well, you know, I never divide photographers into creative and uncreative, I just call them photographers. Who is creative? How do you know who is creative or not? There were photographers I met in Europe, but I wasn't really excited by them. I did go to see a photographer in Dresden, and I thought he was kind of a hack. I guess that Edward Curtis must have been the first one that I really recognized as being what I would call a really good photographer.

You worked for Curtis after you graduated with your B.S. in photochemistry, or was it chemistry?
I had just gotten a B.S. in chemistry, and I was finished in three and a half years, so my major advisor said that I could take time off if I got myself a job, which I did.

And that job was . . . ?
One semester I worked for Curtis for nothing, and then the girl who was the printer got married and they gave me the job. I stayed until I got a scholarship and went to Europe.

Why did you choose chemistry in college?
There was nothing else to choose. They didn't teach art. They didn't teach anything that was near photography at that time, you know. Chemistry was good because you had to make your own formulas. You didn't have it in a bottle like you do now. Everything is easy now.

Can you remember your first published photograph?
You know, Margery Mann can tell you that, I can't. She keeps track of them. I don't pay any attention to statistics.

What was it that drew you to Germany from the printing shop of Curtis?
Well, for one thing they had this wonderful course at the Technische Hochschule in Dresden, and my major advisor at the university knew about it. When I got the scholarship, he sent me first to Leipzig, where he had a lot of friends. I had

some very interesting experiences there. I don't know that I should tell this, but I was put into the arms of some women. One of them was a modiste of the latest order; she didn't believe in making dresses for corseted women, and corseted women were the fashion of the day. But, when she discovered that I had never worn a bone corset, I became her model and she took me to a big show in Dresden. Mind you, this was completely without being paid, even for my fare, and I put on one dress after another for her fashion show. I never got anything out of it but a thank you.

Did you have your own cameras with you at the time?
I always had my cameras! I didn't travel without them, I had a whole trunkload. I had a 5 x 7 inch view camera, and of course, we used plates. It was pretty horrible. It's easy now. Yes, I can travel very light now.

Did you meet any interesting people in the photographic world while you were in Europe?
I met scientists, and I did go to see August Sander later. I had never seen his work when I went to see him. You know, I feel as though I should have bought something when we were there, but I didn't see anything I wanted to acquire. I'll tell you, that man did not know the good from the bad. He was a portrait photographer and he showed us stuff, and we assumed he was saving his best and not putting it up for sale. Maybe he didn't, I don't know. He looked to be in very straitened circumstances. You see, he was burned out of his town by the war and he lived alone upstairs in a farmhouse. His wife had died, and he really was in an unhappy situation.

When you first went to England, you met Alvin Langdon Coburn, didn't you?
Yes, I remember exactly where he lived. When I went to his house he wanted to give me a book. When he left the room to get it, his mother said to me: "You know you'll never be as good as Alvin!" And I said: "Well, I hadn't thought of that!" All I wanted to be was a good photographer, and I never thought of anything else. But she had a watchful eye

over him, if you ever notice the photograph of them together. Well, he finally got married when she died.

Did you meet anybody else while you were in England at that time? Any photographers?
No. I was pretty ignorant then. I guess all of us are when we begin.

When you came back you opened up a studio—a portrait studio. Why was portraiture so important to you?
It was just a matter of making a living. Besides, at that time, magazines weren't taking work from photographers. Or, if they did, it was hardly ever paid for. But I gave them what they wanted, which I don't think anyone else ever did. I was at once very popular. I traveled on the streetcar, and I carried a straw suitcase because it wasn't as heavy as a leather one. I packed a 5 x 7 camera in it, twelve plates, and a collapsible tripod. I went to a house and photographed whatever they wanted photographed—usually the children, or Mama and Papa, everybody at home—proofed it, printed it, and was paid very little!

At that time did your portraiture have a soft-focus, pictorialist style?
In 1910 I had a Pinkerman Smith lens and I used it a lot, but not for portraits. I had a sharp lens for those.

Was that unusual at the time?
No. I think all the regular studios used sharp lenses.

During that time, did you ever meet Stieglitz?
I saw Stieglitz when I came home from Europe.

When he was at the Photo-Secession Gallery?
No. Let me think. I don't believe I went to see him then, I was too scared.

Why were you so scared?
I don't think I knew any more than his name.

On your way back, you paid a visit to Gertrude Käsebier, didn't you?
Yes, I did. She was printing with platinum, and she had one eye covered by a patch, since she had gotten platinum poisoning. She had touched her face or eyes at some point when she was printing. I was always very, very careful. But some people are allergic to it, anyway. If you take up the paper, which has a powdery feel to it, and spread it around with your fingers, you can be sick.

Did you show her any prints?
No. I didn't have anything to show her, it was just a social call.

Did you see Stieglitz's magazine, Camera Work?
I subscribed. You know, the other day I was offered fifty dollars for each copy. I think it's a pity that the value has gone so sky-high. I don't know if it'll last, everyone thinks it will, but the dealers are really avaricious, and they are popping up everywhere.

What painters did you see in New York?
Marin and Dove.

Did that kind of work have any meaning for you?
Oh, yes!

You went to a lot of galleries in Europe, didn't you?
Of course, and I saw a great show in Dresden. You know that photographer, he did fashions for women. Not Cecil Beaton—Baron de Meyer. It was all kind of overpowering to me.

It was shortly after this time that you got married, wasn't it?
1915. I was just a hack portrait photographer then.

You gave up full-time photography to bring up a family. Was this frustrating for you?
Not at all, not at all. It was just that I couldn't do everything at once. I didn't give up photography. I had three children

under two years of age, and I didn't have a darkroom. Whenever I would photograph, I had to have it developed downtown, that kind of thing. My husband was a designer for a
billboard company; then he got a job with a girls' school in
Piedmont; finally he got a job teaching at Mills College. From
then on, I became a photographer, but I still had the kids
around. We had a big yard with lots of places to play and
they would be allowed to go free in the garden, but I didn't
go in the darkroom when they were on the loose. I photographed them, at the same time I did most of my flower things.
Ron and Pad, my twin boys, were great persons for hunting
for things that interested them and that were interesting to
me, too—such as snakes, which they carried home in their
pockets. Pad was very good at holding their tails, so I would
get them on a log of wood and he would hold the tail through
a knothole.

What was it like to work for Edward Curtis?
Well, it wasn't like working for Edward Curtis at all. It was
just working. Someone said to me once: "You must have
known Edward Curtis very well." I said: "Well, in two years
I've met him only twice."

Why was that?
He was never at home. He was a photographer in the field.
But the man that was in charge of his studio was a marvelous
person, I will never forget him, his name was Muhr. I hit it
off with him, and he did everything for me. In my time, from
1907 to 1909, Curtis used a $6\frac{1}{2}$ x $8\frac{1}{2}$ inch view camera (it
was before the 8 x 10) and this man made a transparency
and then a perfect negative for the large prints. It was uncanny.

What was your opinion of Curtis's photographs?
I thought they were wonderful. He had a staff of people working for him and now, since I'm sure they are all dead, I can
say what I thought about them. He had a schoolteacher,
McBride, whose job was to sit at a desk where she took all
the orders for portraits and sold the prints, too. When she
didn't order the portraits, she would very often shove the
prints away and forget about them. When people came up

and asked for their prints, she would unearth them and we'd get hell upstairs for not finishing the photographs. But, because of her forgetfulness, we'd never even got the order! One day, when I went out at three o'clock, she said: "Miss Cunningham, isn't this rather early to leave?" I said: "I don't think so, for a person who arrives at seven." You see, Seattle doesn't have too much sunlight and a platinum print is better done by daylight than by electricity, so I would be at that studio at seven in the morning if the sun was up.

Was Curtis working exclusively on Indians?
No. It was a sideline with him. The studio was for commercial portraitures.

Did you feel at the time that there may have been some reason to question his exploitation of the Indians?
No, not really. Not at all.

When you left Seattle, you began an interest in botanical studies.
I had always been interested in plants but had never studied them until we came to California, where everything grew so marvelously and I had a domestic life which accommodated something like that. You don't mind cooking, and you don't mind digging, and you don't mind turning and following kids around. I just can't understand women not being able to do it all at one time without complaint. Some of my best stuff was done in the twenties.

What was it like at Mills College?
I was only the wife of a man who was at Mills. I was not a professor. I didn't do anything at Mills. I stayed home and I didn't even go to social events, but even so I had a lot of friends there. Later on I did several jobs for Mills College. I did the photographs for their booklets.

While you were living in Oakland, did you become friends with Edward Weston?
My husband was also an interested addict. He was interested in photography and in Weston's work. When we moved from

San Francisco to that hillside by Mills College, it rained and rained. That day Weston and a friend came to see us, and they were very interested in helping prepare the dinner. We had a meager little supper that night, I think it was one steak, and I cut it into nine pieces and made a stew. Anne Brigman, who was entertaining Weston, also came over. They *had* to be very helpful, so they all washed the dishes after dinner, but the next morning we had no water! You see, we didn't know how limited our water was. The person from whom we had bought the place didn't really let us in on his secret, and we were too ignorant to ask. The thing was that there was a well, and it automatically pumped into the tank in the top of the garret, but that amount was the result of quite a number of days of pumping. So we never ever could make it up, and all our washing had to be done by hand at the stream at the foot of the hill. You can't imagine. Women nowadays wouldn't take it at all. I must say, I didn't enjoy it.

Did Weston come to know your work?
The classic letter of all time is in the museum at Eastman House. In 1928 Weston came back from Mexico through Los Angeles and he went to a show at the Los Angeles County Museum and he wrote me a letter. He said that everything in the show was dreadful until he came to one of my pictures. He said: "If you keep up that standard, you will become a great photographer." Very patronizing, don't you think? I'd worked twenty years longer than he at that time, but he'd never seen my pictures before. You see, when he first knew me, I was just a *hausfrau*. What I was doing wasn't revealed to the world then.

You and your husband helped sustain Weston. You bought prints from him, didn't you?
Yes, we did.

Did he collect any of your work?
Edward could never afford to buy anything from anybody. I never heard of him doing so.

What do you think was the need for such a grouping as f/64, tenuous as it was?

I think it was the motivation of Willard Van Dyke. You know, it wasn't such a marvelous show. Henry Swift was a member of the group and he was the only person in the group who had money. He had real money, and he bought. When he died, it was his wife that gave the work of the group to the San Francisco Art Museum, and every once in a while they show it. It's been a long time since I saw it, but I don't get any great lift from it.

Regarding Group f/64, was there something in the air that made you all want to go toward the more precise, to render the greatest detail?

It seems to me that everybody, regardless of how they feel, is affected by what's going on around them. I can't re-create my feelings about how I happened to do this or that, because a lot of my work was done without any motivation other than just what I call having a good time and fooling around. And that was when I did the soft-focus thing of two people who were friends of mine. We went to a country place where a woman who liked us very well fed us and took care of us while we photographed and fooled around. That was in 1910. I was just an amateur, and it didn't become popular. Now folks think it's good. Avedon is doing that kind of thing for *Vogue* and I'm having my old Pinkerman Smith lens remade!

You seemed to have developed the camera view for abstraction on the West Coast almost before Weston.

I don't know when I did anything. I did things by instinct. I remember photographing things at Mills College when I first went there that no one ever bothered with, like the stairway in the old Art Building. Well, that's a classic now. The building's torn down and I gave all the extra prints I had to Mills this year. But I think I'm going to file the others because they'll be valuable for people to use.

What commercial work were you doing during the Depression?

I worked for *Vanity Fair*. That's the only magazine I ever

worked for. It was published by the same people that published *Vogue*. That was around 1931. They asked me what subjects I wanted. I said: "Ugly men." I got Cary Grant and a lot of people I wish I could look up now. I'd be very pleased to see how much they have aged. There was another one who was a red-headed man and looked exactly like one of my own kids. I treated him like that. He was James Cagney. He said to me when I left: "You know, you are the only photographer who hasn't blown a fuse in my house." And I said: "I know why— I use daylight!"

Did you get involved with the Farm Security Administration?
No. I missed it by refusing to do it. I did go on one trip with Willard Van Dyke. We went to see some Brookland people, out of work, who revived an old mill. Dorothea Lange and I were both on that, and Professor Taylor asked us to go down to do the workers in the valley. But I couldn't because I had three kids in school then and they needed a little more of me at home, and so I didn't go. I wouldn't have gone for it like Dorothea did. She had a real appetite for it. She liked that quick shooting, and she didn't mind the hard work either— she loved it. It was her making, actually.

How did you and Dorothea get along? Were you ever photo-graphic rivals?
Never. We were very good friends. When she was married to Maynard Dixon, we would go to a certain place in the summer and she would invite my twin sons to stay with her. She had her kids too, but they were younger than mine, but she loved them.

What documentary work have you done?
My trust wants me to get up a show of local things. They said to me, "You don't have to call it a documentary, just call it 'Walking around San Francisco.'" I once said to Margery Mann: "Well, I'd like to do that," and she said: "Forget it. You're not a documentarian." But what she meant by that is that I don't stick to any one subject. I don't take, for instance, certain miseries of the world, like children that are left without parents, and so on. You know, a documentary is only interest-

ing once in a while. If you look at a whole book of Dorothea's where she has row after row of people bending over and digging out carrots—that can be very tedious. And so it's only once in a while that something happens that is worth doing. Now I have one documentary photograph that I think is good. It was taken under the Queensborough bridge in New York City—a man sleeping on newspapers. Of course, I've never had a 35 mm., and I have never run around like Cartier-Bresson. None of his later work equals his first. He'll never do the man jumping across that puddle a second time. That's really it.

Isn't there a conflict between what you photograph instinctively and what might be called your commercial work?
Well, I don't say I work instinctively when somebody asks me to do a portrait. Actually, I am beginning to hate it. I've already advertised this fact widely. I am not going to photograph anybody who has money and hates his face. That's it. I'm not going to be conned into doing it because of money. I ought to be in a position where I can have a few choices. At first, I never had any choice, and I did the best I could, but believe me, I've had plenty of disappointments from people who don't like their faces.

Do you think a sense of humor is necessary to stay professionally, or aesthetically, alive in the business?
I think a sense of humor doesn't hurt anybody. I think you can make fun of these people when they sit down and say to you: "You're getting the wrong side of my face." If anybody said that to me now, I'd tell them the sitting was finished.

What is the fascination for you in portrait photography?
Money! Money! Money! That's what I went out for. Now that I've made it, it's simply a livelihood. It sounds avaricious, but I've never charged as much as I could have.

Have you involved yourself with causes, like women's suffrage?
I'll tell you, my introduction to women's suffrage was at Hyde Park Corner in 1910. You couldn't believe that, could you? Well, the women used nice language then, no matter what

they were doing. They let themselves be chained to the fence at Buckingham Palace, but they still remained ladies. I wouldn't consider our present movement of that order.

So you haven't any sympathy for women's lib?
No. I don't condemn it, because what they're doing is a good thing. It's going to do something for the cause of women. But I don't like obscene language, and I don't like rough manners, and I don't want to attach myself to it and be one of the voluble ones. I just take things as they are. I'm a worker, I'm not a woman any more than I'm a man. In fact, some people think Imogen is a man's name, but you know what it is—best woman in Shakespeare, that's what my father called me. A princess daughter of Cymbeline.

When did you start teaching?
I never started teaching. I just got snatched into it. I never had a real teaching job, I just do bits and pieces. I have a semester somewhere, a month somewhere, a workshop somewhere.

This started about when?
I'll tell you, we did a night school, somebody and I, at a place downtown in San Francisco. You know, I'm very bad on time —I've spent too much of it living to know when it happened.

What other kind of photographic work were you doing during the Depression?
I was the wife of a professor, so I never knew there was a Depression. We were so poor, and we were so accustomed to it, that we didn't know that anybody else was poor. And you know, that's really true. A person who has a regular job, no matter how low the salary is, still lives. I didn't try to make much money actually and I charged for what I did, but so little that when you look at it now, it's unbelievable.

Did World War II have an effect on your work?
World War II certainly did. I was then working at a studio

down on Montgomery Street and living in Oakland, and I photographed an awful lot of Navy and Army people.

How did you come to live in this beautiful house in San Francisco?
Someone found it through an advertisement. My eldest son was an architect and he designed it for me. It took about a year to get me in. And, of course, there were a lot of funny things that we didn't do because materials weren't available. I had the whole front yard designed by a landscaper and paid in photography. That's one time when it was a good trade.

It seems that after the war you began, on a personal basis, to photograph a lot of artists, writers, and painters of the area?
This simply happened to me. As a matter of fact, I've very seldom gone out for people, they come to me. Now, when I did Gertrude Stein, that was for a man who was writing something about her. I photographed her when she was staying at a hotel here, and I thought it would be a wonderful idea to have the distance of the city behind her. I took her out on a balcony. I was using film in an 8 x 10 camera and I had taken one or two shots out there when Miss Toklas came out and said: "Miss Cunningham, you have three minutes," and I said: "Miss Toklas, this sitting is finished!" I grabbed my camera and came in. Miss Toklas was a very hard gal to deal with.

What was it like photographing Stieglitz?
It was quite simple. I went to New York with a great bunch of 8 x 10 holders, but no camera. I went into his place several times before I asked him. I didn't ask him if he remembered me from 1910, like students do to me. When I was tired, I sat down on the floor because there were no chairs. He came in and I could see that I had done something that other people didn't do, and that made him like me, so he was really very agreeable. He let me use his camera. And I must say, it was as much corroded as my darkroom clock now. You could hardly read the openings and it had a bulb release,

and I'd never used one in my life. This was 1934 and I had no meter. There were no meters then. I did seven shots, and they are all different. The one that I felt most for is not the one that Ansel picked out to use in a pamphlet he got out at the time of the Fair. The one that I like is the one that is in my book.

Did O'Keeffe ever see the work?
She had everything and gave all of it to the Yale museum. And the same happened to the Stein stuff. I sent all of it off. The letters that Miss Toklas wrote to me were charming, but you have to have a magnifying glass to read the writing and it was on tissue paper. But they're very charming and sweet. I've been reading her letters lately to some friends. She seemed to have a great many friends that she wrote devotedly to. She had a nice life, but she had a long, slow death.

Did anything come out of your session with Stieglitz? Did he become interested in your work at that time?
Not at all.

Did he see it?
Well, he had seen it. He picked out something that I don't care for myself. It's two calla lily leaves. Later Steichen picked up more of my stuff that Stieglitz was interested in.

Were you in the great "History of Photography" exhibition that Newhall put together at MOMA in 1937?
Well, I can't imagine that I wasn't, since the Museum of Modern Art already had some of my stuff.

What do you consider has been your major philosophical concern as a photographer?
Have a good life and let other people have one, too. I don't interfere with anyone. I'm not jealous of anybody. I just believe in working. I'm not one of those romantic explainers of my own individual point of view.

There seems to have been one photograph that touched off almost a philosophical concern, if not controversy—the famous portrait of Morris Graves.

I think you are a very special person to divine it that way. I don't get that. There's always some special person who likes Morris. Now you know, the ones that sell more than Morris are my father in the woodpile, and my mother and father and the cow. Those were buried from 1923 to 1970. I had them wrapped up with some kid shots that I did at the barn, and now they're very popular. And so, of course, is my "Magnolia." It's too popular!

You've captured the essential qualities of some of the great working American artists of the times—Roethke, Graves, Stieglitz.

Roethke was a very difficult man, but charged with energy. He was a very special person. You see, I photographed him in his hotel and those were just head shots, so I took him to an alley downstairs where there was a wall. I said to Mrs. Roethke: "Oh, I have a crack coming out of his head," and she said: "Very appropriate." You know, he went off into terrific depressions and had to go to the hospital. He had the saddest life I've ever come in contact with. His wife was marvelous, really marvelous.

What are the sort of things, essential qualities maybe, that you look for in a person when you take his portrait?

You know, I don't. People ask me funny questions like that. I don't direct what I want of them, I let them do it, and when I see it, I take it. And if I don't see it, then it doesn't get taken. The thing that's fascinating about portraiture is that nobody is alike.

Ansel once said to somebody that I was versatile, but what he really meant was that I jump around. I'm never satisfied staying in one spot very long. I couldn't stay with the mountains, and I couldn't stay with the trees, and I couldn't stay with the rivers. But I can always stay with people, because they really are different.

In your long life, you've seen photography reach increasingly larger audiences. Do you feel that this is a good thing, and if so, how would you like to see it develop?

Well, I have no rules for the world. But I do think that the popularity of it is too sudden. There is an exaggeration of its importance. There are too many people studying it now who are never going to make it. You can't give them a formula for making it. You have to have it in you first, you don't learn it. The *seeing eye* is the important thing!

I'd like to see portrait photography go right back to Julia Margaret Cameron. I don't think there's anybody better. Do you? Though now we have the technique to overcome the things that she shouldn't have done. But she certainly saw people!

Do you think she exercised any influence on your photography?

No. I saw her work too late in my life. I was already on my way up then. But I do like her stuff tremendously. People ask me who is my favorite photographer, and I say, Don't ask me a question like that—somebody will be jumping on me. I can't talk about my colleagues.

Are there any people today whose work is especially meaningful to you?

Well, I wouldn't be telling you if I knew. I have a lot of photographic admirations. I like a lot of different people. I can tell you the ones I don't like, though. I have a few very pointed aversions, people who got popular for doing a certain kind of flip stuff, like Avedon. He's my present aversion, and I love disliking him because I hope I'll meet him someday. Another aversion of mine is Les Krims—he's very popular now—the one who photographs his mother nude. I understand he even sprayed his wife with some sort of spray.

What do you think of other contemporary trends?

Oh, there are so many. I think the cheapness of the nude, the way in which it's been handled, that disgusts me. This is an age of vulgarity and eroticism, digging it up from anywhere. That's not my idea of aesthetics.

What are your feelings on photographic education?
There are an awful lot of teachers right now. I asked someone the other day: "What did you learn from your teacher?" and she said: "Well, she helped me a lot in seeing." I won't say that they can't be helped a lot, but it seems to me there has to be something else. I believe in a little self-education. Kids who go to school expecting it all to be put in their heads— that's abominable, and it can't be done. You have to do a little work on your own. Last summer at Yosemite I lent a boy my 4 x 5 camera, which is very precious to me. He said: "What do I do with this now?" and I said: "Unscrew it and find out for yourself. Unscrew every screw and find out." Why shouldn't he learn how to collapse a camera? Why should I teach him that? You mustn't treat a child as if he's a nitwit; tell him something and let him go at it. I don't believe we do enough self-education. People want to have an exhibition as soon as they get out of school. Why do they want to be exposed to the public immediately? They don't realize that some of it should be thrown away. I told the boys up there at Yosemite that everything you do in class is to be put in the wastebasket. They didn't see that at all, though.

Do you think that they should be educated in the way that you were educated, as an apprentice for a while?
There's no chance for that now. People won't take an apprentice on. But, of course, this boy who works for me, spotting and mounting, he's learning something. I don't hesitate to talk to him about anything.

Have you any interests outside photography? You are renowned as a cook, aren't you?
I'm not as good a cook as I was, but then at ninety-three I'm not interested in food any more. But I'm going to get out a cookbook, not on my own, someone is going to use my name

and my recipes, and that's kind of class. It's going to be called *Beg, Borrowed and Stolen.*

I used to sew, make clothes, and all that kind of junk, but my pet avocation now is jam-making.

What future plans do you have for your photographic work?
I've started on a subject now, but I don't know whether I'll be able to do it. If I do, it could be said to be thematic, and I've never taken on a theme before. The theme will be old people.

My son thinks I ought to give up everything, get myself a little 35 mm., walk around town and have fun, have the film all developed and proofed by someone else and never do any darkroom work. I'm perfectly willing to give up the darkroom, it's really tiring. I don't think I could take to a 35, I'm going to stick to 2¼. It's like an eye-level camera to me.

Did your Guggenheim award come as a surprise?
Well, very few people have gotten it at the age that I was. I think I was eighty-seven. That is kind of old!

What was it for?
To reprint some of the stuff I've never printed before. I thought I'd done a bang-up job, but when I got it down to the archivist who's now working for me, she unearthed stuff that I didn't even remember. I'm making loads of prints of them, and I'm going to make a show out of it.

It seems to have taken the establishment a long time to have finally come to grips with the force of your work. Does this bother you?
I've just been interested in photographing. I've never gone out of my way to get any great result. And I don't think it's anything against me. I just feel that it's more the way things normally happen.

It seems that for over seventy years you've been on the edge of the avant-garde in photography.
People say it now, but they never thought of it before.

Does that amuse you or irritate you?

No, it doesn't bother me. Nothing bothers me. Why should I care?

You just go on working for the joy of it?

Well, you see, I never started out the way some kids start out now, saying that they want to be the greatest photographer and so on. I understand that there are some great photographers who have that self-important feeling, but I don't see any reason for it. I think they're just people, and when they call me a famous woman, I say: "You don't know what fame is." It never comes to you till you're dead, so I've got a while yet!

Why do you feel it's so important to get your archives settled and a trust established?

This is an entirely commercial idea. I'm a businesswoman. People want my stuff and I'm going to let them have it. Now, if they don't want it and the thing fails, well, I won't be here to worry.

When you look ahead to work to be done, do you see yourself continuing to do portraits?

Well, I can't see how anybody ninety-three can look ahead, at any rate long-term. I'm going to do what I can, when it happens. I'm not going to hunt up very much of anything. My family is very much concerned that I should take a little time off and have fun, but I don't know how. I've been so steadily motivated that it's very hard for me to enjoy what you would call complete leisure . . . I think I'll just make jam!

March 1975

BOOKS OF CUNNINGHAM PHOTOGRAPHS

After Ninety. Introduction by Margaretta Mitchell. Seattle: University of Washington Press, 1977.
Homage to Imogen (special issue of *Camera* magazine). Lucerne, Switzerland, October 1975.

Imogen Cunningham. Millerton, New York: Aperture, Volume 11, 1964.
Imogen Cunningham: Photographs 1921–1967. Foreword by Beaumont New-
hall. California: Stanford University Press, 1967.
Imogen Cunningham: Photographs. Introduction by Margery Mann. Seattle:
University of Washington Press, 1970.
Imogen! Imogen Cunningham Photographs 1910–1973. Introduction by
Margery Mann. Seattle: University of Washington Press, 1974.

Wynn Bullock

(1 9 0 2 – 1 9 7 5 / A M E R I C A N)

Paul Hill

Did your family have any influence on your going into photography?
My family mostly wanted me to become a professional man—
a lawyer, for instance. My mother was a judge for thirty years.
My family thought that art was something to admire but not
to follow. Actually, I had no idea myself, because I was a
singer for years. I sang professionally on Broadway for four
years and then I spent three years in Europe. But my family
wasn't too pleased with singing as a career, either.

What kind of singing did you do?
I was interested in classical and concert, but I had to earn a living so I got a job in the *Music Box Revue* way back in the Roaring Twenties—they were pretty roaring, too! It was the biggest musical production in New York, and in the country for that matter. They'd never had an understudy for the leading tenor, which I couldn't understand, so I just learned his part by standing in the wings. The leading tenor was very fond of drinking and I was sure that some nights he just wouldn't make it. I arrived one night to find no leading tenor. I had never had a rehearsal with the orchestra, and never tried the clothes, but I offered to go on. He didn't recover for a week and I sang, apparently with success. At the end of the run, he was offered a big contract somewhere else and they offered me his place. I took it. That was the first year, but my mind was always on classical. Broadway was purely to make money, but it was a very exciting career.

During your singing career, did you develop an interest in photography?
Not until I went to Paris for about a year and a half to study with a leading coach. I lived only a block and a half from the Louvre and I had to pass it every day to go to the studio. I became enormously interested in the work of the impressionists and the post-impressionists, and I was particularly interested in the fact that they had revolutionary ideas that accorded with what to my mind was our contemporary culture, the scientific culture. Their interest was in light and how light and color were used in ways that the greatest painters had never understood before. Cézanne said that up until his time artists drew their pictures in perspective and then painted them. He said: "No. You paint and draw at the same time because different colors can come forward and back. If your perspective is contrary to the color you are using, there is a contradiction." That excited me. I got from that the exciting idea that paintings had a life of their own, because the colors moved back and forth—there was movement. And so from there I bought a camera. I just started taking pictures, never

thinking I would become a photographer. When I went to Italy I bought a Leica and then a Zeiss camera. I still studied singing, but I started taking pictures now on purpose, developing the film in the sink of a hotel room. I had them printed in drugstores since I didn't have an enlarger. That was my real start in what became a deeper and deeper involvement in the issues of art.

When was this?
1927 or 1928.

While you were in Europe, did you see the work of any of the photographers there?
No, I never bothered. I just went out and enjoyed looking and taking pictures. I lived in Italy for about a year and a half, and then Germany. When I went to Germany I became more interested in the technical side, because they had such fine cameras there. I never took it too seriously, but I was terribly excited about the visual world of the painters and the fact that some way or another they felt that they were more a part of the world they lived in than the people who worship the past. That excited me.

Do you remember the first serious photograph that you took?
While I was in Paris, I took a picture—not badly composed, except I had no technical training—of a man fishing on the river Seine. I also took pictures from the end of trains going through Switzerland, but they were mostly regular snapshots. I was serious while I was doing it, but my technical accomplishment was zero.

Was it upon your return to the States that you began to think seriously of doing photography?
The Crash of 1929 forced me to take over the family real-estate business, which I did for about seven or eight years. But I also built myself a darkroom and kept on taking pictures, just for my own pleasure. Then I began to buy books and read about photographers.

Do you remember which ones?
I remember Feininger wrote a book on solarization. I was very much interested in the fact that the painters didn't copy nature but gave a picture a kind of life of its own. They did this by distortion and use of color, as I said, to make colors actually move forward and backward by choice. I was interested in that in a kind of intuitive way, but I didn't know enough about photography to experiment.

Did you see the work that was going on at that time—like that of the Farm Security Administration?
No, I was not aware of it at all, because I had a big job taking care of a business which was maybe $100,000 in debt. I was completely absorbed in it, and every spare moment I had I would go out to take pictures for pleasure: the countryside, portraits of friends, my family.

Did you come in contact with Alfred Stieglitz?
No. Painters interested me much more than Stieglitz. I cannot say that I wasn't aware of Stieglitz. But I lived in a town in West Virginia with no library of photographic books, and so I just worked on my own.

What was it that finally caused you to go to school to study photography?
Well, after finally getting the business back into good enough shape to give it to the bank, I went to California. My family talked me into studying law, so I went to U.S.C. Law School. As I told you, my mother was a judge and although I was not really talked into it, I had been brought up all my life with this idea of the professional man and the proper way to make a living. But I just wasn't suited to the law. Although the law is absolutely essential to me, I found it to be a compromise, as you can't have laws that will fit exactly the circumstances of the individual. I began to argue with the professor. I only studied law for about six months, and one day I just decided to finish with it and become a photographer. So I walked out, left my books, and went over to the Art Center

School (it's Art Center College now). It was a very sought-after school by photographers. It was small at the time, and their first-year class was filled, but they said: "If you can make a go in the second year, we'll try you out." So I started in the second year and then finished the third, which was the end of the degree. My future was set; I knew I was going to be a photographer.

Did you have any early influences as a student?
Oh, yes, very definitely. The influence that the painters had on me began to emerge, and it was then that the technique that I really went to the school to learn became good enough so that I could begin to experiment. I did all kinds of experiments, particularly with solarization. The other students started to get interested in what I was doing, but the head of the school called me in and told me that I had to stop it because it was interfering with my studies. I didn't think so at all, because I was doing very good work. So I just went out on my own and I don't think I brought in my personal work. There was one teacher, whose name was Edward Kaminski, who encouraged all types of experimentation. He was a kind of inspiration to the students because he encouraged them to become involved in going out and looking. And so, when school was over, the work that had been rejected by the school formed my first show at the Los Angeles County Museum. It was all solarization and experimental work.

What date was that?
That was in 1941. I kept on experimenting while trying to earn a living doing straight commercial work.

Was it right after you graduated from school that you got into commercial work?
Yes.

And what kind of commercial work was it?
It was portraiture. But then I became very interested in the fact that no one had ever really written anything on solariza-

tion indicating how to control the process. In my work I discovered what I felt was the law of light and chemistry that controlled the process.

This was while you were doing your commercial work?
Yes. I spent six or seven years earning my living while also working on solarization and its patent. It took me seven years to patent it. The Patent Office sent me every conceivable kind of patent, but they really had nothing to do with it. Some of them were close, but they weren't the same process. English patents, German patents, and so on. They turned me down about three times, and finally I went to Washington and appeared before the appeal board and they granted me the patent. I was given the patent in England and in Canada. The English were more interested in it than the Americans. So I wrote two articles for the British Medical Society, which they published.

I was divorced at that time and I had to begin all over again financially. I had to concentrate on the business end of photography. I didn't do certain sorts of commercial work. I don't like the intent of advertising which sets out to sell something and not to reveal whether it's good or bad. It never did appeal to me. Also, art directors who try to mix fine art with advertising art. During the war I enlisted, but I kept my business going by hiring someone. Then I became the photographer for the battalion that I was in, and then someone at Cal. Tech. became extremely interested in my control of solarization. He persuaded the Army to let me go so that I could do work for the war effort in air plants.

Your interest in the scientific part of photography has been with you from almost the very beginning?
It was scientific on one hand, but I have never been bothered by mixing science and art. There is a confusion about fine art. What is art? What is aesthetics? I studied semantics and I feel that words are used too loosely. For example, art to me— if I can give any definition of art at all—simply means skill.

Skill in what?
Skill in whatever you do. In other words, if you are a fine

painter, then you have the skill, both the mental as well as the manual. In other words, if you call it *"fine art"* you get into value judgments, but at least you know what skill means. I would ally art to something rational.

At this time I kept on with my personal photography, but it was purely for myself. My professional photography I deliberately made very commercial so that if someone wanted anything photographed—a house, an interior, a piece of machinery, or whatever—I would do the job as best I could to suit him. But when I photographed for myself, I photographed for myself. When I say for myself, it was not just for personal gratification alone, it was really a form of seeking answers to things.

Philosophical answers?
Inevitably philosophical questions or answers arose. I believe that man is not the center of all things. He's not quite the important person people think he is in spite of his mental capacities. I believe he's a part of nature, distinctive and special in his own way, as are all forms of life.

Was it in your student days that you began to feel the need to have light become the subject matter in your work?
Yes, I took my first light pictures then.

That marks you as a fairly unusual person, to use such an insubstantial or immaterial subject matter.
To me it was the source of all material, because everything is formed of energy, and radiant energy is light.

Why did you become interested in photographing nature?
I always loved nature as a boy. For example, I marveled when I was in Southern California. We would go out into the desert and find discarded bottles. Occasionally we would find a piece of glass that might have been out there for fifty years. Well, light and time had changed it and given it beautiful colors. To me this was a kind of miracle. I've always been interested in light.

How have you seen light evolve in your work?
Even though I find I learn more from painters, philosophers,

and scientists than I do from photographers, I have never had a temptation to become anything more than a photographer, because that's what photography is—a light medium. I didn't rationalize it. I think my interest in light was a natural interest from the very beginning.

I found that the only thing I ever got from my commercial work, outside of the money, was that I had opportunities to experiment technically. My personal work helped my commercial work, as the commercial work helped my personal work. My personal work trained my eye. Toward the end of the period that I was doing commercial work, I found that I used to just set up the camera, and almost immediately I knew what I wanted to take. That was eye training which I gained from my personal work.

Was it as a result of your understanding of painting and the qualities of light within the painting structure that your personal work moved toward the abstract, the non-representational?

No. I was simply excited by the fact that the painters didn't violate the medium. In other words, they didn't try tricks and contrivances for effect but developed themselves intellectually. Actually, Van Gogh, even though he had deep emotional problems, was a highly intelligent, literate person, and it was the same way with Gauguin, but not so much with Cézanne, strangely. I found that the painters were more in tune with the great and profound changes that were taking place in our world. For example, when they were studying the structure of matter, they would go into crystals. Cubism was really formed out of that. The painter wasn't afraid of the scientist. They exchanged ideas; they reinforced each other. I have the feeling that photographers have not done this except for the very fine scientific photographers. The skill that I am talking about in photography is not just technical skill to reveal matter in a literal sense, but somehow to permit a person to be able to live, and live more in peace with the world he's in now. I feel that photography is more the language of this period than any other. As far as I am concerned, a great deal of the painting of the last fifteen or twenty years has been bad. The one thing that painters can't do that photographers can do is to inject a profound sense of realism into the images they create.

Has realism, or the concept of realism, been important to you?
Enormously. But, when it comes to distortion, control of tone and light itself, I feel that the painter has the advantage over the photographer, because his is the plastic medium. But the photographer can achieve a great sense of realism, which I think is so terribly important. It is the strength of photography. By realism I mean that the light you see something by is the light that the picture is taken by. And so this becomes more real to the viewer, because you know that it is true. For the last twenty-five years, I have adhered almost exclusively to the straight image.

What was it that originally impelled you to set aside your development of the abstract as a concept and move toward the straight image?
Actually, I didn't set it aside, I just decided that solarization does not have the power to create the subtle and beautiful light values and nuances that a straight photograph has. I don't think solarization has the power to create this realism. Solarization produces a controlled image in the darkroom. This is not to say that I think this is wrong. Heaven knows, I went through fifteen years of it, and as I say, my patent still stands and I think it always will, it's the only way to control solarization. I simply felt that the artist could do distortion better than the photographer because he has this plasticity which can control the nuances. When he wants to change something in the tone values, he can paint over it. But the photographer doesn't have the same absolute control in that area of symbolism.

Was it your association with Edward Weston that began to make you rethink this idea?
Weston was the first person, I think, who really convinced me.

Although, during the forties, when I was doing my commercial work, I knew all about Stieglitz, Strand, and Weston. I admired their work tremendously, particularly Weston's mastery of the scene. I had never analyzed the word "scene," and for two years after I first met him, I more or less began to copy his work without realizing it.

When did you first meet him?
About 1948 or 1949. And during those two years I didn't make a single picture that was good enough for a show. I'd had a number of shows of experimental work, but my new work just didn't satisfy me. Weston's work inspired me, but knowing him more and more, I found that he was entirely different from me. He was never one to talk a lot, but he wrote a lot, and that was his way of expressing himself. One thing he did say was that it didn't matter what you took: it was the way you took it. In other words, any object, whether it was a toilet, a rock, a woman, or an artichoke! When I tried it out, it didn't work for me; but then my mind didn't work that way, and I didn't know why at the time. When I actually began using an 8 x 10 camera he didn't tell me his methods of processing; another photographer did. I found that they were superb quality negatives, but I wasn't getting the pictures that I wanted. So I simply stopped for a while and began going over the same territory that he'd been going over for twenty-five years, and that I'd been going over for two years, to see if I could find some answers—and I did. I didn't rationalize them, I didn't try to use logic. I'm not one of these people that think their reason and intuition are in conflict; I think that one supplements and complements the other.

I went out and began relooking. My whole philosophy up until that time had been to look, to see things that were interesting and to arrange them. So I was always looking for an interesting object that I could arrange in the ground glass. But even that didn't produce the results that satisfied me. Very gradually I began not to think of objects any more but to think of events. I never heard Weston talk about events. When I looked at objects, I thought: What is it I'm really looking for? Then I began to realize I was looking for qualities. Qualities simply being the nature or character that belonged to or distinguished a thing. One of the first things I discovered was that all things had spatial qualities. I don't know how long it took, I can't remember now, maybe three or four months, for this idea to become stronger and stronger and stronger. I got more and more excited about it. As I got excited about it, I began taking pictures again, and my pictures immediately began to change. Space to me had a great importance. You don't look and arrange, you have to perceive; and perception is quite different from seeing, and apperception is still another thing. While I was taking pictures, I wasn't necessarily thinking about them philosophically, but even so, this was a whole new world of thinking for me. I was convinced that space was not what I had always been taught (something infinite)—it was just the opposite. Space for the photographer, or anybody, was finite, definite; there was no space without objects. In other words, you can only perceive space if there are objects. The quality of that space depended on how you perceive the dimensions of these objects. I wasn't analyzing it then as I now can, it was just intuitively felt. When I thought of space, I immediately began—after a period of two or three months—to think that you couldn't have space without time, because if you have no time, there's no time for space. And if you have no space, there's nothing for time. They co-existed, but they were independent—they had independent significance. This was perhaps the turning point in my career.

Your work altered from this point on?
Completely.

In what manner?
I began making good pictures! The pictures that I had been taking had not satisfied me. I think we have to satisfy ourselves first, because if you take the opinions of others, pretty soon you'll become totally confused! My pictures immediately began to be accepted all over, where before they hadn't been

(except the experimental ones), and even the experimental ones weren't accepted like these new pictures.

Do you see this as being a time when you began to have some feeling about the relationship between what might be called objective reality and an emotional understanding toward the thing itself? Is there a relationship between the two?
I think that there's a definite relationship, but it has taken me twenty years to come to it. I was constantly being asked what I was thinking about while I took the pictures. I discovered that people find it very difficult to talk about space and time. To me, space and time became the most natural things in the world, and I couldn't understand this opposition. But it didn't change anything; people kept asking me to lecture, and I would lecture on space and time. I was just going over some old tapes and one of them was from 1950 and I was talking about space-time then. What I feel is that the picture-taking process, anyway a greater part of it, is an intuitive thing. You can't go out and logically plan a picture, but when you come back, reason then takes over and verifies or rejects whatever you've done, So that's why I say that reason and intuition are not in conflict—they strengthen each other.

If you went out with all the confused amount of data you have to photograph, can you imagine trying to analyze it all? You would never get anywhere. You have to treat it intuitively, but when you come back, how do you judge it? Part of it is intuitive, and reason is partly intuitive, but reason also demands some kind of frame of reference, for thinking, for rejecting, for accepting. If there is no frame of reference, then it is just blind value judgment, and I don't believe in that.

Was it during the time you were developing the space-time theory that you began to see yourself as a philosopher-photographer?
I've never thought of myself as a philosopher, or as a scientist, because I'm neither of these things. I have never studied philosophy. I have read a lot of philosophy because I dis-

covered that the things that I felt about space and time have been reaffirmed by the greatest minds of our era. Philosophers accept it, scientists accept it, psychologists, I think, accept it. They are having this program on television, *The Ascent of Man* by Bronowski. He was saying things that I felt intuitively all my life, and more and more in the last twenty years, since we have been living in a relativistic age where there are no absolutes. Space was treated as an absolute, absolutely infinite, which is an absurd concept. You can think of it psychologically, but you can't, in any way, think of it in terms of perceiving it or saying what it is, except that it's more space than you can comprehend. But that doesn't mean it's infinite, because you don't know what infinite is! I don't worry about the infinite, I worry about the finite, because there's so many finite things to develop that man can never have enough time to develop even if he lived two hundred years, or a thousand years! Think about the things you can do something about.

Is your theory essentially practical?
Very practical, but no rules, definitely no rules. Space is a faculty, it's a form of perception—it's the only way you can perceive the physical world.

You mentioned the word "apperception." What does that have to do with your theories?
Well "apperception" is strange. In the last month, I've had three or four lectures and I've used this word and asked the audience how many understood it. Practically 99 percent did not know what apperception was. It is a very important word, but like so many words today, if you look it up in the dictionary, you become quite confused. One college dictionary says apperception is conscious perception, but they also add that you are consciously aware of an idea that adds to your previous knowledge. Well, that is enormously important. Here is this word that represents a concept, a natural faculty that we can all develop just like we can develop perception of space, like we can develop the perception of time, because time is nothing more than changing space and this simply is

the four-dimensional happening that we remember. Certain things you remember are important, some are not important; certain things in the natural world impress you more than other things in the natural world. But if you develop a sense of time, as I conceived it in photography, you develop your perception of spatial elements, you develop a sense of time which is the events that mark it and that can only be marked by changing space. It's the relationship of these things that you develop a sense of. And no one is teaching it! In other words, they are not teaching photographers how to develop their own powers.

This is a teaching concept you've been engaged in, then?
This is what I think is important, because for years and years I have talked about certain concepts that are defined by the term "space-time" but none of these things are new. But they are new to the photographer. I have yet to talk to a photographer who talks about space.

Then there is reality and existence, order and ordering— these are all very important concepts. In my lectures I have been talking about these things and here's what I now tell the students: The eyes of the photographer are directed on objects accessible to observation upon their apperception and conceptual formulation. In the attempt to give some visual order to the confusingly immense body of observational data, he uses a storehouse of concepts he has observed since childhood. Since conceptions become so habitual, he seldom concerns himself with, or is even aware of, their never-ending problematic character. As a result, he gives to these concepts, or tools of thought, the kind of absolute value not to be doubted. He has good reason to do so, because how could he use his eyes and mind to photograph even simple subject matter if he analyzed his every act and visual response. However, growth in photography requires that the photographer engages in the critique of the transconcepts so that he may not be unconsciously ruled by them. This is especially true when the consistent use of traditional habits of thought leads to paradoxes difficult to resolve. Paradoxes have developed at various levels of my development as a photographer. First, when I began to find instructional education in conflict with my own experiences of the visual world. The conflict I had to resolve was to conform to commercially oriented photographic education long enough to improve my technique, while at the same time following my own desires to explore new and exciting ways to photograph that had little to do with selling photographs. I was forced to walk a narrow path, as I was threatened with expulsion when following my own ideas. Second, some years later, another conflict surfaced when experimental work that I had been doing failed to satisfy me. Throughout my development in photography, whenever paradoxes occurred, I used nature itself as my principal teacher—going out into the fields, along the seashore, and into the mountains and forests, letting them speak to me. As a result, perception sharpened and new ideas began to formulate.

Up to a point you can use traditional ideas, you can use academic training, you can use all these things if the results satisfy you. But what if you reach a point where your pictures aren't coming up to the standards you think they should, or they are not nearly coming up to the level of photographers you admire—not that you want to copy them, but to their level of visual expression? When that comes, you're faced with a problem, aren't you? That's what happened to me, as I told you before. I don't think you can copy anyone. I don't care how good they are. I didn't try to copy Edward Weston, but I was enticed into copying him for two years. Then, when I began to think space-time, as I told you, I began to make pictures that really changed my level of thinking and visual expression. It was then that Edward told me not to take those pictures. It was the only advice he ever gave me! I know what he meant. He would take simple objects and photograph them in a most magnificent way. He had a sense of space that was almost unbelievable, but he never thought about events, as far as I know. It doesn't mean that his pictures don't evoke a sense of events, because every picture does. But there's one thing in apperceiving space and apperceiving events—I don't think he apperceived events, because he never talked about them. And then I began to think of events as well as space. Then he said: "You're getting too complicated; you're taking pictures that people won't understand easily." My feeling about Edward is that he was the end of the great period of photographing objects for their external, beautiful qualities. He was not involved in the internal, which is more philosophical. I think Whitehead said: "Not only is the world more mysterious and queer than you think it is, but it's queerer than you can think it is." Well, the externals just simply don't tell you this mystery. You see, there's a strange paradox. People usually think that when they go inward, they become introspective or they become mystical. I'm not mystical and I'm not introspective. What I felt was that my mind could have an "eye" which could go farther than my physical eye. I didn't have to respond to what I perceived in terms of the external qualities of things. There is no life without change. All right, you try to make pictures that evoke the sense, not only of the external, but of this thing that you feel inside, a thing that your eye can't see directly but your mind knows it's so. This, to me, is not introspective, this is real. The last few years I've defined reality and existence, but some people wonder what reality and existence have got to do with photography—it's purely philosophical. I don't think so at all. It is philosophical, of course—everything to me is philosophical, if you want to treat it that way. People we call philosophers are just the ones that go more deeply into things. Reality, to me, became enormously important because reality and existence had always been equated—I'd been taught to equate them—and I think people do equate them. In other words, if a thing is real, it exists. Of course it exists, but there's an independent significance between the two that is just as important, and this is the only original idea or concept that I've ever had. I know people think about it and talk about it loosely, but I haven't heard anyone come out and say it. Existence, though technically of reality, has an independent significance because it is really the unknown. Your faith and your reason tell you that there must be some source for what is real to you, but what's real to you is only of your senses, brain, and mind. All those things that exist out there are not real to you at all till they are sense-perceived, and once sense-perceived and remembered, you have ideas about them, beliefs about them, and that's what reality is all about. So, the point is, you develop your realities, you don't develop your existence at all, because that's taken care of by the supreme being, you don't have to worry about that. Reality is an on-going process that can be developed, and developed, and developed.

Do you see your photographs as completed absolute statements?
No, I don't. I'm completely against all absolutes. Defining reality and existence doesn't mean that's the way it is, but at least it makes sense to me. The common idea about composing is that you have power over objects to compose them. I think this is putting the cart before the horse. Before you can compose, you've got to perceive—there's nothing to compose till you do. I wasn't thinking of reality then, I was thinking of perceiving, and space is one of the things you perceive when you look at the physical world. In other words, there's no way to see anything except in terms of its edges, planes, and thicknesses. These are the spatial elements. You don't have to analyze—it's impossible even if you try—these spatial elements, but you are aware that that's what you are really trying to express—some of these relationships—because you're expressing what you're perceiving, so you're trying to develop your perceiving. The first thing that happened was that I began to think of space, space seemed to be infinite, then space became finite, and I began reversing everything. So space became not only the objects you perceive, it also became the air. You could feel the air so you know that it's physical. You can see its manifestations when the fog comes because the air supports it, and this adds a kind of mysterious dimension of space. And then light itself is the most spatial event in the universe.

What was it that impelled you to use nature as your main motif? Was it because it held light in a way that appealed to you, or was it because of the mystery of nature?
To me, what we call nature is not just what we see but what we now know through the aid of optical infinites and so forth. That has evoked a sense of mystery because most of what's in

the world we don't even see. The scientist and the philosopher began to prove these invisible things and this is what science was all about. As soon as philosophy solves something, then it's no longer philosophy, like mathematics was once philosophy, astronomy was once philosophy—once certain fundamental concepts were established and accepted, then they became sciences, no longer philosophy. To me an artist who isn't a philosopher isn't an artist. Edward Weston developed this great sense of space to the point that he saw simple things in ways that other people couldn't see them. But he made an irrelevant statement—"Composition is the strongest way of seeing a thing"—which doesn't mean a thing. What he really meant was that if you develop your sense of seeing, then you can develop fine composition. But he didn't say that.

What did Weston feel about your theories?
He wasn't interested, and I didn't discuss my theories with him, but I did show him my pictures. And when I began taking the pictures that I am known by, like the "Family of Man" picture, for example, he said: "Too complicated." It's true, it's a very controversial picture. But I don't care if a picture is controversial. I don't have any set beliefs, because my beliefs change like everything else in my mind changes. But hopefully they grow. When taking that particular picture, I was thinking: Here is the forest and nature that I love, but as well, I was thinking of the concept of opposites. If I put a human figure in the forest, I have different events—the human event and the natural event. But the human event is natural too.

Do you feel your work delves into the mysterious?
Not just the mysterious. I have an enormous curiosity. It has been said that photography, unlike science, has styles that change, but it doesn't grow. Heinecken said: "I do not equate progress with growth." Well, I find that a completely meaningless statement. Now I agree with him that growth doesn't mean advancement. It can mean growth the other way. It can be growth and deterioration. But if a high jumper grows in his ability to jump, he progresses higher. A baseball player,

a tennis player, a scientist progress and have things that they can show that exhibit some progress over what they have done before. Art is a much more difficult thing to judge in this sense, but each individual can detect it whether or not his faculties are becoming more acute or whether they are dimming. Now space is a faculty, time is a faculty, opposites are a faculty— they're relating things. I don't say what's good or bad. The result and time itself will have to prove that. But I know that when I began thinking of space, I began to see things as I never saw them before. I call that progress.

Was what you never saw before the mysterious?
No. I think everything is mysterious. It's just a matter of your power to perceive it. For example, the trained gardener can perceive things that I can't perceive at all. In other words, he sees the condition of a plant because he's studied what things do to plants, and he can make plants grow in a way that I can't. He's progressed further than I have in plant growing.

To me everything in art is a symbol, it's never the thing. The photograph of the tree is not the tree, the painting of the person is not the person. The only thing that can change is the person and his power to create symbols. Once the symbol is created, it's not changed, except that the material gets older. The symbol, however, doesn't change. I believe that symbols are more important than the people. They have more power to influence the world than the people who create the symbols. Why is it that all the great philosophers, scientists, painters, and so forth still have this great influence? It's because of the symbols they've left us. That's why I say: Develop your faculties, because all you are creating are symbols anyway.

Do you think that symbolism is photography's most powerful inheritance?
This is where reality comes in. The light you see a thing by is the light a photograph of that thing is taken by, and no other medium can say that. Everyone knows that, because there's a certain kind of one-to-oneness about a photographic symbol that doesn't exist in any other form of symbolism.

You must realize that with the exception perhaps of Minor White you are one of the very few people who has ever directly stated the potential for the direct symbolic power of the photograph. Do you see any relationship between your work and White's?

Philosophically, yes, but only to a degree. Minor has created magnificent photographs. He's got a fine eye and he writes well. But he and I part company philosophically when he ends up being mystical. To me symbols do not define things, things define symbols. The photograph does not define the tree, the tree defines the photograph. Now, you can alter it when you print it, you can do all the things that you want, but nothing will match the mystery of the tree. I don't think anything can be beyond what it is. In other words, a tree can't be more than a tree; light can't be more than light. That to me is pure mysticism.

Does it interest you photographically?

Not really. When you talk about the light of the spirit, I would rather talk about reality and the senses, brain and mind that you can do something about—not the spirits floating around in a vague vacuum that no one knows anything about. But people have this deep urge for mysticism, so I don't ignore it.

That's odd, because your work has often been called visionary. How do you react to that?

I don't think it is. I think that Edward Weston's pictures were mystical to most people because his sense of space was beyond their sense of space. He could see a shell, or whatever, and see it lighted, and this sense was beyond other people. That was a mystery. I am as interested in space as anybody—I've been talking about it for the past twenty-five years—but space is simply the first three dimensions of time. So I'm interested in all four dimensions and the expression of them, and if there's any mystery to my work, I think it's because I've learned to relate events more than other people, and this includes space-time. I don't call that mysterious, as a matter of fact, it's a kind of quiet relationship if you just open yourself up to it.

Does that opening up involve a recognition of the unconscious in any way?
Certainly. I'm a great believer in the power of the unconscious. I think that we are controlled to a far greater degree than we know by the unconscious. This certainly isn't a new idea, but it's not mystical. This is again the senses, brain and mind. This is part of our reality, part of the things that we can delve into, as did the physiologists, all of them.

Do you think that part of the evocative power of your photographs is this intuitive recognition of essences of the unconscious?
I certainly think the unconscious affects me profoundly, but I think it's been the development of the sense of space and time which I don't think we're all endowed with. I was trained not to develop it, and I think everyone is in some sense trained not to develop it, but it's their greatest power because it's their most natural faculty.

Stieglitz first used the word "equivalent" in a photographic context...
I think maybe the greatest thing that Stieglitz ever did was to just bring to the surface the meaning of the word "equivalent."

Do you find that the concept has any meaning to you?
Profoundly. I was working almost exclusively on it for the last three or four years before I stopped photographing.

What does the idea of equivalence mean to you? Is it philosophical?
Now remember, philosophy is simply the body of our beliefs. There's nothing mysterious, it's not separate from anything else, it's not separate from psychology. Psychologists are philosophers, scientists are philosophers, even in the *Encyclopaedia Britannica*, when they list Russell and Einstein, they say: ". . . mathematician, scientist, philosopher." They didn't

use to do that, but this is the wonderful thing about our modern day and age. Practically all scientists are philosophers because they are dealing with the inner theoretical world. They don't know what light is, they don't know what gravitation is, but the power of the mind is so great in these great intuitive men that they have accomplished miracles even though they still can't say exactly what they've done.

Is part of the accomplishment a recognition of a fragment of the idea of the equivalent?
No. Beaumont Newhall defined the equivalent. You photograph something for its own qualities, but in photographing it, there's something in that thing that evokes a stream of consciousness about something that is not directly related to that thing. With Stieglitz it was the cloud, and he could see forms in the cloud. The cloud itself is beautiful, but then the forms in the cloud became equivalent to what? Equivalent to memories, to something unconsciously felt, subconsciously felt, maybe something subliminal? We are bombarded by these things all the time, so in a way I think the most fruitful field for expressive photography is in the field of equivalents.

Could this be the direction of your major endeavor now?
I think that the equivalent is bringing me back from just the mystery of nature—not man as nature, but nature other than man—to the nature of man. This, I am profoundly interested in. Also the miraculous things man can do.

Do you see your work, then, as statements about the human condition?
I see my work as an expression of manifestations, of positive thinking, of positive belief in the powers that we have, rather than going off into mystical vague terms.

You say that you haven't been taking any photographs recently?
No. Not for a year and a half.

So, how are you occupying your time at the moment?
I've had to do a lot of printing, a lot of lecturing, a lot of

writing, and I've put out two books. Right now nothing would please me more than to just quietly go out and photograph again, and quietly go out and think.

Are you unable to go out and take pictures?
I had an operation for cancer in 1973, and it was a very serious one. But I had a young doctor who was really great and who did a marvelous job. I had three major operations in three weeks and then a year later an exploratory major operation. Fortunately, they didn't find any recurrence—but you never know. It was cancer of the colon. For years, due to the fact that life itself excites me so, I've been getting tense, and I've been getting fibrillations.

What has been the most difficult thing in sustaining your creative life?
I've never found it to be difficult. I've just felt the interference of things. Demands for good shows, demands for good prints, the necessary demands of making a living. But the actual experience of working has been a joy.

Are you pleased that photography has been reaching an increasingly wide audience? If you are, how would you like to see this increasing awareness developed?
I feel that photographers of the future should not do the things Stieglitz did, not the things Edward Weston did. They should have more to do with symbols. But for me the great strength of photography is its reality. However, I think we have to evoke new symbols—equivalence is one of them—that expand our minds so that we may be more at home in this scientific and terrifying age we live in.

Do you see photographers as being able to fulfill that need?
I think so, but I don't think they're doing it. I think most of them are doing the opposite.

Do you mean the younger photographers?
Yes, particularly those younger photographers who are presenting political and social manifestations of all the things

that are wrong in the world. That has a useful purpose, but I personally think that if you keep doing it, you lose part of your life. I would rather think of the more positive things, the things that can develop, and then maybe these other things can be changed. Just continually being anti . . . I'm pro.

What work do you see as having the most profound effect on twentieth-century photography?
Strand's work, of course. But I think he did his best work in his early days. I saw one of his retrospective shows, and in some way or another those tremendously strong portraits and beautiful scenes he did in his early days became a kind of a formula. I like Bill Brandt very much because he captured some of the qualities of the true English culture, even with his simple pictures like "The Maid at the Window." I like that much, much better than his picture of the man on the bicycle, which is kind of propagandistic. Then his nudes are very beautiful, although I think they are similar to Matisse in the distortion; but he did them magnificently well photographically. So Brandt is one of the people I like very much. Weston, of course, is the one who reached the peak of being able to express the world's external qualities more beautifully and stronger than anyone I know. I don't share the same worship of Stieglitz that many people exhibit. I feel that many of his photographs are very beautiful—I like the horses steaming in the snow. But "The Steerage" is just another good picture, not one of the greatest. I feel that he was maybe the last, maybe the best, of the romantics. His recognition of the modern painters was a very, very important thing here in America.

Do you see yourself as an explorer with the camera?
The world is so mysterious. If you grow, you grow with your own powers, your own faculties; space is one, time is another, recognition of reality now becomes one. You can develop your sense of different realities, but you can't develop existence. So you come to principles that are in harmony with your nervous system and with your experience. I feel that this is the direction that photography is going to have to take,

because the external world has been photographed until it's simply repeated and repeated and repeated. Reality can change. If you develop your own powers, you can develop your realities to express things symbolically.

March 1975

BOOKS OF BULLOCK PHOTOGRAPHS

Introduction to Wynn Bullock: Twenty Color Photographs and Catalogue. California: Saisset Art Gallery and Museum, University of Santa Clara, 1972.

The Photograph as Symbol. Massachusetts: Artichoke Press, 1976.

The Widening Stream. Text by Richard Mack. Peregrin Publications, 1965.

Wynn Bullock. Text by Barbara Bullock. California: Scrimshaw Press, 1971.

Wynn Bullock. Text by David Fuess. Millerton, New York: Aperture History of Photography Series, Number 4, 1976.

Wynn Bullock: Photography, a Way of Life. Text by Barbara Bullock-Wilson. New York: Morgan and Morgan, 1973.

Minor White

(1 9 0 8 – 1 9 7 6 / A M E R I C A N)

Paul Hill

Did you get involved in photography as a child?
My maternal grandfather was an amateur photographer. He used to hand-tint glass slides. I can remember my grandmother spending evenings binding the two pieces of glass together with black tape, and I learned to do that when I was six or seven. I was given a box Brownie at about nine or ten. When I started going to college, I was making snapshots and having them finished at the drugstore.

Do you remember what you photographed then?
The ones I recall are of my buddy and my grandmother in my grandmother's garden. Later on I was photographing little waterways and a creek near my house. I was living with my parents in Minneapolis at the edge of town, so the creek and the countryside were very close.

Were there any photographic images that you took at that time that mean anything to you?
I remember one in particular—the bend of the creek. There were some willows hanging over it. I'm sure that photograph's been lost, but that's the one that stays in my head.

You were how old at this time?
Sixteen or seventeen. I started college when I was eighteen and I can recall that I had to stop photographing—I must have been doing more than I should—in order to give more time to college.

Why did you study botany at college?
The influence of a teacher I happened to like very much and who took a liking to me. And Grandmother's garden was a very important part of my life.

Minor is a strange first name. What is its origin?
All I know is that it is an old family name. It belonged to a great-grandfather, but I don't know much about it. I never bothered with family history.

Why didn't you study an art subject at college?
I think my interest in botany started in high school and continued in college. The art influence was there, however. My grandfather was a house contractor and he had his offices in a well-known art gallery in Minneapolis. So, weekend after weekend, I would go there and wander around the gallery. I saw all kinds of art until I was about twelve. Thereafter, I didn't get associated with art very much except through music. I was given piano lessons and was very interested in classical music—I still am.

Did you do much photography while you were at the University of Minnesota?
I learned the processes in developing film, making prints, and all that. My work was with photomicrographs of algae and various other plant forms. It was all done on glass plates.

Did you find it easier to express yourself through words at that time rather than visual imagery?
While I was at college it was all scientific photography. There was no attempt at self-expression. When I got out of college— it was right in the middle of the Depression—I almost immediately turned to writing verse.

Why?
Not having a job and not knowing what to do with myself, that was the only free thing I could do. I had no money for photography. So for the next four or five years I did no photography at all and I spent all my free time writing.

Did you read a lot at this time?
Oh, yes, I have always read. I go to bed with a book every night. About that time I was reading literature—all the romantic novels—but nothing about photography.

Did you immediately start writing lyric poetry?
It was primarily philosophical.

What do you mean by that?
We were always talking about deep, profound, magnificently spiritual ideas.

How old were you at this time?
Mentally, about two! I was a typical teenage kid of the 1930's.

Did you get a job?
I got a job as a house boy in a private club and I graduated to being a bartender, a waiter, and a cook. That went on for five years, making almost no money. I managed to save about

$125 and I bought an Argus camera, a couple of rolls of film, and I got on a bus and went to Portland, Oregon, and settled there—again with no money. It was a very tight squeak there for a long period.

Why Portland, Oregon?
Just a fluke. I had a letter of introduction for Seattle and I stopped at Portland. Then I heard something about the Rose Parade, which was in about three weeks, and I thought I'd stick it out for that. I was staying at the Y.M.C.A. and photographed the parade. By that time I was so short of money I had to get a job, so I stayed in Portland.

Would it be at this time that you were involved in composing your "Sonnet Sequence"? Did you think at that time there might be a relationship between sequencing visual imagery as well as words?
No, I had no such comprehension at all.

What was it that you found so interesting about lyric poetry?
I did it because I wanted to. I have no other recollection.

Had you come into contact with the nineteenth-century American transcendentalist literature?
I read it before I went to college. It didn't make too much sense to me—a little over my head.

Did you get involved with photography as a means of earning a living in Portland?
When I left Minneapolis I decided to be a photographer. I'd tried poetry for five years and that didn't get me anywhere, so I tried photography. I realized that I could shift over to photography, although it would probably take me five years to do it; I felt that there was an essence of something that I knew I would do in photography, but I didn't know how. While I was writing a verse, I'd get hold of the feeling of poetry. It was very strange—even spiritual. I'd done a lot of reading on what poetry was all about, and I thought that all

I had to do then was just change the medium. I knew what I wanted to say.

I was photographing a lot, and I borrowed another camera and photographed still more and moved around the city and made a lot of photographs. Then I got on the W.P.A.—Works Progress Administration—as a creative photographer. Also, I was constantly having shows and I was closely connected with the Oregon Camera Club. Once I was working for the W.P.A., I had enough time and enough material to undertake photographing the iron-front buildings. That was the first project I did for them, and the second project was the waterfront. But it was the iron-front buildings that really mattered. Out of that grew the opportunity to do a teaching tour of the art centers, and there were three of them around Oregon teaching photography. I got over to Le Grande Art Center, which was having trouble with the director. By some fluke or other I got the job of director in 1940; so I was teaching the photography course and also running the whole thing. This included art, painting, basket-making, weaving, even children's clay-modeling.

Did you see any photographic work at that time that meant something to you?
The Oregon Camera Club subscribed to every publication in the world, I think. There was a constant influx. *Camera Craft* was published in San Francisco at that time. That's when I ran into Edward Weston's first book. That bowled me right over—that was about the best stuff I'd ever seen in my whole life.

Did this response that you had to Weston's work equal the feeling that you said you had right from the beginning: that you could do something with the camera?
I don't know whether it did or it didn't. I can't recall.

Did you get a taste for teaching at that time?
Yes, I did. When I was in college I used to tutor a lot, and I always expected to go into teaching.

When you made the transition from poetry to photography, you felt that you were able to say or do a thing with the camera. Could you say what that thing was?
I felt that I had learned what poetry was. This was an experience I can't get into words—it was an experience within myself. I think in an earlier period I had a similar experience with music. I realized that I would never have been much of a pianist, I couldn't do it. But I learned, one afternoon, how to bridge. I knew just how to do it so the bridge would work. Then I stopped playing, and I stopped reading music. That same point happened when I was working with poetry. I came to the point where I could say: "Now I know what 'X' is, I'll learn how to do it in photography."

So there was this peculiar assurance, which I didn't recognize at the time. I went ahead into photography in a blind way. It was the same kind of decision when I went into college and I decided to drop photography in order to learn whatever one has to learn in college.

At the Le Grande Center you also got quite involved with radio broadcasting, didn't you?
Yes, I had to write a program once a week.

On what?
On any of the things that were going on in the Arts Center. It might have been on art, it might have been on dancing. That went on for quite a spell, and most of it was terrible.

Why did the job at the center finish?
The draft came along and I had to leave, but I did spend some time in Portland, where I got a job as a department-store Santa Claus. I was dressed up in these robes, with pillow stuffing—I was as scrawny as a bean pole at that point—and sat there talking to the kiddies.

I also had an exhibition at the Portland Art Museum. It went on just before I had to join the Army. Also, at that time I photographed two houses. That was the last job I did, although I was working with the Portland Civic Theater during that period. I was doing theater photography a good deal just before I left.

You were very interested in the theater at that time. Did you ever have a yen to be an actor or a director?
No. Even when I was in high school I used to help build the sets, paint them, and so on, but I never had any inclination to get on stage in front of an audience and do anything. But backstage I had a great time doing the lighting and all of that.

When I look back at the time when the war started, I realize that I had touched on practically everything I have ever done since. From then on it was a case of moving in on one part or another and continuing it.

What did you do during World War II?
I was in Intelligence at regimental and corps level. I was close to the front lines but I never actually got into combat. I didn't have to shoot somebody or get shot at.

What sort of photography were you involved with at that time?
I had a very sympathetic captain and he saw to it that I had the opportunity to photograph—mostly portraits of officers and soldiers. I ran a little studio down in one of the towns in Hawaii. I processed there and I was practically out of the war for some time doing that.

Did being in the Army have any emotional effect on you in terms of your work?
It did, but I don't know how to explain it.

Did it shape you in any way?
I think it shook me more than shaped me, but having the opportunity to photograph for several months right out of basic training was very helpful. There was no evidence of it affecting my work very much.

One of your first sequences was titled "Amputations," wasn't it?
Yes. There had been an earlier one done around a Y.M.C.A. camp up in the mountains in the middle of the winter. Every-

thing had been given to the Y.M.C.A., the negatives—it's all lost now. But that was the first one.

"Amputations" pertains to work that you did directly while in the service, then?
All the portraits do.

The style was extremely confessional.
It always has been. That sequence came together in about 1947 or 1946. There were something like fifty poems and fifty pictures.

Was it your experience during the war that led to your converting to Catholicism?
No. This came from a girl friend I had when I was living in Oregon. She was a Catholic and we used to talk about it once in a while. When both of us found ourselves heading for the Army, we had a long weekend discussion in which she very powerfully and sincerely urged my taking up the Church. She had all sorts of fine arguments as to why I should. When I got in the Army I became acquainted with our chaplain. I talked with him a little while and he thought it would be a fine idea, too—obviously! I looked at it from the standpoint: Well, I ain't got anything else to do in this damned Army, so let's get into this business of religion; and since the Catholic religion is the most complicated and the most authentic from my viewpoint, let's try that one. So I did. I was baptized and all sorts of things went on. I used it very faithfully while I was in the Army, but when I got out of the Army I drifted right out.

Was it an intellectual or emotional response that drew you to Catholicism?
It was both. This chaplain was a very strange person, as he seemed to be about the weakest thing I'd ever seen in my whole life. You couldn't imagine anybody being more dependent on something. I thought that anybody who could be that weak, that inefficient, had to have something going for him! We had very fine conversations together. At that time services were very primitive—a small table under the sky; and

that I could cope with. But when it came to huge churches, cathedrals, and that sort of stuff, it just seemed so remote. Maybe that's just an excuse. I just drifted out for reasons I don't understand.

Were you interested from the beginning in the ritual, the ceremony, of church proceedings?
The ritual, because it had been quite primitive under those circumstances, and that was all right; I could cope with it. When it got very elaborate, it lost me somehow. I'm sure it was the contact with the chaplain himself that had a great deal to do with it. The immediacy of the situation.

After the war, what did you do?
I realized that I should get started in school someplace. I came back to Washington and almost immediately got on a train as fast as possible to New York City and Columbia University, where I enrolled for some extension courses. For one year I studied under Meyer Schapiro in Art History. He was my advisor for a paper on Edward Weston. I also worked with the Newhalls at the Museum of Modern Art. I was copying a lot of cartoons and slides. I did a lot of copying photography for them on a regular basis. It was a way to make some money. I really caught up on art history.

How did you know the Newhalls?
I was already recognized as a photographer with my traveling shows at the W.P.A. The Newhalls had taken two photographs of mine from Oregon for a little book. So I was a name for them before I arrived, and when I landed, they took me under their wing immediately and we got along really well from the start. There were no problems about getting along with the Newhalls. Beaumont was just back from the war when I arrived. That was an extremely exciting rebuilding for me. I met Stieglitz, Strand, Ansel Adams, Callahan, Smith, Barbara Morgan, Georgia O'Keeffe, and anybody who was there in New York at the time. I was also elected to the Photo League. I went to see Stieglitz in his little gallery and I had three or four conversations with him. Within a five-minute period Stieglitz got me moving again. I had always had this sensation

that while in the Army something had died, or at least gone underground. Stieglitz came along and reactivated something.

Was there a crucial phrase, sentence, or word even that really rekindled that fire again for you?
I asked if I could be a photographer, and Stieglitz said: "Well, have you ever been in love?" and I said: "Yes," and he said: "Then you can be a photographer."

Why did you do a paper on Weston?
The reason for picking Weston was a retrospective show of his work that year at MOMA. It was a big show and there was plenty of stuff I could work with.

Did you work with Nancy Newhall on the show?
Not really. I just stood around watching her move one photograph here, and one there. I certainly learned that when she moved one thing to go with another it was magic. All of a sudden it would come together.

Did you feel that you were appreciating the formal combination of two images, or was it a more emotional response to their positioning?
Emotional response. She was working with highly formal images. I could just see by how she put them together what a whiz she was at it. She was superb. I had already been hanging exhibitions back in Oregon, with artists, and I'd learned a good deal about it from them. You don't put two green paintings beside each other, and that kind of thing. I worked with Nancy from time to time for many years. When I was in Rochester I had lots of shows to do—twelve major shows a year and some little ones. I had lots of practice.

Did Weston see your paper?
Much later; I wrote it twice. Weston saw it, but didn't particularly approve. He said: "You've made some silly mistakes." Of course, I thought it was the greatest paper that had ever been written and wondered why somebody wouldn't publish it. It never has been published—which is just as well!

Were you working on certain photographic ideas at that time?
When I came to New York I said, I'm not going to photograph New York, but I did a little. I photographed the interior of my own small room that I had when I was at Columbia, and Fifty-third Street, which I photographed in the snow. The things that attracted me most were the lights in the windows of the tall buildings at dusk. I did quite a number of portraits, including one of Meyer Schapiro. Photography wasn't dominant, though. It never dominates my life; it just has to be done along with a load of other things.

Had you seen any of Stieglitz's New York pictures?
Oh, yes, the museum had some, and I managed to see a few things at the gallery.

Did the idea of the equivalent mean anything to you then?
Yes. I had read *America and Alfred Stieglitz* when I was in Oregon, and the idea of equivalent really hit me very hard; and one other phrase of his—"You can imitate everything in art except spirit." Those two ideas were what I took from him.

Why did you move from the East Coast to the West Coast at that time?
I had had the promise of a job at the museum in Portland, but during the year in New York that job dissolved. Then Ansel Adams was starting his photography program in California. I met Ansel and he accepted me. I immediately went to San Francisco, and on my birthday I started teaching there.

That's the California School of Fine Arts, now the San Francisco Art Institute?
Right.

Was it at that time that you cemented your close relationship with the West Coast tradition, exemplified obviously by Ansel Adams and Edward Weston?
Yes. In New York I had seen Edward's show and really studied it. I haven't studied a show that well since. I arrived

in San Francisco in July, and in December four students and I went down to see Edward. We had a marvelous afternoon out on Point Lobos. From then on I saw a great deal more of his work. I used to take classes down to him at least once a year, although he was pretty frail. We went down there three weeks in a row and talked and looked at his photography. That was also the time I started photographing Point Lobos. I was fascinated by it. That one year, 1946, was a very crucial one. It solidified the idea of the equivalent for me. I became very much closer to the Newhalls and that is when my curatorial career began to get underway. Strand, Stieglitz, Weston, and Ansel all gave me exactly what I needed at that time. I took one thing from each: technique from Ansel, the love of nature from Weston, and from Stieglitz the affirmation that I was alive and I could photograph. Those three things were very intense. And I also got an interest in the psychology of art from Meyer Schapiro.

Did you find all of these understandings culminating in any-thing?
They culminated in the sequence "The Song without Words." The pictures were taken mainly around the San Francisco area. As soon as that was done, there was recognition, psychologically anyway—everybody recognized that this was quite something.

Who recognized it?
The Newhalls did, and photographers, students, and friends realized it, too. I realized that I had come home to something.

Wasn't it fairly unusual to teach a course in photography in an American school at that time?
Yes, Ansel had started a few months before I arrived and for a while we were teaching together. I can remember the first morning I heard the photographic theory of the Zone System explained, and I thought, Why didn't I think of that?—it's so easy! And so that afternoon I started explaining the Zone System to people.

When Ansel left the college and you took over the running of the course, what ideas of your own did you institute?
I introduced my ideas instantly. I didn't have to wait until he left. I lived next door to him and we were good friends and we just talked and talked all the time. He wanted to teach in what he called the conservatory method, like music. I had learned at Columbia the psychology of reading images and I brought all that into it. Ansel knew nothing about that. He and I would give assignments. I was teaching every day and three nights a week, and I didn't get much chance to do any photography. I was completely immersed in teaching.

What sort of assignments did you set the students?
They were architectural assignments—but the equivalent was always right there. They had to find the essence. Ansel would go up to a building and insist on orientation shots so you knew what the building was. I always insisted on moving in to get the details, and if you could get any equivalents out of them, so much the better. Between the two of us, it worked out pretty well. Then the students would be sent out into various parts of San Francisco to do a week or two documenting an area. I would do a critique of every person on each assignment, as well as the general critique for the whole group. The critiques would run from nine in the morning until five in the afternoon. I didn't leave a photograph unscathed! (Finally, I learned to stop that a little bit.) So while they were out photographing, I was always talking to two or three of them. I never got out on these trips, but I got to see San Francisco because they photographed it for me.

Did you develop the theory of "the sequence" alongside the equivalent?
There was never much theory of the sequence—they just did it. I just did it. I don't recall students doing much with sequence when I was out there.

Single-image work, then?
Mainly. We did groups of things. Assignments such as five to fifty photographs out of area A, or something like that. Or

take one object, photograph it for what it is and photograph it for what else it is, and then photograph an equivalent of it. Then make a fourth photograph which is an equivalent of the equivalent. That really threw them!

Did they present them on a wall in exhibition style?
As I recall I never looked at unmounted photographs. We put them upon a little ledge with the lights on them, and we discussed them. Sequencing of a sort was done. I suppose I moved things around—I don't particularly recall that. Mostly I talked about individual photographs. About how this one got along with that one.

But not in terms of the whole?
I didn't as a rule. The spring exhibition was always a whopping big thing. There would be a large hall, and photography had one wall and our own studio. It was a big studio—two stories high and lots of light. It was at that time that I began to really practice what I had learned in New York in terms of putting photographs together. And under those conditions many students worked on putting their own shows together.

So then maybe what you learned from Nancy Newhall was grouping photographs rather than sequencing them?
Yes, because she was working with single images. They were not sequenced. Edward Weston never made a sequence in his life. I used to ask him about sequencing, and he'd say: "Oh, yes, I made a sequence." And he'd bring out three photographs of the same person in three different positions. That was his idea of a sequence.

Did any particular motif draw you more than any others— the landscapes or the city?
I would generally photograph nature. I didn't photograph the city a lot. My preference would always be to go down to Point Lobos to photograph. But after three years I got tired of Lobos. There's lots of places up and down the coast which I photographed. Then I'd get hungry for the city and I'd photograph the city, too. In numbers I suppose there are as many

of one as there are of the other. There are a lot of little corners around San Francisco I just loved to take pictures of. In that little corner over there there's a photograph, I would think, and someday I'll find it. Well, sometimes I did and other times I didn't.

Were you looking for still lifes?
I worked with a view camera all the time, so I would say yes.

Not the spontaneous human document?
No. I didn't do that until I started working with the smaller camera, about 1948, I guess.

At this time had you been exhibiting fairly frequently . . .
I don't recall when I first had an exhibition in San Francisco. "Amputations" was to be shown at the Legion of Honor Museum, but at the last minute they said: "Can we show it without the verse?" I said no, so it wasn't shown.

What was the objection to the verse?
The verse was too controversial. It was all about war—too controversial.

Was there a pacifist overtone to it that might have offended people at that period of time?
I didn't ask questions, they just said they weren't going to show it with the words; and I said: "You are going to show it intact or you aren't going to show it at all."

Did the concept of an exhibition mean anything specific to you? What did you want from them, and what did you get out of them?
I had done a lot with the Oregon Camera Club. We had yearly exhibitions and I always took part in them, and in the Y.M.C.A. Camera Club small exhibitions too. All I understood by an exhibition was that it was a way of getting in front of the public. I liked the stuff I did in eastern Oregon. It was stuff that was meaningful to me—expressive—and it was a

means of getting it shown. I had no fancy ideas about what I was supposed to do with it other than to get it on the wall so people could see it.

Was there anything you wanted them to do?
Be seen. Sure, I had read about equivalents and all those sorts of things, but they were photographs that were primarily expressive. I thought: Let's get them out. I didn't have any specific idea about what they were supposed to do to anybody except express aesthetic pleasure, if you can call it that.

Did you exhibit within the concept of the equivalent to evoke some sense of equivalency from an audience response?
I may have had such a notion. They were more about essence rather than equivalence at that point.

And what exactly was this essence?
I'll show you a picture that will tell you what essence is. I usually missed, of course, if I tried deliberately to get the essence of something.

It did not necessarily have to do with the materialistic fact of things being in front of the camera?
Let's look at Edward Weston's photographs. How would you define those facts? I was in love with all the stuff I saw. I was interested in communicating what I was looking at—a nice tree, a nice building, and all that. It was pretty straight photography.

No implication of it being more than "the thing itself"?
I would say that in the photography done while I was up in Oregon there was no attempt at equivalence. I knew about it but I was more concerned with Weston's approach, or Ansel Adams's approach, to the straight photograph. It wasn't until I got back from the war that I began to use the equivalent. I didn't know much about it—I postponed using it—I had no interest in it yet. But there were many things in the war that I had not been able to photograph and so then I began to use

equivalents. There were a few photographs I made of clouds when I first got back to San Francisco. They looked something like Stieglitz's.

Did you ever publish the sequence that you did in San Francisco, "Song without Words"?
It was exhibited, but it wasn't published until *Mirrors, Messages and Manifestations*. Here was a set of photographs that came out rapidly. I looked at them and sequenced them, and showed them more as Weston showed his photographs—"Here it is!" Even though I began to know about sequencing and equivalents, I wasn't trying to impose equivalents on people. In the classroom you talk about equivalents—is it one or isn't it? But to get it up on a wall in an exhibition you can't go around and ask the people, Is it an equivalent for you, or isn't it?

But you did set it up as a sequence when you put it up on the wall?
That's true. It was a sequence.

Would it have been the first conscious public exhibition of a sequence by you?
No. My first one was done when I was in Oregon. That was intended as a picture story.

About this time, in the early fifties, the publication Aperture *appeared. How did the idea of such a publication emerge?*
That came out of the one and only photography conference held at Aspen, Colorado, by the Container Corporation. One afternoon there was a discussion of a publication with the Pictorial Society of America or the Pictorial Photographers of America—something like that. They had a publication, and there was a large round-table discussion about a different sort of publication. No one seemed to want to go ahead and do anything. Someone said: "Let's just sabotage them and work from within!" But that idea got dropped. A few months or weeks later, Nancy Newhall, Ansel, and I were in Ansel's

house and the idea of a publication emerged once more. They'd thought it through two or three years prior to that with a magazine they were going to call *Light*. I remember them pulling the first little pieces of it out. We then got busy and called Barbara Morgan on the phone, and Dorothea Lange came over, and one of the wealthy women who lived over in Ansel's area came over—she got a lawyer in, and a designer, and a couple of other people, and some students. There were seven or eight people. We sat down, talked it out, and decided to do it. Ansel said he would write twenty-five letters asking for twenty-five dollars each, and that's how it got started. At this point the question of who was going to edit it came up. Strangely enough, everyone was much too busy, but apparently I had less to lose since I was practically broke and the money I was making at school didn't help much. So, by default, I ended up being the editor. They all promised that they would come and help me when we got the material together.

Was there a guiding concept?
Yes. It was an angel with pink wings and a long tail with a point on it! We talked about what we thought *Aperture* ought to be: excellent reproductions of the finest photographs, superb articles, and a journal for discussion.

It sounds something like what Alfred Stieglitz tried to do with Camera Work. *Did you have that in mind?*
Of course, everyone was aware of what Stieglitz had done. It would be the obvious thing for that group of people to want to do. But it became, very quickly, just a one-man operation. It was not a forum for discussion, it became Minor White's private journal.

What did Minor White do with it?
He just made it his own private property. It was my growth. People who took photographs I wanted to show landed in it. My own stuff landed in it, from time to time, and everything I was doing with photography I was putting into it. It was a beautiful teaching device for a while.

It seems that in the middle sixties you began to promote, very powerfully, an idea that you summed up in the term "reading photographs." Could you talk about what that means?
It came about very easily. Studying with Meyer Schapiro and the Newhalls, I was dealing with photography on a curatorial level—exhibitions which we had to write the contents for.

You try to view a photograph and experience it, and then you try and communicate that experience to somebody else, not in photographs, but in words. It's a thing that the critic and the art historian have to do all the time.

Two years after Aperture *started, it almost folded. Was one of the reasons that it had become Minor White's "private journal," or was it purely financial?*
There was a meeting in New York of all the board members, except me—I couldn't afford to go to New York that week. I got a letter back saying that we were going to discontinue it. It wasn't financially feasible and it couldn't be kept going. There were all kinds of reasons why they didn't want to do it. But they said: "If you want to keep it going, it will be all right and we will try and help out." At that point Shirley Burden showed up and began to pick up the tab, which was very little in those days—$500 a year or something. That's how it kept going.

How did the move from California to George Eastman House come about?
The director of the California School of Fine Arts seemed like he wanted to get rid of me, and I can well understand why he would. I didn't like him very much! I wasn't playing politics and all of a sudden I found my course canceled in October. I got on the telephone to Beaumont and said, "Do you need anybody over there?" and he said: "Get here as fast as you can." So that's how I got there, and I started to function as a curator. I had a little training from working with the Newhalls in New York. It was interesting not to teach for a while, but I got pretty lonesome. So when an opportunity arose at Rochester Institute of Technology to teach a course

in photojournalism—why not? I don't know anything about photojournalism, so I should be the ideal teacher for it! And so with a wisecrack like that, I started my career at R.I.T., which continued to be a series of wisecracks!

What would be the most exciting projects you did during that time at G.E.H.?
There was a constant stream of major exhibitions and innumerable little ones. I think the most spectacular was the "Family of Man" show. They had to use the entire museum to get it in. The show happened to fit amazingly well. Steichen saw the show and said it was the best installation he had seen outside MOMA. I'd seen it in other museums where they had pasted it up on the wall, which was hideous. It was the most spectacular exhibition that we gave.

What did you feel about the "Family of Man" exhibition?
I had all kinds of feelings about it—good, bad, and indifferent! The hanging of it was a very exciting experience. I really felt that it was a magnificent show.

Many of your contemporaries feel that it put back the art of photography many years. Do you think this is a correct criticism?
I don't know whether it is or not. After all, this was an exhibition not for the aesthetes in photography but for people. It may have put the aesthetic thing back a little bit, but that didn't hurt. It was good to have that setback.

Is it important to you that an exhibition can, in fact, attract a lot of people who are not aesthetes of photography?
Yes, of course, I think it is extremely important. Steichen was very conscious of that, and he tried to make an exhibition which would perhaps take us away from further wars and show people what they are. It did show that vast numbers of people could be very excited by a photographic exhibition—it was at their level. Not the aesthetic stuff but very straightforward semi-photojournalistic documentation. Some of it,

though, was really magnificent aesthetically. The design was a very active one and you didn't have to stop and look at the pictures very long.

About this time you got interested in Eastern philosophy and religion. How did this come about?
Barbara Morgan had a large branch of what's sometimes called Burning Bush. She gave it to Nancy Newhall, and somehow within a few days she gave it to me. It was late fall and we had some magnificent frost and the branch was covered in it —I made a picture of it called "Ritual Branch." That coincided with a gift from Nancy Newhall of a book called *Mysticism*. Then someone showed up on my doorstep with two books, *The Doors of Perception* by Huxley, and *Zen in the Art of Archery*. John Upton was living at the house that year and he was studying mythology over at the University of Rochester. I picked up Underhill's *Mysticism* and read it with great interest. I got interested in Zen and mysticism in general. Zen seemed to be something I could get my fingers into. And then, within two years, Walter Chappell showed up from the West Coast and told me about an experience he had had with a Gurdjieff group in New York. He was talking along fine and all of a sudden I couldn't understand what he was talking about. I said: "Why don't you back up and start over again." He started all over again and at the same point I blanked out on him again. I couldn't make out what he was talking about. We ended up very angry that afternoon! That was my introduction to it, but I couldn't grasp what he was saying. He came back several years later to Rochester and I talked to him a little more about it, and this time it made a little more sense. Then we got a reading group going and someone came up from New York to help out on that. I attended these first few meetings and then evaporated from the scene. That was my real introduction to Gurdjieff and it constituted a profound change in a lot of the things I did. Finally I came to a decision to connect myself with something. If there had been one in Rochester I would have gone to a Zen group. But since there wasn't and the Gurdjieff group interested me, I started working with them, and have ever since.

*Was it at about this time that the idea of "camera conscious-
ness" began to be a thing that concerned you?*
I think the idea of "camera consciousness" began to emerge
around 1965 or 1966, at about the time I began to move to
M.I.T.

*There was something that you mentioned recently that seemed
to impress you in a book on mysticism. It was a statement . . .*
The statement was—I can't quote it exactly—"the mystic
could understand the artist, but the artist couldn't understand
the mystic." When I read that I said: Well, I don't believe
it. It wasn't until I began to have inner growth—I won't call
it spiritual experience—that I began to realize that a mystical
quality wasn't showing up in photographs.

What do you mean by this?
Where I was in my "inner landscape"; the sequences weren't
doing it. Take the 1968 sequence (the last in my book), which
certainly reflects a given state of mind, but it's a long way
from what's going on inside.

*Was the experience akin to anything that you had discovered
in music that made you stop studying music, and in poetry
that made you stop writing poetry, and then in photography
that seemed to culminate in a meeting with Stieglitz?*
There was a moment one morning when I was aware of something inside moving into place and filling up a gap. It was
very powerful. It was akin to what Stieglitz had done. He filled
a hole there somehow. It was the same kind of thing, but it
had nothing to do with photography. It just simply happened
inside and there was no exterior anything at that moment.
I asked one of the Gurdjieff teachers about it later, and she said
quite emphatically: "There is a throne and whoever is supposed to sit on it finally came and sat on it." She explained it
that way. That was a profound moment but it had no relationship with photography. But it did have a relationship to
the work I was doing with this woman. It came through the
disciplines we had been working on. I no longer remember

the date, but I do remember it was prior to my moving to Boston, maybe 1962 or 1963.

Why did you resign from George Eastman House?
The major reason for resigning was that I just couldn't stand the director. I just couldn't take that man any more. I worked at Eastman House for over three years, and I was in Rochester eleven. All of these growth things were done while I was teaching.

There seems to be an incredible sense of urgency about this time. You seem to be looking at things like the I Ching, *investigating Zen, investigating Gurdjieff and also hypnosis. Why?*
I think it is just a natural eclectic tendency. I tried everything. I tried them on photography to see whether they fitted or whether they wouldn't.

Did you use these things as teaching aids as well?
Very often I would.

Did you find that any of them were successful?
They were all very useful—I still use most of them.

How was hypnosis useful?
It's a means of concentration. One goes into some kind of a state—not exactly a trance. I'd been trying earlier to establish a way of reading, or viewing, photographs, and arriving at and interpreting an experience. It's the experiential attitude I was always trying to get at. I looked at hypnosis from the outside and I thought: This is just a fast way of doing it. For years I would have people gather around a photograph in a classroom or in a house and look at it for an amount of time and then try and talk about it. When we got the hypnosis technique going, we reacted pretty passively. It was a technique where we could relax all energies. You learn to be very passive with the image until things talk to you—and sooner or later they do. But the intent always was: how to get involved with images as an experience.

Did you feel a little strange trying to confront people with images when they were in a state of hypnosis?
I played with this for several years. In one of the workshops in Oregon around 1960, I met a professional hypnotist who uses it for his medical operations. He sat in on one of my lectures and grabbed me by the scruff of the neck and explained to me a lot about hypnosis! It helped a lot, and he was most useful because he realized that I was up to something that I wasn't too sure about; so he helped me get sure about it. In 1963 or 1964 there was a national convention of hypnotists, and he said would I mind showing this technique to a group of them. I demonstrated this thing for about three hours. Different methods, with and without music, single images, sequences, the whole thing. When we started out he said: "Professor White here has a means we would like you to look at. It seems to be hypnotic and we would like to know whether it is or whether it isn't." The conclusion was that what I was doing was hypnoidal, but not hypnotic. They recognized that instead of putting people under a state of heaviness and under the control of the hypnotist, we were doing the opposite; we were going toward lightness and turning the student over to the influence of the image, not the hypnotist.

Do you ever see a relationship between this and the way Stieglitz was said to have some sort of hypnotic effect on people?
Probably not, but he may have had a hypnotic effect on people. I realized after a while that all I have to do is just talk for a little while and I've got everybody hypnotized! I think Stieglitz probably did the same without even intending to. I suddenly woke up to the fact that I'd been doing it for years and didn't even know it!

At this time you got very involved with the workshop system. Do you feel that this is a better way of teaching photography than in a more institutionalized way?
It's an alternative, neither better nor worse. The first workshops occurred in San Francisco. Then from time to time

people have lived with me. I've never been married so there's always been room for someone around. 1959 was the first time we held a living-in workshop (for five people). There's always a workshop going on. It served two things—companionship and being able to teach people more directly and more intimately than I could do in an academic situation. I couldn't go as far in an institution—I couldn't use hypnosis as much, and I couldn't do this and I couldn't do that. I wanted to take things further. Paul Caponigro was working with me for two summers, which was just right. A person being with me for a year, or a year and a half, was always too much—I used to dominate.

What did you teach in the workshops?
Experience of the subject while photographing it and while looking at the images—and anything else that came to mind. We'd talk about graphics, about design, about history, whatever was on my mind. There was never any fixed course. If I was working with *Aperture* they would hear about it, and sometimes they would help.

Was it during the workshops that you began to develop the theory of taking and viewing photographs in a state of heightened awareness?
The 1959 workshop made it a pretty conscious affair. Up until that time we had been doing something like it, but in a very passive way. I have a feeling that a person looking for a good photographic education should have workshops with various people, plus academic training during the same period of time, say, three or four years. Most people don't make workshops quite as intensive as I do. You just simply live, sleep, eat photography for five, ten, or fifteen days. You do nothing else. The work we can accomplish is just unbelievable. The hypnosis starts on the first evening and goes on until the last. For example, we may photograph water as your partner and photograph your partner like water. Anything I think up. But it's the intensity of it. We used to feel so high on the last night—and without pot or alcohol or anything like that. I discovered that that was a great mistake, however, so I started

making the high peak about two days, or even three days, before the end. I would literally coast them down, so when they left they didn't drive off a cliff or things of that sort!

You've never been tempted to use drugs in these sessions?
I was anti the drug scene right from the very beginning, although I did try some once just to see for myself.

You seem to have four simultaneous careers: as a photographer, as a teacher, as an editor, and also as a critic. Do you have any specific feelings about what a critic, who is also an editor, should be?
He should know something about photography as a craft, even if he decides not to be a photographer. He should also know all about art history and photographic history. He should know his photographers extremely well. He should be the photographer's best creative audience and know when a photographer is slipping. He should be able to come to grips with a photographer's most sophisticated, and even his obscure, meanings.

Does anybody ever fulfill that?
I don't think anybody ever can.

Is there any recent criticism that you think is outstanding?
Probably the best piece of criticism in photography today is *Looking at Photographs* by John Szarkowski.

Why do you say that?
Because it's the best! He is looking into the photograph. He's telling you where it fits in. Above all, he's talking about the photograph, which most critics don't do!

You had a tiff fairly recently with the critic A. D. Coleman. What do you think of his writings?
I have read some of his stuff and I have a feeling he's saying a lot of the right things in terms of how to deal with photography in general. His estimates of various photographers are sometimes pretty good, but at other times something rather

important is missing. He obviously comes out of what we used to call the "trashing school," and he's still anti-institution. His criticism of me was relatively justified, but he just let go and made many mistakes. He did raise the major question of editorial photography, though.

Coleman talked about the editorial ethic that you have firmly established in terms of making exhibitions and catalogues . . . The very interesting thing is that I don't do it any differently, or any more effectively, than *Life* magazine did. Or take, for example, the type of exhibition we did for M.I.T. The theme was set out and people would make photographs for the exhibition. A lot of others would just look through their files and pull out what they could, and still others would just grab anything and send it, regardless of whether it had anything to do with the theme or not. My problem then was to take the body of photographs, look at all of them, several hundred or so, and try to extract out of that a good show, which would have some bearing on the theme. In going through, I could say: "Well, this obviously does not belong to the theme, put that aside. This one might, this obviously does." This meant I did have some kind of preconceived notion of what the theme was to look like. But I still depended very heavily on the photographs to do it. They would be cut down, and down, and down, and then sequenced until an orchestrated set of photographs was present. Obviously, the people who send the photographs in are not going to object to having their photographs used in relation to somebody else's photographs, because they know beforehand that that's going to happen. The result amounts to giving the person who plays the editor permission and material to build something. If the editor could have photographed it, he would have, given the time. I could have done one of these themes, but it would have taken me five years to do it. This way I have the assistance of five hundred, eight hundred, or a thousand photographers. With the photographers, the editor becomes the owner of that exhibition, but the organization of it is his.

Now, A. D. Coleman's objection to all that, I think, goes back to his feeling of the importance of the photographer and photographer's ego in all of this. The photograph can launch the photographer and no one else can touch it. I may not have clarified it very well, but it's something like that. He also feels that the intentions of the photographer determine what the photograph means, which from my standpoint is absolutely idiotic, because all too frequently the intentions of the photographer do not come through. If the photographer can't get his intentions across, he still has the image; then anybody can use it any way they want to. As there are infinite numbers of photographers, all of them repeating themselves and each other all of the time, one has a very wide choice. There is a certain anonymity which comes about in the nature of the medium itself these days. There's just so much of it.

There have been periods in art—for example, cathedral building—when the craftsman never signed his name to anything. That was a group activity. In the case of an exhibition such as this, my name is on it, and the photographers' names are on it. We haven't become so enlightened that we could put on an exhibition without names. The possession, which is attributed to the editor, is quite real. If the intentions of the exhibition are worthwhile, then the use of the photographs in that exhibition can be thought of as being well used. Now, people who submit to such an exhibition probably agree that it is worthwhile, although there is an awful lot of: "Get my stuff on the wall, anyhow. I don't care what anybody does, just get it on the wall!" Unfortunately, that ego problem is there.

Editing photographs in exhibitions and books is an activity we are doing a lot of these days. A lot of young photographers are doing their own editing. I think this is terrific because it's a damn hard thing to learn, and very few photographers know anything about it. Ralph Gibson seems to be doing pretty well at it. I don't know how he's learned it, whether it's just intuition or what.

Getting back to the critic: he is the most responsible single individual in photography, because he has a responsibility to photographers, to himself, to his audience, and to photography. A photographer has, primarily, only a responsibility to himself and his audience. I feel that the critic should not be an artist, although he can't help being one. A critic of art of any form obviously is involved with it and I suppose is one in his own way. But it's a peculiar role; it's not a productive role, it's a coordinating role. It's more an evaluation of things. He is involved on a much broader base than the individual artist. He needs to encourage the artist, stand up for his rights to be himself. He needs to be a student of creativity. The psychology of creativity itself is a topic he should be involved with.

Was it during your time at R.I.T. that you started to introduce rhythm and movement into your classes?
That was not done at R.I.T. It was done in my various private workshops.

What was the reason for that?
In 1961 or 1962 I gave a workshop in the mountains outside Los Angeles. It was a family camp kind of thing, and they taught all sorts of things, largely on a family basis. They had a dance group up for a week, and this group put on a performance in which the director stood on a podium and lectured while his dancers illustrated everything he was talking about. It struck me as just fine and I got well acquainted with him. Sometime prior to that, up in Portland, I had been having people try to interpret an image with music, and I was having people dance improvisations of a slide or a photograph. Well, this particular chap I talked to caught on very well, and he took time off one morning to work with us. We made some sketches of things—heightened awareness, etc.— and then we brought the sketches to where he was. First thing you know, all of us were dancing to the sketches. It was an incredible morning, because you could see the equivalents from one to another. It was just so obvious. That's what we were driving at, an equivalent in dance to something visual.

Did it take a while for visual people to overcome a natural embarrassment in terms of public movement?
There were some difficulties, but within a little workshop those things break down very fast. They say you can do anything in

a workshop. It just suddenly grew out of the idea of the equivalent, and for several years it was done in the workshops by various dancers. Then I started doing it at M.I.T.

How do the students at M.I.T. find it?
They love it! They think it's great.

I'd been trying to get out of Rochester for many years, but could never land a job. All of a sudden I had a telephone call from M.I.T. I was delighted to get out of Rochester. The change fitted my inner growth precisely.

I'd been teaching commercial and professional photography, more or less, for many years. Even though I was teaching creative photography, the photographers I was dealing with were going to go into professional photography. Now, R.I.T. is a highly technologically oriented place which turns out superb craftsmen. I'd come in, close the door, and make them be creative photographers for the rest of the morning. They'd open the door in the afternoon and be technicians again.

In moving to M.I.T. the whole objective changed from teaching future professionals to using photography as a way of teaching technologically and scientifically minded people something about seeing creatively. The key phrase was: "We are trying to provide an opportunity for our scientists, our engineers, and our humanists to observe creativity in some other field than their own."

For some reason or other, that just fitted what I wanted to do. I think I felt a certain pressure of trying to get creative photography across to people who would necessarily have to drop it in order to become professionals in New York City, in advertising, photojournalism, and so on. At M.I.T. there was no such problem. I made it just as creative as I could. The following year we introduced about four courses, which included something called "Evaluating Photography," which was semicritical. Then I began to bring a dancer in to try to bring body movement into the matter of seeing. We took this highly intellectual bunch and made them see with their bodies. They accepted it very readily. Within four years it had grown into a Creative Audience class, in which the photographer induces heightened awareness in himself in order to have an experience of the thing he is going to photograph. And a person who is just going to look at photographs can do exactly the same thing. I figure it is creative to be able to induce that state, because it puts one in touch with deeper places in oneself. One can get in touch with the Creator within oneself. I always use a dancer who understands what I'm doing and who understands what they're trying to do. We're really teaching movement, not dance. I'm teaching seeing, not photography. The whole emphasis is on the expansion of the seeing process, and learning to bring in what is going on in the body, to become aware of it, and to reach a consciousness of it. Conscious photography, then, is being aware of one's body while making, or looking at, photographs.

Does that make a person more able to respond, though not necessarily to understand?
Oh, yes, absolutely. We don't necessarily get an understanding, but it leads to it. Gurdjieff's ideas are involved in this quite deliberately: one of the ideals of Gurdjieff is to function as a whole or total human being, which for the sake of convenience is broken up into three parts: the intellect, the emotions, and the sensations—head, heart, and body. There's a lot more to it than that, but that's enough to start with.

By getting people to look at images and to become aware of their body reactions, they are being asked to add their body to their sensations and their intellectual activity to that. The idea is to be able to respond on all three levels simultaneously. Nothing comes first, except in our education—the head comes first then, by accident. We teach our body through our head. So we're trying to introduce a connection between all these centers. You start either from the body or from the head, and get them both going, and very often the emotions come in of their own accord after that.

As in an intuitive response—the emotions bursting forth as intuition?
No. We don't have much control over our emotions, they come and go, and we go along with them. We do, however,

have some control over our thinking, and we can become conscious of our bodies. By getting head and body conscious and functioning, the emotions sometimes arise of their own accord. But that isn't intuition. The emotions are something else. Because I know something about it and my body has a sensation of it, very often I begin to get emotional.

Sensory and intellectual responses are catalysts for the emotions?

No, they're just parts of the recipe. You put in so much butter and so many eggs, and something else emerges—you have an idiot, you have a cake, you have an experience, or you have something which is full. I mean, it can be a total experience. We're leading to a total response, and we have to start with people who are using their heads a lot. The intellectual knowledge they know very well—it's amazing how much. We try an experiment: we look at a photograph or a slide and then we talk about it. They've been looking at photographs all their lives, they respond to them, and analyze them. We do the same thing in a state of heightened awareness.

How does the state of heightened awareness come about? You induce it?

It's definitely induced. I use a very definite relaxation-rebound technique. We look at a different image, and people will always say: "I get more out of it under this condition than any other." Their intellect sees more at that point. Mostly they're talking out of their heads. Now, through dance and movement practice, which takes just a few weeks, people begin to realize that the image is reaching their body and they begin to find out how. They move or take positions that relate to the experience of what they're looking at. This doesn't cut out the intellectual aspect of it at all, it adds to it. We begin to realize that the emotions emerge when you're doing the other two things. They emerge of their own accord sometimes, but not always. There seems to be no direct way of getting that emotional side. You can't just command them and say emote that image! If you do that, nothing happens.

Wynn Bullock uses the word "apperception" with regard to his own philosophical approach to photography and space/time. Do you use this approach in your Creative Audience classes?
I never use it myself, but maybe I could find a way of using it. As an aside: I try to read what Wynn says but I usually end up getting only the dimmest glimmer of what he's driving at. Maybe when he reads what I write, he has the same problem!

The comparison has been made with your own approach to photography and Bullock's, but he seems to think that you part company when it comes to a comprehension of existence. He felt at variance with the spiritual and religious side of your philosophy. What do you feel about this?
It makes me wish I'd never used the word "spirit," because I don't think we do part company on that at all. "Spiritual" is a word that people always misunderstand. They impute things to it which should not be imputed. I've used such words as "creative" and "spiritual" rather freely because it's useful —but they always need to be defined very carefully. In the past few years I tend to stay away from "spirits" and "spiritual." People who have not gone into disciplined esoteric work generally have the weirdest idea of what "spirit" is. I have been defining "creative" ever since I came to M.I.T. as anything which brings us into contact with our Creator, either inwardly or outwardly. That's an unusual definition of the word "creative," because "creative" sometimes means putting things together that haven't been together before.

I think this definition very clearly states what I'm driving at in teaching, in my photography, in the criticism, and in the picture editing I've done. I try to find this Creator in everything I do. This is the way that you can move through photography, or anything else that you're doing, toward locating that aspect which is ever-present and ever-hidden from us. My philosophy of photography since I came to M.I.T. is tied up in that definition. That's what I am driving at. All the activities I do take me in that direction.

At some point in Rochester in the 1960's I looked at myself

very carefully, and I thought: What in hell am I doing teaching anybody anything about photography or anything else? This came from a prolonged observation of what I am, and the realization that it ain't much! This is a common experience for people involved in the disciplines of esoteric teaching, this sense of nothingness—"I am nothing." I have seen other people have that same experience, whether it was esoteric or not. My thought was Why am I teaching? I have nothing to teach. Then I remember feeling one day: Why am I going to school this morning? Why don't I just go down to school and resign the whole thing and go do something else? But by the time I got to school, I got over that! I have a sense underneath that there is a nothingness and yet there is something there. I couldn't define it any more clearly than that. At around that moment I began to realize that all my knowledge, everything that related to photography, and my success as a teacher, were things that were really going for me. As a teacher I'd grown. I thought: Don't drop it, stay with it. You really don't have anything else you can do. It was at that point that another leaf unfolded which showed me that the inner growth would continue to unfold, that the teaching would remain where it was, that the photography would remain where it was, more or less. All these things that I had were my means of expression—my means of communicating whatever was going on inside. There was a real change. I was standing aside, no longer just caught in teaching. I taught when I wanted to, even though it may have been as often as before. I wasn't compelled by anything, I was choosing to do it. Everything I'm doing is to bring to people what I know of creative photography.

There is a purpose behind this choice?
A certain amount of ego gratification, but that's not the major reason.

What is?
Meeting one's Creator through an art medium is useful to everybody.

Do you feel that this might seem subversive, using photography as a vehicle for your religious beliefs without actually coming out and saying so?

Well, one has to keep that very quiet! That's why I want to get away from the word "spiritual," because people mix it up with religion. I don't like the word "religion," but I don't mind using the word "sacred."

Do you equate that with what you call "camera work"?

Camera work is like equivalent, it works at many levels. Equivalents can be on a graphic level or they can be on a sacred level. Camera work is primarily interested in fine, beautiful, aesthetic, and somewhat sacred photography. Camera work does not, however, automatically mean sacred photography.

What do you mean by sacred *photography?*

Sacred photography tries to lead the photographer toward a recognition that there is a hierarchy of forces. There are lower levels which are not sacred, higher levels which are sacred, and still higher levels that we don't know anything about. There's an ordinary level of life and there's an extraordinary level of life. When you start talking about sacred photography, you are talking about religion. I think that any art medium is "a step on the way," and to many artists this is their ultimate expression—a sacred one, in some form or another. A lot of the highly expressive painters who are only after ego expression, or seem to be, very often touch on the sacred without really intending to.

In terms of literature, would you say that maybe the steps that Carlos Castaneda talks about are applicable here?

Of course. He's talking about esoteric knowledge, esoteric disciplines, and he's putting it in a form that somehow this generation seems to go for. Many of the photographers I've taught are still involved and their work deals with the sacred. Paul Caponigro, especially, realizes that is what he's driving at in photography. He's also a Gurdjieff student and we've talked to each other very clearly on those levels. We're both after the same thing.

Do you believe that an existentialist can get as much from the images that you produce as someone who relates to sacred photography?
I'm not too familiar with existentialist philosophy. If you use the word experiential, then I'll say yes. A person can experience things for what they are and can go deeply enough into what is behind any form. When he meets it, of course, he meets his Creator. You can call it sacred, you can call it experience, whatever. The ultimate experience of anything is a realization of what's behind it.

Is it necessary to hold religious views to really appreciate a sacred photograph? Or can you appreciate it if you do not believe in any higher being?
I think if a person does not believe in any higher being, then he can't see it. He can't imagine such a thing exists, or won't admit it. Therefore, he never can see it.

Is it essential for him to see it while viewing a photograph?
No. The photograph may not have it, either. As you look at photographs and at things to take photographs of, you begin to recognize that this is an ordinary situation, this one is a little extraordinary, and this very extraordinary. You begin to realize that there may be this same force behind absolutely everything. We keep saying this one has it, this one doesn't. I use the word "presence," which simply means the same thing. This has presence, and this one does not. And what is that presence? That presence is something sacred, it's our Creator, or it's another force, it's grace. Through the centuries there have been many names for it. If you give a person a word for it, he doesn't see it, or he says he sees it, but he really doesn't. You have to work for it.

Are you saying that, like beauty, presence is in the eye of the beholder?
No. If the eye of the beholder does not have that capacity, then a person can never see it.

Do you feel, though, that the less informational subject matter there is in an image, the more successful it is as an equivalent?
It's simplified. It does not make it more of anything. I always feel that it's pretty hard to predict what a photograph is going to do to whom.

Mirrors, Messages and Manifestations was probably the first body of your own work to be seen.
Correct.

Why did you wait so long before you published?
I could not find anybody to publish it. I'd have been perfectly willing to publish twenty years earlier than that! It's just as well I waited, I think.

The book has a title that's reminiscent of Jung's posthumous autobiography, Memories, Dreams, Reflections. *Did this influence you?*
I have read Jung. I was conscious, of course, of his book.

Do you see your book as autobiographical?
What else?

Is there an essential overall theme that you see revealed?
You've read it?

Indeed.
Then you know more about it than I do!

You've said that personal photography continues to be a statement of position. Could you say what your position is now?
I don't think I will ever manage to get my position appearing in photography or in my photographs. I am attempting to be in contact with my Creator, asking and allowing that to tell me what to do. I'm trying to be in contact with something that is ultimately wise and follow its directions, instead of trying to be so self-expressive. I've gone through all that. I need now to work with this something, to make things go differently. Or maybe not differently, I don't know what it'll do.

How would you like to see photography develop?
It makes absolutely no difference what I want it to do—it's going to do what it's going to do. All I can do is to stand back and observe. I can control my photography, I can do what I want with it—a little. If I can get into contact with something much wiser than myself, and it says get out of photography, maybe I would. I hesitate to say this, because I know it's going to be misunderstood. I'll put it this way—I'm trying to be in contact with my Creator when I photograph. I know perfectly well it's not possible to do it all the time, but there can be moments.

Is there any work that you are particularly interested in?
Whatever my students are doing.

There seems to be a passing on of certain sets of ideas and understandings. Do you feel yourself to be an inheritor of a set of ideas or ideals?
Naturally. After all, I have two parents, so I inherited something. I've had many spiritual fathers. The photographers who I have been influenced by, for example. There have been many other external influences. Students have had an influence. In a sense that's an inheritance. After a while we work with material that comes to us and it becomes ours, we digest it. It becomes energy and food for us, it's ours. And then in turn I can pass it on to somebody else with a sense of responsibility and validity. I am quoting it in my words, it has become mine, and that person will take it from me, just as I have taken from people who have influenced me. Take what you can use, digest it, make it yours, and then transmit it to your children or your students.

It's a cycle, then?
No, it's a continuous line. Not a cycle at all.

November 1975

SELECTED BIBLIOGRAPHY

Mirrors, Messages, and Manifestations. Millerton, New York: Aperture, 1969.

The New Zone System Manual, by Minor White and Richard Zakia. New York: Morgan and Morgan, 1976.

Rites and Passages. Introduction by James Baker Hall. Millerton, New York: Aperture, 1978.

Zone System Manual. Dobbs Ferry, New York: Morgan and Morgan, 1968.

Beaumont Newhall

(B O R N   1 9 0 8 / A M E R I C A N)

Paul Hill

You were at Harvard University in the late twenties. What did you study?
I studied the History of Art, and took my bachelor's degree in 1930, my master's in 1931.

Who were you studying under?
Well, there were a number of professors. The one most important to me was Paul J. Sachs. It was my ambition at that

time to become a museum worker and Paul Sachs gave a remarkable course in this subject. Most of the museum directors in America, of my generation, were trained by him. As far as the formal art history was concerned, the most important people were visiting professors.

When you graduated with a master's degree, was it difficult to get a job at that time?

It was thanks to Paul J. Sachs that I got my first job, as lecturer at the Philadelphia Art Museum. I arrived for work in September, but on New Year's Eve, I received word from my superior that they would like me to continue but they wouldn't have any money to pay me with. Finally, Paul Sachs found me another job at the Metropolitan Museum of Art in the Department of Decorative Art (there is no longer such a department); this was the part of the museum that looked after the sculpture, all kinds of furniture, and things that were called in those days "Decorative Arts." My particular concern was The Cloisters. This was a private museum that Mrs. Rockefeller bought for the Metropolitan as a branch museum. It was my job to be the curator. I was very excited at the age of twenty-three to have a museum of my own. But when I arrived, all the plans were altered; this little museum was closed and plans were set for building a magnificent new museum, which we know today as The Cloisters.

I researched the architecture of that strange area between France and Spain called Catalonia. I got into it and designed stuff, and I did the conservation and the research, and I loved it. This lasted until they thought I should do some further studies. That's how they let me know that their money had run out. The reason the money ran out was not due to the Depression, but because Mr. Rockefeller was so unhappy with the head of the Department of Decorative Arts that he took his money away—three million dollars—and they felt (I found out years later) that a twenty-three-year-old kid just couldn't be trusted with that sort of news. They had to keep it secret—so little Beaumont was out of a job and he went back to Harvard.

I tried to get a job but I couldn't. I did get a fellowship to study in Paris, and that was a fine experience—very intense, of course—learning the history of art. They had lectures in the morning, and in the afternoon you would go and see the real thing. Then I was fortunate enough the following year to receive a fellowship to go to the Courtauld Institute, and that was another great experience. In the meantime, I completed my residence at Harvard for the Ph.D. and was about to take my finals and write my thesis when the Museum of Modern Art offered me a job as librarian. Of course, I took it at once. I was not really qualified as a librarian, but the museum was very small in those days: I was the sixteenth member of the staff. That was in 1935, and I got so wrapped up in the museum that I forgot all about my Ph.D. That also began a whole new life for me with my future wife, Nancy. I used to say that in those days the Museum of Modern Art was like the early Christian Church. There was a sense of dedication, a real gospel kind of attitude. We would drum up the public. At the time of the Van Gogh exhibition, we hung up a great big flag with "Van Gogh" on it, and the Fifth Avenue Association said: "You can't do that." I said: "Since when is Fifty-third Street Fifth Avenue?" "Any merchant who is one hundred yards from Fifth Avenue is automatically subjected to our rules." So we got out a tape measure and measured it in their presence.

Then we had this great show of Cubism and Abstract Art. We imported abstract sculpture and the U.S. Customs wouldn't accept that because they were non-representational. So I photographed them and we sent a newsletter around saying that this was hardware! Alfred J. Barr, Jr., was the guiding spirit of MOMA in those days. This is before the present building on 11 West Fifty-third Street. It was in a mansion belonging to one of the Rockefellers, who made it available for the purpose of a museum. It was a beautiful white house. We ripped out old fireplaces and tried to make it as modern a gallery as we could, and it was tremendously successful. Perhaps I should say that my salary was very modest even in those days—it was $25 a week—and to eke out my salary, I photographed the exhibitions, simply record photographs of the exhibitions. I fixed up a darkroom in the men's john (the staff were very obliging about it) and I had a shelf over the water closet—it was a little tricky, but you could unzip yourself! I got paid two dollars a negative. My interest in photography was not only in taking pictures; I was developing an interest in the history of photography. My first published article was a review of a German history of photography, in 1934 or 1935.

In 1934 I was privileged to represent the Harvard graduate students at a meeting of the College Arts Association. It was the custom for the chairman of the department to choose one student, who was allowed to choose any subject he wished. Paul Sachs asked: "Well, what are you going to lecture about?" I said: "I would like to lecture on the relationship of photography and painting." Paul Sachs was so shocked by this that he had to sit down, but he agreed to it, and I gave the paper. To my delight, it was published in the magazine that's now called *The College Art Journal*. That's as far as I got academically with the history of photography.

Alfred Barr stopped me one day in the corridor and said: "Would you like to do a photography exhibition?" This was in the late spring of 1936. I said: "Yes, of course I would." He said: "We always had plans from the very inception of the Museum of Modern Art to include photography with sculpture, machine art, and theater, and other unconventional fields for museum collections and exhibitions. What do you want to do?" I said: "I think it would be a good idea to look at the medium from its beginning until today." He said: "That's fine. You get $5,000 for the exhibition." That was very unusual in those days—it's the equivalent of $20–$25,000 today. And then he said: "You'll have to travel abroad." Such a fact had never occurred to me. So on the strength of that, I called up my fiancée, Nancy, who was living in New England, and said: "Now is the time for us to get married, and we'll go abroad for our honeymoon." So I telegraphed my parents, and we were married on the first of July. Nancy always said that when she married Beaumont, she married photography. She also took her first photograph the day after we were married.

Why was Alfred Barr so interested in photography?
Alfred Barr was very broad in his knowledge and in his interest in modern art. He was also very much influenced by

what was happening in Germany. Germany in the 1920's had the most progressive museum displays, and in Germany photography was being considered along with architecture, sculpture, and so forth. Indeed, the most important force in the German art world of the 1920's, and even earlier, was the Deutsche Werkbund. That was a term used for what was the equivalent of William Morris's Arts and Crafts group. The group published a magazine called *Die Form*, and in this magazine were photographs and discussions of the machine as an object of beauty. They organized a colossal exhibition of photography in Stuttgart in 1929 called "Film und Foto." This had over five hundred photos in it. Edward Weston, for example, selected photographs to represent the West Coast, and Edward Steichen, the East Coast. Alfred Stieglitz would have nothing to do with it, though. Photographers from all over the world contributed.

So that was part of Alfred Barr's background, and he found he had a man on his staff that he thought qualified to do this. He had a magnificent trust in me—I'll never forget it. He gave me complete authority to do the show the way I wanted to, and that was really quite remarkable when you consider that at that time I was only twenty-seven years old!

It was the custom at the Museum of Modern Art to publish a book with each show. Each book contained a listing of the objects, reproductions of selected objects, and long essays. I did a book for the exhibition called *Photography 1839–1937*. I began writing the book on Thanksgiving Day in 1936 and it was published on St. Patrick's Day, March 17, 1937. I don't know how I could possibly write and have a book in print in these days in such a short space of time. This was due to two things: I was so young that I didn't know better, and the printers and binders were just waiting for work. Nowadays, a publisher waits for the printer and binder to find a slot.

Well, the book came out and the show went up. The show filled the entire building. It was spectacular and well mounted. At MOMA the entire staff helped each other. I worked on the Cubism and Abstract show, but when you were director of an exhibition, you were the number-one man—you were as high as the director of the museum—it was a beautiful, beautiful thing. The exhibition was very well received. All the art critics reviewed it, including Lewis Mumford, who was with *The New Yorker*, and his review was really magnificent. The show traveled throughout the country for two years, and that really launched photography at MOMA.

How did you collect work for the show?
Well, in France there was a man named André Lejard, who was the managing editor of *Photographie* and he knew the photographers, so he very kindly set up dates. I stayed at a little hotel, and every hour on the hour, practically, I would see someone. So that's how we collected in France. In London I worked with the Royal Photographic Society. I didn't go to Germany, and I think that was a mistake. I don't think the German representation was too good, but Moholy-Nagy helped me to get a lot of people. Moholy himself was great. He was a fine person and my teacher. He was really a good teacher in an informal sense. But what was more important than that was the research. I had done work in the library of the French Society of Photography, then the library of the Royal Photographic Society. I was able to work in those two libraries, and having access to the shelves, I was able to browse. I really taught myself. You might like to know that I started the research while I was laid up in a hospital, following a minor operation. My young bride used to come to visit me, and I would say: "Nancy, will you go to the library and bring back so and so." And then I would read. I would start to read about seven o'clock every morning, read straight through the day, and she would come, and I would say: "Oh, hello, dear. Nurse, give Nancy a ginger ale. Now where was I?" I have often thought that they must have given me a drug, because I was just a demon. These books were all in German and French— nothing in English at all—and I read them all from cover to cover. I think when you go into a field you must plunge in and just plow right through it. It makes every other book you read afterward very easy. It's like going to a city—when I used to travel in France or Germany, I would take a sight-seeing bus just to get the feel of the place, and then I would go off on my own. The most important part of the European

trip was the research that I did in these libraries. There was nothing comparable in this country.

You can read French and German?
Certainly. I wouldn't be where I am if I couldn't read French and German.

What were the exciting things that were happening in photography about that time?
The really exciting thing was the Farm Security Administration in this country. Indeed, the time I started was the same year that Roy Stryker started. I didn't know about his work at all, although I did show the work of Walker Evans and Dorothea Lange. I would say that the most exciting things that happened at the tail end of the twenties were three movements: "straight" photography (at its height at that time), experimental photography, and photojournalism.

"Straight" photography was very doctrinaire. It was related to the theory of "form follows function," which we see in architecture. Group f/64 had just made its mark and I was very pleased that Adams and Weston had contributed to the MOMA show. Both of them contributed more than photographs; they contributed their knowledge, and the work of other people. Another was Moholy-Nagy. He was the representative of the experimental school, which was concerned with the use of materials and was really (as one looks back upon it) just as painterly as the work of the turn of the century. Moholy and Man Ray were two leading photographers, but both considered themselves painters first and photographers second. That was going on; then there was a third thing—and I didn't do very well by it. That was photojournalism. I was particularly impressed by a magazine, a very short-lived one, that was called *Vu*, meaning *seen*. It was produced by a very great magazine editor, whose name doesn't seem to be remembered—Lucien Vogel. He was Paris editor of *Vogue* magazine and founded this little magazine *Vu*, which was patterned directly after the German illustrated press. This magazine was so good that Henry Luce tried to buy it out. He copied it, though; and it was the prototype of *Life. Vu* collapsed because they lost all their subscribers. They were too radical—they believed in the Communist side of the Spanish revolution.

How did you meet Weston and Adams?

We met Ansel in 1939 in New York City. Ansel had come to visit New York at the time we had the gala opening of the new MOMA building. He wanted to see us, so we invited him to lunch and met him under the marquee at the museum. He had just bought a new tripod and was very proud, and he marched along with it as if it were a cane. We went down the street to a French restaurant. We just liked each other then and there.

Who was the first creative photographer you met?

That's a good question. I suppose it would be Alfred Stieglitz. I first met him when I was a graduate student doing my master's work in 1931. Every spring the graduate students would go to New York with Paul Sachs; he would take us to private collections, galleries—it was a great experience. We got to meet the people who sold pictures and we were trained in how to buy pictures. We would go around on our own to galleries, and I went into a place that I had never heard of—An American Place. There on the walls were photographs of New York City by Alfred Stieglitz, and also some of his earlier work. I was absolutely gripped by these pictures. I didn't know who Stieglitz was, but this little old man with white hair, wearing a cape, was there chatting to people. I asked him a question: "What kind of filter did you use making these pictures?" He said: "That has nothing to do with the case, young man!" He really gave me a dressing down for even thinking about the technical problems. There was another man there from the Museum of the City of New York. He said to Mr. Stieglitz: "These are the most magnificent pictures of New York. I would like to have a set for the museum. Can you knock us off a set from your negatives?" "Young man, how many prints do you think exist of the photographs?" He said: "Oh, I don't know." "Young man! Just one, and they are not

going to be shown at the Museum of the City of New York!"
That was quite an experience. That was the first time I met
up with creative photography. There's no question about that
at all.

*You asked a question about filters. That gives the impression
that you had been involved in photography before 1931?*
Oh, I had messed around with photography all my life. My
mother was a photographer, and a pretty good one, too. Her
gods were Gertrude Käsebier and Clarence White. When
Father built the house—he was a physician and had a very
large house—he built a large studio on the third floor. The
studio was for Mother. It had a skylight and a darkroom fully
equipped. But Mother gave up photography at the time of
World War I when chemicals were very scarce because everything for photography came from Germany (Kodak didn't
begin to make its own chemicals until after World War I).
What little got through was for military purposes only.

Well, here was all this abandoned stuff and Mother had no
interest in it. She didn't show me her work, and she didn't
care about my work at all. She had gone into needlework. I
taught myself photography, and started out with Mr. Kodak's
instruction book, *How to Make Better Pictures.*

I must tell you about a very important part in the formation
of my career. I am quite surprised that I can put my finger
on the moment that creative photography impressed me. It
was in 1926. I had left preparatory school and was about to
enter Harvard. A roommate of mine at Andover lived in
Salem, Massachusetts, and we visited back and forth. I could
cover the ground in my little Model T quite quickly and so
we would stay at each other's place. I was spending the weekend with him and we went to the movies and saw a film called
Variety, starring Emil Jannings. I was absolutely gripped by
the visuals; it was photographed by Karl Freund. I was so
gripped by this picture that I went to see it again and again
and again. I would drive to outlying neighborhood theaters to
see it. There was no such thing in those days in America as
special theaters that showed art films. All of these experimental
films were shown in ordinary movie houses. *Potemkim,* for

example, was shown on Broadway along with vaudeville and so forth. There was no such thing as art, it was just film.

I got this tremendous desire to make films, but I didn't have any way to make them, or anybody to teach me. I didn't even have any money to buy films, so I made films with a still camera. I did crazy angle shots and so forth. I must have seen *Variety* a dozen times. Then at Harvard, it was, to me, a great, great privilege to be able to use the books in the largest university library in this country. You would simply call at the desk, write out a slip, and then wait for a page to bring the book. One day I noticed a new German book, *America: Picture Book of an Architect*; the architect was Erich Mendelsohn, one of the great modern architects. He had come to America and photographed skyscrapers, the lights of the city in time exposures (which gave streaks of light), grain elevators, and factories. This book just gripped me. Those two things started me, there's no question about it. My dear mother just happened to give me the facilities. I never knew anybody that was interested in photography during my four years at Harvard. I thought I could maybe get some tips on how to make my things better from taking courses at the Camera Club in Boston, but I realized that would be futile. So I taught myself—I just limped along really.

The Harvard art course was very difficult to get through—you have to literally know, by heart, thousands of images. We had a special room with tables in the library and heaps of photographs on gray cards. We would just sit there, afternoon after afternoon, looking at them, passing them around, quizzing each other, and memorizing them—incidentally, they were all in black and white, there were no color reproductions. Every so often, just for human interest, they would throw in a photographic portrait of an artist. Well, I was a great admirer of Daumier, and I saw this lovely portrait of him which I recognized as being the work of Carjat, because of a book that I had reviewed in 1934. I looked at this picture rather more carefully than my fellow students and I saw a signature, an original signature "à mon ami Lavoignat—Daumier" signed by Daumier to his wood engraver. I took it to Paul Sachs and said: "Look what I've found." He had it framed and hung in his office within a day.

Now, to get back to when I was standing with Ansel under the marquee at the Museum of Modern Art at the time of its opening in 1939. It was there that we established our friendship. Then comes the year 1940, when my aunt's legacy enabled Nancy and me to travel. We were going to Oregon to visit my cousin, and then we were going to Los Angeles to visit her uncle. We were going up the coast and home through the Canadian Rockies. The tickets had all been bought, the schedule done and everything. We took a very slow train—five days —it was cheap and we spent as much time stopping as traveling. There were no bathrooms on board, and when we arrived in San Francisco, the first thing we wanted was a bath. So we told the taxi man to take us to a hotel. We rang up Ansel and he asked where we were staying. We told him the name of the hotel and he said: "Oh, my God! Don't make a move, I'll be right there." The hotel was in the red-light district!

Were there any other art historians working in the same area?
Only one. And that was Heinrich Schwarz, the author of the book on David Octavius Hill.

Was he putting shows together?
Photography was only one of his interests. He was basically interested in collecting prints in all media. But he did have the great acumen to recognize that photography was an art form to be handled in the same way as other arts. An art historian is a very special person and it is a very special discipline. It is not related to criticism. Roger Fry, in my opinion, was not an art historian. He was a very great critic, and wrote on Julia Margaret Cameron.

Let's get back to San Francisco. Ansel Adams took us around. He is one of the most beautiful people—so generous. He introduced us to many people and the most important person he introduced us to was Edward Weston, who was in San Francisco giving a lecture with Ansel at a local camera club. Ansel drove Edward back home to Carmel and we went along with them. Edward was very polite, but there was not very much talk about photography. We arrived quite late at night and we were met by this beautiful young girl with long flowing hair; she was Edward's wife Charis. We were made very welcome, had some coffee, and we went to our hotel, which was walking distance from Edward's home.

The next morning we went to Edward's and we walked down to the shack which had been built by his sons. The shack was just one great big space in which they lived, with two smaller areas of equal importance—a bathroom and a darkroom. In one corner was the kitchen and in the other was a double bed. There was a fireplace, a phonograph, and a table on which was placed some fruit. There was a typewriter on which Charis was writing an account of their trip on the Guggenheim Fellowship, which was published as the book *California and the West*. Edward said: "I'm going out to photograph on Point Lobos. Would you like to come and photograph, too?" So we went along, Nancy with her Rolleiflex and me with a German Voigtländer folding camera. I felt a bit silly with my little bitsy camera alongside his 8 x 10. But Edward made no wisecracks about this at all, he respected us. We photographed, had some lunch, and then Edward said: "Aren't you going to develop your film?" He asked me if I would like to use his darkroom. Later I realized that this was indeed a real kind of friendship. Someone said that to use someone else's darkroom was like lending a toothbrush. He showed me how he operated. He would develop his 8 x 10's in a tray, but his 4 x 5's he would develop with hangers in his developing tank, which was a secondhand car battery with the partitions cut out.

So I developed my little pictures and he said: "Aren't you going to print them?" So next day I printed. Well, I was brought up in those days by Alfred Stieglitz—I used to photograph for *him*—and there was no dodging. It was absolutely straight contact printing. "If you don't get it in the negative, my boy, you didn't get it!" But Alfred Stieglitz dodged his negatives! This is not generally known. It is very important to understand that he underdeveloped, and then, in daylight, locally intensified with mercuric chloride. I am reminded, parenthetically, that Ansel sent me a letter from the ex-husband of Diane Arbus saying: "I thought I had mastered the Zone System but I simply cannot understand how Alfred Stieglitz got such tone values." And Ansel said: "I'm stumped.

I can't answer this question." And I wrote to Arbus telling what I knew and he sent back a letter of absolute shock. But I didn't know about this control until after Stieglitz's death. Paul Strand told me.

Back to Edward Weston. He looked at my prints. He was very, very courteous about them. He asked: "Why didn't you do some dodging here and there?" "Dodge, Mr. Weston, dodge!" So he laughed and showed me how to do it. He printed by contact printing in a frame with a bare light bulb above, and then he would introduce hand movements and a number of neat devices he designed—pieces of paper of various sizes on bits of wire. He was my teacher in photography. So that began a close relationship with Edward Weston in just those few days. We canceled the trip and stayed with Edward in Carmel Highlands until the last minute. It was an experience that shaped our lives.

Edward made my portrait. He didn't make snapshots—he wasn't trigger-happy. Anyway, we sat out in the patio and he made some dozen exposures and he made proofs of them on daylight paper. It was a good picture of me at the period because I am going backward, hand on my chin. I am not forward, I look very retiring, very much the young scholar.

We went back to New York, via Yosemite. Ansel very generously drove us there. And there at Yosemite a very important thing happened. We were talking with Ansel about our desire to form, at the Museum of Modern Art, a true photographic center. Ansel had outlined almost a blueprint of what we wanted to do in his first technical book, *Making a Photograph.* He was very interested himself. I can see him now, having a drink at his lovely place in the very heart of Yosemite Valley. He said: "Well, let's call David McAlpin." And with that he tossed his ice into the bushes and lifted the long-distance phone. He got in touch with his good friend David McAlpin. David had met Ansel through Georgia O'Keeffe. David and O'Keeffe and one of the Rockefeller boys would go off on camping trips. David was a man of considerable means and generosity. Ansel told him of our idea, and he said: "Fine. I would very much like to meet your friends Beaumont and Nancy." When we came back to New York, he invited us to lunch at the University Club and we outlined our plan. He thought about it and then offered the Museum a thousand dollars. So I proudly went to the director and he said that we would have to find out what the donor wanted us to do with the money. David said: "It is just for the photography. Do what you want with it as long as it is related to photography." I immediately spent $500 for Moholy-Nagy's one-man show. I spent the thousand dollars quite quickly. I discovered later that he had given the Metropolitan Museum the same amount, and he had sat back to see how the money was spent by each institution. The Metropolitan husbanded the money and made it last about ten years. I went out and spent it in six months! A photography committee was set up, McAlpin was chairman. Photography at MOMA was founded by myself—myself means Nancy and I—Ansel Adams, and David McAlpin. We founded a department of photography and I was appointed curator. This was the first time that a major museum had founded a department of photography equal to other departments, like painting, sculpture, architecture, and so on. The museum had showed its commitment to photography through the great show of 1937 and the Walker Evans exhibition (which I had nothing to do with), which was a very important and beautiful show. That was organized by Thomas Dabney Mabry, who was an associate director of the museum, and Lincoln Kirstein (he and I were classmates at Harvard).

How did World War II affect you?
It was obvious that I would be drafted because of my age. I was thirty-four, and Nancy and I had no children. I volunteered because we were fighting against great injustices and I felt strongly about the horrors of Nazi rule. Heinrich Schwarz was expelled from his post as director of the Belvedere Museum in Vienna because he was Jewish. However, we managed to bring him to America.

The war had a real meaning for me. I finally received a mail-order commission as a first lieutenant. I was leaving a unique job at MOMA and there was nobody to take the job except Nancy. It took a bit of persuading. I think if they hadn't taken her, the Photography Department would have just been washed up. But it was very difficult for Nancy. She knew how to put on an exhibition, and she knew photography, but she didn't know much about working with other people, against opposition. Nobody was jumping up and down in excitement about photography like they are now. Even in my wildest dreams thirty years ago, I would never have thought that photography would become so popular. Nancy built up the whole center beyond what I had started and she introduced the teaching of photography. She got Ansel to give workshops using the museum darkroom.

I have always been the historian and Nancy, throughout her life, the creative one. The two of us worked as a beautiful team, and without Nancy I would have been a pretty stuffy art historian. She carried on in a brilliant way.

I was overseas in North Africa and in Italy as a photo-interpreter. It was my job to study aerial photographs and from them to deduce what the enemy was doing. It was fascinating work. While I was in America on leave, the war finished in Europe. I was then being groomed for the job of photointerpretation officer to study Japan, as we did not know the railroads network. We had been using inaccurate maps. The whole thing was set up so that I would train my own group, and I was about to leave when the war was over.

When I got back I rejoined the museum. I tried my best to get the museum to hire both of us, but MOMA, although it was a liberal institution, would not hear of a husband-and-wife team. If only Nancy and I were not married and lived "in sin," we could have worked together. That was a bitter disappointment to both of us. It bothered Nancy very much, but there was nothing I could do about it. So I took up my job and Nancy began to work with Paul Strand. Then came a blow: here I was, finally getting on my feet again, when I was told that Edward Steichen had been made Director of Photography. This was completely over my head. It had never been discussed with me. I thought that I was head of the department that Ansel, David, Nancy, and I had founded. No, I was to work with him, as curator. He would bring glamour and a lot of money, and they thought that Kodak would give $50,000 a year. I was to be the intellectual and Steichen was to be the leader. I could not take this, so I resigned. We had a resignation party and everyone from the museum came over. A good friend brought over a whole case of champagne. We had a great party, and that ended an important part of my career.

There now began a new period in the life of both Nancy and myself. Incidentally, although there was all this political trouble with my departure from MOMA, I was almost immediately asked to contribute an introduction to the exhibition of the work of Henri Cartier-Bresson, with Lincoln Kirstein. I have been connected ever since with the museum in a semi-official way, and presently I am on the Photography Committee.

At that time I received a Guggenheim Fellowship and my plan was to write a book on the daguerreotype in America. When I received the Guggenheim I intended to do it, but I had just agreed to do a new edition of my history for MOMA. The plan was that I should simply add a chapter to bring the book up to date. So I wrote the Guggenheim Foundation to ask if I could use the grant to write this new edition. The Director of The Foundation wrote back: "Change your project as you wish, but please tell us where to send the check!" The reason he had asked for my address was that I had written from Black Mountain College. In 1946, Nancy and I were invited by Josef Albers to spend two weeks as the guests of the college to give three or four lectures on the history of photography. There was no pay, but the opportunity to live in the country was too good to miss.

I announced that I would not be talking about the technique of photography, but if any students were interested, they could always talk to me afterward. There were about twenty students who wanted a course in photography, but it was not really possible to do that then. So the following summer Albers invited Nancy and me to spend all summer there. It was then, as I was going to write the new chapter, that I discovered that the book was not very good! I can't understand why people pay extra money for a first-edition Newhall when he put so much time into making the second edition so much better! Anyway, I taught there, and it was the only time that I have given a course in photography. But I had too many students.

I had forty-five, and the darkroom could only hold six. So I developed a technique that I think is unusual. We would spend the morning setting up the view camera, looking at the ground glass, and focusing. Then I told them that I wanted them all to go away and I would do the developing. The next time I showed them the negative, and we looked at the negative in relationship to the place where they photographed. Then I showed them how to print it. By working in yellow light they could see what they were doing and they could see how to handle the materials and the solutions. Within two weeks I got them going pretty damned well.

It was a very hard period and I was not able to spend much time on the book. But I spent the whole of the next year working on *The History of Photography*. I also began research on the daguerreotype in America, which was to appear fourteen years later. My publisher was very, very patient! He was Charles Duell. I said that I would return his advance, because I couldn't meet the deadline. He said he wouldn't accept a penny back and that I was under no obligation to finish the book. I look back on that time as a steady creative period.

Just as I was wondering what to do next, Eastman Kodak Company approached me to set up the collections and make an exhibition in a new museum of photography that they had already established at Rochester, in the former residence of George Eastman. The house is a large building with fifty rooms, and it was a "white elephant." It had been left by George Eastman to the University of Rochester as the residence of the president. But it was expensive to maintain and not suitable, so the university turned the house over to a board of trustees that had been formed to operate a non-profit-making institution. Their first idea was to hire me on a short-term period to arrange the exhibitions, but I wouldn't go because they didn't offer me enough money. It took them a year to find out that I was the best qualified person to do it. So they increased my salary to a more attractive one and gave me a permanent job. Nancy and I moved to Rochester in the fall of 1948.

We began to reconstruct the house to make it into a museum, to collect material, and to build up the whole program. It is the most important museum operation in the field of photography. I was working directly under a Kodak executive—General Oscar Solbert, and the word "general" must never be omitted, because he was a West Point product and he learned a great deal about how to be aggressive! It was a difficult relationship. Eastman House would not have come into being or existed without General Solbert. He knew nothing about photography and he left that side of it to me, which was fine.

The problem was the running of the place. Kodak's first idea was to have an entirely technological museum, and there was no space to show photographs. I was in despair until a very wonderful man, Professor Clarence Kennedy of Smith College, who was a very skilled photographer of works of art, came to Rochester to work in the research laboratory on some kind of reproduction process. He said: "Just find twelve feet and you'll get photography established." So I tore out three closets and made a bay and put up small exhibitions.

Pretty soon my director got a quarter of a million dollars from a relative of George Eastman to build a theater. The attic of that theater was to become a photographic gallery. It was a very poor gallery, but it was something. Kodak had no idea what a museum operation was. They were generous but they never really understood. I began to develop ideas that went far beyond what they had in mind. We also wanted a membership association because our money came entirely from Kodak, and we established George Eastman Associates who would each pay five dollars a year. Instead of spending our publicity budget on handouts that would disappear, we talked about the history of photography in a little magazine called *Image*. And that started out being printed in the house, with one of the guards as the printer. He brought over his whole printing press. It was a four-page thing, and was entirely written by me. Sometimes it was signed and sometimes it was not! We distributed it free at first until we had a following; then we charged for it. Also, we were able to increase the size of it.

The money for the museum came from the Eastman Charitable Trust and the staff were not Kodak employees. It was a separate organization and in no way, throughout my twenty-three years there, did Kodak ever direct or censure our work or order what we were going to show. And that included showing material from its competitors, including Polaroid, De Vere, and so on. This irked some of the sales staff at Kodak, but they had no say whatsoever. We built up the publications and the exhibitions to show to an audience larger than that in Rochester alone. I also gradually increased the staff. The most important addition to our staff was Minor White, who came to Rochester from teaching at the San Francisco Art Institute. He had been invited to the Institute by Ansel Adams, who had stimulated the interest in photography there, and had raised the money for the darkroom facilities. He stayed with us for many years, and was in charge of *Image* and exhibitions of contemporary work. He founded a small gallery in which he would put the work of people he thought promising. One of the most famous photographers launched through the gallery was Paul Caponigro. Minor eventually left Eastman House because of his growing interest in teaching.

The interest in photography as a form of expression—as a creative art—was introduced to the Rochester Institute of Technology almost exclusively by Minor White and Ralph Hattersley. It was a great step forward. For Minor it was really the start of the extraordinary work that was to be done in teaching as well as in his own creative work. Minor hired an assistant in order to ease the load of running *Image* and the exhibitions. That was Nathan Lyons, who is a very industrious man, a brilliant man. He did a very fine job indeed. He built the magazine up to a handsome quarterly. The trustees discussed the problems of the expense and felt that more people would be reached by supporting book publication; and so *Image* came, temporarily, to a close—it has since been revived.

So we began to give a book a year to our members. My *History of Photography*, which was co-published with the Museum of Modern Art, was one, but I think without question that the most important publishing job that Nathan did was *The Daybooks of Edward Weston*, which no other publisher would touch. We financed publication of volume I on Mexico —my wife, Nancy, had edited this during Edward's lifetime and we had hoped that we would be able to interest a publisher because, in that period of his life, Edward was not able to work and he needed money, and his various friends tried to get an income for him, but nobody would touch the *Daybooks*. The book became very successful—so much so that a publishing house, Horizon Press, asked if they could co-publish volume II. That was how this classical work appeared in public. Since then, of course, it has been republished by Aperture in both hardcover and paperback editions. In my experience it is one of the books that has been most influential for students, because they are able to see in its intimate pages many of the questions and the problems that they face. I've often said that this book is the equivalent of the journal of Eugène Delacroix.

We also brought out *Photographers on Photography*, edited by Nathan Lyons; then we did a handsome book on Aaron Siskind, in connection with a major exhibition of his work. We also had many major shows that circulated around the country. Nathan Lyons had a particular interest in the younger photographers and in the trends that were developing. He put on a group exhibition on one aspect that he gave the name of "social landscape" to—Garry Winogrand, Lee Friedlander, Diane Arbus, and Robert Frank. These people were concerned with the human scene. He also put on an exhibition of those who looked upon photography in opposite ways—the classical "straight" photography and the experimental, mixed-media approach. I think it's important that these trends were recognized very early at George Eastman House. Unfortunately, Nathan resigned and began teaching at the Visual Studies Workshop, which he organized and founded in Rochester. That happened in 1969.

Another activity that happened at Eastman House that was of great importance was the frequent conferences we would hold. Eastman House is an ideal place for meetings, and for years organizations such as the National Press Photographers Association of America and the American Society of Magazine Photographers had made use of the Dryden Theater with its large parking space. Nathan was particularly concerned with teaching and invited the leading teachers of photography in institutions of higher learning to come to Rochester to get together to discuss their common problems. At this period photography was just being introduced into the local universities and schools, and there were problems. It was felt that a common front would help solve these problems. The meeting was extremely successful and the body wanted to form into a society and hoped that Eastman House would support them. I told them that I didn't think that was a good idea. I said: "Let's not get organized until we've had a chance to think it over." In the following year, they met in Chicago, independently of Eastman House, and formed the Society for Photographic Education. I still feel that it was a very wise thing that this group became autonomous, but it was brought into being by Eastman House, which I don't think is generally known, and by Nathan Lyons.

I would say that the major exhibition that I directed for Eastman House was "Photo-Eye of the Twenties." This was a joint exhibition organized by me for George Eastman House and the Museum of Modern Art. Working together meant that our budget was more than twice what I could have had in Rochester. I chose some two hundred photographs from international photographers with some of the greats—Edward Weston, Brett, Stieglitz, and then from the other side of the water, Moholy-Nagy, Man Ray, August Sander, and a whole host of people. Really it was a description of the style of the 1920's, and at the Museum of Modern Art I was given the opportunity to design the room in which it was to be held. We built a dramatic display with slanting walls at right angles so that no walls touched each other. Many images of the twenties existed only in the printed book, because the bombings in the war had destroyed the negatives of some of the most important works. So I had to use the reproductions, and it is one of my principles in museum work that you do not show reproductions, because the reproductions invariably lower the quality of the originals. But in this case we segregated them completely, because at that time Kodak had just put on the market a daylight screen for projection. A remarkable thing, because in sunlight you can project a color slide and still see it quite clearly.

So we hung the projector in front of the window, and right opposite the window we put the screen. There was one problem with this projection system and that was that the viewers have to be on a central axis. If you see it from one side, it's just a gray screen—so we built two screen walls so that the visitor had to go around the corner to see it. This also had the advantage that people on Fifty-third Street, when it was in New York, could see it.

We showed the pioneers of twentieth-century photography —Paul Strand's work of 1915, and Coburn's early abstract work, and so forth. This was an extremely successful show and it traveled for two years around the country. I had hoped to do a book on this show, but commuting from Rochester to New York, and running Eastman House, and teaching school, was all a bit more than I could handle. So the book was postponed, but I hope some time to revive it and to at least put on record, in book form, the photographs that were chosen. That was a very pleasant association working at the Museum of Modern Art and establishing a close link between Eastman House and the museum, which still, I'm happy to say, exists.

In 1971 I retired from George Eastman House. I had announced to the trustees some three years earlier my intention of retiring early. I felt that I had established Eastman House and that it was in good hands and would continue. I wanted to write and teach, so the trustees asked if I would find a new director for them. When Van Deren Coke heard of the resignation of Nathan Lyons, who was the associate director of G.E.H., he applied for the job. I met him in Chicago and we had a whole day of discussions. He was very excited by it and took the job. So that was the opportunity for me to leave. Van Deren Coke was teaching at the University of New Mexico, where he was professor of Art and director of the university museum. He introduced photography into the curriculum and built it up from simply a non-credit, one-semester course to its present high level of teaching.

It had not occurred to me to go to the University of New Mexico; as a matter of fact, I had no idea where I would go after my retirement! I thought something would come along, but I hadn't given it too much thought because I would be able to spend time doing my writing. But my wife, Nancy, and I enjoyed a holiday on a ranch in Arizona—a lovely vacation place right in the desert. Van quietly suggested that New Mexico wasn't very far from Arizona, and perhaps on my way back, I'd like to look over the old school. He hadn't made up his mind whether he would take the job at Rochester permanently or not. So consequently I called up the dean, Clinton Adams, from Arizona and was warmly received by him. He asked me to give a lecture and I gave a gallery talk on an exhibition of the Farm Security Administration photographs. I gave my lecture and everybody seemed to like it, and next day I spent all my honorarium—fifty dollars—at the Quivira Bookshop on photographic books. At lunch the chairman of the University of New Mexico Department of Art opened discussions about my joining the faculty. They asked me to teach whatever I wanted—a really remarkable offer. Nancy had stayed at the ranch, and I called her up and she agreed at once. This was, of course, the most important teaching job I had ever had.

My background in teaching was quite extensive. In 1952 I was invited by the University of Rochester to give a course in their extension school, which they called the University School. I had six students to begin with; the following year I had fifteen students, and the University of Rochester Art Department asked if I would teach a course in the history of photography. I was quite willing to do this, and the Art Department put it up to the Committee on Academic Policy. They ruled: "Not possible. This is not a trade school. Photography cannot be possibly considered as a proper discipline for the Department of Arts and Sciences." At that time the Rochester Institute of Technology was seeking accreditation from the state of New York because it was founded purely as a technical school and no degrees had been offered. To give a degree, you have to meet certain standards, and they asked if I would give a course in the history of photography. I felt that this was a better use of my time than continuing a noncredit course, and so I gave a compulsory course on the history of photography to unwilling students, but I found that with a little bit of drama I could hold their attention, and I developed a style of integrating photography with the other arts and indeed with other aspects of human endeavor. It was particularly important to do this at R.I.T. because the students were, at that time of transition, of a very low caliber and they were underprivileged intellectually. For instance, one of the R.I.T. students boarded with Nancy and me, and he showed me the books that they had—*Reader's Digest* was required reading, for example! The course in the history of art covered painting, sculpture, architecture, and music in one semester. So I felt a certain moral obligation to help these fine young people. And I think that's really when I first came to be interested in teaching.

Then Nathan Lyons, in 1967 or 1968, conceived the idea of a new kind of school—a visual-studies workshop—which would cover all graphic techniques and which would be very loosely structured, with opportunities for the students to pursue their particular interests. He had interested the State University of New York at Buffalo in offering a master's degree, but the studying would take place in Rochester. I was asked by the State University of New York at Buffalo if I would become a visiting professor. Every time I'm a visiting professor it seems that it's the other way around, because in this case the students all visited me and I never set foot on the Buffalo campus.

This was my first graduate teaching—we had seminars and I had a general lecture course. The seminars were particularly interesting and important—we had five students—and these five students would sit around the table in my office and each person would take some aspect of the history of photography and report upon it in depth, and then we would discuss it altogether. I think the students who came out of that workshop were quite remarkable. It was a great experience to be able to have the luxury of so few students and a marvelous library—Eastman House has one of the great photographic libraries of the world.

Regarding Eastman House, I certainly should have mentioned the building up of the library and the collections which, except for a great collection of French material purchased by Kodak in 1939, contained very little photographic material in image form. I was able right away to get some important American collections. I acquired the entire collection of Alden Scott Boyer, who perhaps had the largest private collection in the United States, which in a great impulsive moment he gave to us. He'd lost his wife and had no children and he was very much concerned about what would happen to his things, so he wrote me a letter: "If you want my collection, now is the time to talk." I called him on the phone and he said, "Well, do you want to buy it, or do you want me to give it to you?" I said: "I want you to give it to me, naturally." "That's what I like—plain talk!" So I spent that summer in Chicago, and when the time came to ship it back home, it filled four and one half tons of truck. That was really the foundation of the photographic library at G.E.H.

We had some beautiful seminars at Eastman House for the Visual Studies Workshop/State University of New York students. Barbara Morgan, for example, came and talked for three hours without stopping—a magnificent presentation. I brought in a stool, and she looked at it and said: "What's the idea of bringing in that dental chair—I don't want that!"

As an example of what can be done with such fabulous resources as Eastman House possesses: when we talked about Eugène Atget, I didn't use any slides at all—we put three hundred original Atgets on the walls of the classroom! Then we had another great experience when Stefan Lorant, formerly the editor of the Munich *Illustrierte Zeitung*, and one of the pioneer picture editors, brought one of the pioneer magazine photographers—Felix Man—to talk to us. They both spoke English very well and we had the little camera that Man began to work with, the Ermanox. We set it up on a tripod so he could show us how to operate it. He told us that he never went on an assignment with more than twelve glass plates, each $1\frac{5}{8}$ x $1\frac{1}{2}$ inches. He covered a picture story in twelve shots. A young embarrassed photographer from *The New York Times* with two Leicas slung round his neck was dancing around all over the place, and every so often Felix Man would say: "It's no use you taking so many pictures, young man." I think that was the only seminar in the history of photography that was covered by *The New York Times*! Well, that was the type of teaching I did in Rochester.

Now I'm at the University of New Mexico and I am totally dedicated to the assignment of teaching young people something about the history, the philosophy, and the aesthetics of photography. My teaching is based upon the experiences that I had in Rochester, but it's more intense, and because it's a full-time job, it's more difficult, because at the moment resources are inadequate, though in the last three years remarkable improvements have been made. We have acquired three very fine collections, particularly in books, and the collection of original prints is growing into an excellent teaching tool. There's hardly any type of photograph that we cannot show the original prints of to the students. The enthusiasm of the students for photography is remarkable, as is the interest in the history of photography. As far as I know, the opportunities given by the University of New Mexico are greater than any given to any other photographic historian. I do not know of any other university in the country, or in the world, that has three Ph.D. candidates in the field of the history of photography within a department of art history.

Over the years, my views on the history of photography have obviously changed, and the views of those concerned in the history of photography have also changed. This is a natural process and history must be rewritten. It is a surprise to me that nobody else has written a history of photography from my particular vantage point: that of the art historian. There have been other histories of photography written, and very fine ones, but they are more archaeological and encyclopaedic, such as the very fine volume published by Helmut Gernsheim and his wife, which is loaded with far more material than there is in my history of photography.

It was a deliberate decision on my part to make my book fit into the more literary type of history, and to try a very difficult thing, which I still have not completed to my satisfaction: tracing the stylistic development of photography and its relationship to other media. I think one of the great problems in history writing is that you always start with a body collected by somebody else. I relied in my early work on the European books that I have mentioned—the great two-volume history of photography by J. M. Eder and a French one by Georges

Potonniée. Many of the illustrations in my book were the same images that they had published. There is a tendency for writers to go to secondary rather than primary sources, and that's what I was doing when I started. I was able to touch original documents during those few weeks of intense research in England and France, but by and large, it was the secondary source that I followed. This was true also of the writers of history who followed me.

My collection of pictures has been drawn upon very heavily, particularly by Peter Pollack in his *Picture History of Photography*. Thus, we are in danger of creating what my dear wife, Nancy, used to call "chestnuts"—the same old pictures over and over again. There is a definite demand for a certain number of masterpieces to be reproduced. After all, if one is writing a history of architecture, you cannot eliminate a picture of the Parthenon or one of the great Gothic cathedrals. Happily we are learning. We are seeing more images than ever before, and it is very interesting to me that so many of the important photographers of the past have been rediscovered by photographers themselves. For example, one of the great classical pictures of the American landscape is the photograph by T. H. O'Sullivan of the Canyon de Chelly made in 1873. It was Ansel Adams who brought this picture to my attention back in 1936, when he very generously lent to MOMA his copy of the album of original prints, which was published by the United States government.

In the field of photojournalism, and particularly in documentary, the work of Jacob Riis is of the utmost importance. Sociologists had known the work of Riis and his book *How the Other Half Lives* as a classical work of sociology in the crusade to improve the living conditions of the Lower East Side in New York City. It was again a photographer, Alexander Alland, who found that the negatives that Riis had taken were still in existence. He printed them and brought this great body of work to the attention of the art world. Two photographers, Man Ray and Berenice Abbott, literally saved the priceless heritage of the prints and negatives of Eugène Atget. It was largely Berenice Abbott and Walker Evans who recognized that the historical photographs of the American Civil War had aesthetic quality. For example, Alfred Stieglitz had no knowledge whatsoever of Brady and all the cameramen that were under his employ.

I am constantly on the alert for new faces because I don't feel that we have yet really touched what I suppose one might call the visual vocabulary. I don't know how to describe the evaluation—I think it is a creative process that is beyond verbalization—that a critic, picture editor, museum curator, or historian of photography finally arrives at; this is a process that one develops—it's connoisseurship, to borrow a word from art circles. It's having a great acquaintance with a tremendous number of images and being able to compare them. How does A stand with B? Is A simply a follower of B? In what way is A different from B, and what are the qualities that really make up the excellence of A and B? What is their individual contribution and what is their position in respect to the overall aspects of the culture of the time?

I have many good friends, whose names I will not repeat, who have been disturbed and unhappy that I have not been able to include their work in my publications. It's unfortunate, but that's the way it is. I have to maintain a kind of personal integrity, and, of course, accept the responsibility. But then my views change. It's necessary for the historian to try to sort out these changes, and the value of these changes.

In this interview I want to stress the importance to me of my late wife, Nancy. Nancy, as I said earlier, often said that when she married me she married photography, and it is very difficult to separate my work from hers. Basically, Nancy was the writer and she worked with photographers on many projects; she was also a great exhibition organizer. She was not at home on the lecture stage or doing formal teaching— she left that to me. But in the informal classrooms she was extraordinarily fine. She was shy about speaking in public, but in the kind of environment that we have created here in Albuquerque, she was able to make beautiful presentations. She died in an accident while we were on vacation in 1974, ironically on the very spot she had written about so beautifully—Snake River and the Grand Tetons—in a book with photographs by her very close friend Ansel Adams. We were floating down the river looking at the ecology and what was happening to the rushing waters, when the boatman, who was a knowledgeable young man, pointed to a tree that was leaning over the river. He said: "You know, that tree is going to fall." And it fell that instant. Nancy was very seriously injured and died twelve days later. I learned afterward that she would never have been the same again—so it was a blessing. Her relationship to me was that of a dear wife and also a very close colleague. It was a collaboration that enriched both of us and she cannot be left out of any account of my career. She helped me enormously in my writing, and I helped her. There was not one thing that either of us did that did not involve the other. I'm very happy that her last book, a beautiful biography of Peter Henry Emerson, is now out.

While we are talking about the problems of history writing, one has to consider the future. I think the historian must never fix his plans only on the past—he must have an overall feeling of the importance of history. I was changing my views when I wrote my last edition in 1964. For instance, I did not feel that photo-montage was a kind of photography. I now feel that it is important to include a passage on photo-montage because it wouldn't exist without photography, without the multiplication of imagery providing the material from which the monteur creates his montage. Also, photography's close relationship to film; there will be a chapter on that in the new edition. Another thing that I now feel should be greatly expanded is the history of ways of reproducing images other than by the silver print; in other words, the photo-mechanical processes.

Also, I will deal with the book form. There must be a considerable discussion on the book as a vehicle which every photographer of any importance has chosen. Just look over the list of photographers who have been concerned with the book—P. H. Emerson, Alvin Langdon Coburn (who went to the extent of mastering the hand photogravure, and running the press himself for two of his books), Edward Weston, and Ansel Adams, who has mastered the knowledge of printing to such an extent that he has won the respect of pressmen. His last book was beautifully reproduced, and this was largely due to his own intense preoccupation with the quality of printing—he worked very hard on that. There were many trips from Carmel to San Francisco (where the printers were), to be there at the moment when the presses were rolling. Walker Evans's concern with the book—we can go on and on. . . . We should know how photogravure and photo-lithography came about, the aesthetics of book design, the sequencing . . .

Nancy was certainly one of the great book designers, having created the Sierra Club format with *This Is the American Earth* and particularly the biography of Ansel Adams, *The Eloquent Light*. Maxime Du Camp's Mideast travels appeared in 1852 in a very beautiful book with one hundred original photographs, and this is the only source that historians have used to represent this great photographer. There are five hundred original negatives in the Institut de France that nobody has looked at. Another good example is the Victor Hugo photographs. Victor Hugo's son Charles, and his father's friend August de Vacquerie were amateur photographers and they made, undoubtedly under the direction of Victor Hugo himself, some extraordinary pictures; these are only known from an album in George Eastman House and from a book published at the turn of the century. Nobody that I know of has gone to the Victor Hugo Museum in Paris and had a look at them.

Why is there not a collection of photographs by Emile Zola? He made thousands of negatives. We have not yet been able to find more than half a dozen of the photographs by the French painter Degas, but one day we may come across a case of these. The period now in the history of photography is one of a much greater search and follow-up evaluation. I think some of the evaluations so far have been very weak. I once bought about twenty-five of the Edward Curtis gravures in Boston for $1.50 each (these are now the property of the University of New Mexico), but I don't think that he was such a great photographer. Adam Clark Vroman is much better.

Right now, we are in the process of exploring and digging and I believe that the photographs and stature of Charles

Lummis will emerge. One of my students is doing a thesis on him and is gaining access to a large quantity of his work. I casually mentioned Lummis to Barbara Morgan, who was discussing Curtis's pictures with me. I said how I felt that Curtis's were sentimentalized, that the Indians are wearing an ancient costume, that the whole attitude, his attitude, I think, was not nearly as deep as Vroman's and Lummis's. I said that one day I thought Lummis was going to be the man, and she said: "He was the person that got me interested in Indians!" He mapped out a whole trek that she and her husband, Willard, made in New Mexico, and it was through Lummis's knowledge of the Indians that they gained access to places not usually possible to visit, particularly to photograph. What a fascinating exhibition it would be of these three photographers—then it would be possible to stand back and see if my judgment is correct.

I want to mention the matter of writing. This might not seem necessary in an account of my career as a historian, because one perhaps takes it for granted that a historian can write. But I soon learned that one cannot take writing for granted, and of course, one of the great influences was Nancy —in my opinion one of the greatest writers on photography. She brought to her writing a poetic quality that is beyond my capabilities. I do want to have on record my friendship with Ferdinand Reyher, a Hollywood scriptwriter and novelist—a play doctor, as they call it, who would be brought in at the last moment to patch up Broadway tryout productions. He was a very gifted writer, although his work is not well known. In the 1940 period, in the Guggenheim days, when I was free-lancing, he decided to spend two years, which he could comfortably do, writing a book on photography which would be called *Tintype*. He needed background research and his cousin suggested that I could put him on the track. So we began to work on *The History of Photography* together and it was very enjoyable. He said: "Now I just would ask you not to discuss your book with me until it is finished and ready to go to the printer. We can talk about anything you want to except any problems with writing that book—that's your problem!" At last the book was done and I was just about ready to take off for Black Mountain College, and then to Rochester for this new job. I called him up and said: "Ferdy, haven't you been able to read my book yet?" He said: "Well, I just got through the first chapter." I said: "Oh, come off it now. I cannot afford to wait around like this!" And so he said: "Come down and we'll talk about it." I went down to the Hotel Chelsea, where he lived, every morning for two weeks while he studied the first chapter only. I had to bring every single book from which I had quoted and we discussed why I had used this quotation and not that, why I had editorialized—opened my big mouth —when my hero spoke better than I did. We worked over that thing a solid two weeks and he said: "Now you've got the idea, rewrite the whole book!" So I spent all summer rewriting the book. *The History of Photography* was deliberately planned with the help of a storyteller; and I think one of the problems we face today, particularly, I am sorry to say, in the academic world, is lack of attention to real writing—the choice of words, the pace, the transitions—which are particularly difficult. I know Nancy was struggling with cutting the second volume on Ansel Adams. It was too long and she realized it, and everybody realized it. The publishers felt it would be a quick job just to "blue pencil" it, but she was such a beautiful writer that the pace and sequencing had to be worked out with transitions, otherwise it would be a fragmentary thing.

History is research, and history is interpretation, and history is presentation—in that order. Research is the easiest to learn and the most fun. The interpretation becomes difficult and the presentation requires a real stage setting and careful structuring. Even the shortest piece I do is structured: it has to have a beginning, middle, and an end.

There was one other thing I should have talked about when we were talking about collecting, and that is the present-day photographic market and what has happened to this history of photography within the last few years. We saw that in 1934 the young art historian Beaumont Newhall was allowed to make a presentation of photography, although there was no way to study at any higher institution in this country. I have told you that in 1954 the University of Rochester would not consider the history of photography as a suitable discipline. We now have a completely different situation where more and more universities are taking up the history of photography. We have the creation of a chair in the history of photography and modern art at Princeton University. They have established it with a large sum of money from David H. McAlpin and it is now occupied by Peter Bunnell, a student of mine at the Rochester Institute of Technology. My *History of Photography*, which used to sell about a copy a day, is now on press for a third reprinting (fourth edition) of 25,000 copies. This is a completely different picture, and I think it's very important that we should try to figure out what has happened. Why this sudden interest in what was such a specialized and little-recognized field?

Part of it has to do with the art market, and that's something we don't like to think about. It's absolutely true that the financial aspects have a great deal to do with our appreciation of art. Those who invest in art will often turn it over to museums—the tax deduction is a financial break—and to a certain extent, what a picture brings in the auction sales is an indication of the taste of the moment. The increase in the value of photographs has been unbelievable. I told you about the Curtis pictures I bought for $1.50—they were valued two years ago at $150, today they would be twice that. There is a photograph on the wall of my house by Julia Margaret Cameron of Mrs. Duckworth. We bought this in the 1950's from Helen Gee, who ran a photo gallery and coffee house in New York City. We paid $75 for it. A similar print was sold recently at Sotheby's for $3,750. The photograph of the Canyon de Chelly by O'Sullivan that I mentioned earlier was purchased by me in Washington for one dollar, and it is now worth between five hundred and a thousand dollars. Just last month a photograph by Paul Strand, a platinum print—and, of course, since a platinum print is no longer possible, this has unique quality—was sold for $10,000. This is the highest price ever paid to a living photographer for a photograph as a work of art. Every time I see the price of an Edward Weston photograph, I think of our dear friend hardly able to scrape along. His photographs were valued by two different dealers— I think there were eleven pictures—at $5,000! That was just last year. Today they would be double that, and in Eddy's day $5,000 would have been an absolute godsend. All of this has a bearing on the history of photography now that photography makes news on Wall Street. There is also a tremendous interest in collecting of cameras. To me this is a separate field, and although the instrument that the artist uses is of importance, the history of that instrument itself leaves me a bit cold. It's the history of technology, and the only way to write the history of cameras, which has never been done, is perfectly simple. How do you see the image? You would begin with the Kodak No. 1: You just hold it at arm's length and point it in a certain direction. But people were missing Uncle Ed and Grandma, so Eastman then brought out a new model with a V scribed on it, and you just centered it. And then there were the models in which you would look through sights like a gun through a frame, across to the ground-glass image. But the actual collection of cameras is dull to me . . . I like to drive automobiles, not look at them!

We historians must be very careful that our work is not chauvinistic. It should be international in scope unless you draw it with certain guidelines. But it does happen that my history of photography may appear chauvinistic, because, as far as I can see, the strongest photographers have come from this country. Or let us put it another way: more strong photographers have come from the United States than from any other part of the world, though I would like to disprove that. I would like to see more work from Europe, but England has very little. Why is that? France has only a handful; Germany, I don't know . . . Renger-Patzsch and Steinert.

I think one of the reasons for this present passion for photography is the mania for what is called "collectibles" now going on in this country. We should not think that only photographs and cameras are going up in price. Take antique silver, for example—it has trebled in value over the last three years.

Focus has been put on photography because never in the history of the world have people seen so many camera images. Do you realize that in the average American household today the family spends most of the evening looking at pictures? Some of that rubs off. I think that the students' interest in photography is because they have been brought up in a world of images. We are just learning what photography is, and the analogy which I can use is in the technique of writing. There was a period in our history when the man who could write was a very special man, as those who were literate were in the minority. Now, by and large, in our present culture everybody can write. In Africa that's certainly not true, but it is in this country and in Europe. We have come, over the centuries, to realize that writing is a technique which can be used in a hundred different ways. It can be used to report the news factually; it can be used to express one's innermost thoughts in poetry; it can be used to send messages and communications. Today, when we say that this man is a writer, we are talking about a special person—an artist. The shopping list of my housekeeper cannot be compared with a poem by Dylan Thomas. In photography, we haven't yet learned to separate it out. Anybody can have a camera, anybody can make a picture. People are told photography is so simple, but the fact is that photography, because of that very reason, is excessively difficult. And that is where we have to struggle. We cannot accept the work of journalists as literature, except now and then; in the case of Cartier-Bresson, and in the case of Eugene Smith. But the trouble is that people think that concern with people is what makes photography an art. That's not true at all. There's a place for that, there's a place for Ernest Hemingway's columns filed from Europe for the Toronto *Daily Star*. That's part of literature. Perhaps we're getting to the point where we recognize the "literature" of photography.

I am very proud that it has been my privilege through tremendous opportunities given to me by the Museum of Modern Art, and by every institution that I have worked for, to have helped bring about something of a recognition of photography —but it's only the beginning. The more nearly complete histories of photography, the more developed histories of photography, will be written by my students; and that is why I am so concerned at the moment about teaching and about writing the next book.

March 1975

SELECTED BIBLIOGRAPHY

Airborne Camera: The World from Air and Outer Space, by Beaumont Newhall. New York: Hastings House and George Eastman House, 1969.

A Collection of Photographs, by Beaumont and Nancy Newhall. Millerton, New York: Aperture, 1969.

The Daguerreotype in America, by Beaumont Newhall. New York: Dover, 1971, 1976.

Dorothea Lange Looks at the American Country Woman, commentary by Beaumont Newhall. Los Angeles: Ward Ritchie and Amon Carter Museum of Western Art, Fort Worth, Texas, 1967.

Frederick H. Evans, by Beaumont Newhall. Millerton, New York: Aperture, 1973.

The History of Photography: From 1839 to the Present Day, by Beaumont Newhall. New York: Museum of Modern Art, 1964.

The Latent Image: The Discovery of Photography, by Beaumont Newhall. New York: Doubleday, 1967.

Masters of Photography, by Beaumont and Nancy Newhall. New York: A. W. Visual Library, 1958.

On Photography: A Sourcebook on Photo History in Facsimile, by Beaumont Newhall. New York: Century House, 1956.

Photo Eye of the 20's, by Beaumont Newhall (catalogue). New York: Museum of Modern Art, 1970.

Photography: A Short Critical History, by Beaumont Newhall. New York: Museum of Modern Art, 1937.

Photography at Mid-Century. Edited and selected by Beaumont Newhall. Rochester, New York: George Eastman House, 1959.

T. H. O'Sullivan: Photographer, by Beaumont and Nancy Newhall, with an appreciation by Ansel Adams. Rochester: George Eastman House and Amon Carter Museum of Western Art, Fort Worth, Texas, 1966.

William H. Jackson, by Beaumont Newhall and Diana Edkins, with a critical essay by William L. Broecker. New York: Morgan and Morgan and Amon Carter Museum of Western Art, Fort Worth, Texas, 1974.

Index

Abbott, Berenice, 17–18, 129, 206, 403
Abu Simbel, 195
Adams, Ansel, 41, 125, 129, 149, 214, 235–6, 238, 241–2, 248–9, 275, 285, 306–7, 346, 348–50, 353–5, 383–4, 387–91, 395, 403–6, 408
Adams, Clinton, 399
Adamson, Robert, 183–5, 187–8
Adenauer, Konrad, 194
"Adet," 95
Adhemar, Jean, 194
Afterimage, 236
Agee, James, 278
Agence Rapho, 85–6, 90, 95–6, 100
Albers, Josef, 115, 121, 392
Album, 168
Alland, Alexander, 403
Alliance Photo, 95
Almassy, Paul, 209
Almer Coe Optical Company, 229
Alvin Langdon Coburn, Photographer (Gernsheim), 208
America and Alfred Stieglitz, 348
America: Picture Book of an Architect (Mendelsohn), 386
American Ceramic Society, 139
American Museum of Natural History, 290
American Place, An, 217, 238–9, 384
American Society of Magazine Photographers, 396
Americans, The (Frank), 272
"Amputations" (White), 344–5, 352

Anderson, Paul, 284
Annan, Craig, 183–5, 187
Annan, Thomas, 185
Aperture, 275, 396
Aperture, 354–6, 362
Aperture History of Photography series, 75, 76n
Arbus, Diane, 41, 272, 388–9, 396
Architects' Journal, The, 177
Architectural Review, The, 177, 181
Armitage, Merle, 220
Armory show (1913), 11
Art Center (California), 17
Art Center School, 316–17
Art and Photography (Scharf), 199
Art Through the Ages (Gardner), 134
Arts Council of Great Britain, 70, 168, 192
Ascent of Man, The (Bronowski), 325
Ashton, Leigh, 192
Aspen Institute for Humanistic Studies, 128
"Assassinated Worker, The" (Bravo), 231
Atget, Eugène, 17–18, 41, 48, 98, 108, 198, 206, 401, 403
Atlantic Richfield, 130
Avedon, Richard, 30, 301, 308

Baer, Morley and Frances, 219
Bailey, David, 30
Bailey, Oscar, 152

Barbey, Bruno, 71
Barr, Alfred J., Jr., 379–81
"Battles and Games" (Smith), 146
Baudelaire, Charles, 107
Bauhaus, 81, 112–24, 131, 138,
    140–1, 161, 164; see also New
    Bauhaus
Bavarian State School of
    Photography, 161
Bayer, Herbert, 111–31, 163
Beame, Abraham, 49
Beaton, Cecil, 21–31, 97, 166, 193,
    297
Beautiful London (Gernsheim), 177
Beethoven, Ludwig van, 264
Beg, Borrowed and Stolen
    (Cunningham), 310
Bell, Clive, 182, 193
Bell, Quentin, 182
Bell, Vanessa, 182–3
Berliner Illustrierte, 163
Berry, Ian, 71
*Bibliography of British Books
    Illustrated with Original
    Photographs, A* (Gernsheim), 208
*Bibliography of British
    Photographic Literature, A*
    (Gernsheim), 208
Bibliothèque Nationale, 41
"Birds, The" (Doisneau), 84
Bischof, Werner, 96
*Bistro-Tabac (*Brassaï), 42
Black Star Agency, 55, 57
"Blind Woman, The" (Strand), 4
Bloomsbury School of Photography,
    53
"Bohemia" (Rousseau), 234
Bolaffi-Arte, 191
Bonnard, Pierre, 39
Book of Beauty (Beaton), 25

Boubat, Edouard, 92
Bourke-White, Margaret, 258
Bourne, Samuel, 183
"Bowls" (Strand), 5
Boyer, Alden Scott, 401
Brady, Mathew, 199, 404
Brancusi, Constantin, 4, 11
Brandt, Bill, 17, 28, 57, 166, 236, 336
Braque, Georges, 4, 18, 39
Brassaï, 17, 37–42, 47, 80–1, 85 92,
    101, 104
Bravo, Manuel Alvarez, 224–36
Breton, André, 75, 230
Brett Weston Photographs, 219–20
Breuer, Marcel, 114–15, 120, 124
Brigman, Anne, 300
British Broadcasting Corporation
    (BBC), 53–5, 202–3
British Film Institute, 193
British Medical Society, 318
British Museum, 188–9
British Royal Family, 29–30
Brodovitch, Alexey, 39
Bronowski, Dr. Jacob, 325
Brower, David, 244
Bruce, David, 188
Bruehl, Anton, 140
Bruguière, Francis, 135–7, 140
Bullock, Wynn, 126, 313–37, 370
Bunnell, Peter, 409
Burden, Shirley, 356
Bystander, 55

Cachin, Françoise, 75
Cagney, James, 302
California School of Fine Arts, 348,
    356
California and the West (Weston),
    388
Callahan, Harry, 346

Camera, 208–9
Camera Club (Boston), 386
Camera Craft, 342
Camera Work, 3, 184, 283, 297, 355
Cameron, Julia Margaret, 182–3,
    187, 198, 308, 387, 409
Cannes Festival, 41
Canyon de Chelly, 286, 290, 403, 409
Capa, Cornell, 276
Capa, Robert, 58–9, 63–4, 66–7, 95
Caponigro, Paul, 250, 362, 372, 395
Carjat, Étienne, 386
Carlyle, Thomas, 183
Carroll, Lewis, 186–7
Cartier-Bresson, Henri, 17, 39, 47,
    63, 65, 74–9, 87, 92, 95, 99, 106–8,
    198, 217–18, 227, 229–30, 236,
    277, 291, 303, 392, 411
Castaneda, Carlos, 372
"Cathedral of Socialism"
    (Feininger), 112
Cendrars, Blaise, 85, 93–5, 107
Central School of Classic Art, 226
Cézanne, Paul, 4–5, 11, 314, 320
Chagall, Marc, 46
Champs délicieux, 166
Chappell, Walter, 358
Charles-Roux, Edmonde de, 96
Charlot, Jean, 212
Chemische Versuche (Schulze), 186
Chicago Art Institute, 137
Chicagoan, The, 135
Chisso Corporation, 278–80
Christian IX, King, 61
Churchill Club, 177
Churchill, His Life in Photographs
    (Gernsheim), 177
Churchill, Randolph, 177
Churchill, Winston, 176–7
"City Hall Park" (Strand), 3

Clark, Sir Kenneth, 177, 192–3
Clark, Lady, 177
Clerque, Lucien, 209
Clifford, Charles, 163
Clift, Bill, 250
Cloisters, The, 378
Clore, Charles, 203
Coburn, Alvin Langdon, 116, 191,
    295, 398, 405
Coke, Van Deren, 151–2, 200, 398–9
Coleman, A. D., 363–5
Coleman, A. D., 363–5
College Art Journal, The, 380
Colliers, 135
Columbia University, 151
Combined Societies, 168
Comptes Rendus, 189
"Concerned Photographer, The"
    (Smith), 276
Concerning the Spiritual in Art
    (Kandinsky), 112–13
Concise History (Gernsheim), 197
Container Corporation of America,
    125–7, 354
Contrejour, 236
Conversations avec Picasso
    (Brassaï), 42
Cooling Gallery, London, 24
Cordier, Pierre, 209
Corot, Camille, 42
"Country Doctor, The" (Smith),
    264–6, 269
Country Life, 177, 181
Courtauld Institute of Art, 117
Cox, Trenchard, 201
Craig, Gordon, 136
Creative Arts, 135
Creative Camera, 208
Creative Photography group, 168
Creative Photography (Scharf),
    199

"Creative Photography, 1826 to the Present," 205
Cros, André, 209
Cubism and Abstract show, 379, 381
Cubists (ism), 4, 123, 320
Cunningham, Imogen, 249, 293–311
Curtis, Alfred, 283
Curtis, Edward, 286, 294, 298–9, 406–7, 409

Dadaism, 10, 15, 18, 118
Daguerre, L. J. M., 184, 191, 199
Dali, Salvador, 25, 127
Dame, Die, 162–3
Danielle's, 10
Darwin, Charles, 183
Daumier, Honoré, 386
David Octavius Hill (Schwarz), 187–8
Davidson, Bruce, 249
Davies, Sue, 168
Daybooks (Weston), 135, 222, 395–6
de Brunoff, Michel, 96
"Decadent Art" exhibition, 163
"Deed of Demission" (Hill), 185
Degas, Edgar, 75, 406
de Gaulle, Charles, 57, 62
Delacroix, Eugène, 42, 396
Delano, Jack, 5
Delius, Frederick, 263
Delphic Gallery, 239
Delpire, Robert, 65–6
De Meyer, Baron Alfred, 27, 297
Design, 137
Deutsche Werkbund, 381
deYoung Museum, 214
Dictionary of National Biography, 183
Dieuzaide, Jean, 209
Dilaccer, Antoinette, 188

Dityvon (Raimond-Dityvon), Claude, 106
Dixon, Maynard, 302
Doisneau, Robert, 65, 80–110
Doors of Perception, The (Huxley), 358
Dove, Arthur, 3, 297
Drawing from the Cast (Gardner), 134
Du, 48
Du Camp, Maxine, 406
Duchamp, Marcel, 11, 17
Duckworth, Julia, 183, 409
Duell, Charles, 393
Dumont, René, 78

Eastman, George, 394; *see also* George Eastman House
Eastman Charitable Trust, 394
Eastman Kodak Company, 241, 246–7, 393–5
Ecole de Photo de Vaugirard, l', 103
Emerson, Peter Henry, 179, 198, 405
Encyclopaedia Britannica, 197, 208, 333
"Entrants de Mondrian" (Kertész), 47
Entretiens (Breton), 75
Erdekes Ujsag, 45
Erwitt, Elliott, 91
Ethical Culture School, 1
"Evaluating Photography," 367
Eder, Joseph Maria, 195, 402
Edward VII (Gernsheim), 190
Edward VIII, King, 54
Edwards, Emily, 229
"Egg Slicer, The" (Weston), 135
"Egyptian Family" (Rodger), 66
Einstein, Albert, 333
Eisenstaedt, Alfred, 62, 123, 163

Eisenstein, Sergei, 123, 213, 231
Eisner, Marie, 63
"Elephants Have Right of Way," 66
Elizabeth, Queen (mother), 29
Elliott, Dr. Andrew, 184–5
Eloquent Light, The, 406
Evans, Walker, 5, 125–6, 230, 249,
    278, 383, 390, 403, 406
Excelsior, 84–5
Expressionists, 117, 147
"Eye of Paris, The" (Miller), 42

"Family of Man," 66, 126–7, 232,
    265, 330, 357
Farm Security Administration
    (F.S.A.), 5, 52, 198, 229, 255,
    288, 302, 316, 383, 399
Fashion and Reality (Gernsheim),
    191
Feininger, Lyonel, 112, 316
Fenton, Roger, 183
Festival of Britain exhibition, 184
Fichter, Robert, 152
Fieger, Erwin, 198, 209
"*Film und Foto*," 119, 212, 227, 381
"Flea Market, The" (Doisneau), 84
*Focus on Architecture and
    Sculpture* (Gernsheim), 177–8
Fondo Editorial de la Plástica
    Mexicana, 232
Fontana, Franco, 198, 209
Ford, Colin, 188, 201
Form, Die, 381
Forth, Robert, 156
Fountain Press, 178, 196
Franco, Francisco, 267
Frank, Robert, 270–2, 274, 276, 396
Franklin College, 161
French Society of Photography, 98,
    194, 382

Freund, Karl, 385
Friedlander, Lee, 396
Friends of the Bauhaus, 115
Frith, William Powell, 183
"Front de Seine" (Doisneau), 99
Frontier Films, 6
Fry, Roger, 182, 387
Futurists, 13

Gal, Pino dal, 209
Garbo, Greta, 30
Gardner, Helen, 134
*Gardner's Photographic Sketch
    Book of the War*, 186
Gauguin, Paul, 320
Gauthier-Villars, 189
Gee, Helen, 409
George Eastman Associates, 394
George Eastman House, 205–6, 243,
    300, 356–7, 360, 393–8, 400–1, 406
George IV, King, 29
Gernsheim, Alison, 179, 186–92,
    194, 201–4, 208, 402
Gernsheim, Helmut, 160–210, 402
Gernsheim Museum of Photography
    Foundation, 204
Gianella, Victor, 209
"Giant, The" (Smith), 147
Gibbs-Smith, Charles, 196, 201
Gibson, Ralph, 272, 365
Gilpin, Laura, 282–91
Goslin, Nigel, 188, 203
Goya, Francisco José de, 7, 14
Graffiti, 42
Grant, Cary, 302
Graves, Morris, 307
Grimes, Sam, 245
Gropius, Walter, 113–15, 117–18,
    120–1, 124
Grosset, Raymond, 90, 95–6

Grosz, George, 118
Group f/64, 214, 285, 301, 383
Guggenheim Fellowship, 220, 310, 392
Gurdjieff, G. I., 358–30, 368, 372

Hagemeyer, Johan, 213, 218
Harper's Bazaar, 16, 34, 39
Hartley, Marsden, 3
Hastings, MacDonald, 57, 202
Hattersley, Ralph, 152, 395
Häusser, Robert, 209
Ház, Nicholas, 145
Heartfield, John, 118, 163
Heckroth, Hein, 174
Heinecken, Robert, 330
Hemingway, Ernest, 411
Henry Miller: Grandeur Nature (Brassaï), 42
Herrigel, Eugene, 147
Herschel, John, 183
Hicks, Wilson, 259
Hill, D. O., 183–5, 187–8, 198, 387
Hine, Lewis, 1–3
Hiro, 34
Histoire de Marie, l' (Brassaï), 42
"Histoire d'un soldat, L'" (Stravinsky), 115
History of Photography, The (Gernsheim), 178, 184, 188, 190–1, 195–7, 199, 208
History of Photography, The (Newhall), 393, 395, 407–9
History of Photography (Stenger), 172
"History of Photography" exhibition, 306
Hitachi, 276–7
Holiday, 219

Hopkinson, Tom, 193
Hoppé, E. O., 166, 168
How to Make Better Pictures (Kodak), 385
How the Other Half Lives (Riis), 403
Hugo, Charles, 406
Hugo, Victor, 77, 406
Hull House, 229
Hundred Years of Photography, A (Moholy), 165, 172
Hutton, Kurt, 55
Huxley, Aldous, 358
Huxley, Sir Julian, 194

I Ching, 360
Idylls of the King (Tennyson), 182
Illustrated, 63
Illustrated London News, 177, 289
Illustrierte Zeitung, 401
Image, 394–5
In Wildness (Porter), 243, 251
"Indian Family" (Rodger), 66
Indiana University, 145, 150–2
Ingres, Jean Auguste, 12
Institute of British Photographers, 162
Institute of Contemporary Arts, 168
Institute of Design, 125
Itten, Johannes, 113, 115, 117, 121

Jackson, W. H., 290
Jacobi, Lotte, 150
Jannings, Emil, 385
"Jardin" (Prévert), 102
Jeffers, Robinson, 213
Jewish Museum, Smith exhibition at, 277–8
Johnston, J. Dudley, 167, 201

Julia Margaret Cameron
  (Gernsheim), 178, 187
Jung, Carl, 374

Kalvar, Richard, 106
Kaminski, Edward, 317
Kandinsky, Vasili, 112, 115–17, 121
Kane, Art, 126
Käsebier, Gertrude, 3, 283, 285, 293,
  297, 385
Kelley, Sir Gerald, 193
Kennedy, Clarence, 394
Kepes, Gyorgy, 141
Kertész, André, 38, 44–9, 80–1, 123
Keystone Agency, 46
Kirstein, Lincoln, 78, 390, 392
Klee, Paul, 113, 115, 117, 121
Korff, Kurt, 163
Krims, Les, 308

Labyrinthe, 42
Ladies' Home Journal, 64
La Faille, Georges, 104
Lamartine, Alphonse de, 107
Land, Dr. Edwin H., 244
Land Birds of America, 245
Landau, Ergy, 85
Landry, Bob, 57
Lange, Dorothea, 5, 249, 277, 302–3,
  355, 383
Lartigue, Jacques-Henri, 33–5
Lazar, Arthur, 250
LeBas, Boy, 23–4
Leclerc, Colonel Jean, 57, 62
Lecuyer, Raymond, 94
Léger, Fernand, 94
LeGray, Gustave, 184
Legion of Honor Museum, 352
LeGrande Art Center, 342–3

Lejard, André, 382
Le Querrec, Guy, 106
Lerski, Helmar, 163
Let Us Now Praise Famous Men
  (Agee and Evans), 278
Levy, Julien, 78, 127, 206; Gallery
  of, 47–8, 230
Lewis Carroll—Photographer
  (Gernsheim), 187
Lhote, André, 74–5
Library of Congress, 290
Life, 47, 55–8, 60–2, 90, 99, 256–61,
  264–7, 269, 271, 274, 279, 289,
  364, 384
Life and Landscape on the Norfolk
  Broads (Emerson & Gernsheim),
  179
"Life in Paris" (Doiseau), 96
Light, 355
Lissitzky, El, 118, 166
Listener, The, 54
Living Birds of the World, 245
Living Insects of the World, 245
London Salon, 166–7
Looking at Photographs
  (Szarkowski), 363
Lorant, Stefan, 55, 163, 401
Los Angeles County Museum, 317
Lower Animals, The, 245
Luce, Henry, 56, 58, 60, 383
Lummis, Charles, 406–7
Lyons, Nathan, 150, 152, 395–8, 400

Mabry, Thomas Dabney, 390
McAlpin, David, 389–91, 409
Macbeth, 136
McCarthy, Joseph, 7
MacPherson, Robert, 183
"Magnolia" (Cunningham), 307

Magnum, 63–4, 66–8, 71, 95, 269–70

Magritte, René, 123

Maher, Herbert, 126

"Maid at the Window, The" (Brandt), 336

Making a Photograph (Adams), 389

Malevich, Kazimir S., 118

Maltan, Josef, 114

Man, Felix H., 163, 187, 401

Man Behind the Camera, The (Gernsheim), 178

Manet, Édouard, 14

Mann, Margery, 294, 302

Marey, Étienne Jules, 189

Marginalia (Moholy), 165

Marin, John, 3, 297

Marshall Field's, 139–40

Mary, Queen, 29

Massachusetts Institute of Technology (M.I.T.), 359, 364, 367, 370

Massey, Vincent, 169

"Masterpieces of Victorian Photography," 192

Matisse, Henri, 18–19, 39, 336

Meatyard, Ralph Eugene, 152

Memories, Dreams, Reflections (Jung), 374

Mendelsohn, Erich, 386

Messerli, Niggi, 209

Metropolitan Museum of Art, 19, 390

"Mexico," 230

"Mexico Photographs" (Bruehl), 140

Meyer, Hannes, 118, 121

Michaelson, Kate, 188

Michals, Duane, 91

Miller, Henry, 42

Mills College, 299, 301

Minamata, 261, 269, 276–80

Minamata (Smith), 275

Minicam, 143–5

Ministère des Sports et de la Jeunesse, 87

Ministry of Information (London), 28–9

Mirrors, Messages and Manifestations (White), 354, 374

Modotti, Tina, 226–8

Moholy, Lucia, 118, 165–6, 172

Moholy-Nagy, László, 114–19, 121, 123, 137–41, 143–5, 163, 165–6, 198, 382–3, 390, 397

Mohr, Jean, 209

Mondrian, Pieter Cornelis, 46

Montgomery, General Bernard, 61

Moore, Raymond, 209

Morgan, Barbara, 212, 346, 355, 358, 401, 407

Morris, William, Arts and Crafts group of, 381

Muhr, Adolf, 398

Mumford, Lewis, 382

Munkacsi, Martin, 45, 75, 123, 163, 255

Musée de l'Armée, 87

Museum of the City of New York, 384–5

Museum of Modern Art (MOMA), 19, 46–7, 78, 124–5, 205–6, 227, 232–3, 306, 346–7, 379–84, 387, 389–92, 395, 397, 403, 411

Museum of Modern Art (Moscow), 232

Museum of Modern Art (Stockholm), 206

Music Box Revue, 314

Muybridge, Eadweard, 199
Mydans, Carl, 258
Mysticism, 358

Nadar, 188
Napoleon, 40, 87
Nast, Condé, 48
National Buildings Record (NBR),
  175–7, 181
National Collection of Photography,
  193
National Endowment of the Arts
  grant, 220
National Gallery, exhibition at, 177
National Geographic, 66, 243
National Institute of Art (Mexico),
  232
National Portrait Gallery, 30, 168
National Press Photographers
  Association of America, 396
National Science Foundation, 250
National Treasury (Mexico), 225
National Trust, 201
Navahos, Gilpin and, 286–8, 290–1
Nègre, Charles, 199
"Neue Sachlichkeit," 116, 162
Neusüss, Floris, 209
New Bauhaus, 125, 139–40, 142–3
"New Objectivity," 116
New Photo Vision (Gernsheim),
  168, 175, 178
New Vision, The (Moholy-Nagy),
  137–8, 142
New York School, 10–11
New York Times, The, 401
New Yorker, The, 135, 382
Newhall, Beaumont, 18, 78, 125,
  179–80, 191, 195–8, 206, 218, 306,
  334, 346, 349, 356, 377–411

Newhall, Nancy, 7, 78, 179, 217–18,
  243–4, 346–7, 349, 351, 354, 356,
  358, 379–80, 382, 387–93, 395,
  398–400, 403–8
Newsweek, 256
Niepce, Joseph N., 191, 201
Noel, Frank ("Pappy"), 254–5
Nubas of Kordofan, 63–5, 71–2
"Nude Descending the Staircase"
  (Duchamp), 11
Nürnberg, Walter, 166
"Nurse-Midwife" (Smith), 265–6

Observateur, L', 91
"Oeil de Paris, L'" (Miller), 42
Ohio State University, 137
Ohio University, 151
O'Keeffe, Georgia, 239–40, 306, 346,
  389
Olga, Princess, 29
"One Hundred Years of
  Photography," 193
Optical Society of America, 247
Oregon Camera Club, 342, 352
Orozco, José Clemente, 212, 226
O'Sullivan, T. H., 403, 409
Oxford University Press, 196

Paepcke, Walter, 127–8
Painted Walls of Mexico, The
  (Bravo and Edwards), 229
Painting and Photography
  (Gernsheim), 200
Palacio de Bellas Artes, 227
Parc Montsouris (Prévert), 102
Paris after Dark (Brassaï), 38
Paris de Nuit (Brassaï), 38, 41, 81,
  101

Paris secret des années (Brassaï),
30, 40, 42
Parkinson, Norman, 30
Paroles en l'air (Brassaï), 42
Payant, Felix, 137
Pencil of Nature (Talbot), 184
Penn, Irving, 30, 96–7
Penrose Annual, 139
"People Are People the World
Over," 64, 66
"Pepper" (Weston), 135, 156, 158
Peter Grimes (Britten), 264
Pevsner, Sir Nikolaus, 169, 177, 193
Photo Eye, 138, 213
"Photo-Eye of the Twenties," 397
Photo League (New York), 231, 346
Photograms of the Year, 167
Photographers' Gallery (London),
168
Photographers on Photography
(Lyons, ed.), 396
Photographie, 382
Photography, 165
Photography 1839–1937 (Newhall),
381
Photography Is Not Art (Ray), 13
Photo-Secession Gallery, 2, 4, 13,
283, 296
Piaf, Edith, 105
Picabia, Francis, 11
Picasso, Pablo, 4–5, 11, 18, 38–41,
93
Picture History of Photography
(Pollack), 403
Picture Post, 55, 57, 99
Pioneers of Photography (Scharf),
200
Pittsburgh (Smith), 268–70, 274
Point, Le, 91
Pollack, Peter, 403

Pompidou Center, 101, 104
"Pont Transbordeur, 1928, The"
(Bayer and Moholy-Nagy), 119
Popular Photography, 196, 274
Porter, Eliot, 129, 237–51
Portland Art Museum, 343
Portland Civic Theater, 343
Potemkin, 385–6
Potonniée, Georges, 402–3
Prévert, Jacques, 93–5, 102, 107
Priestley, J. B., 193
Prinet, Jean, 188
Prinsep, Val, 183
Putnam, Brenda, 285, 287

"Quais, The" (Doisneau), 84
Queen Victoria (Gernsheim), 190

Rabelais, François, 107
Radio Times, 54
Rado, Charles, 85–6, 90
Ray, Man, 9–20, 126, 166, 198, 383,
397, 403
Red Shoes, The, 174
Renault factories, 82, 85–8, 97
Renger-Patzsch, Albert, 163–4, 198,
410
Renoir, Jean, 77
Renou en Colle, 230
Revolutionary League of Writers
and Artists, The (LEAR), 228
Reyher, Ferdinand, 407–8
Riboud, Marc, 71
Richter, Hans, 166
Riis, Jacob A., 199, 403
Rimbaud, Arthur, 107
Rio Grande, Gilpin and, 288–90
"Ritual Branch" (White), 358
Rivera, Diego, 212, 226–7, 229–30
Road to Survival, 250

"Road to Victory" exhibition, 125–7
Robinson, H. P., 198, 209
Rochester Institute of Technology
   (R.I.T.), 356–7, 366–7, 395,
   399–400, 409
Rockefeller family, 378–9, 389
Rodger, George, 50–73
Rodin, Auguste, 4, 12
Roethke, Theodore, 307
"Romanticism and Classicism in
   Photography," 152
Ronsard, Pierre de, 107
Roots of Heaven, The (Gary), 250
"Rose Petals on the Beach"
   (Porter), 242
Rosebery, Lord, 176
Rosenblum, Walter, 152
Rothermere, Lady, 192
Rothermere, Lord, 194
Rothman, Henry, 231
Rousseau, Henri, 234
Royal Academy, 167
Royal Photographic Society
   (R.P.S.), 72, 166–8, 177, 185, 188,
   193, 200–1, 382
Russell, Bertrand, 333

Sachs, Paul J., 377–8, 380, 384, 386
Safranski, Kurt, 163
"Sahara, The" (Rodger), 66
Salomon, Erich, 163, 198
Salon de l'Escalier, 48
Sander, August, 163–4, 295, 397
San Francisco Art Institute, 348, 395
Sargent, John Singer, 13
Schad, Christian, 116
Schapiro, Meyer, 346, 348–9, 356
Scharf, Aaron, 199–200
Scherman, Dave, 57
Scherschel, Frank, 57

Schlemmer, Oskar, 115, 117
Schulze, Johann Heinrich, 186
Schwarz, Heinrich, 185, 187–8, 387,
   390
Schweitzer, Albert, 65, 264, 267–70,
   272
Schwitters, Kurt, 118
"Seasons, The" (Porter), 243
Selassie, Haile, 62
Self-Portrait (Ray), 15
"Sense of Abstraction, A" exhibit,
   150
Servadi, Walter, 152
"75,000 Miles to War," 58
Seymour, David "Chim," 63, 67, 95
"Shadows of the Porch Railing"
   (Strand), 5
Shahn, Ben, 5, 126
Short Critical History (Newhall),
   179
Sierra Club, 243–4
Silent Spring, 250
Silvester, Hans, 100, 209
Silvy, Camille, 184
Sinsabaugh, Art, 152
Siqueiros, David Alfaro, 226
Siskind, Aaron, 149, 152, 198, 396
Sketch, The, 22, 25, 55
"Sleeping Boy, The" (Kertész), 45
Smith, Aileen, 275, 280
Smith, Henry Holmes, 132–58
Smith, Juanita, 267–8
Smith, W. Eugene, 65, 253–81, 346,
   411
Snow, Carmel, 39
Snowdon, Lord, 203
Society for Photographic Education,
   151–2, 397
Sokolow, Anna, Dancing Group of,
   229, 231, 234

Solarization, 316–18, 321
Solbert, General Oscar, 394
Sommer, Frederick, 129, 150
"Song without Words, The"
    (White), 349, 354
"Sonnet Sequence" (White), 341
"Spanish Village, The" (Smith),
    259, 265–7
Spencer, Dr. A. C., 165
Stadlen, Peter, 174
Staley, Norman, 141
Stanfield, Clarkson, 187
Statesman and Nation, The, 177
"Steerage, The" (Stieglitz), 336
Steichen, Edward, 3–5, 13, 27, 66,
    125–7, 136, 147, 150–1, 194, 198,
    206, 232, 259–60, 264, 285, 306,
    357, 381, 391
Stein, Gertrude, 305–6
Steinert, Otto, 198, 410
Stenger, Dr. Erich, 163, 172, 191,
    195
Stephanie, Gerry, 152
Stephen, Leslie, 183
Stern, Seymour, 213
Stieglitz, Alfred, 3–5, 11, 13, 78,
    125, 140, 151, 198, 217–18, 222,
    238–40, 249, 284–5, 296–7, 305–7,
    316, 322, 333–6, 346–9, 354–5,
    359, 361, 381, 384, 388–9, 397, 404
Strand, Paul, 1–8, 77, 125, 198,
    217–18, 222, 227, 231, 236, 241, 249,
    277, 285, 322, 336, 346, 349, 389,
    391, 398, 409
Stravinsky, Igor, 115
String Quartet No. 14 (Opus 131),
    (Beethoven), 264
Strong, Roy, 188, 202
Stryker, Roy, 5–6, 288, 383

Studio, The, 164
"Sudan Family" (Rodger), 66
Sudre, Jean P., 209
Summerson, Sir John, 175
Surrealism, 18, 25, 48, 75, 123, 230
Swift, Henry, 301
Swiss Foundation of Photography,
    208
Szarkowski, John, 47, 206, 363

Talbot, W. H. F., 184, 197
Tales of Hoffman, 174
Tant qu'il y aura des bêtes
    (Brassaï), 41
Tatler, The, 22, 25, 55
Tennyson, Alfred Lord, 182, 187
Thackeray, Anne, 182
Thames & Hudson, 200
Theatre Arts, 135, 137
This Is the American Earth, 406
Thomas, Dylan, 411
Thoreau, Henry David, 243, 246
Those Impossible English (Bell
    and Gernsheim), 182
Time in New England (Strand and
    Newhall), 7
Times, The (London), 177, 193–4
Tintype (Reyher), 407
Toklas, Alice, 305–6
Toronto Daily Star, 411
Transmutations (Brassaï), 52
Tropic of Cancer (Miller), 42
Twelve Seasons, The, 250
"291," 2–4, 284
Tzara, Tristan, 166

Uccello, Paolo, 14
Uelsmann, Jerry, 126, 152
Ullstein, Ludwig, 163
Underhill, Evelyn, 358

UNESCO photographic conference, 194

University of New Mexico, 398–9, 402

University of Texas, 203–7

Upton, John, 358

Utopia or Else (Dumont), 78

Uvachrome, 162, 164–5

Vacquerie, August de, 406

van der Post, Laurens, 64

van der Rohe, Mies, 121

Vandivert, Bill, 56, 63

Van Dyke, Willard, 214, 217, 301–2

Van Gogh, Vincent, 320; exhibition, 379

Vanishing Navaho, The (Gilpin), 288

Vanity Fair, 136, 301–2

Variety, 385–6

Victorian Society, 202

Vie Ouvrière, La, 99

Vigneau, André, 81, 83–5

Village Romeo and Juliet, A (Delius), 263

Visual Studies Workshop, 396, 401

Viva, 106, 109

Vivex, 165

Vogel, Lucien, 383

Vogue, 16, 26–8, 34, 96–7, 99, 122–3, 301–2, 383

Vortographs (Coburn), 116

Vox, Maximillien, 87

Vrai, 87

Vroman, Adam Clark, 406–7

Vu, 46, 383–4

Wadenoyen, Hugo van, 168

Walden (Thoreau), 243

Wales, Prince of, 54

"Walk to Paradise Garden, The" (Smith), 263

"Wall Street" (Strand), 3

Warburg Institute of Art, 162, 175–6

Warhol, Andy, 12

Washington Square (Kertész), 48

Watts, G. F., 183, 187

Wave, The (Strand), 231

Weber, Max, 284

Weil, Dr. Ernst, 184

Welpott, Jack, 158

West, Benjamin, 283

Weston, Brett, 211–23, 241, 397

Weston, Charis, 387–8

Weston, Cole, 218–19

Weston, Dody, 218–19

Weston, Edward, 41, 83, 135–7, 140, 149, 156, 158, 167, 198, 211–14, 216–20, 222, 226–7, 248–9, 255, 299–301, 321–2, 327–8, 330, 332, 335–6, 342, 346–9, 351, 353–4, 381, 383–4, 387–9, 395–7, 405, 409–10

Weston, Elinore, 218

Wheeler, Monroe, 78

White, Clarence, 3, 152, 385; school of, 283–4

"White Fence, The" (Strand), 5

White, Minor, 2, 129, 150, 152, 241, 248, 250–1, 332, 338–75, 395

White Sands Portfolio (Weston), 222

Whitehead, Alfred North, 328

Wild, Hans, 56

Winogrand, Garry, 396

Wittkower, Dr. Rudolf, 175

Woolf, Virginia, 182–3
Works Progress Administration
  (W.P.A.), 215, 342, 346
World Exhibition of Photography,
  163
World War I, 5
World War II, 6, 28–9, 168–74, 244,
  259–61, 284, 304–5, 343–4, 390–1

Young, Charlotte, 186
Y.M.C.A. Camera Club, 352

Zaluka, Leo, 135
Zen in the Art of Archery
  (Herrigel), 147, 358
Ziff-Davis, 260
Zola, Emile, 406

A Note about the Authors

Thomas Joshua Cooper was born in 1946. He graduated from Humboldt State University in Arcata, California, and received his Master's Degree, with Distinction, in Photography from the University of New Mexico at Albuquerque. In 1976, he was awarded a Photography Bursary by the Arts Council of Great Britain. This is Britain's highest honor in the arts for photography and it had been awarded only once before. Mr. Cooper has had numerous one-man and group exhibitions in Europe and the United States. His work is in many museums, including the National Gallery of Canada, the State Museum of Fine Art in Santa Fe, New Mexico, La Bibliothèque Nationale in Paris, and the Victoria and Albert Museum in London. In 1978, Mr. Cooper was awarded a National Endowment for the Arts (NEA) Photographers Fellowship.

Paul Hill was born in Ludlow, England, in 1941. He trained as a reporter and worked on local papers for six years. He has freelanced as a photographer since 1965 for, among others, *The Observer*, the BBC, *The* (London) *Sunday Mirror*, and the *Financial Times*. He is a former secretary of the British Society for Photographic Education. Mr. Hill is chairman of the Support for Photographers Committee of the Arts Council of Great Britain. Until 1978, he was Principal Lecturer in charge of the Diploma in Creative Photography Course at Trent Polytechnic in Nottingham. Mr. Hill has shown his work extensively in Europe and the United States. He is currently owner of The Photographers' Place, a workshop and study center in Derbyshire.